THE PUBLIC SOCIOLOGY DEBATE

THE PUBLIC SOCIOLOGY DEBATE

ETHICS AND ENGAGEMENT

Edited by Ariane Hanemaayer
and Christopher J. Schneider

UBCPress · Vancouver · Toronto

22 21 20 19 18 17 16 15 14   5 4 3 2 1

Printed in Canada on FSC-certified ancient-forest-free paper (100% post-consumer recycled) that is processed chlorine- and acid-free.

Library and Archives Canada Cataloguing in Publication

The public sociology debate : ethics and engagement / edited by Ariane Hanemaayer and Christopher J. Schneider.

Includes bibliographical references and index.
Issued in print and electronic formats.
ISBN 978-0-7748-2663-1 (bound). – ISBN 978-0-7748-2665-5 (pdf). –
ISBN 978-0-7748-2666-2 (epub)

1. Sociology – Philosophy. 2. Sociology – Methodology. 3. Sociology – Moral and ethical aspects. 4. Sociology – Study and teaching. 5. Applied sociology. I. Hanemaayer, Ariane, 1984-, author, editor of compilation II. Schneider, Christopher J., author, editor of compilation

HM511.P82 2014   301.01   C2013-908757-5
C2013-908758-3

Canadä

UBC Press gratefully acknowledges the financial support for our publishing program of the Government of Canada (through the Canada Book Fund), the Canada Council for the Arts, and the British Columbia Arts Council.

This book has been published with the help of a grant from the Canadian Federation for the Humanities and Social Sciences, through the Awards to Scholarly Publications Program, using funds provided by the Social Sciences and Humanities Research Council of Canada.

UBC Press
The University of British Columbia
2029 West Mall
Vancouver, BC V6T 1Z2
www.ubcpress.ca

To our parents, Glenda, John, Kathy, and Jim, for teaching us the value of education

Contents

Foreword / ix
MICHAEL BURAWOY

Acknowledgments / xix

Introduction: Burawoy's "Normative Vision" of Sociology / 3
ARIANE HANEMAAYER and CHRISTOPHER J. SCHNEIDER

Part 1 Debating the Normative Dimensions of Professional Sociology

1 Returning to the Classics: Looking to Weber and Durkheim to Resolve the Theoretical Inconsistencies of Public Sociology / 31
ARIANE HANEMAAYER

2 Public Sociology, Professional Sociology, and Democracy / 53
AXEL VAN DEN BERG

Part 2 Critical Reflections on the Possibility of Public Sociology

3 *L'Ouverture des bouches:* The Social and Intellectual Bases for Engaged and Public Social Theory / 77
SCOTT SCHAFFER

4 Precarious Publics: Interrogating a Public Sociology for Migrant Workers in Canada / 108
JILL BUCKLASCHUK

5 Reflections on the Theory and Practice of Teaching Public Sociology / 132
SUSAN PRENTICE

Part 3 Blurring the Line between Policy and Public Sociology

6 Public Sociology and Research Ethics / 153
ANNE MESNY

7 Coral W. Topping, Pioneer Canadian Public Sociologist: "A Veteran Warrior for Prison Reform" / 175
RICK HELMES-HAYES

Part 4 Innovative Engagements in Public Scholarship

8 Social Media and e-Public Sociology / 205
CHRISTOPHER J. SCHNEIDER

9 Public Ethnography as Public Engagement: Multimodal Pedagogies for Innovative Learning / 225
PHILLIP VANNINI and LAURA MILNE

Conclusion / 246
ARIANE HANEMAAYER and CHRISTOPHER J. SCHNEIDER

Epilogue: Student Reflections on a Public Sociology Course at UBC, Okanagan Campus / 252
KYLE NOLAN

Appendix 1: Theory and Practice of Sociology Syllabus, University of Manitoba / 257

Appendix 2: Public Sociology Syllabus, UBC, Okanagan Campus / 263

Contributors / 276

Index / 280

Foreword

MICHAEL BURAWOY

The debate surrounding public sociology will not stop. Unlike other debates, this is one in which all can and have participated – junior and senior, student and educator, teacher and researcher, members of elite and non-elite universities, citizens of the Global South and the Global North. It is a debate that involves not just sociology but, potentially, any academic discipline. Indeed, it can be extended to the very nature of the university. This volume of essays from Canada testifies to the openness of the debate, for it embraces positions that defend, in turn, professional sociology, policy sociology, critical sociology, and public sociology to the varying exclusion of the others. Indeed, as I have argued before, Canada is uniquely placed to push the project of public sociology forward not only because of the healthy balance that exists between public sociology and the three other types of sociology but also because Canada is well situated geopolitically to recognize the challenges of an unequal world, which has meant that, in the past, it has played an important role in global affairs.

One reason the debate continues is that public sociologists interrogate the very foundations of sociology as a discipline. By asking "Knowledge for whom?" and "Knowledge for what?" they question the foundations that have often been sealed or subject to the dictates of the anointed. The debate can be disruptive, especially for professionals who want to get on with their scholarly pursuits and not be bothered with the meaning of our enterprise. But we live in a time when we have to examine what we are up to as our own existence as autonomous academics is threatened by the very forces we study, not least markets and states.

To be more specific, the democratic ethos of science that Axel van den Berg so rightly and energetically defends is actually under threat not just from within – through the monopoly of academic capital and the hierarchies it spawns or the misuse of science for political ends – but also from without. Indeed, this threat from without is a major impetus behind public sociology, which we can better understand by broadening the scope of the democratic ethos that underpins academic work. A good place to begin is Robert Merton's famous identification of the normative bases of science: universalism, organized skepticism, disinterestedness, and communism. Universalism subjects truth claims to pre-established impersonal criteria. This is van den Berg's principle of value neutrality that minimizes bias in the conduct of science. Organized skepticism gives pride of place to critical thinking, taking nothing for granted. It is threatened by attempts at outside control, especially when science moves into new areas or takes new directions. Disinterestedness is the absence of interests other than the pursuit of knowledge, assured through competition and "rigorous policing."* Finally, communism is the common ownership of knowledge that ensures scientists will be rewarded by recognition or esteem but not with rights of private ownership.

In formulating the normative foundations of science in the late 1930s, Merton was, indeed, concerned to defend the integrity of science against fascist regimes and, to a lesser extent, Stalinism – political regimes that determined who should practise science for whom and for what. But Merton was no less concerned with the threat posed by the rationalizing tendencies of liberal democracies. Here, he was following in the footsteps of Max Weber, who devoted much energy to defending university autonomy against state encroachment. Weber was one of the few academics to actively defend colleagues who were persecuted for their politics (Robert Michels) or their religion (George Simmel). Today, Merton's four foundations are coming under attack from a different source – namely, state-led financialization of the university, in which the production and dissemination of knowledge becomes a commercial proposition, turning the university from a public into a

* See Robert Merton, "The Normative Structure of Science," *The Sociology of Science: Theoretical and Empirical Investigation, Social Theory and Social Structure* (Chicago: University of Chicago Press, 1973), 276. The article was originally published in 1942.

private good. The speed and form of this financialization varies from country to country, but few are able to escape the pressure. Although Canada is lagging behind England and the United States, the process is nonetheless happening here too.

As soon as the university becomes a self-financing operation, it searches for new sources of revenue (increasing student fees, knowledge in the service of industry, corporate donors) and cost-cutting devices (increase in the number of temporary employees, distance learning, various forms of outsourcing). Disinterestedness and communism are thereby easily discarded, but universalism and organized skepticism are also threatened by a parallel and connected process of rationalization. In competing for limited funds, universities have entered into the game of rankings, which involves elaborate and costly manipulations, subjecting scholarship to short-term calculus of arbitrary criteria that determine what counts as knowledge. The combination of commodification and rationalization has led to the polarization of conditions of higher education at every level: within and between disciplines, within and between universities, within and between countries.

The university as we know it is being gradually (or sometimes rather quickly) thrown into the arms of state and market. Academics face a number of choices: to passively watch the process unfold, to actively participate in its promotion, or, alternatively, to uphold the university's public character and defend its autonomy by building countervailing alliances with publics that are experiencing similar pressures of marketization and rationalization. Public sociology, then, is one conduit for such conversations with publics that involve diagnoses of the broad direction of society. Of course, developing such public conversations is easier said than done, as the essays in the volume point out. Sociological diagnoses have to compete with so many others in the public sphere and are easily crowded out, especially as they are often at odds with common sense. We so often offer messages that few want to hear. The public sphere is so dominated by corporate visions of the world that it sometimes appears as though sociologists seek to impose their views on the world when they are simply trying to get a foot in the door.

To avoid competition in the public sphere and circumvent the concentration of communicative power, sociologists can opt for organic rather than traditional public sociology, unmediated rather than mediated engagement. This is the idea of public ethnography that Phillip Vannini and Laura Milne advance in their essay on different modes of engagement. It does sound attractive but, as Jill Bucklaschuk points out, there are real limitations to public ethnography as many publics are simply inaccessible. Even when publics are accessible, they often demand that sociologists deliver something tangible, which turns sociologists into policy scientists. No less important, as Anne Mesny shows, the university itself can put up resistance to any such organic public engagement by restricting research relations to a narrow model defined by the biomedical sciences.

But there is one arena in which sociologists, and academics more generally, do have a comparative advantage, and that is in the area of teaching. The educator has a captive audience that can make the relationship undemocratic and hierarchical, a condition that may be necessary to get the sociological point of view across. The sociological perspective is not a natural one; it is not common sense. Its achievement requires sustained and disciplined work. Susan Prentice reflects on her own teaching of public sociology, linking it to feminist methodology and highlighting how its practice varies with the public standing of sociology itself. There is a second approach to the relation between teaching and public sociology – less the *teaching of public sociology,* whether by example or in theory, and more *teaching as public sociology,* in which students are seen to be a public, carrying their own lived experience that teachers can elaborate. Teaching becomes a way of connecting the personal troubles of students to public issues, micro experiences to macro forces – an analysis in which students can actively participate. In this view, teaching becomes a triple dialogue: a dialogue between students and teachers, a dialogue among students, and in its most adventurous forms, a dialogue between students and secondary publics.

But what is this sociology that is being used to elaborate students' lived experience? Or, as Ariane Hanemaayer asks, where is the sociology in public sociology? By this she means not just the sociological understanding of the world, but a reflexive understanding that positions sociology in general and public sociology in particular. I have already suggested that a sociology of the university in crisis points to the commodification of the production and dissemination of knowledge that is threatening not only our own discipline but the university itself. This is but part of a much broader social theory within which knowledge is but the latest factor of production to be commodified.

Indeed, the history of capitalism can be seen as successive waves of commodification and decommodification. We are in the midst of a third wave of commodification, what I call third-wave marketization, that involves the extensive and intensive (re)commodification of labour (the fall of unions and social security, the rise of precarious work, casualization, informalization, etc.), of nature (land expropriations for profit in China, India, Latin

America; carbon trading to justify emissions; privatization of water, etc.), and of money (making profit from loans; derivatives with increasing debt of individuals, organizations, and countries). Whereas states were active in resisting, containing, and redirecting second-wave marketization, they are now in a collusive relationship with markets, and are more likely to promote rather than contain commodification. Or, even worse, they are expelling populations from having access to labour markets, creating dangerous wastelands and new forms of debt in processes I call ex-commodification.

With the commodification and ex-commodification of each of these factors of production, their use value is undermined: knowledge cannot serve the public interest; labour cannot labour effectively; nature cannot sustain human existence; money serves to increase debt, bankruptcy, and financial crisis. Such a theory of capitalism points to the long-term destruction of human society. The interests of humanity are, indeed, at stake. Here, sociology has an important legacy to uphold. If there is one thing that Karl Marx, Max Weber, Émile Durkheim, and Georg Simmel have in common, it is the critique of the overextension of the market, what Karl Polanyi called the disembedding of the market from society. Their solutions may have been different but their diagnoses share this suspicion of market fundamentalism. This tradition continued into the twentieth century. Talcott Parsons launched his magnum opus with an uncompromising critique of utilitarianism, and Jürgen Habermas was equally uncompromising about the dangers of the overextension of system logic that would colonize the lifeworld. Pierre Bourdieu spent the last ten years of his life in a relentless assault on the destructive powers of the unregulated markets, which distinguishes him as a sociologist from Scott Schaffer's other two public intellectuals, Jean Paul Sartre and Václav Havel. Behind Zygmunt Bauman's liquid modernity lies the market unfettered from its social moorings. In other words, sociology's abiding legacy is the critique of the market. Its standpoint is neither that of the economy nor that of the state but that of civil society – that problematic defence against overreaching markets or states. This is the sociology, or rather a sociology, behind public sociology, and why public sociology continues to be on the agenda and will continue to be as long as we face third-wave marketization.

What might such a vision of public sociology look like? A course I taught in the spring of 2012 at Berkeley with my colleague Laleh Behbehanian attempts to develop such a theoretically rooted conception of public sociology. We called it "Public Sociology, Live!" – an example, perhaps, of what Christopher Schneider calls e-public sociology. The idea was to use cases of public sociology from all corners of the earth to generate a multi-sided global conversation. Every week, twenty Berkeley undergraduates would read, comment on, and discuss the writings of a chosen public sociologist in preparation for a Skype conversation with that person. The sociologist would open up with a fifteen-minute lecture, followed by forty minutes of discussion with the students, all of which was video recorded, downloaded to the Berkeley YouTube channel, and posted on the International Sociological Association website (http://www.isa-sociology.org/public-sociology-live/). The video was watched by hundreds of people (and subsequently thousands) but in particular by six parallel seminars in Barcelona, Oslo, Sao Paulo, Tehran, Johannesburg, and Kyiv. The participants discussed what they heard and saw, summarized their discussion, and posted the summaries on Facebook (http://www.facebook.com/groups/259654060772916/). We did the same in Berkeley, but students also had to post their own individual comments in response to the summaries from the other seminars. Conversations were then supposed to flow.

This sounded like a fine idea! Students would be able to engage with some of the great living public sociologists on our planet, who, in turn, wouldn't have to leave their living rooms to partake in the seminar (although, given the difference in time zones, they might have to host the seminar in the wee hours of the morning). While parallel seminars meet on a more or less regular basis, there was not the intensity of dialogue for which we had hoped, due perhaps to the way the course emerged. Laleh and I determined who the public sociologists would be, the direction of the conversation, how it would take place, and so on. This design only underlined the global inequality we were addressing in that it was the concentration of academic, social, and technological capital at Berkeley that made the course possible in the first place. There was a further asymmetry to which students called our attention – they did not participate in public sociology, which became the prerogative of sociologists from elsewhere.

Now that I have a better sense of what is technically feasible, the course could be redesigned to elevate the level of participation on all sides. But let us consider the cases themselves as they point to the abiding dilemmas of public sociology as presented in the chapters contained in this volume. We can start with land struggles in India and Latin America. Nandani Sundar, having spent a decade researching scheduled tribes in Chhattisgarh, describes the way the indigenous community is not only facing land expropriations but is immersed in a violent war waged between Naxalites (Maoists) and state-sponsored Special Police Agents. It is, indeed, difficult for the community to speak out about its victimization, and, whenever Sundar enters the area, she puts her own life in danger. Her public sociology is not to engage the local community but to engage India in a public discussion of the atrocities being perpetrated. She writes in newspapers; she gives interviews on the fate of her community. She even partakes in and wins a legal battle in India's Supreme Court against the provincial government for violating the constitution. But all to no avail. César Rodríguez Garavito describes a parallel engagement in Colombia. Here, an indigenous community faces flooding from dams but simultaneously lies at the vortex of a civil war between left-wing guerrillas and the paramilitary. It is a treacherous terrain – he calls it, appropriately enough, a "social minefield" – for everyone, not least the sociologist who in this case works with NGOs through appeals to international law.

Turning from land expropriation and commodification to questions of labour commodification, Pun Ngai and her collaborators in China enter the dangerous terrain of labour relations, drawing attention to the exploitative practices of the giant corporation Foxconn, which makes the parts for Apple Computers and others. In 2011, a spate of suicides spread through Foxconn and drew attention to the deplorable conditions in these anonymous factories, which employ several hundred thousand young workers. Pun Ngai and her colleagues, working with undercover students, have publicized their research findings. Armed with theories of the labour process, local engagement in the hidden abode of production leads to traditional public sociology, but of a rather activist character.

Sari Hanafi conducts a parallel project in the Palestinian refugee camps in Lebanon. Working with the inmates (a difficult enough project in itself), he courted the wrath of the Lebanese government by exposing the limited rights of employment and education. Demonstrating just how complex such situations can become, he also found himself to be the object of hostility from Palestinians who wanted to protect "the right to return." Contradictory forces present the public sociologist with multiple dilemmas, which is not an indictment of public sociology but of the world.

Engaging finance capital is even more difficult as its machinations are conducted behind closed doors. This can call for extreme measures. Walden Bello broke into the World Bank to uncover documents about its financial support for the Marcos dictatorship – documents that provided the basis of his co-authored book *The Development Debacle,* which became an underground bestseller in the Philippines. When truth and power are locked together, it takes force to extricate one from the other, but this wouldn't get past any internal review board. On the other side of the fence, Frances Fox Piven, with a long history of engagement with welfare rights movements and right-to-vote laws in the United States, deploys her theory of interdependent power to address questions raised by the Occupy Wall Street movement.

These projects of public sociology involve a complicated relation between local engagement and wider dissemination. Michel Wieviorka explains this well in distinguishing between the production of knowledge (professional sociology) that indeed can involve direct participation in communities and its wider dissemination (public sociology) through various media. Thus, he has tried to educate French publics about the dark side of society – terrorism, anti-Semitism, racism, and violence. For Wieviorka, however, even professional sociology – the methodology of "sociological intervention" developed by Alain Touraine and his collaborators – is accountable to publics in that it defines the relevance and validity of scientific research, moving it closer to organic public sociology. Indeed, sociological intervention seems very similar to Ramon Flecha and Marta Soler's "critical communicative methodology," in which sociologist and public engage in the co-production of knowledge. They show how it is possible to establish close relations with even the most alienated publics, such as the Roma people in Spain, and how the ensuing dialogue can provide the basis for policy change at the level of the European Union.

These intricate cases of public sociology raise many difficult questions, especially concerning the division between public sociology and politics. The distinction can best be understood in terms of intersecting fields. Public sociology may engage with publics; it may serve clients but it does so while still being accountable to the academic field of sociology, the professional findings, and foundations of sociology. Politics, on the other hand, operates according to the logic of the political field – the way interests are pursued and political capital is accumulated. It is possible, as Bourdieu argued, that academic capital can be converted into political capital for more effective participation. The relationship between public sociology and political engagement cannot be understood outside the relationship between fields. Where the fields virtually coincide, as they often do in authoritarian regimes such as the Soviet Union, all sociology is immediately political. In liberal democracies, the space for an autonomous professional and critical sociology is enlarged while the terrain of overlap, where public sociology easily becomes politics, is reduced.

At the same time, as I have been at pains to argue, both academic and political fields are increasingly overdetermined by the economic field. Politics is answerable to financial capital, which sidesteps and, therefore, restricts democratic processes while the university is increasingly having to act as a corporation, strategizing in the market and, therefore, changing its organization from one that nurtured education and research to one that is self-financing. This subversion of the university elicits the support of academics who stand to make short-term material gains but to the long-term detriment of the university's capacity to produce knowledge that will solve the pressing problems of third-wave marketization. This direction of development is justified by orthodox economics and rational-choice political science, which are themselves contested within their disciplines. But we need to develop an alternative sociology that provides the foundation of alliances not with corporate elites and state nobilities but with broader publics whose livelihood is being threatened by third-wave marketization. As Rick Helmes-Hayes has made so clear from his biographies of John Porter and, here, of Coral Topping, Canadian social science, including that of Quebec, has a long history of being concerned with issues of public importance and has not been reluctant to enter political debate without sacrificing the professional and scientific content of its research. Long may it continue!

Acknowledgments

This book project coincided with a public sociology course held in the spring of 2011 at the University of British Columbia, Okanagan Campus. As best we can determine, it was the first publicly accessible undergraduate public sociology course of its kind offered anywhere in Canada. We gratefully acknowledge the generous funding support from the Irving K. Barber Endowment Fund at the University of British Columbia to foster exceptional and innovative undergraduate learning experiences. We would like to acknowledge the following sociology professors for their participation in the course: David Altheide, Ronjon Paul Datta, Aaron Doyle, Jeff Ferrell, Joe Kotarba, Tara Milbrandt, Nancy Netting, Carrie Sanders, Paty Tomic, and Patrick Williams. We thank the following media for promoting the course: AM1150, CBC Radio, Castanet Media, Kelowna Capital News, Shaw TV, and 103.9FM The Juice. We especially wish to recognize and thank Jessica Samuels (formerly of AM1150) for her ceaseless efforts in promoting the course.

We wish to acknowledge the University of British Columbia for the generous funding support it provided through the Irving K. Barber School of Arts and Sciences, the Office of the Provost, and the Department of Sociology (Unit 6), Okanagan Campus, which enabled us to hold a public sociology workshop at the UBC Okanagan campus in March 2011. Ariane Hanemaayer organized much of this workshop and also helped design the public sociology course (see Appendix 2) and is acknowledged here for her efforts. We also wish to thank Kyle Nolan for his skilful documentation and logistical execution of the events during both the public sociology course and the workshop. We remain especially grateful to Cynthia Mathieson, Peter Wylie, and Peter Urmetzer for their support of this book project and its related endeavours.

We also thank our editor at UBC Press, Melissa Pitts. Melissa has been instrumental throughout this project, and we thank her for her help, support, and patience. A big thanks to UBC Press production editor Lesley Erickson and to copy editor Joanne Muzak. The anonymous peer reviewers provided very helpful and thoughtful comments, and we are thankful to them. We also wish to acknowledge Sherry Fox, office manager of the Canadian Sociological Association, for her help in promoting a panel discussion at the 2012 Congress of the Humanities and Social Sciences in Waterloo, Ontario, to further explore and debate the work presented in this volume. We thank Axel van den Berg, Jill Bucklaschuk, and Scott Schaffer for joining us and participating on this panel.

We owe a special debt of gratitude to contributors Rick Helmes-Hayes and Anne Mesny for their support and guidance along the way. In this regard, we also wish to acknowledge Gray Cavender and Nancy Jurik. There are, of course, many others, aside from the contributors, who have helped shape and inform our interest in and ideas about the public sociology literature (whether directly or indirectly), including David Altheide, Doug Aoki, Michael Burawoy, Ronjon Paul Datta, Neil McLaughlin, and Tara Milbrandt. We also wish to acknowledge our siblings, Kiara and Kevin, and thank the Hanemaayer and Schneider families for their support.

Many of the ideas and debates expressed in this book emerged over good food and wine shared at RauDZ Regional Table. Special thanks go out to the RauDZ staff, Chef Rod Butters, and Audrey Surrao for hosting the participants of both the public sociology workshop and the course.

THE PUBLIC SOCIOLOGY DEBATE

Introduction

Burawoy's "Normative Vision" of Sociology

ARIANE HANEMAAYER and CHRISTOPHER J. SCHNEIDER

This book invites sociologists and sociology students to consider what is at stake in debates about public sociology. What kind of sociology are you committed to, and how do your sociological commitments inform sociological practice? This book explores the normative dimensions that ground or shape sociological inquiry and its practice in the public sociology literature. Normative commitments have a variety of valences and dimensions; they concern questions of the good, the moral, the ethical, and the political dimensions of normative statements (Woodiwiss 2005, 5).

The normative component of sociology and its practice has various dimensions; a normative position is a socially determined perception that enriches our capacity to make judgments as people but also as sociologists, including the very sociology that we choose to practise. This practice can include ethical, moral, and political statements. Those statements that are grounded by the normative dimensions of sociological practice are ones that tell us what *ought* to be or *should* be the case in the social world. Subsequently, ethical judgments (what one ought to do or should do) made by sociologists have commitments that lie in the normative dimension of sociological practice, such as when a sociologist makes recommendations for social change. Statements that concern how or that sociology ought to work towards ending human suffering constitute normative recommendations.

A recent sociological research study published in the peer-reviewed journal *Social Science Research* provides a concrete example that highlights the various dimensions of normative statements. In the article, author Mark Regnerus (University of Texas at Austin) (2012, 752) argues that there are "consistent differences" between "children of women who have had a lesbian relationship and those with still married (heterosexual) biological parents." While Regnerus is careful not to explicitly suggest "that growing up with a lesbian mother" causes less than desirable outcomes in child development, his conclusions about same-sex marriage and heterosexual marriage suggest that "the empirical claim that no notable differences exist must go" (766).

The publication of this article caused considerable controversy. A *New York Times* article (Oppenheimer 2012) reported, "Two hundred scholars signed a letter attacking his paper and the journal." Further discussions emerged regarding the ways that cultural or religious values influence scientific research. What we draw attention to are the normative implications of sociological research. How do we, as sociologists, evaluate the research and make recommendations therein? How do values play into scholars' and news media's response to Regnerus's conclusions? We contend that these are the issues that highlight the following dimensions of the normative commitments of sociology:

1 The sociologist's ethical obligations: Should sociologists, based on these scientifically valid and representative data, have a duty to act against homosexual couples raising children?
2 Normative sociological judgments: Should homosexual couples be able to raise or have children if these children *might* suffer potential harms?
3 The influence of obligations and judgments on our political projects: Does sociology as a discipline have a duty to make policy recommendations that forbid or encourage same-sex couples to raise children in light of these data?

The answers to any of these questions are complex and illustrate the importance of examining the normative commitments of the discipline of sociology more broadly. (We do not endorse the above recommendations. The Regnerus conclusions are meant to highlight what is at stake when social science data are linked to normative statements.)

Recent debates in the sociology literature concerning public sociology, popularized by Michael Burawoy's work on the subject (2004, 2005a), have normative underpinnings, asking what role sociology should play in the broader social sphere and how its research may be used (or should not be used) to make desirable and viable social change. At the core of the public sociology debates are questions concerning the normative dimensions of sociological practice: how and under what circumstances should (or shouldn't) sociologists advocate for social change? And how does our research translate into social transformation, or not? Responses to these questions, including those that range from lukewarm to heated, can be located in the "well over 100 essays" scattered throughout books and journals written by sociologists around the world on public sociology (Burawoy 2009, 450).

Public sociology and its corresponding debates are engaged with the normative, moral, ethical, and political valences of the discipline. Essential to its approach, public sociology, as conceived by Burawoy and others, deals with questions of the moral worth of sociological knowledge and seeks to correct social conditions identified as social problems using political intervention. The central aim of public sociology is to correct – that is, to make better social conditions for the betterment of humanity. Such "corrections," however, are guided by normative assumptions and serve as a reflection of the moral standards of a given point in history. We can engage with the public sociology debates, for example, by addressing the theory behind the argument and examining the practical action of public sociology (for a good example of public sociology in action, see Nyden, Hossfeld, and Nyden 2012). Engaging the literature of public sociology, this book explores the theoretical debates of public sociology and examines the normative foundations of ethical judgments made by sociologists. This volume raises questions about and considers some of the normative features of the debates. How and why, for example, do we do sociology? And how do these processes inform our ethical judgments as a discipline, particularly as they relate to formulating a stance for (or against) making recommendations for social or political change? Exploring how normative commitments underlie sociological statements and decisions in the field of public sociology is a basic goal of this book. We, of course, do not mean to imply or suggest that there is an absence of discussions about the normative in the public sociology literature (these discussions are paramount). Our task, rather, is simply to make discussions concerning the normative valences of the discipline of sociology its core premise. To do so we first consider Burawoy's 2004 presidential address to the American Sociological Association (2005a) in relation to the normative dimensions of sociological practice.

In his address, Burawoy introduces his version of public sociology by dividing the discipline into four categories of sociological practice: professional, critical, policy, and public sociology. These four categories have unique research questions and approaches; each approach constitutes different commitments for sociological practice. This is the fourfold division of labour for sociological thought and practice, Burawoy (2005a, 15) unapologetically tells us, and it is his "normative vision" of the discipline. While Burawoy concedes that public sociology has no inherent or "intrinsic normative valence" (8), the practice of sociology is nevertheless "nothing without a normative foundation to guide it" (16). Although some scholars agree with this normative vision and others do not, these debates indicate that the normative dimensions of the discipline are both important and contested commitments that are foundational to sociological practice.

Of particular concern for us is that, while the practice and teaching of public sociology continues to expand, we feel that renewed interest in debates surrounding its practice can refocus scholastic and practical attention upon the ethical commitments that doing any version of sociology (be it professional, critical, policy, or public) entails. Our purpose here is not to provide a comprehensive or robust overview of the public sociology literature. Rather, we aim to further explore how one's sociological commitments raise additional questions about how one can (or cannot) make ethical judgments regarding the translation of sociological research into recommendations for social change.

Here, we draw from the works of Burawoy and others to refocus attention upon the normative implications of each of these four forms of sociological practice. We then anchor each chapter in the context of the ethical foundations that underpin the four forms of sociological practice in an effort to bring to the forefront some of the concerns of these tensions in the public sociology debate.

Assessing the Normative Underpinnings of the Public Sociology Debates

Each form of sociological practice, as conceived by Burawoy (2005a), is guided not only by its perspective on the nature of social reality and its subsequently informed research program but also, importantly, by its normative commitments and assumptions. These commitments can be located in the "fundamental character of our discipline," which, according to Burawoy (2005a, 11), consists of the cooptation of Alfred Lee's (1978) "knowledge for whom?" and Robert Lynd's (1939) "knowledge for what?"

Taken together, Burawoy argues, these two questions organize the discipline into four sociologies that are instrumentally guided by the auspices of either (1) the production of knowledge for the sake of an end goal (e.g., for the category of professional sociology, this is knowledge for the sake of knowledge, while for policy sociology it is the production of knowledge for a client) or (2) the production of knowledge for the sake of its usefulness in generating change (be it disciplinary, e.g., critical sociology, or the broader social world, e.g., public sociology). While Burawoy (2005a) calls this second classification "reflexive," because, he says, "it is concerned with a dialogue about ends" (11), we note that the endeavour of reaching these ends (i.e., change) nevertheless remains an instrumental and normatively grounded task.

Burawoy's 2004 presidential address presented a call for sociologists to unite under "a shared ethos," one that underpins the "reciprocal interdependence of professional, policy, public and critical sociologies" (2005a, 15). While this "call to arms" seeks to clarify the place of sociological knowledge and understanding in the broader academic and everyday worlds, it also produces conditions for new questions to emerge. How do sociologists make ethical judgments concerning the relationship between sociological research and its methods and making recommendations for social change? And under what conditions (if any) should sociologists intervene in political and social change?

Responses to such queries are always driven by our normative assumptions of the social world – that is, what ought to be and what should be. For instance, Burawoy's very own disciplinary (i.e., Marxian) commitments inform his perspective (see Nielsen 2004), when he indicates that sociologists should intervene when the "invasion of market forces" (Burawoy 2005a, 21) give rise to "market tyranny and state despotism" that threaten the "interests of humanity" (24). For Burawoy (and those in agreement with his position), this line of reasoning extends to sociologists who understand that their efforts must have a moral obligation to stop the proliferation of social problems, injustices, and inequalities for the sake of the betterment of humanity. We may be, nevertheless, left uncertain by what is meant by "humanity" (see van den Berg, Chapter 2, this volume).

Two basic questions guide the conceptual theme of this volume: How do we, as sociologists, study, know, and learn to recognize what these "interests of humanity" are? And how do we know what is best for humanity? These questions, we contend, ask how our sociological research and our commitments to practising a specific kind of sociology are linked to our ability to make ethical judgments – real, desirable, and viable recommendations for social change. It is our sociological practice that grounds our ability to make political or policy statements, and our sociological practice is the groundwork for how we, as sociologists, understand the social reality in which we may wish to intervene.

Consider an excerpt from Charles Ellwood's book *Sociology and Modern Social Problems* (1910, 218):

> Popular education on the old lines can never do very much to solve the negro problem. This does not lead, however, to the conclusions that all training and education for the negro race is foredoomed to failure. On the contrary all the experiments of missionaries in dealing with uncivilized races has led to the conclusion that an all-round education in which industrial and moral training are made prominent can relatively adjust to our civilization even the most back-ward of human races.

How are the interests of humanity, in this case the lack of morals of the "most back-ward of human races," learned, identified, and designated for correction? How did Ellwood, a professor of sociology at the University of Missouri, arrive at this determination in the early twentieth century? And how do contemporary sociologists like Burawoy and others then determine what is best for humanity in the present (or future, as the case may be)? Perhaps to better understand this ongoing process we might inquire as to how normative judgments are both encouraged and implied in the debates about the practice of public sociology. If we are to preserve the foundations that produce the possibility for the production of sociological knowledge at all, such questions precede the possibilities and challenges of sociology as well as the consideration and deliberation of its use for generating social change.

This volume engages with questions surrounding the relationship between sociological research and generating normative, political, or policy recommendations, inquiring into the relationship between doing (sociological) description and making prescriptions (for social change). Investigating and elucidating the relationship between the study of the social world (and its various phenomena) and the ethical, moral, and normative commitments that emerge in the execution of any political project, advocacy, or activism is necessary to provide a decisive rationale for proceeding prescriptive statements.

As Burawoy and others suggest, sociologists are already engaged with the communities that they study in various ways, be it in producing disciplinary knowledge about their socially constituted troubles, critically assessing their foundations for the production of that knowledge, providing policy recommendations to clients, and engaging with publics. To elucidate the nature of the relationship between sociological research and recommendations for social change, sociologists must explicitly examine the grounds upon which desirable and viable normative judgments can be made.

The debates over public sociology vary historically. For instance, Canadian sociology differs from its US counterpart (Helmes-Hayes and McLaughlin 2009), and other national sociologies differ dramatically from that of the United States (Burawoy 2005b, 2008, 2009). But the underpinning of ethical obligations and the moral good and relevance of doing (public) sociology and sociological research is a consistent theme across the literature. These questions have a history that dates back not only to the beginnings of American sociology (e.g., Chicago School) and Canadian sociology (e.g., see Helmes-Hayes, Chapter 7, this volume; Helmes-Hayes and McLaughlin 2009) but also to the development of the object and task of sociology, particularly in the works of Saint-Simon, Comte, Marx, Weber, and Durkheim (see Hanemaayer, Chapter 1, this volume).

While the purpose of this book is not to provide a history of ideas regarding the status of morality and its place in sociological thought, we do want to emphasize that the discipline has inherited a professional obligation (or normative question) to concern itself with the relationship between the production of sociological knowledge and its use for generating social change, as exemplified by the public sociology debates. This question is not so easily navigated, however, as we have seen with the hot and cold endorsement of Burawoy's call for sociology to take bolder action to become involved in problems of social justice. The nerve that appears to have been struck by Burawoy's statements on public sociology demonstrate the contested nature of the relationship between sociological research and the grounds upon which recommendations can be made, whether sociological description makes it possible, or if it is the duty of sociology to make prescriptions for the betterment of humanity. The chapters included in this volume engage with issues of knowledge production and social change.

Public Sociology: An Opportunity to Debate Research and Recommendations

The idea for this volume crystallized during the spring of 2010. The *Canadian Journal of Sociology*'s 2009 special issue on public sociology, "Public Sociology in Canada: Debates, Research and Historical Context," stoked the flames of our collective enthusiasm for the subject. While our individual interests in public sociology differ, we realized that a comprehensive work that set out to interrogate the normative dimensions of doing public sociology was lacking. We see the need to develop the theoretical relationships among ethics, perspective, and practice in order to consider how these relations contribute to one another, and how debates about the "status" of public sociology have emerged from this process. We find it somewhat troubling that the practice of public sociology, in its various forms, forges ahead of such concerns, many of which remain unquestioned and unresolved.

We surely do not need to convince readers of this book of the fact that public sociology is more popular than it has ever been. Various texts have taken up the public sociology debate, producing numerous scholarly articles and special edition journals devoted to the subject (e.g., see *Social Problems,* 2004; *Social Forces,* 2004; *Critical Sociology,* 2005; and *Canadian Journal of Sociology,* 2009). Additionally, several edited volumes have also focused specific attention upon public sociology (e.g., see Agger 2007; Blau and Smith 2006; Clawson et al. 2007; Jeffries 2009; Nichols 2007). Other books, such as those aimed at undergraduate students, encourage and promote the development of public sociology (see Nyden, Hossfeld, and Nyden 2012).While these texts invariably advance the debate, no one collection of articles or edited volume has directed sole attention upon or raised questions about the normative commitments that doing any version of sociology entails.

To reiterate, we do not mean to suggest that ethics is absent from the debates. In fact, the notion of ethics is in many ways central to the ensuing debate. The necessity of instituting a form of value-laden sociology as a disciplinary practice to directly contrast with the existent and rigid model of objective sociology is one of Burawoy's basic positions, as expressed in his 2004 presidential address and reiterated elsewhere in his published work (see Burawoy 2005a, 2005c, 2005d, 2006, 2009).

Proponents of public sociology continue to implement its practice with increasing frequency. For instance, the foreword to a more recent "how-to" public sociology manual endorsed by Burawoy and directed primarily at undergraduate students reads, "Public sociology. It has been done. It is being done. And you can do it" (Nyden, Hossfeld, and Nyden 2012, xiii). Public sociology has even moved beyond debate and practice to include international university undergraduate and graduate programs that offer courses, certificates, specializations, and even degrees, including a PhD (e.g., George

Mason University). This institutionalization, of course, does not mean that the moral issues of the debate have been resolved.

Some have accepted Burawoy's "normative vision" while others have challenged or dismissed it. Abbott (2007, 197), for instance, calls Burawoy's description of sociology a "moral enterprise" whereas Goldberg and van den Berg (2009) suggest the promotion of public sociology is "morally dubious" (765), while others have simply stated that "public sociology is not for me" (Nielsen 2004, 1619). Despite these and other such statements, Burawoy (2007, 244) argues that even those "who make no mention of the division of labour [fourfold typology] or who seek to abolish it nevertheless reproduce its elements," a conviction that suggests that the normative commitments of sociology are an essential part of the fabric of our discipline.

It has been suggested that the very "disciplinary core" of sociology appears to be at stake in the nature of the public sociology debates (Brint 2005, 48). The relationship between sociological research and recommendations – description and prescription – continues to be a prescient issue in the discipline because to abandon our sociological principles in favour of prescribing moral judgments is to abandon our disciplinary ethos. For our discipline to "flourish," we need to inquire into the basis upon which normative recommendations can be made, otherwise, in the words of Burawoy (2005a, 8), "why should anyone listen to us rather than the other messages streaming through the media?"

The chapters in this volume engage questions surrounding the nature of sociological research and its relation to ethical judgments, an implicit conversation that is ongoing in the public sociology literature. The struggle over the definition of sociology ensconced in the "public sociology wars" (Burawoy 2009) can be reconceptualized as debates over the relations between the divisions within the discipline, on the one hand, and how each has its own commitments to the question of description and prescription, on the other hand. Regarding the latter distinction, no single volume has collectively addressed this vantage point. Whether one ought to behave like a public sociologist, and what exactly this means, are important questions to consider more seriously. The basic aim of this book is to interrogate some of the ethical, normative, and political challenges that underscore the public sociology debates. We situate each chapter in relation to the normative commitments articulated in the public sociology debates and Burawoy's division of labour. Doing so helps to elucidate the normative vision Burawoy has for the discipline and its division of labour. It also helps to situate the chapters in relation to the questions that the normative valences raise pertaining to the ethical obligations of sociology, the basis for normative judgments, and the relationship between research and recommendations for political and social change.

Overview of This Volume: The Division of Sociological Labour

To demonstrate how this book is a necessary engagement with the debates by considering public sociology and its commitments to normative practices and prescriptions, we illustrate, using Burawoy's (albeit, some suggest, problematic) division of the discipline, and show how each version of sociology grapples with the relationship between issue and intervention, description and prescription, and research and recommendations, which, we contend, relate to the normative dimensions of the public sociology debates. We detail how some scholars have defended their own type of sociology in relation to the public sociology mandate – the use of sociological knowledge for normative prescription – and show how each category conceives of the scientific and ethical obligations of the practice of sociology. It is worth repeating that our intention is not to provide an exhaustive review of the public sociology debate but, instead, to explore how such responses connect with the *kind* of sociology we choose to practise and *how* we choose to practise this sociology.

Professional

According to Burawoy (2005a, 10), all four categories in the sociological division of labour rely on the "true and tested methods, accumulated bodies of knowledge, orienting questions, and conceptual frameworks" of professional sociology. It is in the category of professional sociology where sociology derives its conceptual foundation for making sound investigations into the nature of the social world: "As sociologists we not only invent new categories but also give them normative and political valence" (Burawoy 2005c, 323). Burawoy's project aims to take the analytic and conceptual groundwork laid by professional sociologists beyond its academic relevance.

Burawoy is clear that it is our moral obligation as sociologists to give the knowledge produced by our work political use – taking our research and giving it moral traction (2005a, 2005c), no longer "abstain[ing] from political engagement" (2005f, 80). But this is no easy task, as the scientific nature of research is to describe rather than declare. On what grounds can professional sociology move beyond the scientific nature of its methods, categories, and analyses and "valorize the social" (2009, 469)?

Seeing how professional sociology provides the backbone and standards for all sociological practice (Burawoy 2005a), it would be the task of professional sociology to determine how, and if, certain concepts and categories have relevance to those publics that sociology studies. For professional sociologists, any knowledge of the normative valences of the social world or professional practice would arise from the methods, knowledge, questions, and conceptual frameworks generated by the scientific study of social reality.

But what is preferable to the public sociologist? And how do we know? Ask those who are skeptical about the role of professional sociology and its relation to public sociology and activism. Bell (2009, 102) puts it like this: "If public sociologists are concerned with the 'betterment of society,' then we must ask what is better? And how do we know? I propose epistemic implication as a method of objectively testing value judgments. Using it, public sociologists can examine proposed images of the good society and objectively evaluate the moral claims on which they are based." By using the epistemological judgments of professional sociology, we can objectively test what values ground various claims. The methods of sociology provide the foundations upon which statements presented for consideration may be critically evaluated. This sentiment is shared by others. Professional sociology is considered useful, indeed necessary, to the practice of public sociology, primarily because it "imposes" (Touraine 2007, 78) "true and tested methods" (Burawoy 2005a, 10) that "provide a theoretical lens for identifying research problems" (Hu 2009, 259). It is suggested that professional sociology is neutral in its methodological collection of data but is motivated to engage in political projects through public sociology (Piven 2007), a sociological practice committed to making social change for the betterment of humanity (see Burawoy 2005a, 2005c, 2006). Elsewhere, Blau and Smith (2006, xvii) report that "over the past decade social scientists have increasingly abandoned their claims to moral neutrality, indebted to the honesty of those who led this shift: scholars who openly advocated racial, gender, and labor justice ... [engage] issues from a perspective of responsibility and a commitment to justice, *which is to say, an ethical perspective*" (emphasis added). Burawoy and his supporters seem to agree that professional research has an important task in making moral judgments, but that it remains an ethical imperative for sociologists to concern themselves with issues of social justice. Indeed, Burawoy (2005g, 154) is very clear that we must "build up professional sociology as the moral and not just the structural core of the discipline."

Of course, others are hesitant about the role of professional sociologists in activism and social change. Massey (2007, 145) says, "sociologists should – indeed must – speak forcefully on important issues whenever they have something to say, but they should do so as individuals and not collectively as a profession." Professional sociologists would not speak from the ethos of their discipline, but they would speak as politically involved citizens. Patterson (2007, 181) describes professional engagement as "the kind of public sociology in which the scholar remains largely committed to the work but becomes involved with publics and important public issues as an expert," which sees the professional sociologist as a kind of consultant to those who seek the advice of sociology on various social issues to generate change. The disciplinary struggles over public sociology seem to rely upon the acceptance of professional sociology.

In Chapter 1, Ariane Hanemaayer asks a "guilty" question about the metatheoretical foundations of the public sociology programme: is public sociology sociological? By examining Burawoy and some of the subsequent statements about public sociology, she contends that public sociology is overdetermined by its normative valences, that Burawoy's advocacy for sociologists to make ethical judgments risks jettisoning our sociological judgments for normative ones. Hanemaayer endeavours to retrieve the sociological and metatheoretical commitments of public sociology by considering how two classical theorists (Weber and Durkheim) dealt with questions concerning the ontological and normative dimensions of sociological practice, theorizing a public sociology *avant la lettre*. By drawing on the sociologies of Weber and Durkheim, Hanemaayer demonstrates not only how the relationship between research and recommendations has been a central question for development of the discipline since its creation but also how doing sociology principled to its metatheoretical commitments allows sociologists to make sociologically sound ethical judgments about the social phenomena they study and the happenings of the social world.

In Chapter 2, Axel van den Berg asserts that the debate over the disciplinary struggles (see Burawoy 2009), particularly those concerning professional sociology, in fact lie much deeper than professional privilege. A lack of commitment to a fundamental democratic worldview is what the kerfuffle over public sociology really seems to be about. In this chapter, van den Berg, himself a self-proclaimed professional sociologist, contends that the debate is really a "fundamental disagreement over the relationship between (social) science and democracy." Professional sociology should involve the elevation and celebration of value neutrality because, van den Berg argues, while there may be "plenty of values, or nondemonstrable judgments, that the members of the audience will have to agree on to start with, such as the existence of a shared ... reality," these agreements inform a "democratic epistemology" – one not present in Burawoy's (2005a, 24) declaration of sociology as representing "the interests of humanity." Van den Berg outlines the manner that professional sociology (short of Burawoy and his supporters) can and should remain value-neutral, rather than "overdetermined" by the normative valences of public sociology, as Hanemaayer would argue. For professional sociologists, the basic concern throughout the debates, van den Berg surmises, is that the "dubious aspects of public sociology will lead to a throwing out of the baby of inclusive methodology with the dirty bathwater of its always imperfect realization."

Critical

Burawoy's (2005f, 73) category of critical sociology "exposes and engages the assumptions, often the normative assumptions, of professional sociology." This type of sociology is charged with the task of analyzing the normative foundations that constitute the "truths" generated by the rigorous methods and scientific epistemologies of professional sociology. Critical sociology appears to be the normative underlabourer of those engaged in professional projects: "For critical sociology truth is nothing without a normative foundation to guide it" (Burawoy 2005a, 16). By doing the critical questioning of the knowledge produced by professional research, critical sociology provides the grounds upon which public sociology may be undertaken: "Critical and public sociology, on the other hand, interrogate and even call into question those very ends, the normative foundations of professional and policy sociology. Critical sociology is a normative dialogue, primarily among sociologists and conventionally directed to professional sociology, whereas public sociology is dialogue primarily between sociologists and publics about the normative foundations of society" (Burawoy 2005d, 380). Those who have taken issue with Burawoy's formulation of the critical tradition in sociology (see, for example, Morrow 2009; Feagin, Elias, and Mueller 2009) note that examination of the normative foundations of professional sociology goes for public sociology as well. It is not as simple and clear-cut as Burawoy seems to suggest. While Burawoy's categories may render professional sociology as the type that generates knowledge about the values of a society, group, or subculture, critical sociology exposes the normative commitments of any endeavour in sociological research. Any translation of these normative interests in sociology or the values of those under study requires reflection as well, as put forth by Morrow (2009) and others. Further, public sociology, some contend, is not an exception to the rigorous questioning of the critical condition: "In the course of his analysis [Burawoy] more or less conflates the normative, the moral, and the political under the one head of the critical" (Abbott 2007, 197).

Glenn (2007, 221) also shares uneasiness about the mapping of the critical category as she points out how "power and hierarchy are embedded in the [fourfold typology]." Those who share a commitment to sociological reflexivity, one where the very values and assumptions set forth in any statement of truth are questioned, are cautious about any translation of these normative concerns to public sociology and its practice. For instance, Jeffries (2009) and Nichols (2007) each suggest that the critical commitments demonstrated in Sorokin's work offer a way to think about the ethical principles in an engagement with any kind of social change or "alternative vision of the good" that can provide a "compelling moral vision of a better world" (Jeffries 2009, 118).

Continuing this thread, others, such as Feagin, Elias, and Mueller (2009, 84), argue that the "standpoint and starting point of a critical public sociology should be the creation of a counter system framework focused on social justice and democratic group pluralism," "because societies continue to be fundamentally defined by injustices structured along class, racial, and gender lines." The research that generates knowledge about social reality has its own normative valences, and the critical tradition, according to its supporters, is not only able to expose those values and commitments, but can also provide the methods for theorizing an alternative version of those values, which can then be translated to political projects undertaken by public sociologists (see Collins 2007; Piven 2007; Feagin, Elias, and Mueller 2009).

The concern with political recommendations is one for public sociology, guided by the ethical principles and values researched and developed by the professional and critical traditions. In our discussion above, we see the hesitation to include normative recommendations as part of a sociological project as defined through professional sociology. With the critical category, however, supporters conceive of its project as elucidating the normative aspects already present in the undertaking of any sociological project, as those projects themselves have normative commitments, values (i.e., what is "worth" knowing) that can be translated to making political recommendations and proposing alternatives to the current conditions structuring any group of study (e.g., society). The relationship between sociological research and normative recommendations is one of ethical principles: assessing the normative valences of any research problem to theorize alternative conditions to better humanity as a moral good requires a reflexive relation to the generation of any truth statement.

In Chapter 3, Scott Schaffer explores how social theorists can resume critical engagement in the everyday world. To comprehend this process, Schaffer draws on Schalk (1991) to suggest that we can learn from the intellectual engagement of Sartre, Bourdieu, and Havel to generate a basis for involvement in social action. Schaffer contends that such a task remains "just as important" in our social assessment of the proper relationship between social theorist and publics. An ardent supporter of this form of public engagement, Schaffer asserts that "left intellectuals *should* be engaged in public life in a way that speaks with those on the 'front lines' of movements for social justice and social change" (emphasis in original). While Schaffer is concerned with how "thinkers can either mobilize elements of their body of work or foster a societal position in order to serve as interlocutors in public debates," Jill Bucklaschuk contends that intervention must also include more inclusive frameworks that "explore the implications and complexities of engaging marginalized groups as publics."

At the heart of Chapter 4, Bucklaschuk considers the choice to actively include those at the fringes of society, those rendered most invisible by their temporary migrant social status. These individuals play a key role in social, economic, and political development, on the one hand, while they simultaneously lack these very same resources to be "actively involved in dialogue" in addressing matters of concern, on the other. Although Bucklaschuk believes that sociologists should and must play "an important role in exploring and collecting their experiences and bringing public awareness to the inequalities and injustices they face," she is quick to remind us that our assumptions about the ethical dimensions of our sociological statements might actually do harm as we cannot make publics "visible just because we believe they would benefit from such a process." Rather, Bucklaschuk highlights the importance of "multi-actor collaboration" in addressing the concerns of marginalized publics, and, while Bucklaschuk does not challenge the legitimacy of public sociology, as others in this volume do (see van den Berg and Hanemaayer), a consistent theme concerning the democratic engagement of knowledge creation as critical engagement is present. Critical democratic engagement can also consist of teaching practices, an area explored in Chapter 5, presented by Susan Prentice.

Prentice describes how a graduate course she organized was structured in such a way that it served as a unique space of critical sociological inquiry. Prentice asserts that "a public sociology classroom is best thought of as a critical space of 'traditional' learning and teaching." While public intellectuals have an active and critical role in different societies (see Schaffer, this volume), the same cannot be said of North America, and, therefore, "internationalizing learning and teaching public sociology," argues Prentice, remains an important endeavour. The ethical decision to "take a stand" in the classroom is an important decision that should not be taken as an opportunity to "'imprint' [one's] personal political views because such moves are irresponsible, coercive, and undemocratic in the context of a classroom." The ethical position taken by Prentice is clear: critical sociology should facilitate teaching to better "interrogate the foundations of social science inquiry, including those of public sociology itself."

Policy

Policy sociology is one in service of a client. The client guides the generation of data, often the methods desired, as well as the purpose for which the data will be used. Statistics Canada is one example of such a version of the policy sociology category. A few of the mandates of Statistics Canada are to analyze economic performance of the country and to create useful policies to maintain Canada's economy (Statistics Canada 2009). For Burawoy (2005e, 431), policy sociology "at its core [concerns] no dialogue about normative assumptions." Because any research project is undertaken to produce knowledge for the purposes and interests of a group, like the mandates of Statistics Canada, there is no space for normative or critical reflection – just for following the procedure and interests of the client.

Stinchcombe (2007, 136) notes that "the deep problem with ... policy sociology is the same as the problem of economics: its truths must be truths about the future." Stinchcombe (2007, 141) continues, "If it is true that only theory, not facts, can deal with the future and that much public discourse is about what sort of future we ought to have, how can we get out of the box of the institutionalized rigidity of our imagined futures?" In pursuing truths about that which has not yet come to pass, clients may employ sociologists as they can provide the research that policy makers can use to put forth recommendations for legislative or legal change. But the ways these recommendations are generated (by sociological principles) are of no concern to the client; it is the result that counts. There is little room for reflection in policy research, Burawoy contends: "Of course, it may not be simply the structure of our discipline that handicaps us in the policy field, but also the messages we carry ... We must ask whether our message is also too left of publics let alone states? Can we produce the ignition to spark the conversation?" (Burawoy 2005c, 321-22).

In policy sociology, the normative dimensions exist but are determined by the interests of the client, as the client is the one who decides what the knowledge is for (in Burawoy's terms). Questions concerning how the discipline may remain ethically principled when pursuing policy work, or if policy sociology is a worthwhile endeavour, will always remain in service to another master (i.e., not the interests of "humanity" per se).

In Chapter 6, thinking through Burawoy's statements about the discipline and its thwarted relation to policy sociology, Anne Mesny explores the "distinctions between public sociology and policy sociology." She uses the policies regarding ethical conduct for research involving human participants as a starting point. In Canada, these principles were established in 1998 by the Tri-Council Policy Statement, which provides regulations that scientists should follow regarding relationships with researched human subjects. Mesny contends that there remains a "discrepancy between the ethical issues that are acknowledged" by university research policies and "the ethical issues that [scholars] actually encounter," a process that includes working with participants that are vulnerable but also those that are powerful, such as policy makers. Mesny argues that the "distinction between public sociology and policy sociology is certainly not as clear-cut as Burawoy suggests" and contextualizes these differences in terms of the usefulness of sociological knowledge, on the one hand, and for whom, on the other, and the role of university ethics boards in the process. She concludes that "conducting research that is immediately relevant for research participants should be seen as *one* type of research among other types of equally legitimate research."

In Chapter 7, Rick Helmes-Hayes, an admitted supporter of public sociology, argues that the ethos of a value-committed science was at one time a basic and acceptable practice of Canadian sociology. While Schaffer (this volume) focuses upon three non-Canadian scholars to argue that left intellectuals should critically engage with publics, Helmes-Hayes highlights the work and engagement activities of Coral W. Topping, "the first and only sociologist at the University of British Columbia between 1929 and 1954." This chapter provides an account of Topping's style as a public sociologist. Topping used public engagement but with the express commitment to bring changes in the form of policy, particularly in relation to prison reform.

To be certain, Helmes-Hayes does not suggest that Topping was a policy sociologist (nor do we) – far from it. Topping did not work for any client. Rather, he suggests that Topping's "efforts as a tireless and effective advocate" for the humane treatment of criminals and juvenile delinquents in Canada ushered in policy changes that dramatically altered "the organization and running of the nation's carceral institutions." These changes, Helmes-Hayes tells us, now serve as the "basis of Canada's current correctional system." While Topping was not a policy sociologist, his "highly moralistic" efforts as a public sociologist, Helmes-Hayes suggests, were historically not "too left of publics [or] states" (Burawoy 2005c, 321-22) to be institutionalized in the form of policy in Canada's correctional system. Indeed, as Helmes-Hayes argues, the moralistic messages that sociologists once carried were in fact "once an accepted and useful part of mainstream sociological practice."

Public

Public sociology, according to Burawoy (2005a, 5), is not the "negation of professional sociology." Rather, public sociology "aims to enrich public debate about moral and political issues by infusing them with sociological theory and research" (Burawoy 2004, 1603). The purpose of public sociology is to engage those beyond the academy to stimulate dialogue about matters of "public importance" (Burawoy 2005a, 7). Public sociology is value-laden and driven by the moral position of the sociologist. The explicit purpose of public sociology is to generate social change for the "good of humanity," even while the good of humanity may remain unclear or potentially undemocratic (see van den Berg, this volume).

There are two basic forms of public sociology, traditional and organic (Burawoy 2005a). With traditional public sociology, sociologists publish material intended for audiences beyond the academy. These publications can include books or opinion pieces in newspapers that are accessible to publics, or anything published in "plain English" (Gans 1988, 6). Publishing on the Internet in the form of blogs or even open-access journals has expanded these possibilities for sociologists (see Schneider, this volume). The organic form of public sociology occurs when a sociologist "works in close connection with a visible, thick, active, local, and often counter-public" (Burawoy 2005a, 7). Counterpublics can include groups that seek social change on behalf of human rights organizations, for example; counterpublics are making sure not to "confound human rights with the rights of states and markets" (Burawoy 2006, 4).

The tasks of the organic public sociologist, according to Burawoy (2005a), include, on the one hand, engaging in a dialogue with these groups, while on the other hand informing them of our work. The goal of this process is to make these groups visible in the public sphere in order to facilitate social change. In this way, the sociologist acts as translator of sociological research and a politically transformative liaison (Burawoy 2007). The interest of the sociologist determines not only his/her sociological perspective but also his/her organic activities.

For Burawoy (2007, 241), "sociology ... harnesses that science to its earlier moral concerns in order to give vitality to public sociology." Professional and critical sociology breathe life into the public sociology project, providing the information and normative commitments necessary for engaging in public activism and advocating for social change. The normative valences of the practice of public sociology are not intrinsic or essential (i.e., the same across all research endeavours), but public sociologists remain committed "to dialogue around issues raised in and by sociologists" (Burawoy 2005a, 8). Those who support the practice of public sociology contend that those who "pretend that politics and morality do not influence the form and impact of our research ... [are] blind to social reality. Thus, to name ourselves as public sociologists means, first and foremost, to be more *explicit* and *reflective* about what we are *already* doing" (Hays 2007, 87, emphasis in original). Given the argument set forth by Burawoy and others, public sociology and its practice bring out the normative dimensions of a discipline that already exist. The public sociologist is the translator and transformer. She translates research, developed through sociological methods, into real recommendations with the aim of transformation – namely, addressing social problems and political issues and moving towards the betterment of humanity.

Other scholars remain less enthusiastic about the normative sociological features emphasized and valorized by public sociology. Smith-Lovin (2007, 129), for instance, notes, "If we take as the core enterprise of sociology the accumulation of knowledge about social processes, the accountability to publics is a problem for scientific sociology." While acknowledging that the use of sociological knowledge ought to benefit and be accountable to those who are under research, she notes that there is some hesitation about the ability "to judge our contributions based on that relatively traditional, conservative, professional goal in order to sustain the legitimacy and internal consensus that allow us to sustain the discipline" (Smith-Lovin 2007, 132). As Bell (2009, 103) puts it, any public intervention requires a validity, a "*reliable and valid futures thinking* and objective *value judging*" (emphasis in original).

In being accountable to publics with the goal of ameliorating their social situation, there arises one of our key questions regarding how research and recommendations are linked: by what standards can sociology make value judgments objectively? Glenn (2009, 135) provides nine "standards for distinguishing between good and bad public sociology": much of what he says "deals with how public sociologists strongly committed to their ultimate values may be able to gain a reasonable degree of objectivity about effectiveness of the different means being advocated and used for the attainment of the goals they believe in" (139). These discussions surrounding the criteria for objective and desirable intervention take the value and validity of Burawoy's normative vision of the discipline seriously. Burawoy's supporters believe sociology will foster the development of a more democratic society.

Wallerstein (2007, 174-75) reminds us that "we can never come close to ... a more reasonable accommodation of multiple readings of the good, and therefore ultimately a democratic political system if there is not greater openness in our public discussion." Wallerstein recognizes that what is good for humanity is subject to socially constituted values, but conversation about those values, as stimulated by sociology, is a worthwhile pursuit. Others, such as Patterson (2007, 176), agree: "I firmly believe that the public use of sociology, properly executed, is part of a communicative process in the public sphere that is necessarily democratic in both intent and consequence." The greatest contribution public sociology can make to the broader social world is that "it can potentially ... [develop] a more intellectually oriented public sphere" (Furedi 2009, 172). The rationale for public sociology is that sociology makes the world better by creating democratic engagements through public interaction with sociologists and education (Leonard 2009, 240; cf. Mills 1959, 187-88).

Public sociology makes no apologies for its normative commitments to making a better world, as it sees the relationship between doing sociological research and making recommendations for transforming the social world as unproblematic and, indeed, a moral imperative of the discipline more generally. As Agger (2007, 2) puts it, "my project is unashamedly normative: I contend that sociology should take the lead in building a democratic public sphere."

In Chapter 8, Christopher J. Schneider outlines how social media, and social networking sites more specifically, expand opportunities for public sociologists in the public sphere and offer a novel way to connect research and recommendations. Schneider calls this *e-public sociology,* a hybrid of Burawoy's (2005a) traditional and organic public sociology. Traditional public sociology, for Burawoy, involves sociologists who publish their work in oligopolistic media, whereas organic public sociology includes sociologists who work face-to-face with publics. Social networking sites, Schneider argues, draw from both forms of public sociology, forming e-public sociology, which includes publishing work in accessible public spaces (traditional) as well as interacting with publics through these very same media (organic). Schneider collected data from seventy-five faculty members who responded to a questionnaire that he distributed through various listservs; while his findings affirmed that students are "our first public" (Burawoy 2005a, 7), faculty respondents interacted with the student publics beyond the university only under very limited circumstances. Schneider notes that the "unwillingness to engage with undergraduate student publics in these mediated spaces is not necessarily conducive to bringing sociological knowledge to wider extra-academic audiences," which leads him to conclude that the practice of public sociology between faculty respondents and students remains "limited" and thus not entirely conducive to Burawoy's (2005a) version of public sociology.

In Chapter 9, Phillip Vannini and Laura Milne outline a "new public scholarship" for the future because of an influx of "more students learning the language of the social sciences today than there are journalists, documentarians, think-tank researchers, and policy pundits combined." Vannini and Milne argue that a "public ethnography" is better suited than even public sociology to reach "beyond the confines of academic discourse." They define ethnography as "the in-depth study of people's ways of life, of cultures" and public ethnography as exploiting the potential of ethnographic research that focuses on "describing and understanding social life from the perspective of the people who take part in it." Vannini and Milne suggest that a "multimodal" approach is the best way to translate sociological research and to reach multiple publics. This process moves beyond both writing and interaction to include video and photography but also incorporates platforms such as social networking to help launch these projects into public spaces. Coupled with student engagement and innovative public ethnography, this process, Vannini and Milne assert, can bolster public scholarship across diverse audiences in packages that make sense to members of these audiences.

We contend that the debates over Burawoy's fourfold vision and the division of sociological labour tell us something about the normative commitments of the discipline. To return to the question we asked at the outset: What kind of sociology are you committed to? The chapters that follow provide the reader with a range of responses that each engage with the assumed normative valence of the discipline. Our hope is that this collection will move the public sociology debates in the direction of a more focused and sustained engagement with the normative commitments of sociology. Questions that investigate what role sociology should play in the broader social sphere, and how its research may be used (or not used) to facilitate desirable and viable social change, remain important as these questions inform ethical judgments in practice, statements and recommendations for social change, and sociological engagement in political projects.

References

Abbott, Andrew. 2007. "For Humanist Sociology." In *Public Sociology: Fifteen Eminent Sociologists Debate Politics and the Profession in the Twenty-First Century,* edited by Dan Clawson, Robert Zussman, Joya Misra, Naomi Gerstel, Randall Stokes, Douglas L. Anderton, and Michael Burawoy, 195-209. Berkeley: University of California Press.

Agger, Ben, ed. 2007. *Public Sociology: From Social Facts to Literary Act.* 2nd ed. Lanham, MD: Rowman and Littlefield.

Bell, Wendell. 2009. "Public Sociology and the Future: The Possible, the Probable, and the Preferable." In *Handbook of Public Sociology,* edited by Vincent Jeffries, 89-106. Lanham, MD: Rowman and Littlefield.

Blau, Judith, and Keri E. Iyall Smith, eds. 2006. *Public Sociologies Reader.* Lanham, MD: Rowman and Littlefield.

Brint, Steven. 2005. "Guide for the Perplexed: On Michael Burawoy's 'Public Sociology.'" *American Sociologist* 36: 46-65.

Burawoy, Michael. 2004. "Public Sociologies: Contradictions, Dilemmas, and Possibilities." *Social Forces* 82, 4: 1603-18.

–. 2005a. "2004 Presidential Address: For Public Sociology." *American Sociological Review* 70, 1: 4-28.

–. 2005b. "Conclusion: Provincializing the Social Sciences." In *The Politics of Method in the Human Sciences,* edited by G. Steinmetz, 508-25. Durham, NC: Duke University Press.

–. 2005c. "The Critical Turn to Public Sociology." *Critical Sociology* 31, 3: 313-26.

–. 2005d. "Rejoinder: Toward a Critical Public Sociology." *Critical Sociology* 31, 3: 379-90.

–. 2005e. "Response: Public Sociology: Populist Fad or Path to Renewal?" *British Journal of Sociology* 56, 3: 417-32.

–. 2005f. "The Return of the Repressed: Recovering the Public Face of American Sociology, One Hundred Years On." *Annals AAPSS* 600 (July): 68-85.

–. 2005g. "Third-Wave Sociology and the End of Pure Science." *American Sociologist* 36: 152-65.

–. 2006. "A Public Sociology for Human Rights." In *Public Sociologies Reader,* edited by Judith Blau and Keri E. Iyall Smith, 1-18. Lanham, MD: Rowman and Littlefield.

–. 2007. "The Field of Sociology: Its Power and Its Promise." In *Public Sociology: Fifteen Eminent Sociologists Debate Politics and the Profession in the Twenty-First Century,* edited by Dan Clawson, Robert Zussman, Joy Misra, Naomi Gerstel, Randall Stokes, Douglas L. Anderton, and Michael Burawoy, 241-48. Berkeley: University of California Press.

–. 2008. "What Is to Be Done: Theses on the Degradation of Social Existence in a Globalizing World." *Current Sociology* 56, 3: 357-59.

–. 2009. "The Public Sociology Wars." In *Handbook of Public Sociology,* edited by Vincent Jeffries, 449-73. Lanham, MD: Rowman and Littlefield.

Clawson, Dan, Robert Zussman, Joya Misra, Naomi Gerstel, Randall Stokes, Douglas L. Anderton, and Michael Burawoy, eds. 2007. *Fifteen Eminent Sociologists Debate Politics and the Profession in the Twenty-First Century.* Berkeley: University of California Press.

Collins, Patricia Hill. 2007. "Going Public: Doing the Sociology That Had No Name." In *Public Sociology: Fifteen Eminent Sociologists Debate Politics and the Profession in the Twenty-First Century,* edited by Dan Clawson, Robert Zussman, Joya Misra, Naomi Gerstel, Randall Stokes, Douglas L. Anderton, and Michael Burawoy, 101-13. Berkeley: University of California Press.

Ellwood, Charles. 1910. *Sociology and Modern Social Problems.* New York: American Book Company.

Feagin, Joe, Sean Elias, and Jennifer Mueller. 2009. "Social Justice and Critical Public Sociology." In *Handbook of Public Sociology,* edited by Vincent Jeffries, 71-88. Lanham, MD: Rowman and Littlefield.

Furedi, Frank. 2009. "Recapturing the Sociological Imagination: The Challenge for Public Sociology." In *Handbook of Public Sociology,* edited by Vincent Jeffries, 171-87. Lanham, MD: Rowman and Littlefield.

Gans, Herbert J. 1988. "Sociology in America: The Discipline and the Public." *American Sociological Review* 54: 1-16.

–. 2010. "Public Ethnography; Ethnography as Public Sociology." *Qualitative Sociology* 33: 97-104.

Glenn, Evelyn Nakano. 2007. "Whose Public Sociology? The Subaltern Speaks, But Who Is Listening?" In *Handbook of Public Sociology,* edited by Vincent Jeffries, 213-30. Lanham, MD: Rowman and Littlefield.

Glenn, Norval D. 2009. "Some Suggested Standards for Distinguishing between Good and Bad Public Sociology." In *Handbook of Public Sociology,* edited by Vincent Jeffries, 135-50. Lanham, MD: Rowman and Littlefield.

Goldberg, Avi, and Axel van den Berg. 2009. "What Do Public Sociologists Do? A Critique of Burawoy." *Canadian Journal of Sociology* 34, 3: 765-802.

Hays, Sharon. 2007. "Stalled at the Altar? Conflict, Hierarchy, and Compartmentalization in Burawoy's Public Sociology." In *Public Sociology: Fifteen Eminent Sociologists Debate Politics and the Profession in the Twenty-First Century,* edited by Dan Clawson, Robert Zussman, Joya Misra, Naomi Gerstel, Randall Stokes, Douglas L. Anderton, and Michael Burawoy, 79-90. Berkeley: University of California Press.

Helmes-Hayes, Rick, and Neil McLaughlin. 2009. "Public Sociology in Canada: Debates, Research and Historical Context." *Canadian Journal of Sociology* 34, 3: 573-600.

Hu, Linda. 2009. "Integrating the Four Sociologies: The 'Baigou Project' in China." In *Handbook of Public Sociology,* edited by Vincent Jeffries, 245-62. Lanham, MD: Rowman and Littlefield.

Jeffries, Vincent, ed. 2009. *Handbook of Public Sociology*. Lanham, MD: Rowman and Littlefield.

Lee, Alfred McClung. 1978. *Sociology for Whom?* New York: Oxford University Press.

Leonard, Elizabeth Dermody. 2009. "From Data to Drama: Returning Research to Convicted Survivors." In *Handbook of Public Sociology,* edited by Vincent Jeffries, 225-44. Lanham, MD: Rowman and Littlefield.

Lynd, Robert S. 1939. *Knowledge for What? The Place of Social Science in American Culture*. Princeton, NJ: Princeton University Press.

Massey, Douglas S. 2007. "The Strength of Weak Politics." In *Public Sociology: Fifteen Eminent Sociologists Debate Politics and the Profession in the Twenty-First Century,* edited by Dan Clawson, Robert Zussman, Joya Misra, Naomi Gerstel, Randall Stokes, Douglas L. Anderton, and Michael Burawoy, 145-57. Berkeley: University of California Press.

Mesny, Ann. 2009. "What Do 'We' Know That 'They' Don't? Sociologists' versus Nonsociologists' Knowledge." *Canadian Journal of Sociology* 34, 3: 671-95.

Mills, C. Wright. 1959. *The Sociological Imagination*. New York: Oxford University Press.

Morrow, Raymond A. 2009. "Rethinking Burawoy's Public Sociology." In *Handbook of Public Sociology,* edited by Vincent Jeffries, 47-70. Lanham, MD: Rowman and Littlefield.

Nichols, Lawrence T., ed. 2007. *Public Sociology The Contemporary Debate*. New Brunswick, NJ: Transaction Publishers.

Nielsen, François. 2004. "The Vacant 'We': Remarks on Public Sociology." *Social Forces* 82, 4: 1619-27.

Nyden, Philip, Leslie Hossfeld, and Gwendolyn Nyden. 2012. *Public Sociology Research Action and Change*. Los Angeles, CA: Sage.

Oppenheimer, Mark. 2012. "Sociologist's Paper Raises Questions on Role of Faith in Scholarship." *New York Times,* 13 October.

Patterson, Orland. 2007. "About Public Sociology" In *Public Sociology: Fifteen Eminent Sociologists Debate Politics and the Profession in the Twenty-First Century,* edited by Dan Clawson, Robert Zussman, Joya Misra, Naomi Gerstel, Randall Stokes, Douglas L. Anderton, and Michael Burawoy, 176-94. Berkeley: University of California Press.

Piven, Frances Fox. 2007. "From Public Sociology to Politicized Sociologist." In *Public Sociology: Fifteen Eminent Sociologists Debate Politics and the Profession in the Twenty-First Century,* edited by Dan Clawson, Robert Zussman, Joya Misra, Naomi Gerstel, Randall Stokes, Douglas L. Anderton, and Michael Burawoy, 158-68. Berkeley: University of California Press.

Regnerus, Mark. 2012. "How Different Are the Adult Children of Parents Who Have Same-Sex Relationships? Findings from the New Family Structures Study." *Social Science Research* 41: 752-70.

Schalk, David. 1991. *War and the Ivory Tower: Algeria and Vietnam.* New York: Oxford University Press.

Smith-Lovin, Lynn. 2007. "Do We Need a Public Sociology? It Depends on What You Mean by *Sociology.*" In *Public Sociology: Fifteen Eminent Sociologists Debate Politics and the Profession in the Twenty-First Century,* edited by Dan Clawson, Robert Zussman, Joya Misra, Naomi Gerstel, Randall Stokes, Douglas L. Anderton, and Michael Burawoy, 124-34. Berkeley: University of California Press.

Statistics Canada. 2009. "How Data Are Used." http://www.statcan.gc.ca/.

Stinchcombe, Arthur L. 2007. "Speaking Truth to the Public, and Indirectly to Power." In *Public Sociology: Fifteen Eminent Sociologists Debate Politics and the Profession in the Twenty-First Century,* edited by Dan Clawson, Robert Zussman, Joya Misra, Naomi Gerstel, Randall Stokes, Douglas L. Anderton, and Michael Burawoy, 135-44. Berkeley: University of California Press.

Touraine, Alain. 2007. "Public Sociology and the End of Society." In *Public Sociology: Fifteen Eminent Sociologists Debate Politics and the Profession in the Twenty-First Century,* edited by Dan Clawson, Robert Zussman, Joya Misra, Naomi Gerstel, Randall Stokes, Douglas L. Anderton, and Michael Burawoy, 67-78. Berkeley: University of California Press.

Wallerstein, Immanuel. 2007. "The Sociologist and the Public Sphere." In *Public Sociology: Fifteen Eminent Sociologists Debate Politics and the Profession in the Twenty-First Century,* edited by Dan Clawson, Robert Zussman, Joya Misra, Naomi Gerstel, Randall Stokes, Douglas L. Anderton, and Michael Burawoy, 169-75. Berkeley: University of California Press.

Woodiwiss, Anthony. 2005. *Scoping the Social.* New York: Open University Press.

PART 1

DEBATING THE NORMATIVE DIMENSIONS OF PROFESSIONAL SOCIOLOGY

1

Returning to the Classics

Looking to Weber and Durkheim to Resolve the Theoretical Inconsistencies of Public Sociology

ARIANE HANEMAAYER

Durkheim and Weber conceived of the enterprise of sociology as the scientific study of social phenomena (social facts and social action) and understood sociology to be necessarily engaged in public issues that transcend individual experience. As two of the classical founders of the discipline, Weber and Durkheim were concerned with developing the program of sociology and its relation to social change. Both thinkers understood the development of the object and subsequent program of sociological research as concurrent and intertwined with questions concerning the ethical, political, and normative valences of the discipline. For these early sociologists, doing sociology has political, ethical, and normative commitments specifically grounded in sociological practice.

Debates regarding Michael Burawoy's 2004 American Sociological Association (ASA) presidential address have stirred up much interest and controversy surrounding the endorsement of public sociology by the ASA.[1] Burawoy (2007) advocates for sociological engagement with public issues through practices that he terms *organic public sociology.* He describes this as bringing "sociology into a conversation with publics," a process in which "the sociologist works in close connection with a visible, thick, active, local, and often counter-public" (28). For Burawoy, the relationship between the researcher and the "researched" is "mutual education" to "make a better world" (28). The commitments of public sociology to make a better world, however, prescribe a "sociological" relationship to publics at the expense of metatheoretically grounded and reflexive sociological practice.

In this chapter, I develop the relationship between knowledge and sociologically construed political projects. I argue that public sociology is overdetermined by its normative commitments and is, in fact, ideological, moral philosophy. Following this demonstration, I retrieve the sociological commitments of public sociology by considering the sociological and political practice of Weber and Durkheim. Looking to Weber and Durkheim will resolve both the inconsistencies and the moralizing tone of public sociology.

A Guilty Reading of Public Sociology

This chapter demonstrates that public sociology is not sociological by giving it a "guilty reading," in the Althusserian sense. Guilty readings begin by posing a question to a discourse (in this case, public sociology) about its "relation to its object" (Althusser and Balibar 1997, 14). I do so by asking if the object of public sociology is consistent with the ontological, epistemological, and normative commitments of sociological terrain,[2] as expressed by Burawoy's (2005a) category of professional sociology and the sociological problematics of Weber and Durkheim. I conceive of the "terrain" of sociology by employing the spatial metaphor described by Louis Althusser (Althusser and Balibar 1997), a visuality that represents an epistemological structure where questions are posed and answers may be "sighted." The metatheoretical commitments that comprise a sociological terrain are the production condition for asking and investigating sociological questions in order to say something substantial about the social world and its phenomena. Reading any sociological statement symptomatically "helps to identify its useful parts and to discover symptoms (of incoherence) and to assess whether these merely indicate inadequacies or a point at which discourses intersect" (Pearce 1989, 5). My goal is not to show how public sociology inadequately explains its objects or epistemological terrain; instead, I show how the normative commitments of public sociology are inconsistent with the terrain of its sociological problematic and metatheoretical commitments. I demonstrate how the normative commitments of public sociology are inconsistent with metatheoretical commitments of Burawoy's "professional sociology" category and the sociologies of Weber and Durkheim.

Burawoy's (2005a) public sociology leaves behind constitutive sociological metatheoretical commitments and becomes a movement of advocacy – to make a better world – disconnected from its sociological terrain and amounts to what Durkheim (1982) refers to as moral philosophy. Moral philosophy is the method of the moralists who philosophize on the moral worth of a concept. If the concern of public sociology is making the world a better place, this is an example of a moralist philosophizing, taking as its concern what actions are morally good and worthwhile.[3] I argue that public sociology, while trying to specify how and why sociological practice should relate to broader publics by making the world better, actually generates a series of "oversights" (Althusser and Balibar 1997), unwittingly rendering visible a normative problematic formulated outside of a consistent sociological problematic.[4] In short, the answer rendered by public sociology about how to relate sociological knowledge to broader publics is an answer to a question that belongs to the terrain of moral philosophy.

To make my argument, I read selected materials on public sociology symptomatically to assess how questions and answers are connected (and not), and whether both questions and answers share the same metatheoretical commitments, suppositions that are the production condition for understanding the discourse-object relation. Next, I retheorize public sociology to retrieve public sociology on sociological terrain, specifically the sociology of Weber and Durkheim. I do this by establishing Weber's and Durkheim's respective sociological commitments and explicate what public sociology would look like if practised in each social theorist's sociological terms. Concluding remarks discuss the contours of a sociologically coherent public sociology.

The Programmatics of Public Sociology: A Symptomatic Reading

The public sociology debate touches on significant issues surrounding the sociological production of knowledge, knowledge transfer, and political projects. In Burawoy's (2005a) terms, these concerns are articulated in the relationship between professional and public sociology. Professional sociology is the "accumulated body of knowledge, orienting questions, and conceptual frameworks" carried out by way of "true and tested methods" (10). Burawoy considers professional sociology to be the heart of the discipline, concerned with the methods by which the projects of sociology are accomplished – how knowledge is produced and accumulated. Public sociology, on the other hand, takes as its task the provision of solutions to public and social problems (as discovered and verified by the methods of professional sociology). The goals of these projects are mutually defined through a "dialogic relation between sociologist and public": "the agenda of each is brought to the table, in which each adjusts to the other" (Burawoy 2005a, 7-8). Burawoy distinguishes between the practice of the professional and public sociologist through the idea of the production and accumulation of sociological knowledge. For Burawoy (2005a), the professional sociologist produces knowledge for instrumental purposes – for the sake of knowing more about the social world, society, and so on – whereas the public sociologist is committed to reflexive knowledge, asking what knowledge is for and acting based on that reflection. If the reflexive commitment of public sociology is asking what knowledge is for, then the mandate of public sociology lies in a normative dimension. The public sociologist's orientation to the task of any given project and the knowledge gained from it involves asking what the phenomenon of investigation is and acknowledging that it requires a normative judgment – that something *must* be done, a judgment *must* be made to act on the accumulated knowledge of sociology. Knowledge then becomes subservient to the aim of making normative judgments in providing and proposing solutions to social problems. The public sociologist is not concerned with the social context that makes certain forms of knowledge/statements possible, or more or less influential. Instead, the public sociologist is interested in acting on the knowledge accumulated and produced by sociology and its projects.

This normative dimension of public sociology that I am highlighting also circulates in statements by some of Burawoy's supporters. For example, Smith-Lovin (2007, 125) contends that knowledge "should be used to improve the lot of others, when it is relevant to their potential interests"; thus, moral questions of what knowledge should be for become predominant. Scholars who agree that sociologists should be "sharing insights of sociology with the public and contributing to the common good" caution that this implies thoughtful and critical engagement with publics, not merely sound bites (Hays 2007, 81).[5] While some supporters of Burawoy advise that the public sociology mandate heed such warnings as the problems of truth and prediction (Stinchcombe 2007, 136; Abbott 2007, 200), Glenn (2009, 137), for example, goes on to develop standards for public sociological practice and the role of "experts" providing knowledge to the community: "a good public sociologist will ... refrain from dogmatic adherence to 'derivative values.'" Despite the contradiction that Glenn sets forth in developing a public sociologist who adheres (perhaps dogmatically) to Glenn's own standard of not being "dogmatic" about any "derivative value," he takes up Burawoy's version of public sociology by engaging with the academic dialogue regarding how public sociology should be practised. This line of thinking, while supportive of Burawoy, is also normatively prescriptive. Supporters such as Stinchcombe, Abbott, and Glenn remain faithful to the normative commitments of public sociology, concerning themselves with the necessary use of sociological knowledge rather than questions of how social problems are generated and instead emphasize standards and techniques one ought to adhere to when practising public sociology.

While public sociology seems desirable to sociologists concerned with human rights, public sociology has also met with controversy and its share of skepticism since Burawoy's statements (e.g., 2005a, 2005b, 2007). For example, Collins (2007) suggests that, for the classical theorists, bettering humanity meant doing sociology. Additionally, Brint (2007, 239) comments, public sociology may "undermine the development of our disciplinary core." Brint speculates that public sociology makes trouble for the rigour with which sociologists study and make statements about what is happening in the social world, as well as possible consequences for the discipline's body of research and writing. Both Collins and Brint indicate that sociology is compromised by the overdetermined normative problematic of public sociology,[6] shifting from the sociological concern with "what *is* the case" to the terrain consistent with moral philosophy concerning "what *ought to be* the case."

The Oversight of Public Sociology

The normative commitments of public sociology risk fostering a discipline that is dedicated to the public not through doing sociology and studying the happenings of the social world but through advocacy. To be "for" a public sociology, sociologists represent "the interests of humanity" (Burawoy 2007, 56) by prescribing that sociologists "act in the political arena" (30), and share the "insights of sociology with the public ... contributing to the common good" (Hays 2007, 81). I have briefly shown how public sociology is overdetermined by its normative commitments. In this section I explicate the metatheoretical commitments of public sociology to show how it has left sociological grounds.

The main concern of public sociology is with political intervention (e.g., activism, advocacy) in a social problem. This activity depends upon a model of the dissemination of knowledge, passed from the vast pool of accumulated sociological knowledge (i.e., experts who claim to know how to make the world better) to a public taken to be ignorant but that could be made knowledgeable by an interaction with sociology.[7] The sociological dissemination of knowledge to a public is concerned with advocating for the "good/right" way to live in the world: what *ought to be* in the world overdetermines consideration of what *is* in the world. The problem of producing a better world is associated with knowledge accumulation, its dissemination, and political action. By being engaged in political action, sociologists pass on their knowledge to make a better world under the auspices of public sociology. And the knowledge produced by professional sociology provides the legitimacy and expertise that allows public sociology to advocate for its normative judgments. The public sociologist is committed to a world where more knowledge about the social world produces desirable social change.

Further, Burawoy (2007, 30) acknowledges that "public sociology has no intrinsic normative valence, other than the commitment to dialogue around issues raised in and by sociology." He goes on to say, "In this sense, sociology's affiliation with civil society, that is public sociology, represents the interests of humanity – interests in keeping at bay both state despotism and market tyranny" (56). At first, Burawoy is saying that public sociology is committed to mutual education about the knowledge produced by sociological research. Then Burawoy says that there are normative valences, those of representing "the interests of humanity" against oppression or cruelty (which he associates here with state despotism and market tyranny). Here lies the incoherence with the metatheoretical commitments of sociology: on the one hand, public sociology is committed to an open dialogue based on issues raised by doing sociology. On the other hand, public sociology resonates on another terrain, one overdetermined by normative commitments to make a better world in the interests of humanity.

Burawoy's slip from the sociological problematic to a solution overdetermined by moralizing (doing the right/good thing to end oppression and cruelty) is what Durkheim calls the *ideological method.* Durkheim (1982, 86) notes that it is desirable to use science for the bettering of humanity, but cautions that it is not scientific to classify social phenomena in relation to an "overriding concept" (in this case, the interests of humanity). "The use of notions to govern the collation of facts, rather than deriving notions from them," is not scientific (86). Instead, this is ideological science. When a concept (such as the good/right in the interests of humanity) normatively determines the organization of facts, the concept reproduces itself upon the facts. For example, if a policy maker searches out evidence for why cell phone use while driving leads to poor driving (e.g., motor vehicle accidents) to advocate for creating a law that prohibits the use of cell phones while driving, the collection of facts has been pre-organized by the normative interest in demonstrating that cell phone use produces bad driving. Althusser (Althusser and Balibar 1997, 45) refers to this kind of a priori organization of facts as *dogmatic.*[8] Similarly, public sociology slips into normative ideology because it looks for instances of injustice against humanity (e.g., cruelty, oppression) in the facts or knowledge accumulated by sociology. A scientific (i.e., not dogmatic) sociology would examine the phenomena and events and ask under what social relations the phenomena and events can be understood as unjust as well as examine the social conditions that gave rise to the phenomena and events themselves.

Touraine (2007, 78) anticipates my intervention here and reasons that sociology is committed to "discovering in which sectors of social life 'committed' sociology can most probably make clear the *nature of social problems* and the conditions of politically and morally efficient reform programs" (emphasis added). Here, Touraine marks a break between public sociology and the sociological problematic. The terrain of public sociology is concerned with normative engagements, advocacy for making a better world, acting in a political arena to generate social change. What counts as bettering humanity is understood according to the ideological criteria of acting in the interests of humanity. What might instead be perceived as the strength of the program of sociology is its ability to analyze and explain the circumstances under which certain social phenomena come to be understood as "good" for humanity. Public sociology is not reflexively committed to its knowledge, knowledge objects, or programs for advocating on behalf of publics based on that knowledge.[9] Public sociology is not reflexive insofar as it fails to be critically aware of its own assumptions and preconceptions; it is not concerned with the "interrelationships between knowledge and power that obtain [the sociological] field" (Woodiwiss 2005, 88-89). Burawoy's answer to the question of what knowledge is for assumes that knowledge is separated from its history and its relationship to a broader community, social (inter)relationships, and power. The ideological method of public sociology ignores the facts that produce knowledge about human rights; they are themselves conditions of social relations.

As Nichols (2009, 41) contends, sociologists "cannot be the moral vanguard of humanity, as Burawoy seems to believe," if they are to be committed to doing sociology. A reflexive public sociology is metatheoretically committed to how knowledge about the social world is understood in particular ways by particular publics in contingent circumstances.

The Epistemic Problem of Public Sociology

Agger's (2007) position on public sociology, as proposed by Burawoy, is that positivism remains the problem with public sociology – indeed, with all sociology. As Agger states,

> On the one hand, I welcome discussion of public sociology in the discipline. This helps diminish the emphasis on method that has distracted sociology since the 1970s from broad-gauged issues of practice, problems, and policy. On the other hand, I confess to a degree of cynicism when I see the American Sociological Association endorsing the brand of "public sociology"... I think Burawoy's version of public sociology is problematic, essentially ceding the core of disciplinary power to the positivists who edit the journals and control the major departments. (Agger 2007, 267)[10]

The concern with the improvement of humanity by employing the knowledge of the social sciences is a reemergence of earlier sociological discussions. The discipline of sociology appeared in a historical conjuncture characterized by the rise of the philosophy of the Enlightenment, the decline of Christian theology and the Catholic Church, and the Restoration in France. Saint-Simon and his student, Comte, developed sociology as a normative enterprise that not only collects knowledge about the social realm but also uses that knowledge to better the social world. For these early sociologists, "the world ... contained no natural healing element. The body-social was neither self-healing, nor did it bring into life new social forces capable of providing a natural basis for a new society. New religious and moral principles had therefore to be introduced in order to make the world normal and natural" (Therborn 1976, 222).

Building on these principles of Saint-Simon, Comte's central ideas relate to the evolution of societies through what he termed "theological" to "positive" states (Gane 2006, 2). The "arrival of a new society" would have to be brought about based on the "fundamental characteristics of the new epoch" that sociology could determine (Therborn 1976, 222). Like other sciences, sociology would have a principle role in bringing about this important shift in the social world. Sociology was to revolutionize European society brought by the "triumphant march of reason" (Gane 2006, 3). For Comte, the necessary task of sociology is to use scientific reason to help society evolve, through scientific development, into the positive state (the best state). The object of Comte's sociology is the study of this very transformation between the theological and the positive society: "the correct and objective logic entailed ... first to discover the logic of the past, then that of the future and only then could the present state ... be determined" (3). At this time, the raison d'être of sociology was to determine how to improve the state of society. Comte simultaneously announced the creation of sociology and the completion of its task: the improvement of society to its "positive state."

Further, Comte considered the desire to improve society an innate human drive: "Comte relates all the drive for progress of the human species to this basic tendency, 'which directly impels man continually to improve his condition in all respects'" (Durkheim 1982, 89). Comte's main conception of the human condition was that humans tended towards progress, greater happiness, improving society's conditions. This interest is parallel to Burawoy's project: knowledge to make a better world reflects Comte's principle of the drive of the social sciences as the innate drive to make society better.

Durkheim disagrees with this aspect of Comte's positivism:

> To demonstrate the utility of a fact does not explain its origins, nor how it is what it is. The uses which it serves presume the specific properties characteristic of it, but do not create it. Our need for things cannot cause them to be of a particular nature; consequently, that need cannot produce them out of nothing, conferring in this way existence upon them. They spring from causes of another kind. The feeling we have regarding their utility can stimulate us to set these causes in motion and draw upon the effects they bring in their train, but it cannot conjure up these results out of nothing. (Durkheim 1982, 89)

For Durkheim, the crux of sociology is to explain the relationship between the object or nature of social phenomenon and history – that is, the nature of social phenomena and their conditions of existence (Durkheim 1982). For this reason, Durkheim does not believe that the work of sociology is finished, as Comte declared. Durkheim points out that a concern with the utility of facts, as proposed by Comte, reveals a reflexive problem with sociology. Comte's science is dedicated to the improvement of the human condition through an instrumental relation to knowledge, one unaware of its social relations or historical conditions in the broader social context. A commitment to the normative project of making knowledge useful ignores the social conditions of moral facts. Durkheim supports a form of sociology that is reflexively grounded and committed to exploring and interpreting the broader social history and social conditions that make it possible to understand or explain phenomena in a certain way. Durkheim took what we might today recognize as public sociology seriously, but in different terms; it is not a matter of for whom or for what utility, nor for the improvement of humanity in the sense suggested by Comte and echoed by Burawoy and others.

"To the extent that sociology exists," Durkheim (1973c [1890], 42) states,

> it is more and more sharply separated from what is called, rather inappropriately, the political sciences, those bastard speculations, half theoretical and half practical, half science and half art, which are sometimes still confused, but wrongly, with sociology. The latter, like any science, studies what is and what has been, seeks laws, but is not interested in the future ... This is not sociologist's advice – it will be the societies themselves which will find the solution.

Sociology is concerned with the relation between the phenomenon as it exists (what it is) and how it emerged (its social history); it does not predict the future.

In the second preface to *The Division of Labour in Society,* Durkheim (1984, 1) states that "the sociologist's task is not that of the statesman. Accordingly we do not have to set out in detail what that reform should be. We need only indicate its general principles as they appear to emerge from the facts." Durkheim makes this argument in the context of his discussion of the corporation as an "essential organ of public life" (liv). He concludes that "in the present state of scientific knowledge we cannot foresee what it [the laws regarding the regulation of corporations] should be, except in ever approximate and uncertain terms. How much more important it is to set to work immediately in constituting the moral forces which alone can give that law substance and shape" (lvii). For Durkheim, the role of sociology is demonstrating the conditions that give way to the malfunction of an "organ" of the state/civil society. By locating the conditions that affect the cohesion or functioning of an institution or social phenomenon, the sociologist can demonstrate under what conditions the malfunction can be repaired. The contribution that sociology makes to better humanity is theorizing the possibilities for social change.

Retrieving the Sociology in Public Sociology

In this section, I take the works and sociological terrain of Max Weber and Emile Durkheim and, symptomatically, reread public sociology on their respective terrains and problematics. Agger (2007, 285) asks that "sociology rethink [its] relationship to politics and the public sphere." The slip from public sociology to moral philosophy risks losing the already present, socially construed political commitments of sociology. I contend that it is necessary to retheorize public sociology and its call for political and public engagements by demonstrating how one may do public sociology by doing sociology. Here, I outline Weber and Durkheim's metatheoretical commitments, how each conceived of politics, and what public sociology would look like on their respective terrains.

Public Sociology on the Weberian Terrain

Burawoy's (2007, 30) claim that sociologists must "act in the political arena" and have a "collaborative relation between sociology and journalism" (57) would be supported by Weber's version of politics and sociology. However, Weber's metatheoretical commitments put these obligations in a different light. To begin, Weber's ontological commitments state,

> Sociology ... is a science concerning itself with the interpretive understanding of social action and thereby with a causal explanation of its course and consequences. We shall speak of "action" insofar as the acting individual attaches a subjective meaning to his behaviour – be it overt or covert, omission or acquiescence. Action is "social" insofar as its subjective meaning takes into account the behaviour of others and is thereby oriented in its course. (Weber 1978, 4)

For Weber, the individual (or collections of individuals) engaged in social action is the ontological object of sociological knowledge.

All individual action involves subjective meaning. For Weber, the "social" is the individual's self-understanding in a social context; it is one's relation to the world that is subjectively meaningful. Knowledge is always already possible because of one being spontaneously oriented to a world that one finds meaningful or where one finds meaning. The sociologist studies the social action of an individual or group to find the social value in which the social action finds its significance.

For Weberian sociological investigation of political action, the individual engaged in political practice (social action) is one who is oriented to politics as her vocation. Weber (1946b, 77-78) understands politics as the leadership of or influencing of a political association of a state, "a community that (successfully) claims the monopoly of the legitimate use of physical force within a given territory." Weber describes a social commitment to politics as follows:

> There are two ways of making politics one's vocation: either one lives "for" politics or one lives "off" politics. By no means is this contract an exclusive one. The rule is, rather, that man does both, at least in thought, and certainly he also does both in practice. He who lives "for" politics makes politics his life, in an internal sense. Either he enjoys the naked possession of the power he exerts, or he nourishes his inner balance and self-feeling by the consciousness that his life has *meaning* in the service of a "cause." In this sense, every sincere man who lives for a cause also lives off this cause. (Weber 1946b, 9, emphasis in original)

For Weber, politics as one's vocation is both subjectively meaningful, that "his [or her] life has meaning in service of a cause," and the cause to which one is oriented takes into account the current and anticipated subjective meanings of others. Weber's version of public sociology would consider the public sociologist as oriented to a meaningful political cause; this is similar to Burawoy's version. But, in asking what sociological knowledge is for, Weber cautions that sociologists, as teachers, being like leaders, do not relay worthwhile knowledge to a public, thus telling them what to think and how to act. Instead, the sociologist, as a teacher, demonstrates and offers a way of thinking, which is sociological (scientific) thinking (Weber 1946a, 143-45). In the following passage, Weber outlines the relation between doing sociology and being politically oriented:

> If you take such and such a stand, then, according to scientific experience, you have to use such and such a means in order to carry out your conviction practically. Now, these means are perhaps such that you believe you must reject them. Then you simply must choose between the end and the inevitable means. Does the end "justify" the means? Or does it not? The teacher can confront you with the necessity of this choice. He cannot do more, so long as he wishes to remain a teacher and not to become a demagogue. He can, of course, also tell you that if you want such and such an end, then you must take into the bargain the subsidiary consequences which according to all experience will occur. Again we find ourselves in the same situation as before. These are still problems that can also emerge for the technician, who in numerous instances has to make decisions according to the principle of the lesser evil or of the relatively best. Only to him one thing, the main thing, is usually given, namely, the end. But as soon as truly "ultimate" problems are at stake for us this is not the case. With this, at long last, we come

> to the final service that science as such can render to the aim of clarity, and at the same time we come to the limits of science. (Weber 1946a, 151)

For Weber, science cannot give us a worldview, that is, prescribe the choices we should make or how to act within the world: sociologists are not the world's "demagogue." Instead, sociology places current issues within the context of the social situation, showing ("teaching") inquirers the possible consequences of certain choices and actions. The Weberian public sociologist would be committed to demonstrating (through teaching, for instance) how a sociological orientation to a problem brings out the ethical and moral issues at stake in the social world with each particular choice (as that choice appears in the context of being an oriented course of action). This means, for Weber, showing both the strengths and limitations of each course of action. Doing science is a way of knowing the powers and limitations of each oriented course of action in the world.

The sociologist as politically oriented does not make "academic prophecy ... [as this] will create only fanatical sects but never a genuine community" (Weber 1946a, 155). Weber's version of the genuine community is one where individuals consider choices of action as oriented social action – action that is subjectively meaningful and takes into account the meanings of others, and considers the possible causes and consequences of each course of action. In other words, a genuine community is a community of sociological thinkers in Weber's view. The Weberian public sociologist is not a prophet or demagogue, advocating for any one particular worldview on a given issue; the Weberian public sociologist is committed to demonstrating and teaching the possible ends from each means laid before the group or individual by examining the course of action's dynamics of social context and meaning.[11] Further, the Weberian public sociologist acts after sociological, thoughtful consideration of the choice and circumstance at hand with integrity to the moral excellence of the best, ethical course of action according to the principle of "lesser evil."

For Weber, this notion of integrity is where politics converges with its calling:

> It is immensely moving when a mature man – no matter whether old or young in years – is aware of a responsibility for the consequences of his conduct and really feels such responsibility with heart and soul. He then acts by following an ethic of responsibility and somewhere he reaches the

> point where he says "Here I stand; I can do no other." That is something genuinely human and moving. And every one of us who is not spiritually dead must realize the possibility of finding himself at some time in that position. Insofar as this is true, an ethics of ultimate ends and an ethic of responsibility are not absolute contrasts but rather supplements, which only in unison constitute a genuine man – a man who can have the "calling for politics." (Weber 1946b, 53-54).

The ethics of the public sociologist, then, is intertwined with her action. The ethics of ultimate ends is the public sociologist's (or individual's) orientation to a desired consequence after recognizing its social nature. The ethical responsibility is understood to be a subjectively meaningful orientation, a decision of agency, recognizing its consequences and limitations as well as the strengths of a given orientation to that ultimate end. The public sociologist is a demonstration of ethical action taking into account the broader social world and community. If public sociologists, as teachers, are able to lead by demonstration, being principled to a genuine community, then the political obligations of the sociologist are fulfilled.

This picture of the public sociologist is a contrast to Burawoy's version of Weber's political message. Weber's sociology maintains normative commitments; however, those commitments are in (reflexive) relation to the causes and consequences of present and potential social action, as well as the subjective meanings of others and oneself.

Public Sociology on the Durkheimian Terrain

Like Weber, Durkheim's sociological problematic consists of political and ethical commitments for sociological practice. For Durkheim, sociology is the study of social forces as carried by the degrees of crystallization of collective representations. The social fact is that which is external to the individual and his personality, actions, and practices, and that constrains or influences social activity; social facts are "rules of conduct that have sanction" and real consequences in social life (Durkheim 1957, 2). Morality is a social fact, the body of rules that constitutes, enables, and constrains everyday actors to definite goals, actions, and obligations in and to the social order (Durkheim 1984, 13).

Morality is "the totality of beliefs and sentiments common to the average members of a society" (Durkheim 1984, 38). This totality of beliefs "forms a determinate system with a life of its own. It can be termed the collective or common consciousness ... By definition it is diffused over society as a whole, but nonetheless possesses specific characteristics that make it a distinctive reality" (38-39). The rules that constrain individuals exist as a reality that has real implications for individuals' lives. The rules can be observed and theorized insofar as they exist by the real consequences they have for social action. Action is social because it is constrained and oriented by the collective consciousness *(conscience collective),* which constitutes all dimensions of social life. It is the sociologist's obligation to examine and theorize "how these rules were established in the course of time: that is, what were the causes that gave rise to them and the useful ends they serve" (Durkheim 1957, 1). The sociologist traces the system of the collective consciousness and the causes that give rise to morality to examine "the way in which they operate in society; that is, how they are applied by individuals" (1). For Durkheim (1957), ethics are the individual's obligations to oneself, family, or professional group, as constituted by morality.

Durkheim "claimed that positive social change required a morality that could be reflected upon, criticized and modified" (Pearce 1989, 47). Durkheim's interest in social change, however, was distinct from that of Comte and Saint-Simon. Durkheim was against the popular socialist philosophy of his time. He describes Saint-Simon's socialist program as follows: "Socialism ... is entirely oriented toward the future. It is above all a plan for the reconstruction of societies, a program for a collective life which does not exist as of yet ... and which is proposed to men as worthy of their preference" (Durkheim 1928, 5). Durkheim understood socialism in much the same way as he described moral philosophy. Socialism was not a science: "Science is a study bearing on a delimited portion of reality which it aims at knowing and, if possible, understanding" (5). Durkheim argues that for Saint-Simon and the socialists, there was no limit or measure for the proposed goals. This is the problem with socialism and its moral philosophy: how would it know when it had reached its goal of the just society? For Durkheim, the problem was a methodological blind alley.

A public sociology in Durkheim's terms would be concerned with explaining morality and would examine the history of the social facts that constrain a particular group (and subsequently its individuals), specifically how a particular morality came to be established over time, the causes that led to its establishment, and the ends it serves for both the individual and the state. The Durkheimian public sociologist would demonstrate what possible consequences the function of morality has at the level of the state, institution, and individual. From here, the public sociologist would be able to sociologically explain what is happening and how it came to happen in a given situation: "The problem is to know, under the present conditions of social life, what moderating functions are necessary and what forces are capable of executing them. The past not only helps us to pose the problem – it also indicates the direction in which the solution should be sought" (Durkheim 1928, 201).

In "Individualism and the Intellectual" (1973a), Durkheim examines individualism as a product of social facts, showing its development throughout history, as well as taking it as an occasion to respond to the political climate of his times, particularly Dreyfusard principles (cf. Lukes 1969). Durkheim sociologically explores and defends the implications of individualism to confront "the central issues of the moral basis of individual rights, the limits of political obligation, the legitimacy of authority, the responsibility of intellectuals and the positive implications of liberalism" (Lukes 1969, 14). Unlike Burawoy's appeal and defence of human rights in public sociology, Durkheim demonstrates that individual human rights are constituted and constrained by social and moral facts. As well, the way that those rights came into existence and how they operate in society are connected to their social history. Burawoy (2006) argues that human rights are the basis for a public sociologist's advocacy but does not account for how it is that these rights have come into existence in particular ways and function at various levels of society, for various publics (e.g., for the individual, or for the state). Durkheim maintains that in any given social context or situation in which the sociologist is engaging, it is important to explain the relation between moral facts and individual human rights.

Durkheimian public sociology thus implies making sound judgments about the issue at hand using the scientific method of examination. It is a problem of "practical ethics" to reserve judgment, or, as Durkheim (1973a, 50) puts it, to "yield less easily to the sway of the masses and the prestige of authority." The public sociologist should not necessarily advocate on behalf of what the group under study is asking for, yielding to the sway of the group. Instead, the public sociologist makes sociologically scientific judgments about the social facts, their function in and for the group, and their consequences. From there, the Durkheimian public sociologist – with an understanding of the history of a social fact, its development, and its modes of operation – then makes an ethical judgment about the situation and its effect on the individual and group with whom she is working.

While Durkheim believes that scholars, as citizens, should participate in public life, he clearly states that the scholar and statesman have different orientations of "mind *(esprit)* and will" (Durkheim 1973b, 59). The role of the sociologist is as an educator: "It is our function to help our contemporaries know themselves in their ideas and in their feelings, far more than to govern them" (Durkheim 1973b, 59). Sociology, as a science of morality, can tell us why certain things are understood as moral and others are not by developing the nature and history of moral facts. Durkheim's science of morality invites us to examine how certain conceptions of "making a better world" come to be understood as moral while others do not. It is likely that Durkheim would not agree with Burawoy's project as it currently stands. Unlike the advocacy of Burawoy's project, the ethical obligation of sociological knowledge is to do science. Durkheim argues that the ethical responsibility of the scientist as an educator is to evaluate whether the conditions of existence for moral facts are just and under what conditions those moral facts arose and are sustained, and who benefits (e.g., state, institution, or individual) from them. This intersection of (social) science, ethical contemplation, and education is how Durkheim would conceive of a public sociology.

Contours of a (Retheorized) Public Sociology

Public sociology is the concern with the production of knowledge and its usefulness for generating social change. Public sociology draws on the knowledge produced by sociology, but its problematic is overdetermined by normative commitments and resembles moral philosophy. A sociological vocation dedicated to the amelioration of social problems and public issues is desirable but requires a reflexive relation between the sociologist and the social world to avoid the sociologist's practising ideological science. Generating social change is an important part of the practice of sociology, as Weber's and Durkheim's sociology suggests.

Generating change, Durkheim would contend, comes from thoughtful consideration of the social conditions that produce public issues, and such issues are made visible by doing social science. To conclude, the meta-theoretical contours of a public sociology have strong relations to political and ethical action, namely, (a) by sociologically articulating the social conditions and social relations that produce social issues, facts, and phenomena; (b) through a reflexive relation to the social world (and oneself in it); (c) by resisting the reproduction of ideological categories and concepts; and (d) by being ethically obliged to change the causes of social issues wherever possible through a pedagogical commitment to doing sociology. For Weber and Durkheim, sociology is an obligation to living, understanding, and being within a structured world. Being a public sociologist is to be ethically committed to practising sociology according to one's sociological principles.[12]

Acknowledgments

I am most grateful to R. Paul Datta, Doug Aoki, Tara Milbrandt, and Christopher Schneider for their comments and suggestions on earlier versions of this chapter. I am additionally grateful to the Social Sciences and Humanities Research Council of Canada for funding support. Appreciation also extends to the workshop participants and contributors to this volume for their stimulating comments and conversation.

Notes

1 For examples of texts that engage with the public sociology debates, see Zimmer (2004), and Helmes-Hayes and McLaughlin (2009), Burawoy (2005a, 2005b, 2006, 2007), Blau and Smith (2006), Nichols (2007), Agger (2007), and Jeffries (2009).

2 For my discussion here, *metatheory* refers to the ontological, epistemological, and normative dimensions in any given sociological piece of work. *Ontology* refers to questions and statements regarding what the nature of a social action *is* or what society *is* (Woodiwiss 2005, 9). *Epistemology* is concerned with the nature of what is known about the social world and those objects within it; epistemology is the theory of knowledge (Benton and Craib 2010, 4). Assumptions regarding the best practices for gaining knowledge about the phenomenon of investigation are also epistemological concerns (Woodiwiss 2005, 9). The normative is concerned with what "ought" to be, particularly morality, ethics, and politics (Benton and Craib 2010, 6).

3 Durkheim contests that moral philosophy is neither scientific nor sociological. I return to Durkheim's case against moral philosophy later with discussion of both Saint-Simon and Comte.

4 For Althusser (Althusser and Balibar 1997, 27), an oversight is when an object is "invisible" on a terrain and does not "answer" the question posed by the visuality of the terrain. Oversight is the "production of the fleeting presence of an aspect of its invisible within the visible field of an existing problematic." This is an instance where the text "slips," producing a "change of terrain," as the object cannot be sighted upon the terrain that produced the initial question (Althusser and Balibar 1997, 27). Where there is a slip, the text is generated as the result of an answer to a different question on a different terrain.

5 For a thorough and rigorous critique of expert intellectuals, see Honneth (2009). Honneth contends that public intellectuals of the kind referred to by Walzer (2000) (indeed, Burawoy and his supporters) are able to identify with the public in order to say what is sayable, to "win a public hearing" (Honneth 2009, 183). What Honneth terms the "social critic," however, instead aims at "interrogating the descriptive system" to change the orientation of publics to social systems and culture (Honneth 2009, 184).

6 Translator Ben Brewster summarizes Althusser's concept of overdetermination as follows: "Althusser uses [this] term to describe the effects of the contradictions in each practice (q.v.) constituting the social formation (q.v.) on the social formation as a whole, and hence back on each practice and each contradiction, and non-antagonism of the contradictions in the structure in dominance (q.v.) at a given historical moment. More precisely, the overdetermination of a contradiction is the reflection in it of its conditions of existence within the complex whole, that is, of the other contradictions in the complex whole, in other words its uneven development" (Althusser 1990, 253). In this case, the normative dimensions of the discourse of public sociology (the complex whole) are the conditions of existence (ontology) for the practice of public sociology. The normative commitments determine the projects of public sociology (the ontological dimension is unevenly represented).

7 For a discussion of this relationship between sociologists as "knowers" conveying knowledge to lay people, see Mesny (2009) and Bucklaschuk, this volume.

8 To further illustrate the distinction between ideology and science, Althusser's (Althusser and Balibar 1997, 45-46) method highlights the epistemological conditions that produce research questions, such as the one in the above example – under what conditions do concerns with "good driving" and cell phone use become relevant? Questioning the circumstances and conditions that give rise theoretically (or also, for Althusser, historically) to particular research questions enables one to avoid doing ideological science. Thus, ideological science practically executes the collection of facts by using an overriding concept, whereas scientific endeavours consider the production conditions that render facts intelligible (at a particular historical conjuncture).

9 Burawoy (2005b, 163) defines reflexivity in "third-wave sociology" as "reflecting on who we are and what we do." To take my argument seriously, doing reflexive public sociology means engaging in socially construed political practice. It does not only mean self-reflection on possible bias in professional sociology or policy sociology as doing sociology for ultimate ends of knowledge production or policy production ("instrumental knowledge") (Burawoy 2005a). Doing reflexive public sociology means considering under what social and historical conditions a "common interest in human freedom" becomes a desirable and necessary project (Burawoy 2005b, 165). Under what conditions does human freedom become an issue? How did these conditions arise? Under what conditions might this change? Reflexivity is more than just asking who we are and what we do; it is the metatheoretical commitments that make what we do possible and being responsible and accountable to them in our political activities.

10 The endorsement by the ASA of the "brand of public sociology" may be less of a surprise than Agger (2007) infers. Consider how early American sociologists often employed moralist rhetoric, informing many of their social reform projects during the early days of the academic discipline of sociology (Coser 1978, 287). In the words of early American sociologist Albion Small, who, "in his presidential address to the American Sociological Society [now, ASA], meeting of 1913 ... stated emphatically, 'The social problem of the twentieth century is whether the civilized nations can *restore themselves to sanity* after the nineteenth-century aberrations of individualism and capitalism'" (Coser 1978, 291, emphasis added). Indeed, according to early

American sociologists, society had lost its moral way, and the discipline of sociology would be able to better humanity and restore its morality and "sanity." For a lengthier discussion of early American trends in sociology, see Coser (1978).

11 Further theoretical analysis may very well lead to a version of combating Weber's own pessimism, where we can imagine that being a Weberian sociologist may provide a means of reflecting on the moral good (significance to others) of the ends themselves inherent in any form of rationalization. A Weberian public sociology that provides the theoretical means of questioning the rules and ideological rule following in legal-rational domination may indeed free the individual from the "essentially fixed route of march" in the "machine" of bureaucratic rationalization and instrumental rationality (Weber 1978, 988).

12 For other examples of public intellectuals who are principled to their respective theoretical problematics, see Schaffer, this volume.

References

Abbott, Andrew. 2007. "For Humanist Sociology." In *Public Sociology: Fifteen Eminent Sociologists Debate Politics and the Profession in the Twenty-First Century,* edited by Dan Clawson, Robert Zussman, Joya Misra, Naomi Gerstel, Randall Stokes, Douglas L. Anderton, and Michael Burawoy, 195-209. Berkeley: University of California Press.

–. 2007. *Public Sociology: From Social Facts to Literary Acts.* 2nd ed. Toronto: Rowman and Littlefield.

Agger, Ben. 2007. *Public Sociology: From Social Facts to Literary Acts.* 2nd ed. Lanham, MA: Rowman and Littlefield.

Althusser, Louis, and Étienne Balibar. 1997. *Reading Capital.* Translated by Ben Brewster. New York: Verso. First published 1968.

–. 1990. *For Marx.* Translated by Ben Brewster. New York: Verso. First published in 1969.

Benton, Ted, and Ian Craib. 2010. *Philosophy of Social Science.* 2nd ed. New York: Palgrave Macmillan.

Blau, Judith, and Keri E. Iyall Smith. 2006. *Public Sociologies Reader.* Toronto: Rowman and Littlefield Publishers.

Brint, Steven. 2007. "Guide for the Perplexed: On Michael Burawoy's 'Public Sociology.'" In *Public Sociology: The Contemporary Debate,* edited by Lawrence T. Nichols, 237-62. New Brunswick, NJ: Transaction Publishers.

Burawoy, Michael. 2005a. "2004 Presidential Address: For Public Sociology." *American Sociological Review* 70, 1: 4-28.

–. 2005b. "Third-Wave Sociology and the End of Pure Science."*American Sociologist* 36, 3-4: 152-65.

–. 2006. "A Public Sociology for Human Rights." In *Public Sociologies Reader,* edited by Judith Blau and Keri E. Iyall Smith, 1-18. Toronto: Rowman and Littlefield.

–. 2007. "For Public Sociology." In *Public Sociology: Fifteen Eminent Sociologists Debate Politics and the Profession in the Twenty-First Century,* edited by Dan Clawson, Robert Zussman, Joya Misra, Naomi Gerstel, Randall Stokes, Douglas L. Anderton, and Michael Burawoy, 23-64. Berkeley: University of California Press.

Clawson, Dan, Robert Zussman, Joya Misra, Naomi Gerstel, Randall Stokes, Douglas L. Anderton, and Michael Burawoy, eds. 2007. *Public Sociology: Fifteen Eminent Sociologists Debate Politics and the Profession in the Twenty-First Century.* Berkeley: University of California Press.

Collins, Patricia Hill. 2007. "Going Public: Doing the Sociology That Had No Name." In *Public Sociology: Fifteen Eminent Sociologists Debate Politics and the Profession in the Twenty-First Century,* edited by Dan Clawson, Robert Zussman, Joya Misra, Naomi Gerstel, Randall Stokes, Douglas L. Anderton, and Michael Burawoy, 101-13. Berkeley: University of California Press.

Coser, Lewis. 1978. "American Trends." In *A History of Sociological Analysis,* edited by Tom Bottomore and Robert Nisbet, 287-320. New York: Basic Books.

Durkheim, Emile. 1928. *Socialism and Saint-Simon.* Translated by Charlotte Sattler. London: Routledge and Kegan Paul.

–. 1957. *Professional Ethics and Civic Morals.* Translated by Cornelia Brookfield. London: Routledge and Kegan Paul.

–. 1973a. "Individualism and the Intellectual." In *Emile Durkheim on Morality and Society,* edited by Robert N. Bellah, 43-57. Chicago: University of Chicago Press. First published 1898.

–. 1973b. "The Intellectual Elite and Democracy." In *Emile Durkheim on Morality and Society,* edited by Robert N. Bellah, 58-62. Chicago: University of Chicago Press. First published 1904.

–. 1973c [1890]. "The Principles of 1789 and Sociology." In *Emile Durkheim on Morality and Society,* edited by Robert N. Bellah, 34-42. Chicago: University of Chicago Press.

–. 1982. *The Rules of Sociological Method and Selected Texts on Sociology and Its Method.* Edited by Steven Lukes. Translated by W.D. Halls. New York: Free Press. First published 1895.

–. 1984. *Division of Labour in Society.* Translated by W.D. Halls. New York: Palgrave Macmillan.

Gane, Mike. 2006. *August Comte.* New York: Routledge.

Glenn, Norval D. 2009. "Some Suggested Standards for Distinguishing between Good and Bad Public Sociology." In *The Handbook of Public Sociology,* edited by Vincent Jeffries, 135-50. Lanham, MD: Rowman and Littlefield.

Hays, Sharon. 2007. "Stalled at the Altar? Conflict, Hierarchy, and Compartmentalization in Burawoy's Public Sociology." In *Public Sociology: Fifteen Eminent Sociologists Debate Politics and the Profession in the Twenty-First Century,* edited by Dan Clawson, Robert Zussman, Joya Misra, Naomi Gerstel, Randall Stokes, Douglas L. Anderton, and Michael Burawoy, 79-90. Berkeley: University of California Press.

Helmes-Hayes, Rick, and Neil McLaughlin. 2009. "Public Sociology in Canada: Debates, Research, and Historical Contexts." *Canadian Journal of Sociology* 34, 3: 573-600.

Honneth, Axel. 2009. *Pathologies of Reason.* New York: Columbia University Press.

Jeffries, Vincent, ed. 2009. *Handbook of Public Sociology.* Lanham, MD: Rowman and Littlefield.

Lukes, Steven. 1969. "Durkheim's 'Individual and the Intellectual.'" *Political Studies* 17, 1: 14-30.

Mesny, Anne. 2009. "What Do 'We' Know that 'They' Don't? Sociologists' versus Nonsociologists' Knowledge." *Canadian Journal of Sociology* 34, 3: 671-95.

Nichols, Lawrence T., ed. 2007. *Public Sociology: The Contemporary Debate*. New Brunswick, NJ: Transaction Publishers.

–. 2009. "Burawoy's Holistic Sociology and Sorokin's 'Integralism': A Conversation of Ideas." In *The Handbook of Public Sociology*, edited by Vincent Jeffries, 27-43. Lanham, MD: Rowman and Littlefield.

Pearce, Frank. 1989. *The Radical Durkheim*. London: Unwin Hyman.

Smith-Lovin, Lynn. 2007. "Do We Need a Public Sociology? It Depends on What You Mean by *Sociology*." In *Public Sociology: Fifteen Eminent Sociologists Debate Politics and the Profession in the Twenty-First Century*, edited by Dan Clawson, Robert Zussman, Joya Misra, Naomi Gerstel, Randall Stokes, Douglas L. Anderton, and Michael Burawoy, 124-34. Berkeley: University of California Press.

Stinchcombe, Arthur L. 2007. "Speaking Truth to the Public, and Indirectly to Power." In *Public Sociology: Fifteen Eminent Sociologists Debate Politics and the Profession in the Twenty-First Century*, edited by Dan Clawson, Robert Zussman, Joya Misra, Naomi Gerstel, Randall Stokes, Douglas L. Anderton, and Michael Burawoy, 135-44. Berkeley: University of California Press.

Therborn, Goran. 1976. *Science, Class and Society*. London: New Left Books.

Touraine, Alain. 2007. "Public Sociology and the End of Society." In *Public Sociology: Fifteen Eminent Sociologists Debate Politics and the Profession in the Twenty-First Century*, edited by Dan Clawson, Robert Zussman, Joya Misra, Naomi Gerstel, Randall Stokes, Douglas L. Anderton, and Michael Burawoy, 67-78. Berkeley: University of California Press.

Wallerstein, Immanuel. 2007. "The Sociologist and the Public Sphere." In *Public Sociology: Fifteen Eminent Sociologists Debate Politics and the Profession in the Twenty-First Century*, edited by Dan Clawson, Robert Zussman, Joya Misra, Naomi Gerstel, Randall Stokes, Douglas L. Anderton, and Michael Burawoy, 169-75. Berkeley: University of California Press.

Walzer, Michael. 2000. "Courage, Sympathy, and a Good Eye: Virtues of Social Criticism and the Uses of Societal Theory." *Deutsche Zeitschrift für Philosophie* 48, 5: 709-18.

Weber, Max. 1946a. *From Max Weber: Essays in Sociology*. Translated and edited by H.H. Gerth and C. Wright Mills. New York: Oxford University Press. First published 1922.

–. 1946b. *Politics as a Vocation*. Translated by H.H. Gerth and C. Wright Mills. Fortress, PA: Fortress Press. First published 1919.

–. 1978. *Economy and Society: An Outline of Interpretive Sociology*. Edited by Guenther Roth and Claus Wittich. Berkeley: University of California Press. First published 1897.

Woodiwiss, Anthony. 2005. *Scoping the Social*. New York: Open University Press.

Zimmer, Catherine J., ed. 2004. "Commentaries and Debates." Special issue, *Social Forces*. 82, 4.

2

Public Sociology, Professional Sociology, and Democracy

AXEL VAN DEN BERG

Michael Burawoy has clearly hit a major nerve in the sociological community with his 2004 call for a "public" sociology (Burawoy 2005a). He set off a multinational firestorm of debate between advocates and critics of his proposals from a bewildering variety of philosophical positions. The arguments are recorded in literally hundreds of articles, collections, special journal issues, and even a full-fledged *Handbook of Public Sociology* (Jeffries 2009) and in a major extension of the franchise into a new Global Sociology (Burawoy, Chang, and Hsieh 2010).

In his closing chapter of the *Handbook,* Burawoy (2009b, 467) asks, "What, then, are these disciplinary struggles about? Why are they so intense?" His answer consists of a Bourdieusian analysis of sociology's "academic field" in which the dominant "professional sociologists" fiercely defend their privileged position against attacks from subordinate, exploited, and underprivileged public and critical sociologists (462-67; see also Burawoy 2007). It is a typical sociologizing trick that neatly discredits and sidesteps whatever critical arguments professional sociologists may bring to bear on his notion of public sociology.[1] Rather than respond with an equally disingenuous counter "analysis,"[2] I want to argue here that the conflict's intensity is due to the fact that something far deeper is at stake than simply professional privilege. At the heart of the debate, I think, is a fundamental disagreement over the relationship between (social) science and democracy. And contrary to the impression Burawoy and his admirers try to make – an impression that they themselves no doubt deeply and authentically believe in – the professional sociologists in this debate are the true democrats while the public sociologists appeal, whether they know it or not, to a deeply *anti*-democratic, technocratic strain that has been part of the sociological subconscious since the days of Auguste Comte. Simply put, while Burawoy's "public sociology" seeks to invest its favoured political causes with the authority of sociology, professional sociology is committed to the notion that the ultimate authority to decide on the validity of its findings is the public at large.

As I and many others have pointed out (Goldberg and van den Berg 2009, 768-73), Burawoy advocates a number of quite different things under the label of public sociology. And many of them are more or less innocuous and thus not terribly controversial. These include better marketing of the discipline, sociologists taking on various civic roles, possibly more room in the curriculum and research agendas for applied sociology, and sociologists acting as "traditional" public intellectuals. While Burawoy does occasionally, and rather disingenuously it seems to me, retreat to these fairly inoffensive positions,[3] these are *not* what the heated debate is all about. It is about the two remaining and most distinctive meanings of Burawoy's public sociology: some disturbing aspects of the "organic" public sociology he advocates and the call to convert the discipline of sociology into "a public that acts in the political arena" (Burawoy 2005a, 8) in the service of "civil society" and even "humanity." These two recommendations have profoundly *un*-democratic implications that rest at least in part on a deep misunderstanding of the nature of "professional" sociology. Let me explain.

Democratic "Public" versus Authoritarian "Professional" Sociology

To be sure, Burawoy's attitude towards what he calls professional sociology, or what others would call academic or social scientific sociology,[4] is somewhat ambiguous. At times, he seems to accord it a position of pre-eminence, of the *primus inter pares* without which the other kinds of sociology could not exist:

> There can be neither public nor policy sociology, however, without a professional sociology that develops a body of theoretical knowledge and empirical findings, put to the test of peer review. Professional sociology provides the ammunition, the expertise, the knowledge, the insight, and the

> legitimacy for sociologists to present themselves to publics or to powers. Professional sociology is the *sine qua non* of all sociologies ... the fact is that today without professional sociology there can be no other sociology. (Burawoy et al. 2004, 105, emphasis in original; see also Burawoy 2005a, 10; 2005b, 319; 2005c, 424; 2004, 1611)

But in his more recent reactions to the ongoing debates, and in particular his Bourdieusian field analyses, Burawoy strikes a decidedly different tone. Here he depicts "professional" sociologists as a bullying, domineering, authoritarian elite that seeks to impose its supposedly "value-free" vision of the discipline on all others. Here are a couple of recent examples.

> [The disciplinary field of sociology is characterized by] a set of relations of domination and exploitation ... In the United States the scientific field rests on armies of teachers in state universities and community colleges who teach excessive amounts for modest compensation. More directly, research departments depend on legions of graduate students who not only do most of the face-to-face teaching and grading but also perform mind numbing operations of research. Together, they make possible the scientific practice of the elite ... many "professionals" want to obscure their dependence on cheap labor by confining the definition of the field to "science," and either expel public sociology, as a relatively autonomous form of knowledge, or bring it under their control. (Burawoy 2009b, 453)

> The struggle for public sociology threatens the equilibrium of our discipline, demystifying the invisible domination of professional sociology, compelling it to come out into the open and defend its interests as the interests of all ... We can call these hegemonic strategies, in which the professionals position themselves as representing the interests of all, a war of position ... A more aggressive strategy, that is a war of movement, is to condemn public sociology ... At the extreme public sociology is demonized as "political orientation in non-partisan clothing" ... which justifies infantilizing and sanctioning its supporters, expelling them if necessary. (466)

In short, the "shock troops of professional sociology" (464) wage a "war of position or movement" against public sociology to "maintain the dominance of self-referential professional sociology" and preserve the privileges of the "priesthood of aging white males from the elite departments" (465).[5] Against these forces of oppression, Burawoy's (2007, 250) public sociology seeks "institutional change that will create more freedom for the subjugated."

Contrast this with how Burawoy describes the public sociologists whose advocate he claims to be. As we have seen already, in his eyes, organic public sociologists are an embattled, subjugated minority, either ignored or actively oppressed by the dominant professionals. They are also, contrary to their professional oppressors, deeply committed not to the comforts of the ivory tower but to their chosen underprivileged "publics" on the outside. "Organic public sociologists" are out there with the masses "working tirelessly and invisibly in the trenches of civil society" (2009b, 460). Unlike the traditional public sociologist (read: public intellectual), the organic public sociologist "does not pronounce from the rafters but directly engages with publics in the trenches of society" (452). Not only are such public sociologists working *for* and *with* their respective publics, they are also democratically *accountable to* such publics, unlike the elite professionals, who are only accountable to each other. Thus, "public sociologies march to the tune of dialogic engagement rather than empirical-theoretical knowledge, a consensus rather than a correspondence view of truth, norms of relevance rather than norms of science, accountable to publics rather than peers" (Burawoy 2009b, 466). Contrary to the abstract knowledge of the professional sociologist, evaluated only by his or her peers, public sociologists "pursue communicative knowledge accessible to and accountable to lay publics" (Burawoy 2004, 1611). This is not restricted to the instrumental knowledge decreed to be the only legitimate kind by professional sociologists. For "empirical science can only take us so far: it can help us understand the consequences of our value commitments and inform our value discussions, but it cannot determine those values" (1606-7). Public sociology goes beyond this, actively taking a role and position in the very determination of those values themselves, engaging "publics beyond the academy in dialogue about matters of political and moral concern" (1607).

Now, lest we get the impression that these organic public sociologists would seek to impose their views on their respective publics or try to impose their own particular public's interests on the public at large, it should be clear that public sociologists are deeply committed to democratic dialogue at all times. Unlike their professional nemeses, public sociologists wish to constitute the discipline of sociology and its professional associations "as a public that acts in the political arena" (Burawoy 2005a, 8). Thus, for Burawoy, the American Sociological Association "is a political venue unto itself – a place to debate the stances we might adopt" (Burawoy 2004,

1606). But this must be done as democratically as possible, of course: "We should be sure to arrive at public positions through open dialogue, through free and equal participation of our membership, through deepening our internal democracy ... Public sociology has no intrinsic normative valence, other than the commitment to dialogue around issues raised in and by sociology" (2005a, 8). In Burawoy's view, "from its inception in 1905, the ASA has been a battleground between professionals seeking to centralize control in their hands and countervailing critical voices, calling for internal democracy and stronger public engagement" (2009b, 465).

Furthermore, once the discipline's stances on the correct goals and values have been democratically established, they cannot, of course, simply be foisted upon the wider lay public. "Determining values should take place through democratic and collective deliberation" (Burawoy 2004, 1607), both inside the discipline and its associations and between sociologists and the public at large. This amounts to the democratic process of "public knowledge" creation: "I define *public knowledge* as the discussion of basic values and goals of society between academics and various publics" (Burawoy 2009a, 871, emphasis in original). In short, in contrast to those privileged, domineering, authoritarian, elitist professional sociologists, public sociologists are a profoundly egalitarian and democratic lot, deeply committed to getting their hands dirty with the folks out there and to helping nail down the "basic values and goals of society" through strictly democratic deliberation every step of the way.

The Democratic Ethos of Professional Sociology

Note that Burawoy simply dismisses any claims that professional sociology represents "the interests of all" as obviously nothing but a cloak for a "hegemonic strategy" that aims to preserve professional sociologists' self-interest. He does not provide any specific arguments to refute those claims. In fact, he does not have to because he can quite conveniently lean on a spate of so-called critical literatures, which has become de rigueur in more theoretically inclined circles since the 1960s, denouncing the pretentions of "value-free science" as nothing but a covert defence of the status quo. According to these critics, positivism, or the claim that rigorous methodology ensures some degree of *wertfreiheit* or objectivity, is hopelessly passé.

Burawoy trades heavily on these now fashionable views in order to ridicule any professional sociologists who would defend the primacy of their kind of sociology.[6] Sztompka's naively positivist conception of social science, he Burawoy (2011, 398) informs us, "has been effectively dismantled by diverse schools of post-positivist thinkers that in recent times could start with Karl Popper and include such distinguished philosophers, historians and sociologists as Polanyi, Kuhn, Lakatos, Feyerabend, Shapin, Latour, and Habermas." "The 'pure science' position that research must be completely insulated from politics is untenable since antipolitics is no less political than *public engagement*" (Burawoy 2004, 1605, emphasis in original) so "there is no sociology from nowhere – that is a positivist illusion" (Burawoy 2011, 403). "Recognizing we are part of the world we study, we must take some *stance* with respect to that world. To fail to do so is to take a stance by default" (Burawoy 2004, 1606, emphasis in original). And so on and so forth.

The quotes above allude to the fundamental assumption common to all the currently fashionable critiques of positivism: the insistence that, to use Althusserian language, no knowledge claim is "innocent."[7] From the critical theory of the Frankfurt School and Habermas to postliberal feminism, from Foucauldian poststructuralism to Latourian actor-network theory, they all share a starkly interest-ridden worldview when it comes to knowledge claims. They insist that all such claims must be evaluated first and foremost by the *cui bono* criterion: who benefits? There is no neutral terrain: all knowledge claims serve some interest and by implication must hurt another. Horkheimer's original critique of "traditional theory" is quite clear on this: the positivist claim to describe the world as it is amounts ipso facto to supporting the capitalist status quo, in contrast to "critical theory," which represents a higher order of reason (Horkheimer 1972).[8] While formulated differently in the other literatures referred to above, they draw on the same starkly zero-sum assumption: those who are not explicitly for us (or for the subjugated masses or "change" or "humanity") are ipso facto against us.[9] Put differently, there is no such thing as a politically neutral fact, and any pretence that there is one is inherently misleading or worse.

But however distinguished those "post-positivist thinkers" may be and however fashionable they are among today's cognoscenti, this does not, in itself, render their views beyond question. Merely invoking them (with the important exception of Popper; see below) hardly suffices to relegate all "professional" objections to Burawoy's public sociology to the dustbin of intellectual history as hopelessly passé "positivist illusion." After all, the whole point of the current debate is precisely that "professional" sociologists reject the fashionable view of their kind of social science as just one politically loaded perspective among many. To dismiss this simply by fiat does not really move the debate forward; it just circumvents it.

"Professional" sociologists claim, often with great passion,[10] that they are doing something other than simply trying to force the biased perspective of privileged white males in Western academia on the rest of the world. In fact, they claim no more than what Burawoy concedes in his more charitable moments quoted above: that professional sociology produces the theoretical knowledge and empirical findings, the expertise and legitimacy for sociologists to present themselves to publics or to powers. This is precisely what the defenders of "professional" sociology have argued (see, for example, Brint 2007; Massey 2007; Nielsen 2004; Smith-Lovin 2007; Tittle 2004). But in their view, professional sociology's ability to provide such legitimacy and trusted expertise would be seriously compromised if it were conflated or equated with the political and practical *uses* that can be made of its findings.

So what exactly is this legitimacy and expertise based on? I believe it is ultimately based on modern science's implicit commitment to what might be called a "democratic epistemology," a commitment that has given it its enormous authority and persuasive power in the eyes of the general public. In other words, far from the privileged, domineering elite described by Burawoy, "professional" sociologists subscribe to a fundamentally *democratic* ethos. By contrast, some variants of Burawoy's public sociology suffer from a deep and disturbing strain of *anti*-democratic elitism, one that has been present in the discipline since the days of Auguste Comte.

These are, of course, large claims, and I can only summarily defend them in this limited space. First, what is this democratic epistemology that I say "professional" sociologists subscribe to? Consider the basic methodological principles and practices viewed by such sociologists as forming the core of their science. They consist of a range of techniques to eliminate "bias," including strict sampling and other techniques to ensure "representativity," careful (and, where possible, controlled) observation, strict accountability, replicability, and so on. In other words, the scientific method is an elaborate protocol, always under construction, that is meant to ensure that the results do *not* depend on the preferences of either the researcher or this or that fraction of the intended audience. To put it slightly differently, these methods are meant to ensure fairness in the treatment of different outcomes preferred by different fractions of that audience; they set up the evidential tournament in such a way that all outcomes preferred within the given audience have a fair chance of being supported or refuted. They put all theories favoured within the audience at equal risk. This is what is at stake in eliminating bias in sampling, in carefully considering alternatives in interpreting the findings, in formulating null-hypotheses and strict significance requirements – in short, in paying careful attention to issues of accuracy and representativity. It is what Popper had in mind when he proposed falsifiability as the criterion of scientificity. For Popper (1963, 38), "every genuine test of a theory is an attempt to falsify it, or to refute it. Testability is falsifiability; but there are degrees of testability: some theories are more testable, more exposed to refutation, than others; they take, as it were, greater risks."

Now why do scientists, natural as well as social, put themselves and their often reluctant graduate students through all these hoops? Is it just a shell game meant to fool the members of an unsuspecting public into believing truths that are not theirs, as so many of the postpositivist sophisticates claim? And if so, what accounts for its remarkable success in fooling most of those audiences?

The point of all this effort to avoid bias and ensure representativity is to persuade the members of a possibly skeptical audience of one thing only: that if *they* had stood in the researchers' shoes (or, more likely, sandals), they would have observed the same thing the researcher is reporting to them. Now why do researchers feel called upon to go to such lengths to persuade their audiences of this? Why can they not simply proclaim the validity of their findings by authoritative decree? Because the underlying philosophical principle is that each and every individual in the designated audience, whether that audience consists of fellow scientists or all of humanity, must ultimately judge for him- or herself whether the evidence presented is convincing and the logic compelling.

This is what I mean by a democratic epistemology: to the extent that scientists claim that their findings are valid for all, they can only do so by persuading all that they really are valid from where they, the members of the "all," stand. Ultimately then, the scientific method so dear to "professional" sociologists rests on a commitment to respect the reason and viewpoint – in the sense of the position from which they observe the empirical world – of each and every individual in the designated audience. If the methods do not persuade significant portions of that audience, if that respect is lacking as far as they are concerned, then the researcher stands accused of error or bias, or worse. It means he or she has failed to do his or her job properly.

Note that I am carefully trying to avoid any straightforwardly realist claims with respect to the ultimate reality of the empirical world reported on by the researchers. Nor am I necessarily willing to argue that there actually *is* one single such reality for all audiences or humans, as opposed to the strictly perspectivist position taken by, for instance, postliberal standpoint feminists like Dorothy Smith or Sandra Harding (Smith 1987; Harding 1991, 2004, 2011). All I am saying is that the core methodology of (social) science consists of various techniques and efforts to peacefully overcome at least some of the perspectival differences that divide us. If this fails, all one can do in the name of science is to try again with methods ensuring greater representativity and no more. After that, the only remaining means of "persuasion" is decidedly extra-scientific: appeal to a Higher Authority or force.[11]

Note also that I am not willing to make any strong claims about the possibility of complete value freedom in science, whether natural or social. As Burawoy is fond of pointing out, Max Weber himself strongly emphasized the unavoidability of value commitments for the conduct of (social) science (e.g., Burawoy 2004, 1606).[12] This is why I, like Weber (1949), prefer to talk of value *neutrality:* the point of the methods is to increase the likelihood that the results are neutral with respect to the value differences that divide the members of the audience in question. They are by no means value-free, not least because there will always be plenty of values, or nondemonstrable judgments, that the members of the audience will have to agree on to start with, such as the existence of a shared objective reality, the possibility and desirability of persuading one another peacefully about the nature of that reality, the principle that each rational human being is ultimately his/her own judge in deciding what that reality looks like, and so on. All these prejudgments together form, in effect, precisely the democratic epistemology I am talking about: the belief that each and every human being is the seat of human reason and that there are no legitimate means of persuading him or her of any particular view of objective reality other than those methods that are ultimately based on his or her own perceptions and sense of logic, and therefore rely entirely on voluntary persuasion. Of course, those who refuse to be persuaded can simply reject the scientific method *tout court* and abandon this form of peaceful persuasion for something less pleasant – and/or be viewed as irrational by the rest of us. Alternatively, they can make a claim to the effect that the current methodologies are not inclusive *enough,* which, if found to be a valid objection, necessitates further tinkering with the methods of science to eliminate the source of bias.

There are several well-known objections to this depiction of the nature of (social) science, which we have already encountered in passing. Here I can only briefly touch upon them. First, many will find this description of the practice of science hopelessly utopian and naive in the face of the wealth of social constructivist science and technology studies that have effectively made a mockery of it. This literature shows, its advocates claim, that "that science – sociology included – is not outside society, is not beyond social determination" (Burawoy 2011, 398), that is, that the construction of scientific "facts" involves, and is determined by, a host of social, "extra-scientific" factors.[13] I want to register two counterarguments against this sort of objection. First, let us grant right away that science is *in practice* a social institution like any other, with its high stakes and gross inequalities (in prestige as well as other rewards), and rife with authoritarianism, corruption, and so on. But this is a fairly trivial observation, really. And to use it as a basis for dismissing scientific truth as on a par with any other partial and partisan truth is to succumb to what Thomas Gieryn (1982, 287) has called "the fallacy of 'nothing but-ism'": just because science's quest for impartiality is imperfect does not mean that it does not differ significantly from other institutional domains in this respect. It is a matter of degree, not kind. No doubt some politicians and journalists do their best to carefully check the accuracy and representativity of their facts. But this is not necessarily their principal concern as they need to take all kinds of shortcuts due to political pressures and copy deadlines.[14] Scientists, by contrast, are expected to be first and foremost concerned with accuracy and representativity. As noted, the degree to which they actually are is, to put it mildly, variable. Moreover, if and when scientists are committed to accuracy and representativity, it is not necessarily primarily because of a deep, personal commitment, although there is no doubt some of that, too. It is primarily due to the system of checks and reviews, of criticism and replication by peers that is designed, again, always with variable success, to "keep them honest." And to the extent that the system appears to be working, their findings enjoy an authority far beyond anything a journalist or politician could ever dream of.

Second, since science is a flawed social institution like any other, it is likely to be subject to systematic, socially determined bias. Note that I have been careful so far to say no more than that science seeks to eliminate any privileged position in the evidentiary tournament for any fraction of its designated audience only. If that audience consists exclusively, say, of aging white males with positions in prestigious research universities, then it is quite likely that the supposedly value-neutral scientific results they come up with ignore the perspectives of other social groups and interests, as a long list of feminist critics has pointed out. But this just points to the fact that the audience in question is not inclusive enough. In other words, such criticisms actually endorse the principle of value neutrality, arguing that the science in question ought to have been conducted in a value-neutral manner with respect to the full range of social groups and perspectives that exist within the audience that the researchers claim to address.

This brings me to a second, often-voiced, seemingly more fundamental objection to scientific claims to value neutrality, most forcefully formulated by a variety of critical feminists and postpositivist theorists. This objection is based on one version or another of the perspectivism mentioned above and frequently alluded to by Burawoy. It is a more fundamental objection in that it does not just question the possibility of actually achieving value neutrality in really existing science; it rejects the very idea of value neutrality as a sham, a cover for the interests of the dominant group.

There are, I think, two different ways to interpret this objection. The first might be called "hardline perspectivism." Advocates of this position effectively believe that there are multiple conflicting and irreconcilable truths out there and that the only reason one prevails over another is the societal power behind it. This leads inescapably to a view of (social) science as war by other means. As Harding (1991, 11) puts it, since "neither knowers nor the knowledge they produce are or could be impartial, disinterested, value-neutral, Archimedean," "science is politics by other means" (10). This position is most closely associated with feminist standpoint theories.[15]

Such hardline perspectivism has some very awkward implications for its advocates, however. For one thing, it is oddly self-delegitimizing. If the only reason one (social) scientific theory prevails over another is the brute political power behind it, then this would apply to the critics' own standpoints as well, of course. But then there is really not much point anymore in arguing with one another with the help of logic and evidence. The only sensible remaining strategy would appear to be to take to the streets and slug it out with whatever political and other weapons we have at our disposal.

This brings out another rather awkward implication, however, particularly for those who fancy themselves to be the champions of the oppressed, subjugated, and powerless. For to take such a combative "might-makes-right" stance on behalf of precisely those who are most lacking in the resources to defend their interests on the hard terrain of power politics sounds like a disastrously self-destructive strategy. And, conversely, precisely in the struggle on behalf of the weakest, by far the most promising strategy would appear to be the massive mobilization of the best available, that is, the hardest-to-ignore logic and evidence that social science has to offer.[16]

This may well be why even the most hardened conflict-perspectivist rarely opts for the position that there are simply two or more mutually exclusive, equally (in)valid partisan alternatives out there. Instead, virtually all of them choose the other option, which is to criticize positivism, or current and past uses of the notion of objectivity, for not being inclusive enough, that is, for being biased, which is based, of course, on exactly the fundamental assumptions underlying traditional science. It is also why such criticisms are often quite effective. Thus, Harding (1991, Ch. 6) herself, after much hardnosed philosophical sabre-rattling, ends up arguing for a "strong objectivity." Similarly, Foucauldians and assorted post-whatnot advocates protest the "erasure" of the Other's perspective and demand its inclusion, and Dorothy Smith proclaims the perspective of the oppressed to be superior to that of the oppressor because it incorporates the perspectives of both, thus providing a more complete understanding of the "relations of ruling" (Smith 1987). In other words, such critics of positivist social science merely invoke its own democratic principles against the mainstream's alleged violation of those principles.[17]

In short, none of the often-voiced objections raised against the democratic ethos that I argue underlies "professional" sociology seems to hold any water. At worst, they are self-defeating. At best, they end up reinforcing that very ethos. The same cannot, I think, be said of certain versions of Burawoy's public sociology.

The Not-So-Democratic Ethos of Public Sociology

As noted, a number of Burawoy's recommendations in the name of public sociology are entirely innocuous. They become problematic only where he starts to suggest that public sociologists have a special role to play in the determination of ultimate goals and values of their publics and of society as a whole. Critics have been particularly exercised by Burawoy's call to constitute the discipline as "a public that acts in the political arena" and to turn the ASA into "a political venue unto itself – a place to debate the stances we might adopt."

As we have seen, Burawoy feels that organic public sociologists have a special mandate for engaging non-academic publics "in dialogue about matters of political and moral concern" and that the discipline as a whole has a special role to play in helping determine the "basic values and goals of society" – "through democratic and collective deliberation" to be sure. In this deliberation public sociologists have a particular competence to contribute something called "reflexive knowledge," which deals with the "major issues that affect public life" (Burawoy 2007, 244). In contrast to the old guard of professional sociologists, Burawoy (2004, 1604) claims, the younger generation of sociologists is "less concerned about the purity of sociology as science and more likely to assume that our accumulated knowledge should be put to public use, whether in the form of member resolutions or policy interventions."

Now, everything revolves on what exactly is meant by *knowledge* here. Postpositivist notions of multiple, equally valid knowledges provide a convenient warrant for loose talk about "reflexive knowledge" – as opposed to the "instrumental" knowledge of professional sociologists. But such loose talk simply dodges the crucial issue: exactly in what sense are public sociologists' views of the "basic values and goals of society" grounded in a form of expertise that nonpublic sociologists, or nonsociologists, do not have? Yet this is clearly what Burawoy has in mind: we sociologists, or at least those committed to public sociology, have some kind of special expertise in matters having to do with the ultimate goals and values of our respective publics as well as of the public at large (society or even humanity). If that is not what he means, then it makes no sense to talk about any special knowledge in this context, and the role of sociologists in contributing to the formulation of social goals and values reduces to the kind of extracurricular civic activity and public debating on an equal footing with all other citizens that no "professional" sociologist would have the slightest objection to.

But what could this special expertise with respect to social values and goals be based on? Clearly not just on the research methodologies of empirical science taught in "professional" graduate schools, which, Burawoy (2004, 1606-7) reminds us, "can help us understand the consequences of our value commitments and inform our value discussions, but ... cannot determine those values." Now recall that these methodologies are designed specifically for the purpose of persuading the relevant audience that all pre-existing points of view within that audience are given a fair chance of winning or losing the evidentiary contest. And, by and large, they appear to have the intended effect or, at worst, they provoke calls for their improvement. But what analogous techniques or methods have public sociologists developed to persuade the public at large that their expert views on social goals and values have duly taken into account all relevant points of view? If anything, the hermetically self-referential and abstruse language in which much of their reflexive and critical ruminations are expressed, not to mention the obvious political slant of the "academic left," seem tailor-made to convince the public at large of quite the opposite. There is certainly plenty of anecdotal evidence suggesting this is exactly what has happened.[18]

But in the absence of any widely respected and trusted methods for arriving at truths about goals and values that all citizens will, by virtue of those trusted methods, freely recognize as theirs, on what grounds can the public sociologist still claim any special expertise? Interestingly, both Comte and Durkheim believed that their absolutely rigorous science was capable not only of helping us "understand the consequences of our value commitments and inform our value discussions" (Burawoy 2004, 1607) but also to determine the validity of those commitments themselves. This was the original meaning of the term *positivism* after all. Both Comte and Durkheim thought that sociologists were, or soon would be, in a position to diagnose society's ills in a strictly scientific manner and to prescribe the appropriate cures. Marx, in his own way, had a similarly unshakeable faith in science's ability to both explain and prescribe the proper actions to be taken, and certain prominent followers of his have extended this to proper thoughts as well.

Burawoy's call for a public sociology with a special mandate to pronounce – in the context of free and democratic deliberations, of course – on society's proper goals and values stands firmly within this deeply technocratic and crypto-authoritarian tradition. Although he speaks with the self-assured sophistication of a postpositivist who has moved far beyond the naive scientistic confidence of Comte, Durkheim, or Marx, he still firmly believes that sociology can somehow produce *both* valid explanations *and* correct values and thus solutions. Put differently, Burawoy still insists that sociologists have some special expertise in deciding the validity of societal goals and values, an expertise that is entitled to recognition as such by the lay citizenry. But in the absence of the voluntary and widespread recognition of this expertise by that citizenry, such a claim simply boils down to an attempt to hijack the legitimacy and prestige of "professional" science – which, as we saw, Burawoy is keenly aware of – to provide one's own political views with an extra cachet they would not otherwise have. In other words, it amounts to an attempt to short-circuit the democratic process, not to contribute to it, let alone to deepen it. The self-proclaimed experts in matters of goals and values cannot have it both ways: either they claim a special expertise, in which case their voice should count for more than that of the lay citizen, or they concede that their expertise in these matters is no greater than that of any other citizen, and they must therefore be content with a role in the public arena on the exact same terms as all other citizens.[19]

Thus, in this crucial respect, Comtean positivism and the alleged positivism of today's "professional" sociologists are each other's exact opposites, a fact Burawoy and the postpositivists he is so fond of conveniently ignore. As noted, in contrast to Comte and others, today's alleged positivists believe precisely that "empirical science can only take us so far: it can help us understand the consequences of our value commitments and inform our value discussions, but it cannot determine those values" (Burawoy 2004, 1606-7). And they further insist that sociologists have no business claiming any special expertise beyond this. By conflating the two diametrically opposed meanings of the term *positivism,* Burawoy tries to discredit today's positivists by associating them with their very opposite – Comtean positivism. This is worse than disingenuous. It is only by such sleight of hand that he can write off a critic like Sztompka as the "last positivist," a hopelessly antiquarian Comtean, representing "a disappearing position ... a rearguard action" (Burawoy 2011, 403). Clearly, it is Burawoy himself who, with his call for public sociology to claim a privileged seat at the table where society's values and goals are decided upon, represents the very worst in "the elitism of Comtean positivism" (401).

But then again, do we really need to get all that worked up about the crypto-authoritarian proclivities that lurk underneath the surface of supposedly well-meaning calls for a more public sociology? Surely they are not likely to do much harm outside the walls of the ivory tower? Perhaps not. But they can do a fair bit of harm within that ivory tower and especially to the relation between that ivory tower and the rest of the world. They could rob sociology of what little credibility it still enjoys among the public at large. And in the process, said proclivities may end up robbing precisely the weakest members of society of one of the few potentially effective weapons that can be wielded on their behalf: solid social scientific data and arguments that cannot be easily swept aside.

Conclusion

So let me return now to Burawoy's (2009b, 467) questions: "What, then, are these disciplinary struggles about? Why are they so intense?" While there may be an element of turf- or privilege-protection in the critical responses from defenders of "professional" sociology to Burawoy's clarion call, this cannot, I think, fully account for the vehemence and passion of their arguments. A more likely motivation is the "professional" sociologists' deep worry that the more dubious aspects of public sociology will lead to a throwing out of the baby of inclusive methodology with the dirty bathwater of its always imperfect realization. This would be a great disaster as it would inevitably destroy what little legitimacy and trusted expertise we sociologists still have to offer.

But more fundamentally, I suspect the passionate responses are in large part due to the fact that these "professional" sociologists, myself included, feel Burawoy's call for a public sociology, or at least the questionable part of it, strikes at the very heart of what makes (social) science (social) science: its fundamental commitment to a democratic, fair method of knowledge making. This commitment is, ultimately, deeply political. It is a commitment to a fundamentally democratic worldview, one that is, in the view of these "professional" sociologists, under attack by a public sociology whose commitment to real democracy is shaky at best. This, more than anything, accounts for the vehemence of the responses by a host of otherwise usually dispassionate and even-tempered academics.

But one could also turn the question around: what accounts for the enormous enthusiasm that Burawoy's call has also elicited from sociologists the world over? I can only speculate here, but at least one plausible reason comes to mind. More than any other discipline, sociology has always attracted a large complement of would-be world reformers of all stripes. And at least since the 1960s, calls for more "relevance" have been persistent and loud, particularly among disgruntled graduate students. They have been fond of quoting Marx's famous eleventh and final thesis on Feuerbach: "The philosophers have only interpreted the world, in various ways; the point is to change it" (Marx and Engels 1969, 15).[20] To them, having to go through the hoops of learning rigorous quantitative and qualitative methods seems to be a useless distraction from the much more urgent business of getting on with changing the world. They feel like their youthful idealism is squeezed out of them by the *disciplinary* hoops and hurdles put before them. As Burawoy (2005a, 14-15) himself laments, "it is as if graduate school is organized to winnow away at the moral commitments that inspired the interest in sociology in the first place."

Consequently, there is an enormous pent-up demand for liberation from the oppression of methodological rigour within the sociological community.[21] So the call for liberation, from the president of the American Sociological Association no less, must have felt like a long-awaited vindication to many.[22] Yet, for some of us it still makes sense to try to understand the world a little better before we rush off to change it. And understanding it is hard enough without being constantly drawn into political arguments about the urgent need to set right the wrongs in the world. In fact, understanding the world takes quite a different set of skills from what is required for successfully changing it. And the refusal to recognize the difference between the two can only undermine the successful pursuit of both.

Acknowledgments

I am grateful for the very helpful comments on an earlier draft of this chapter from Jeffrey Alexander, Jean-Claude Barbier, Eran Shor, and Piotr Sztompka.

Notes

1 See also Burawoy's (2011, 402-3) disposal of Piotr Sztompka's criticisms of a distinctive "global sociology" by pointing to Sztompka's Polish origins as the obvious source of his infatuation with all things American.

2 An obvious candidate for such a counteranalysis is the possibility that the call for a public sociology as an alternative to professional sociology has wide appeal particularly among those who are not very keen on subjecting their own ideological prejudices to methodologically rigorous testing.

3 In his 2009 reflections on the "public sociology wars," for instance, Burawoy (2009b, 450, 451) suggests that "For many [critics] communicating our ideas to wider publics puts sociology at risk, threatens its integrity, and jeopardizes its credibility"; and he asks rhetorically, "what has prompted these wars over public sociology, over the seemingly innocent proposal to take sociology's findings, its ideas, its theories beyond the academy, that is to carry on what is effectively its mission of public education?"

4 Burawoy's choice of terminology is far from innocent. *Professional* has clear connotations, especially for sociologists, of an elite enforcing a monopoly on knowledge claims and credentialing practice in a field so as to secure special privileges and status for its members.

5 Burawoy is particularly fond of the term *shock troops* to describe the more energetic of his "professional" critics. My co-author Avraham Goldberg and I are among those who have earned that designation (Burawoy 2009a, 874).

6 Not a little patronizingly, his rejoinder to Sztompka's critical review of the three-volume survey of "global sociology" (Sztompka 2011) is titled "The Last Positivist" (Burawoy 2011). See also Sztompka's own "Ten Theses" (Sztompka 2010).

7 See Hanemaayer, Chapter 1, this volume, on Althusser and "guilty readings."

8 For the distinction between "traditional" and "critical" theory, see, in particular, the essays "The Latest Attack on Metaphysics" (Horkheimer 1972, 132-87) and "Traditional and Critical Theory" (188-243).

9 No doubt unbeknownst to these theorists, this perspective is a direct descendent of the strictly dichotomous worldview of hard-line Leninism (see Kolakowski 1978, 386-89; van den Berg 2003a, 125-26).

10 Burawoy (2009b, 458) appears to think that such passion contradicts the professional sociologists' commitment to dispassionate science (for a similar point against Goldberg and me, see Burawoy 2009a, 874). This is odd. Surely one is entitled to feel passionately about the importance of dispassionate science? I attempt to explain some of this passion in this chapter.

11 For a philosophically much more subtle defence of the distinction between facts and values along these lines – even though there is no hard and fast way of doing so – see Kolakowski (1977).

12 But then, Weber's "Science as a Vocation" amounts to one of the most powerful indictments ever written of precisely the kind public sociology that Burawoy advocates (Weber, Gerth, and Mills 1958, Ch. 5), which Burawoy only indirectly acknowledges, as a minor aside, in brackets (Burawoy 2004, 1606).

13 For some of the classics in this genre, see Barnes (1977), Bloor (1976), Latour and Woolgar (1979), Latour (1987), and Knorr-Cetina and Mulkay (1983).

14 For an interesting defence of (social) scientific practice along these lines, see Pels (2003).

15 See, for example, Harding (2004) and (2011).

16 Larry Laudan (1990, 161-62, 163) makes this point with respect to the widespread infatuation of "the cultural left" with various forms of relativism.

17 In the examples given here, taken from the third-wave feminist literature, the apparent self-contradiction is particularly clear. But others who have embraced a postpositivist position as a way to promote a "progressive" political agenda have inevitably ended up in the same unacknowledged conundrum: having to claim an even *more* inclusive validity for their own position than that falsely claimed by their positivist targets. This is the case, for instance, with Habermas's critical theory (see van den Berg 1980, 1990) and "critical realism" (van den Berg 2003b, 2006). It illustrates, in a sense, how inescapable the democratic ethos really is.

18 As an amusing example, consider this comment by a proponent of the much-debated proposal of the Harper government to significantly increase the severity of the Criminal Code: "Every time we proposed amendments to the Criminal Code, sociologists, criminologists, defence lawyers and Liberals attacked us for proposing measures that the evidence apparently showed did not work. *Politically it helped us tremendously to be attacked by this coalition of university types*" (*Globe and Mail* [Toronto], 9 April 2011, "Unlocking the Crime Conundrum," F1, F5, emphasis added).

19 Burawoy is certainly not alone in trying to square this circle. Elsewhere, I have argued that Habermas's life work consists of a long succession of failed attempts to somehow reconcile the opposites of a firm belief in objectively demonstrable values and a commitment to democratic decision making concerning those values (see van den Berg 1980 and 1990).

20 Not coincidentally, Burawoy's original call for public sociology (2005a) is presented in the form of exactly eleven theses.

21 One of the most popular pieces of postpositivist sophistication among an earlier generation of disillusioned aspiring sociological activists was Feyerabend's *Wider den Methodenzwang* (Against the Coercion of Methods) (*Against Method,* 1978).

22 For some examples of authors welcoming the implied liberation from methodological rigour, see Collins (2007, 104), Hays (2007, 79), and Stacey (2007, 94).

References

Barnes, Barry. 1977. *Interests and the Growth of Knowledge.* London: Routledge and Kegan Paul.

Bloor, David. 1976. *Knowledge and Social Imagery.* London: Routledge and K. Paul.

Brint, Steven. 2007. "Guide for the Perplexed: On Michael Burawoy's 'Public Sociology.'" In *Public Sociology: The Contemporary Debate,* edited by Lawrence Nichols, 237-62. New Brunswick, NJ: Transaction Publishers.

Burawoy, Michael. 2004. "Public Sociologies: Contradictions, Dilemmas, and Possibilities." *Social Forces* 82, 4: 1603-18.

–. 2005a. "2004 Presidential Address: For Public Sociology." *American Sociological Review* 70, 1: 4-28.

–. 2005b. "The Critical Turn to Public Sociology." *Critical Sociology* 31, 3: 313-26.

–. 2005c. "Response: Public Sociology: Populist Fad or Path to Renewal?" *British Journal of Sociology* 56, 3: 417-32.

–. 2007. "The Field of Sociology: Its Power and Its Promise." In *Public Sociology: Fifteen Eminent Sociologists Debate Politics and the Profession in the Twenty-First Century,* edited by Dan Clawson et al., 241-58. Berkeley: University of California Press.

–. 2009a. "Disciplinary Mosaic: The Case of Canadian Sociology." *Canadian Journal of Sociology* 34, 3: 869-86.

–. 2009b. "The Public Sociology Wars." In *Handbook of Public Sociology,* edited by Vincent Jeffries, 449-73. New York: Rowman and Littlefield.

–. 2011. "The Last Positivist." *Contemporary Sociology* 40, 4: 396-404.

Burawoy, Michael, Mau-kuei Chang, and Michelle Fei-yu Hsieh, eds. 2010. *Facing an Unequal World: Challenges for a Global Sociology.* Taipei, Taiwan: Institute of Sociology, Academica Sinica and International Sociological Association.

Burawoy, Michael, William Gamson, Charlotte Ryan, Stephen Pfohl, Diane Vaughan, Charles Derber, and Juliet Schor. 2004. "Public Sociologies: A Symposium from Boston College." *Social Problems* 51, 1: 103-30.

Collins, Patricia Hill. 2007. "Going Public: Doing the Sociology That Had No Name." In *Public Sociology: Fifteen Eminent Sociologists Debate Politics and the Profession in the Twenty-First Century,* edited by Dan Clawson et al., 101-13. Berkeley: University of California Press.

Feyerabend, Paul K. 1978. *Against Method: Outline of an Anarchistic Theory of Knowledge.* London: Verso.

Gieryn, Thomas F. 1982. "Relativist/Constructivist Programmes in the Sociology of Science: Redundance and Retreat." *Social Studies of Science* 12: 279-97.

Goldberg, Avi, and Axel van den Berg. 2009. "What Do Public Sociologists Do? A Critique of Burawoy." *Canadian Journal of Sociology* 34, 3: 765-802.

Harding, Sandra G. 1991. *Whose Science? Whose Knowledge? Thinking from Women's Lives.* Ithaca, NY: Cornell University Press.

–. 2004. *The Feminist Standpoint Theory Reader: Intellectual and Political Controversies.* New York: Routledge.

–. 2011. *The Postcolonial Science and Technology Studies Reader.* Durham, NC: Duke University Press.

Hays, Sharon. 2007. "Stalled at the Altar? Conflict, Hierarchy, and Compartmentalization in Burawoy's Public Sociology." In *Public Sociology: Fifteen Eminent Sociologists Debate Politics and the Profession in the Twenty-First Century,* edited by Dan Clawson et al., 79-90. Berkeley: University of California Press.

Horkheimer, Max. 1972. *Critical Theory: Selected Essays.* New York: Herder and Herder.

Jeffries, Vincent, ed. 2009. *Handbook of Public Sociology.* Lanham, MD: Rowman and Littlefield.

Knorr-Cetina, Karin, and M. J. Mulkay. 1983. *Science Observed: Perspectives on the Social Study of Science.* London: Sage.

Kolakowski, Leszek. 1977. "The Persistence of the Sein-Sollen Dilemma." *Man and World* 10, 2: 194-233.

–. 1978. *Main Currents of Marxism.* Vol. 2, *The Golden Age.* Oxford: Oxford University Press.

Latour, Bruno. 1987. *Science in Action: How to Follow Scientists and Engineers through Society.* Cambridge, MA: Harvard University Press.

Latour, Bruno, and Steve Woolgar. 1979. *Laboratory Life: The Social Construction of Scientific Facts.* Beverly Hills, CA: Sage.

Laudan, Larry. 1990. *Science and Relativism: Some Key Controversies in the Philosophy of Science.* Chicago: University of Chicago Press.

Marx, Karl, and Friedrich Engels. 1969. *Selected Works.* Moscow: Progress Publishers.

Massey, Douglas. 2007. "The Strength of Weak Politics." In *Public Sociology: Fifteen Eminent Sociologists Debate Politics and the Profession in the Twenty-First Century,* edited by Dan Clawson et al., 145-57. Berkeley: University of California Press.

Nielsen, François. 2004. "The Vacant 'We': Remarks on Public Sociology." *Social Forces* 82, 4: 1619-27.

Pels, Dick. 2003. *Unhastening Science: Autonomy and Reflexivity in the Social Theory of Knowledge.* Liverpool: Liverpool University Press.

Popper, Karl R. 1963. *Conjectures and Refutations: The Growth of Scientific Knowledge.* London: Routledge and Kegan Paul.

Smith, Dorothy E. 1987. *The Everyday World as Problematic: A Feminist Sociology.* Toronto: University of Toronto Press.

Smith-Lovin, Lynn. 2007. "Do We Need a Public Sociology? It Depends on What You Mean by *Sociology.*" In *Public Sociology: Fifteen Eminent Sociologists Debate Politics and the Profession in the Twenty-First Century,* edited by Dan Clawson et al., 124-34. Berkeley: University of California Press.

Stacey, Judith. 2007. "If I Were the Goddess of Sociological Things." In *Public Sociology: Fifteen Eminent Sociologists Debate Politics and the Profession in the*

Twenty-First Century, edited by Dan Clawson et al., 91-100. Berkeley: University of California Press.

Sztompka, Piotr. 2010. "Ten Theses on the Status of Sociology in an Unequal World." *Global Dialogue* 2, 2, http://www.isa-sociology.org/.

–. 2011. "Another Sociological Utopia," *Contemporary Sociology* 40, 4: 388-96.

Tittle, Charles R. 2004. "The Arrogance of Public Sociology." *Social Forces* 82, 4: 1639-43.

Van den Berg, Axel. 1980. "Critical Theory: Is There Still Hope?" *American Journal of Sociology* 86, 3: 449-78.

–. 1990. "Habermas and Modernity: A Critique of the Theory of Communicative Action." *Current Perspectives in Social Theory* 10: 161-93.

–. 2003a. *The Immanent Utopia: From Marxism on the State to the State of Marxism.* New Brunswick, NJ: Transaction Publishers.

–. 2003b. Review of *Being Human: The Problem of Agency,* by Margaret S. Archer. *Canadian Review of Sociology and Anthropology* 40, 2: 233-36.

–. 2006. Review of *The Politics of Method in the Human Sciences: Positivism and Its Epistemological Others,* edited by George Steinmetz. *Canadian Journal of Sociology Online* (May-June): http://www.cjsonline.ca/.

Weber, Max. 1949. "The Meaning of 'Ethical Neutrality' in Sociology and Economics." In *The Methodology of the Social Sciences,* edited by Edward Shils and Henry A. Finch, 1-47. New York: Free Press.

Weber, Max, Hans Heinrich Gerth, and C. Wright Mills. 1958. *From Max Weber: Essays in Sociology.* New York: Oxford University Press.

PART 2

CRITICAL REFLECTIONS ON THE POSSIBILITY OF PUBLIC SOCIOLOGY

3

L'Ouverture des bouches

The Social and Intellectual Bases for Engaged and Public Social Theory

SCOTT SCHAFFER

As the works throughout this volume show, debates about the nature, operation, and goodness of public sociology have been rife since the work of Michael Burawoy gained prominence with his ascendance to the presidency of the American Sociological Association in 2004. His famous text, "For Public Sociology" (Burawoy 2005; see also Burawoy 2009a, 2009b), has become a lightning rod for a variety of frustrations, anxieties, and tensions around the position of sociology and sociologists vis-à-vis the general public and has exacerbated concerns about the nature of the sociological endeavour in the United States. The situation is no less prevalent in Canada, where, as Dawes and Helmes-Hayes and McLaughlin have pointed out in their contributions to the special issue of *Canadian Journal of Sociology/ Cahiers canadiens de sociologie* (2009), the discipline is younger, less fully institutionalized, and less fully assured of its position within the academy. Furthermore, the anxieties that attend this situation are always exaggerated by our relative size with regard to our southern neighbours.

It is not as if we have not had public intellectuals in Canada. Three recent leaders of federal political parties, after all, were university professors or well-known intellectuals, and the current prime minister, Stephen Harper, is a trained economist. The trend to have leading political figures who are intellectuals is greater in Canada than in the United States or the United Kingdom, our regular points of comparison. There is a greater range of opportunities in Canada for intellectuals or other thinkers to take the public stage, primarily thanks to the CBC and its Massey Lectures, the Canada Reads debates, and the publicity attendant to the Giller Prize nominees. However, these intellectuals are not sociologists; nor do sociologists readily take their intellectualism public. The question becomes, then, on what basis can sociology become public?

Most of the writers on the matter of public sociology, whether in the United States or Canada, presume that there is something intrinsic to the sociologist that drives them to choose to engage in public sociology. Burawoy's fourfold dissection of the sociological division of labour, for example, engages in a kind of methodological individualism (despite the protestations of some critics that he is engaged in developing a Parsonian universal [McLaughlin and Turcotte 2007]). Burawoy's analysis of the four types of sociological labour – professional, policy, critical, and public – posits these forms of work in terms of the audience of the work, but beyond that, the only possible explanation of how a sociologist comes to address one of these audiences is some characteristic of the sociologist him- or herself. This is certainly true, albeit in a tautological sense: public sociologists engage with publics because they wish to engage with those publics. Abbott's (2007) corrective to this aspect of Burawoy suggests that the inherent value-ladenness of social life is ultimately at the heart of the need to engage sociology with the world it studies, and that this results in a need to make sociology more humane. While I see more value and more room for agreement with Abbott's normative positioning of public sociology, this still raises the question: On what basis or bases can sociology or the field of social theory (in which I work) become more publicly engaged? I argue that there are structural factors at work preventing critical intellectuals from being involved in public life, much of which has to do with the intellectual work done by these people, yet there are deeper foundations for the fostering and flourishing of engaged social theory and theorists. In other words, the ways in which critical social theory has developed since the 1980s have prevented intellectuals from having a professional basis – that is, a basis rooted in the particularities of social-theoretical practice and the products of such practices – for becoming what the French are fond of calling *l'intellectuel engagé* – the engaged intellectual.

This chapter will argue three key points. First, I suggest that left intellectuals *should* be engaged in public life in a way that speaks *with* those on the "front lines" of movements for social justice and social change, rather than speaking *for* them (in a patriarchal "we know what they're really doing" kind of way) or at them (as if the theorists are the vanguard rather than the students or equal participants). Second, I argue that to begin to understand *how* we might become more engaged in public life, we need to examine the ways in which intellectuals in other societies have become engaged in public life since the end of the twentieth century. Third, I contend that the key elements of the engagement of critical intellectuals in other societies include mutually reciprocating elements of the relationship between intellectuals and the broader public, a relationship that can and should be changed starting with the nature and dissemination of intellectual work. In sum, my point is that understanding what intellectual engagement would look like requires an examination of how others outside the Canadian context have become engaged and how we can bring these lessons "back home," and that this step is a prerequisite to becoming *engagé.*

I first examine the concept and definitions of intellectual engagement, arguing that looking solely at what intellectuals do or do not do is insufficient for assessing public intellectualism, and that understanding the bases for intellectual engagement is just as important for the process. An examination of the kinds of structural impediments to public intellectualism is also required, for the prevalence of this type of political activity is dependent on both the will of the intellectual and the structural or societal elements of this picture. The second step in the development of this argument is to examine three ideal types of the social and epistemic bases for intellectual engagement as indicated by some of the more famous European *intellectuels engagés* – namely, Jean-Paul Sartre, Pierre Bourdieu, and Václav Havel. I have chosen two thinkers who are not normally considered "social theorists" (Sartre and Havel) because my primary interest here is in the ways in which thinkers can either mobilize elements of their body of work or foster a societal position in order to serve as interlocutors in public debates. Finally, I return to and modify Burawoy's fourfold model of the division of labour in sociology to indicate particular ways in which I think the experiences of intellectual engagement provided by these thinkers can inform the development of a new group of engaged intellectuals in the Canadian contexts, a group that works alongside those who are on the "front lines" in the quest for a more just society.

The Phenomenon of Intellectual Engagement

Given the late arrival of Canadian sociology to the examinations of the role of public sociology and public intellectuals more generally, and given the parallels between American and Canadian sociology, identified by Dawes (2009) in his analysis of the institutional dynamics surrounding the possibilities of public sociology, I have chosen to look to American works on public intellectualism as an altogether too-rough indication of the state of public intellectualism in Canada. Schalk's *War and the Ivory Tower* (1991) represents one of the more paradigmatic examinations of the engagement of intellectuals in the late twentieth century. Tracing the concept of l'intellectuel engagé back to the Dreyfus affair in the early twentieth century, Schalk focuses primarily on the political activities of French and American intellectuals during the Algerian Revolution and Vietnam conflict (respectively) to explore the possibilities for intellectual engagement today. Schalk's problem, as is mine, is the apparent retreat of intellectuals to the ivory tower in times of relative peace. As Schalk (170) puts it in the conclusion to his work, it is conceivable that intellectuals could "redefine and reenergize themselves, through a resurgence of activism," but in the current era, it appears that intellectuals have become *échaudé* – burned out (169).

To Schalk's mind, intellectual engagement is in some part inherent in the history of "the intellectual class." The first appearance of *les intellectuels*, during the Dreyfus affair, represented a moment at which intellectuals, generally "defined by their more abstract and distantiated social role," left that stance vis-à-vis society and moved to make a political statement (Schalk 1991, 38-40). The symbiotic relationship between the place of the intellectual and the act of engagement that Schalk attributes to French intellectuals in the early 1900s relies upon the role of intellectuals as "men and women of ideas who explore and challenge the underlying values of society" and who have "a normative function: to prescribe what ought to be" (Vogelgesang qtd. in Schalk 1991, 39). Schalk also conceives of the act of engagement as the actualization of that normative function in the form of "political involvements by members of the intellectual class – however broadly or narrowly defined a social group that is widely viewed as not normally prone to descend from the ivory tower into the arena" (Schalk 1991, 40). The new mode of action represented by intellectual engagement involves a paradoxical situation in which the conflicting roles of "thinker" and "citizen" are unified in a new kind of social actor, one that has a sophisticated theoretical or intellectual background and is willing to act in a realm that appears intellectuals usually want nothing to do with – the general activities of the "rabble" and the "political" (See Wolfe 2000, 82).

For Schalk, there are three forms of intellectual engagement that represent increasing degrees of commitment to the position these people take on and increasing willingness to see the particular position enacted as a matter of public policy. The first of these forms, the pedagogic, involves intellectuals doing what they normally do – thinking, critiquing, writing – but doing it in a more public realm than is usual for them, such as in newspapers, periodicals, and other media. The pedagogic form of engagement manifests itself as "calm, rational, frequently scholarly writings ... in an effort to educate the public and persuade the leaders of the governments in question of the errors of their ways" (Schalk 1991, 48). It is, in sum, an effort to teach, to instruct the public as to what will happen should current political and social policies continue to be followed and, in some cases, to provide an alternative path that the writer sees as more beneficial for a society. This position is echoed in Burawoy's (2005) seminal work, in which he develops his fourfold model of the discipline of sociology and his conception of the traditional public sociologist.

The second form of engagement Schalk (1991, 49) identifies is the moral form, a kind of "ethically based protest and a growing sense of outrage and shame." Appearing in France around 1956 and the United States in 1966, moral engagement continued to involve pedagogical attempts at convincing the public and political leadership of the error of their ways and, at the same time, extended into more protest-based activities, such as marches, teach-ins, and other activities that made clear the kind of outrage and dissent required by the historical situation in which intellectuals found themselves. Often, moral engagements were motivated, according to Schalk, by an aggrieved sense of patriotism, the claim that the path that the country was on was "not France" or "not America," and that, to reclaim French or American values, a new social and political policy had to be pursued (in these cases, the granting of independence by France to Algeria and the withdrawal of American forces from Vietnam).[1]

Finally, the third stage of intellectual engagement, what Schalk calls the "counterlegal," sees intellectuals engaging in actions their governments deem to be illegal (ranging from the signing of petitions, which in 1950s France could place scholars in danger of harassment or imprisonment, to participation in protest marches, facilities occupations, other forms of civil disobedience, and the like in the United States) (Schalk 1991, 50-52). While this type of engagement would obviously have fewer participants due to the significant risk involved to person and/or professional position, there were significant numbers of intellectuals who pursued counterlegal strategies of engagement (Schalk 1991, 52). The danger at this level is of making the crossover from engagement to what he calls *embrigadement* –

the abandonment of critical engagement for the sake of the "unquestioning support of a political cause" (52). However, Schalk suggests that the majority of intellectuals who became engaged and reached the moral and counter-legal stages of engagement avoided this danger. At the same time, they saw that *something* had to be done about the violence enacted by these governments (Schalk 1991, 53). Schalk argues that, after the end of the political conflict that required the engagement, intellectuals retreated from political involvement to the ivory tower.

In sum, the kind of political engagement pursued by intellectuals is never coerced. As Schalk (1991, 41) writes, "the intellectual or intellectuals in question are not pushed down the stairs of the ivory tower and out into the streets. True engagement cannot be coerced but is derived from reflection on the external political and social situation and reasonably free decision to become involved." To put it another way, the peculiarities of the institutional position of intellectuals – the tradition of academic freedom, the requirement for the critical evaluation of the world around them, and the theoretical resources to develop alternative understandings of social and political policies – allow them the latitude to decide on their degree of involvement and provide them with a set of resources often unavailable to the general public.

The Last Intellectuals? Structural Impediments to Engagement

Given the institutional position of intellectuals and intellectuals' freedom to engage, why is it that we do not see more frequent engagements or interventions on the part of intellectuals in Canada?[2] There are many entirely valid, and familiar, reasons that academics have not left the ivory tower in recent years, many of them relating precisely to the same kinds of institutional arrangements that make intellectual engagement possible. In particular, changes in the ways that university faculty are hired, granted tenure and promotion, and asked to work give pause to anyone wishing to take a dissenting role in the American public and political scene. After all, the academic freedom given to faculty by way of tenure lies in the hands of more senior and possibly more institutionally ensconced professors; and the very availability of tenure-stream positions is a resource controlled by higher-level administrators, who increasingly treat the university as a business run under neoliberal principles, preferring to hire multiple part-time instructors to positions of insecurity than to create positions for life.

Jacoby's *The Last Intellectuals* (2000) recognizes the drastic absence of what he calls "public intellectuals," those intellectuals who deign to address or elicit some kind of response from the general public. Arguing that an entire generation of potential public intellectuals has disappeared, leaving no one to replace "the last intellectuals" (people like Noam Chomsky, Susan Sontag, and others of the "sixties intellectuals"), Jacoby identifies in particular the ways in which intellectual life has been recast in the last half of the twentieth century. The North American transition from urban to suburban living, which eliminates the possibility of "bohemian" intellectual scenes and leaves most people commuting to a home that, once in, they are reluctant to leave; the demise of smaller literary magazines in favour of scholarly journals; the "managerial revolution"; and the rise of the power of television and its particular mode of discourse – all of these factors play a part in Jacoby's tragic tale of intellectual decline. But more importantly for Jacoby, the changes in how the university operates implicitly dictate that "thou shalt not become engaged in public affairs" to intellectuals.

As Jacoby puts it, the entire mode of existence for intellectuals has been changed in recent years:

> The habitat, manners, and idiom of intellectuals have been transformed within the past fifty years. Younger intellectuals no longer need or want a larger public; they are almost exclusively professors. Campuses are their homes; colleagues their audience; monographs and specialized journals their media. Unlike past intellectuals they situate themselves within fields and disciplines – for good reason. Their jobs, advancement, and salaries depend on the evaluation of specialists, and this dependence affects the issues broached and the language employed. (2000, 6-7)

In particular, Jacoby identifies three key tendencies in the university itself that contribute to the disappearance of the public intellectual. The first is the "publish or perish" requirement in larger research-oriented universities, in which tenure decisions are made predominantly on the amount of scholarly publishing done by junior faculty (and, in some cases, the particular forums in which one publishes, leaving those left scholars with few options to pursue research based on their particular political positions). This evaluation of one's merit as an intellectual in terms of labour productivity results in a shift of the language with which one writes, from a public discourse to the jargon of a kind of "secret society," and results in entire fields of research being oriented to a cabal of specialists, something akin to the phrase "preaching to the choir" (Jacoby 2000, 153-59). The second tendency is the professionalization of most critical forms of inquiry: as Jacoby

(2000) notes, those scholars whose politics might be most critical and most useful for a general public (in particular Marxists) seem most likely to abandon that public for the sake of job security and "institutional clout and prestige" (185), leading to a switch from "the theory of fetishism, which Marx sets forth ... [to] the fetishism of theory" (173). The third pattern is a general "distaste, even contempt, for critical thinking" (Jacoby 2000, 203), both in the university and the general public. Even in research universities, the tendency has frequently been to rely on student evaluations for renewal and promotion decisions, resulting in the perceived need by faculty to not be *too* critical, to provide students with "immediately applicable knowledge," and to prioritize preparing students for careers over preparing them for membership in a larger society. All of these factors impact negatively on those who would be public intellectuals; there is no perceived reward beyond the fuzzy feeling of being a "good citizen" for engaging in political affairs, and there are frequently disincentives for doing so, so why bother?

A further trend, one not identified by Jacoby, is what Soley (1995) calls "the leasing of the ivory tower." Following the decline of funding to American public universities that started in the mid-1980s, universities were forced to seek additional funding from corporations that would endow chairs and establish research institutions intended to further corporate interests within the university (1995, 9).[3] As Soley (1995, 5) writes, "The story about universities in the 1980s and 1990s is that they will turn a trick for anybody with money to invest; and the only ones with money are corporations, millionaires, and foundations. These investments in universities have dramatically changed the mission of higher education; they have led universities to attend to the interests of their well-heeled patrons, rather than those of students." Even when corporations do not directly establish research institutes or endow chairs, their presence can be felt: decreased governmental funding for universities also means decreased public funding for research grants, a gap picked up by corporations; and in addition to the number of publications of faculty members, part of tenure and promotion decisions often includes the amount of extramural grant funding received by scholars. And since tenure-track positions in Canadian universities have been on the decline, replaced by adjunct positions due to decreased funding and the relatively higher number of students that can be serviced by more adjunct faculty, those who are lucky enough to gain tenure-stream positions are most likely not going to do anything to jeopardize them, including speaking their mind on public matters.

We can see, then, that there are structural factors at work preventing the creation of a new generation of public intellectuals. The quest for tenure; the requirements for publishing and grant-earning; the need for the professionalization (and subsequent jargonization) of intellectual writing; and public and student pressures on faculty for immediately applicable knowledge – all these issues face young scholars who would like nothing more than to have a beneficial impact on the world around them. But, there have always been structural factors at work in the university and against public intellectual work, in the United States and elsewhere. Wolfe's lambasting of scholars who are interested in eliminating the various *-isms* in American society through deconstructive and critical analyses, as well as Jacoby's (2000, 195) quite correct observation that describing someone as "a 'man of letters' ... is almost derogatory, hinting of village poets or family historians," go to show that there is something outside the institutional prerogatives of the university that hinders public intellectualism.[4]

Yet the reasons for intellectuals to engage themselves in public affairs are more compelling than the reasons they do not engage, and these reasons need more detailed examination. I believe it useful to explore the engagement of three intellectuals from outside the United States to understand the kinds of motive forces at work in their engagement. These models are, of course, ideal types in the Weberian sense, meaning that they are purified examples insulated from one another; and certainly, once the cases of Jean-Paul Sartre, Pierre Bourdieu, and Václav Havel are detailed below, the purification will be evident. I believe, however, that it is necessary to distill three ideal types of motive forces for two reasons: first, to provide a kind of "role model" of the engaged intellectual, one that my readers can translate into their own experience and particular social and institutional context; and second, to highlight the important role played in intellectual engagement not just by moral outrage, which I am sure many of us share about certain aspects of the world, but also by the particular theoretical stances we choose, the particular situations in which we pursue our research, and the relationship we choose to have with the general public as a whole. To my mind, these factors have just as much to do with the presence or absence of public intellectuals as do the structural and institutional factors discussed above.

Model 1: Sartre – Engagement by Philosophy

Jean-Paul Sartre, by far one of the best-known intellectuels engagés, exemplifies the first model of intellectual engagement – engagement based upon the philosophical and theoretical stance taken by the intellectual.[5] The kinds of engagement Sartre undertook, which mostly resemble Schalk's pedagogic and moral forms of engagement, including public writings and lectures, public forums on the Algeria and Vietnam conflicts, and the refusal of the Nobel Prize for literature and an invitation to lecture at Cornell University in 1965, seem quite clearly to be bound to his philosophical stance. Drawing from his existentialist philosophy, the development of his notion of a "literature of commitment" in the time of *Les temps modernes,* and his conversion to a more Marxist-inflected existentialism, Sartre's basis of commitment is fundamentally theoretical. It lies in his own philosophical and social-theoretical understanding of the world and in the way in which he tried to convey this understanding to the world at large.

Most people who know of Sartre's philosophical work think first and foremost of his work in *L'être et le néant* (1943). This seminal work of existential philosophy, which posits that individuals are eminently free to create the world around them, and thereby are solely responsible for the world they wish to see in existence, provides one element required by a philosophical engagement with the world – namely, a conception of responsibility.[6] For the early Sartre, the issues of freedom and responsibility were existential absolutes; regardless of whether one chose to realize oneself as being existentially free and responsible for the acts predicated on that freedom – in other words, whether one acted authentically with regard to one's freedom or in "bad faith," denying one's freedom and responsibility – one had to deal with the brute facticity of existing in the world (Sartre 1963, part 1, ch. 2). Later, in a corollary to the famous phrase "existence precedes essence," Sartre claims that

> a man is involved in life, leaves his impress on it, and outside of that there is nothing. To be sure, this may seem a harsh thought to someone whose life hasn't been a success. But, on the other hand, it prompts people to understand that reality is what counts, that dreams, expectations, and hopes warrant no more than to define him negatively and not positively ... What we mean is that a man is nothing else than a series of undertakings, that he is the sum, the organization, the ensemble of the relationships which make up these undertakings. (1993b, 48-49)

Following this argument, we can see that the absolute freedom Sartre claims inheres in us by virtue of our mere existence, leading to an absolute responsibility in which "what happens to me happens through me ... Moreover everything which happens to me is *mine*" (Sartre 1993a, 64), would result in a clear basis for engagement in the world around us. If we are authentic beings, then we take responsibility for our actions, and we would want to commit ourselves to acting in the best manner possible.

There is a problem here, however. At this point in Sartre's intellectual development, "Hell is other people" – that is, Sartre cannot yet deal with the presence of others in the world except as facts to be dealt with, unknown and unknowable variables to be grappled with on a case-by-case basis, and generally to be struggled against in the furtherance of one's own existential project. It is not until Merleau-Ponty's (1973, 127) rejoinder to Sartre's radically individualistic existentialism that Sartre begins to deal more beneficially with social relations and sociological phenomena. In *Critique of Dialectical Reason* (1985), Sartre begins to explore the ways in which social groups form out of – and impact on – individual freedom. Moving from the series, in which individuals are related solely by virtue of their non-identity with others, to actual groups that form as a result of the volition of the individuals making them up, Sartre's new sociologically informed philosophy allows for a deeper understanding of the ways in which individual freedom is limited by the particular sociohistorical situation in which it finds itself, the responsibility that one has for the maintenance or transformation of that situation, and the necessity of involving oneself in that situation. The sense of responsibility Sartre developed in his earlier work carries over here, but it becomes more complex. Now, we not only have responsibility for the kind of world in which we want to live but also for the impact of our actions upon ourselves and others.

However, the simple development of a philosophy of responsibility would not appear to be sufficient to justify holding Sartre out as a model of intellectual engagement. Sartre's *Qu'est-ce que la littérature?* (1948) identifies a new "literature of commitment," one in which the author's relationship to the reader is highlighted as a primary element of the text, and one in which "art for art's sake" is an antiquated notion, replaced by the conferral of a particular meaning and perspective, intended by the author. What kind of perspective? To quote from de Beauvoir's reportage, "the true perspective is that of the most disinherited; the hangman can remain ignorant of what he does; the victim experiences his suffering and his death irrecusably; the truth of oppression is the oppressed" (de Beauvoir qtd. in Boschetti 1988, 107). By conveying the perspective of those who bore the brunt of the world on their shoulders, not just in philosophical existence but in their daily lives, Sartre felt that authors could convince their readers to rise to action against the situations of unfreedom in the world. Put another way, Sartre's literature of commitment represents a form of action, the kind of action for which intellectuals are uniquely qualified; and this action is not just necessary but also sufficient for inspiring change in the world (Boschetti 1988, 109).

Sartre's overall goal in his works, according to Boschetti (1988, 108), was the bridging of the gap between *praxis* and ethics – in other words, between some conception of "the good life" and how it should be lived and the kinds of actions required to achieve a concrete state of affairs in which that good life could come into existence. In searching for the balance between ethics and praxis, Sartre saw himself as hope-filled, a "fellow traveler" with those who actively agitated for social change (Sartre and Lévy 1996, 58, 63). While never actively picking up arms, either during the resistance to Nazi occupation of France during the Second World War or in any of the other liberation movements he supported, Sartre continuously argued that a literature and philosophy of commitment was a form of freedom-oriented action, one that he felt could serve the forces of social change and freedom:

> *BL:* How is it that some intellectuals needed something to cling to – needed to find a prop, a basis, in that trash?
>
> *JPS:* Because it was a question of finding a future for society. Society had to stop being the shitty mess it is everywhere today. I didn't think I could change the world all by myself and on the strength of my own ideas, but I did discern social forces that were trying to move forward, and I believed my place was among them. (Sartre and Lévy 1996, 64-65)

In developing a conception of intellectual work and writing that was consistent with his philosophical stance regarding human freedom, responsibility, and the necessity of action to ensure the development of a situation of human freedom, Sartre's engagement by philosophy proved at the very least to detail the ideas of an intellectual committed to hope and to develop a continual critique of the ills of the world and our place in reproducing them.

Model 2: Bourdieu – Engagement by Experience

After his death in January 2002, Pierre Bourdieu's peers throughout the world praised his commitment to acts of social justice. The majority of them who knew him well attributed much of his passion and engagement to one of the core elements of his experience as a social scientist: the effect of Bourdieu's French military experience in Algeria during the 1955-1962 revolution and the impact that experience had on his transition from philosophy to sociology.[7] As Smaïn Laacher, one of his colleagues at the L'École des hautes études en sciences sociales, noted, "L'Algérie lui a collé au corps et aux morts" (Algeria stuck with him in his body and until death) (qtd. in Bernard 2002, para. 1). Starting with his *Sociologie de l'Algérie* (1958), and continuing through his later works on cultural spaces in French society, television, the position of the academic in French society, and ultimately his *Contre-feux* books, Bourdieu's work contained two key elements for understanding his work as an engagement by experience, the second model of intellectual engagement discussed here: a clear theoretical model for analyzing contemporary society and its structures, and a clear sense of the role that the intellectual analyst played in highlighting those structures and the problems created by them.

Bourdieu's key theoretical concept, the *habitus* – the set of "structured structures predisposed to function as structuring structures" (1977, 70) – highlights one of the essential elements that Sartre's more sociological work in *Critique of Dialectical Reason* leaves fallow – namely, how it is that individuals learn to produce and reproduce a social world in the ways they do and the extent to which those individuals can act in line with this "practical mastery, and in particular as an *ars inveniendi,*" or an "inventive art" (Bourdieu 1992, 122). The habitus appears as the site at which the individual can be seen as "social, collective" and taken for granted, as if a "fish in water" (126-27); it is that mechanism by which "social agents are determined only to the extent that they determine themselves" (136), or, put another way, by which individuals as products of history act in relation to definite situations in the world. The habitus, though, is not fully deterministic; instead, it allows individuals to see opportunities, possibilities, and potential meanings for them in the world and to act in field-appropriate ways upon those chances. As Bourdieu puts it,

> Habitus is not the fate that some people read into it. Being the product of history, it is an *open system of dispositions* that is constantly subjected to experiences, and therefore constantly affected by them in a way that either reinforces or modifies its structures. It is durable but not eternal! Having said this, I must immediately add that there is a probability, inscribed in the social destiny associated with definite social conditions, that experiences

> will confirm habitus, because most people are statistically bound to encounter circumstances that tend to agree with those that originally fashioned their habitus. (1992, 133, emphasis in original)

By analyzing the ways in which individuals and groups of individuals respond to social structures, instead of the structures themselves, Bourdieu was able to exclude "the 'subjects' ... dear to the tradition of philosophies of consciousness without annihilating agents to the benefit of a hypostatized structure" (140), reflecting a concern for how people live, deal with the social structures within which they find themselves, and develop the potential for radically transforming those structures.

In large part, I would argue that this concern reflects an overarching concern on Bourdieu's part for understanding the ways in which people respond to conditions of inequality and oppression. Going back to his *Sociologie de l'Algérie,* we find that concern reflected even in his definition of colonialism:

> La société coloniale est un système dont il importe de saisir la logique et la nécessité internes du fait qu'il constitue le contexte en référence auquel prennent sens tous les comportements et en particulier les rapports entre les deux communautés ethniques. Aux transformations résultant inévitablement du contact entre deux civilisations profondément différentes tant dans le domaine économique que dans le domaine social, la colonisation ajoute les bouleversements sciemment et méthodiquement provoqués pour assurer l'autorité de la puissance dominante et les intérêts économiques de ses ressortissants. (1958, 106)[8]

Even in this definition, it is the actions of individuals within the system that are privileged in recognizing that they refer to, and ultimately reproduce, the system itself. These behaviours and social relations, rather than being deduced social scientifically, can be observed in practice, resulting in a quite different depiction of the colonial situation than the one provided by Sartre. More specifically, Bourdieu's analysis of the colonial situation, and ultimately of the habitus and in other contexts, is one that recognizes the general functioning of our manner of existence in the world and the way that we orient to our particular social situations (and here, I think of the kinds of interpersonal and interfield relations discussed in *Distinction* [1987] and *The Weight of the World* [1999]).

By emphasizing the generality of the way that the habitus functions, and by maintaining a concern with actors as opposed to structures, Bourdieu is able to transport his theoretical framework into multiple contexts. It also allows him to understand the particular relationship between the social scientist and the people under study. As Wacquant (1992a, 44-45) recognizes, "it was nearly impossible under the horrendous circumstances by the methodical efforts of the French military to suppress Algerian nationalism, not to be constantly interpellated about the peculiar privilege of the academic who withdraws from the world in order to observe it and who claims detachment from the subjects he studies." Bourdieu's analytic position vis-à-vis his research subjects – and ultimately, his engagement – is thereby one that recognizes the particular position of the scholar and one that enables the scholar to remove him- or herself from the usual position of "an expert, that is, an intellectual at the service of the dominant" (Wacquant 1992b, 53). Instead, the kind of reflexivity required by Bourdieusian sociology ensures that "social science cannot be neutral, detached, apolitical ... [P]roof is the constant encounters it has with forms of resistance and surveillance (internal no less than external) that threaten to chip away at its autonomy and are largely unknown in the most advanced sectors of biology or physics" (Wacquant 1992b, 51), since the sociologist or social theorist is always placed in simultaneously dominant and dominated sectors within the larger field of power (see Bourdieu 1990, 146).

It is this mandatory reflexive awareness that allows Bourdieu to become critically engaged in public affairs and develop what has been called "la tradition 'd'ouvrir sa gueule'" (Bourdieu and Grass 1999, para. 1). In this tradition of "opening one's mouth," the intellectual, by virtue of his or her knowledge and the position he has taken vis-à-vis their research subject, is able to speak out on current public affairs. Wacquant (1992b, 54) characterizes Bourdieu's engagement as "parsimonious, restive, and relatively low-key ... best typified by the somewhat uneasy combination of intense commitment with a rational distrust of organizational attachments." Bourdieu (1998, vii) himself claims that "I do not have much inclination for prophetic interventions and I have always been wary of occasions in which the situation or a sense of solidarity could lead me to overstep the limits of my competence. So I would not have engaged in public position-taking if I had not, each time, had the – perhaps illusory – sense of being forced into it by a kind of legitimate rage, something close to something like a sense of duty." And his own concern was that intellectuals fulfill their "immense historical responsibility" and pursue actions invested with both moral authority and intellectual competence, something Bourdieu was not entirely sure of himself (Bourdieu 1998, ix; Bourdieu 2002, para. 4). Yet Bourdieu was frequently engaged; the obituary section of *Le Monde* on 26 January 2002 includes praiseworthy comments from the president and prime minister of France; the Socialist, Communist, and Green parties of France; the Association for the Taxation of Financial Transactions for the Aid of Citizens; and other unions and organizations. As well, Bourdieu's books on the university system (*Academic Discourse* [1996]), small-scale and apparently invisible forms of suffering (*The Weight of the World,* described in a *Le Monde* editorial as "son manifeste plus éloquent"), and his collected writings on the rise of neoliberal globalizing economic systems and their impacts on the French people (*Acts of Resistance* [1998], *Contre-feux* [1996], *Contre-feux* 2), all go to highlight the degree to which Bourdieu was willing to open his mouth.

In sum, Bourdieu's engagement, as well as his entire social-theoretical framework, appear to be rooted in his particular social scientific experience, "depuis l'Algérie en guerre et l'enseignement en mutation des années 1960, jusqu'à la mise à nu de toutes les misères du monde, celles de la société néolibérale, celles du monde mondialisé des années 1990" (Charle and Roche 2002, para. 12).[9] The encounter between Bourdieu and Hobsbawm in 2001, it appears, made clear what Bourdieu saw his career as being about: no science without engagement, no engagement without science (para. 13). And it is commitment to the mutual intertwining of science and engagement that merits not only his continued importance as a social theorist, but his position as a model for engaged social theory (see also Truong and Weill 2012).

Model 3: Havel – Engagement by Cultural Conscience

The third model of intellectual engagement, which I call engagement by cultural conscience, relies primarily on the perception of the place of intellectuals in a society. This model is most probably the furthest from North American intellectuals' experience (or at least the perception they have of how they are valued by the wider society); after all, as even de Tocqueville pointed out nearly two hundred years ago, the American democratic and egalitarian culture, which Canada has inherited in part, would suggest that no person's viewpoint or ideas should be placed ahead of another's, which encourages the absence of an intelligentsia (de Tocqueville n.d., para. 7-9). Yet, in other societies, there is a peculiar demand placed on the intellectual – to serve as a kind of social conscience, one who can "smell a rat ... and make others smell it too" (Schalk 1991, 170), and who can hold a mirror up to a society and show its members what they have become and the potential direction forward. In our time, one of the most prominent individuals who served this function is Václav Havel, known the world over for his dissenting activities in Czechoslovakia during the Prague Spring of 1968 and the Velvet Revolution that ended Communist Party rule in 1989.

Originally an absurdist playwright in the 1960s, Havel became increasingly involved in politics, starting with the protests of the Fourth Writers' Congress in 1967 against censorship and arbitrary police actions. This engagement continued as Havel became director of the *Tvár* literary magazine and struggled with the Novotny regime to gain Czechoslovak latitude to forge their own version of socialism and loosen the fetters imposed by Moscow (Maxa 1970, 26; Havel 1998, 95; Kusin 1971, 99; 1972, 69, 82). In 1979, Havel was imprisoned for subversion due to his work with the Charter 77 reform movement. In 1989, Havel helped to found the Civic Forum, the human rights group that ultimately toppled the communist regime. He was then elected as president of Czechoslovakia in 1990 and of the Czech Republic in 1998.

Throughout this thirty-year career, which straddled "being a writer" and "being in politics," Havel constantly and consistently criticized the development of mass political parties and the involvement of individuals in political positions they held no real interest in doing anything with. He never thought of himself as politically minded (Havel 1990, 8; 1998, 97); yet, as his official biographer noted,

> For years he criticized the practice of politics as a pragmatic battle for power, whose goal was to gain power by any means; he promoted "apolitical," moral politics, politics based on conscience and truth. Then destiny played him a dirty trick; it invited him to show what *he* could do as a politician. Power dropped into the hands of the man who had written the celebrated essay, "The Power of the Powerless." (Kriseová 1993, 271)

Based on this cursory examination of Havel's political life, we could ask a simple question: What drove Havel to violate his public statements regarding politics and his place in it, which he once likened to a literary critic being called upon to write a novel (Kriseová 1993, 271)? Two better questions, though, manifest themselves if we look beyond the biographical elements of this description. First, could the Czechoslovakian reform movement have come as far as it did if Havel had been replaced by, for example, Dusan Hamsik, Milan Kundera, Ivan Klíma, or Ludvík Vaculík, four other writers involved in the reform movements of the 1960s and on? Or, to put this question in a more incisive way: Was the position of the intellectual *that* important for the Czechoslovakian reform movement, and if so, *then* why Havel?

I would argue, following better scholars of Czechoslovak history than I, that the position of the intellectual – in both a leadership or articulation role for already existing dissatisfaction and dissent and in a leadership role for the reform movement – was critical to the reform movement's success. The intelligentsia – including not just scholars and writers but also what American sociologists would identify as "professionals" – took the position, traditional in Czechoslovak society, of engaging actively with the political leadership in both Prague and Moscow and synthesizing the larger discontent in the society to effect social change beneficial for the population at large.

On at least four separate occasions during the past two centuries – Czechoslovak national resistance to the Austro-Hungarian empire, resistance to the Nazi occupation during the Second World War, the Prague Spring, and the Velvet Revolution (Kusin 1971, 137) – intellectuals have taken up the position of being the "conscience" of Czechoslovak society (Kusin 1972, 167). As Kusin writes, the definition of *conscience* is one that is particularly unique to Czechoslovak society:

> When Jaroslav Seifert, the poet, appeared to those assembled at the Second Writers' Congress (22-29 April 1956) to be "the conscience" of their nation, he was not exhorting them to establish a political watchdog organization to keep an eye on the government. In fact, the writers never constituted themselves as a political organization. Seifert meant something more sophisticated: the concept of "conscience," something intellectual and spiritual which rouses men to be human, humane and genuine, stood opposed to the Stalinist theorem (proclaimed at the Soviet Writers' Congress in 1934 and surviving until the present day) of the literati as "engineers of human souls," a mission seen by many to signify the approach of a mechanical manipulator and maintenance man. (1972, 67)

The place of conscience, then, is a culturally defined and specific place, one that serves, as opposed to Stalinist attempts to construct the "new socialist man," to remind both the general public and the political leadership of their humanity and to cease serving as "mere instruments" of Communist Party policy (Kusin 1972, 81). In part, the resistance of the intelligentsia against the Party represented a power struggle between two particular segments of Czechoslovak society, and the struggle against censorship, in part led by Havel, represents a significant attempt to wrest control over the entirety of society from the Party by transforming culture, seen by Stalinism and neo-Stalinism as "an instrument of politics" (Kusin 1972, 82), into an authentic expression of human existence, the kind of realist writing done by Havel, Klíma, and Kundera, among others.

Yet to represent this solely as a power struggle over who would have the capacity for defining "reality" for the majority of society would seem to indicate that the intelligentsia had their own personal interests at the heart of their concern. However, it appears that this is precisely *not* the case: time and time again, the available research shows that the precise reason for the writers' rebellion was not their own professional interests, but rather the fact that no one in an ostensibly socialist society had the capacity to define their own reality. Hamsik (1971, 161) informs us that "It is a feature of public life in Czechoslovakia that the nation's thoughts, feelings, and endeavours are put better by writers than by politicians." Even in more sociological studies of the Prague Spring, it becomes clear that the intelligentsia, and in particular the writers, "felt the worst 'under Novotny' ... [and] was traditionally inclined to resist this peculiar combination of arbitrariness and stupidity ... The intellectual became the aristocrat of spirit" (Kusin 1971, 136). And in tiring of the "combination of arbitrariness and stupidity," the intellectuals were able to utilize their particular skills – writing, thinking, clarifying, and synthesizing – to channel the dissatisfaction of the larger Czechoslovak society into a coherent form of resistance against the neo-Stalinist regime.

Other sectors of the intelligentsia, including social theorists, became more *engagé* in furthering a democratic socialist reform movement. Mlynár developed the argument against what Sartre would call "the Terror," the absolute cooptation of the members of a social grouping for the sake of pursuing that group's goal, rendering them without freedom (Sartre 1985, 449-50, 577, 582). Mlynár considered "society, not the state, to be the subject of historical development, the 'masses of the working people,' not the state, to be the makers of social relations" and that "man as citizen represents a lower level of emancipation than the man who is a member of an unpolitical society, but he is certainly symptomatic of a higher level of development than the earlier man as a subject, a passive target of subjectivist political and state powers" (Kusin 1971, 107-8). Other social scientists, such as Kaláb and Kratochvíl, began to link social science with an understanding that science, not the absolute power of the state, needed to dictate the direction of social development (101-6). Furthermore, the majority of reformers involved in the Prague Spring were members of the Communist Party, and their theories "were not born *because* their originators were members of the Party, but because – as intellectuals – they felt themselves to have closer ties with Czechoslovak society and the Czech and Slovak nations as basically a unit of European civilization, than with their party" (119; Kusin 1972, 85-89). As such, because of their position in Czechoslovak society as articulators (rather than creators) of the public will, intellectuals were able to serve as "the truly *engagé*" (Hamsik 1971, 12) and at the forefront of the attempts at reform.

This is the bulk of the reason I believe that if Havel had not been at the forefront of the Prague Spring and Velvet Revolution, someone else would have been; in Czechoslovak society, intellectuals are, by virtue of this culturally defined position as the conscience of their society, engaged in public life (almost to the point of it being a burden on writers).[10] In this sense, the *position* of the intellectual in a society may very well be more important than the particular intellectual. Given the responsibility that Havel sees as inherent in the professional intellectual role, intellectuals serve as commentators and critics, reflecting on public affairs at large. And this is the kind of engagement that Havel, since his first presidential election in 1990, has argued that other intellectuals in other contexts should take on:

> That is why I wonder whether genuine intellectuals, philosophers, and poets are not virtually duty-bound to stop fearing and loathing politics and to take upon themselves all the risks and requirements that go with it, even though they find them rather strange. Is it not time for intellectuals to try to give politics a new and, as it were, postmodern face?
>
> Who, for that matter, is better equipped to perceive the global context in which political actions take place, to assume a share of responsibility for the state of the world, and to restore to political prominence values such as conscience, love for one's fellow humans, and respect for nature, for the order of Being, and for the pluralism of cultures? (Havel 1998, 100)

For Havel, the key task for intellectuals is in essence to claim for themselves in a valid and legitimate manner the same kind of role in their own countries that Czechoslovakian society gave them by virtue of tradition, a role in which intellectuals serve as the conscience and reflection of their society, turning diffused disgruntlements and concerns into clear agendas for future social development.

Closure: The Future of Intellectual Work?

If there were ever a time for intellectual engagement, this would seem to be it. The American war on terror and crackdown, whether explicit or tacit, on dissent; the increasing polarization of societies on the basis of racial and ethnic identity, economic status, and belief system; the induced "clash of civilizations" as a result of the appearance of the "us versus them" mentality (Huntington 1998; Said 2002); the increasing sense of disenfranchisement, both political or economic; the global economic disaster from 2007 on; and the increasing global resistance to inhumane economic and political orders, evinced by the Arab Spring revolutions and the Occupy movement – all of these situations indicate a need for the contribution of thoughtful, reflective intervention in these debates by those of us whose profession it is to think critically about society.

The three models of intellectual engagement here suggest particular ways of pursuing a corresponding kind of intervention. It is, of course, easy enough to express something that offends our individual conscience and sensibilities; many of us have written to political representatives or signed petitions to protest something with which we disagreed or to support a policy or program we would like to see. There are North American intellectuals whose public interventions are sparked by these motivations – Noam Chomsky and Stanley Fish being only two of the most immediately recognizable. In Canada, we have the efforts of Charles Taylor and Gérard Bouchard to enable Quebecers to reexamine the fundamental tenets of Québécois society in the work of the Commission de consultation sur les pratiques d'accommodement reliées aux différences culturelles is a recent example in Canada (see Schaffer 2012). However, to base an intervention on our particular philosophical or social-theoretical position or on particular research we have pursued is an entirely different matter, especially if we live in a culture that would seem to repudiate the notion that intellectuals could serve as a society's conscience. The above discussion on the pressures emanating from the general public and the academy against intellectual engagement only serve to complicate matters, leaving us with two issues to struggle against: the sociological issues pertaining to our particular position in the social structure and the cultural issues militating against our more active engagement; and the fact that quite frequently, both in response to these issues and independently, our intellectual work does not frequently allow for our intervention in public affairs.

To most, social theory appears to be dramatically divorced from practical social and political action; it seems as if it is merely philosophy about the social world, and is often treated as something to know but not be specialized in, including in Canadian graduate schools. In part, the former might be true, since social theory is intended to understand general trends and patterns in societies. However, there is nothing in that mandate that prevents social theory from directly addressing matters for public intellectual engagement. In fact, as Kusin's analysis of intellectual work published before the Prague Spring (1971) shows, much social-theoretical work could be translated directly into plans for individual and collective action, including the reorganization of the Czechoslovak political and economic orders in order to create Dubček's vaunted "socialism with a human face."

To my mind, a reciprocal action exists between social theorists (and, more generally, social science scholars) and the general public. The general public tends to distrust intellectuals, in part because it doesn't understand what we've written or what the relevance of those writings might be to people's lives. Intellectuals perceive this distrust as anti-intellectualism, and end up writing in ways that are accessible to specialists (and even those who write for a more general public, such as Chomsky or Fish, tend to write in ways that could be called relatively obfuscatory; see Fish 2002 for an example). This reinforces the general public's perception that we are unconcerned with their lives, and so on.[11] Of course, neither side is particularly correct in these perceptions – but neither is incorrect either, and more needs to be done to break this cycle to augment the capacity for additional reflection and thoughtfulness among members of the reading public (Schaffer 2002).

It is my contention that a combination of the three models of intellectual engagement discussed here will allow for this kind of change. While it would be difficult to automatically and arbitrarily change how the general public views social theorists, it is certainly possible over time to affect this view and enable people to see the relevance of our potential contributions. We do this best in writing; through our writing, we are able, as Havel (1998, 185) puts it, to deliver "a sharp light thrown on the misery of the contemporary soul." However, the mode of writing we tend to pursue, one that seems to eschew clarity and cogency in favour of appearing most erudite, is not necessarily most suitable for addressing the general public. It is entirely possible to be both *intellectual* and *accessible* – and both Bourdieu and Sartre were able to do this in their own manners (Bourdieu in media addresses and public essays and speeches; Sartre through his literary and dramatic works and his contributions to *Les temps modernes*). Given the complexity and depth of their thought, for Bourdieu and Sartre to be able to make their ideas clearly comprehensible and directly relevant to the general public shows that we too should be able to pursue the creation of publicly accessible and relevant social theory.

In particular, this examination of the three models reveals a set of three common traits regarding the relationship between critical social theorists and sociologists and a broader public, traits that highlight the mutually reciprocating nature of that relationship, and traits that can be changed by virtue of changes in the ways in which we work. Specifically, these traits involve the scholars' motivation for writing; their theoretical positioning vis-à-vis the wider public; their intention to be accessible; and the cultural position of intellectuals in the society in question. Of course, and not coincidentally, the very traits that have enabled the scholars examined here to be engaged intellectuals are the same traits that prevent most North American social theorists from becoming engaged.

First, scholarly motivation here refers to not just why one chooses a particular subject to research and write on but also, and more importantly, what a theorist intends to see done with his or her theoretical work. Does a scholar merely wish to understand how some aspect of the social world works and to disseminate that understanding to the community of scholars for scientific evaluation? If so, engagement is most probably not the motivating factor or even the desired outcome. Does a scholar wish to see his or her theoretical work put into praxis in some kind of way, either through changes in how individuals in their community or society live their lives or in having those theories translated into praxis by social movements? In this case, engagement and the observation of a concrete result from the theoretical work would be the motivating factor, taking a step closer to engagement in public affairs than the merely scientific work. Both are, of course, valid in their own right; however, they have entirely different motivating factors.

The second of these considerations concerns the theoretical positioning of the writer, which in part follows the "science for science's sake"/"science for humanity's sake" distinction implied just above. However, it involves much more than a simple positivism/activism distinction. As we saw with regard to Sartre and Bourdieu, their particular theoretical stances enabled them not only to translate their conceptual apparatuses into a variety of situations but also to extend those apparatuses into dealing with questions of what should be done. Given the way in which critical social theory has developed since the 1980s, with the apparent schisms between cultural and political Marxism, the development of poststructuralist and postmodernist theories, and the advent of "identity politics" theories that appear to focus on singular criteria of inequality, it appears that these positions would not allow for or enable scholars to become engaged on the basis of their theory. Despite the tensions between these schools of thought, however, common patterns and parallels can be observed in the mechanisms they describe, and it is these patterns and parallels that I believe can enable social theory to become more engaged.

Third, we need to look at who the intended audience of the work is and how it will respond to what we do. If the intended audience is made up of specialists in the particular field of social theory in which the author works, then the work will obviously have less of an impact on the wider world, in part because it relies on a specialized language, jargon, and an already understood and agreed-upon paradigm for discussing the social world. Social-theoretical work written for a broader audience, though, may very well have a beneficial impact on the larger social world, inspiring the people around us to live their lives and organize their social relationships in new and more just ways. However, this depends on *how* the work is written, *for whom* the work is written, and *why* the work is written in that way; and all of these factors can make or break our relationship with a larger public. This concern with audience and with the translation of theoretical works into the languages of the public sphere goes far, I argue, to correct one of Burawoy's (2005) major weaknesses in his conception of the traditional public sociologist. That model of public sociology "instigates debates within or between publics, *although he or she might not actually participate in them*" (Burawoy 2005, 7, emphasis added). My position is that engaged social theorists have a theoretically principled basis for participating in these debates. Some versions of social-theoretical work (see Abend 2008) are necessarily normative and potentially beneficial for debates about changes in society. These positions need to be articulated for a broader public in terms of very pressing debates about our collective future and in ways that ensure that these ideas are accessible in both linguistic and epistemological terms.

If we bring these three common elements back to Burawoy's fourfold division of labour in sociology, then we find, as Figure 3.1 shows, that ultimately all four (or five, depending on how one thinks about Burawoy's notion

FIGURE 3.1
The goals of sociological knowledge

	Purpose of sociology	Audience	Responsibility	End state
Professional	Knowledge for its own sake	Professional sociologists	Demonstration of validity of knowledge for all recipients	Deep understanding of social forces
Policy	Application of knowledge in form of policy	Policy makers; corporate leaders; other sociologists	Formulation of responsible, reasonable policy	Rational policy development
Critical	Identify causes of social problems	Critical sociologists; members of activist public	Highlighting ways society has "gone wrong," sites for improvement	Critique of social forces to lay basis for improvement
Traditional public	Broader public understanding of social forces	General public	Providing valid insights for public decision making	Fostering reasoned public debate, betterment of society as a whole
Organic public	Assist members of subaltern groups	Subaltern groups; general public; social activists; policy makers	Group(s) for/with whom sociologist acts	Betterment of specific human groups' life

of the "public sociologist") approaches have one core value at their heart – namely, the betterment of society. Whether that betterment comes about through the beneficence of knowledge for its own sake, the rational application of knowledge by policy makers, the capacity for critiquing the ways in which society has failed to fulfill its promise, the provision of scientifically correct information to foster reasoned public debate, or the provision of analyses for the sake of directly improving the conditions of existence of a suffering group, the end state of sociology on this view turns out the same and can be directly tracked to the rootedness of sociology in the "moral sciences" traditions of Kant, Adam Smith, and John Stuart Mill.

In his book *Disrespect: The Normative Foundations of Critical Theory* (2007), Axel Honneth makes the case that members of subalternised groups in society, those who suffer from the social problems we study, those who experience injustice as a form of disrespect, very often lack the language for articulating their experiences of these social problems, which leaves them out of the processes of communicative action that are supposed to take place in a society. I take his general point, though I think it is important to modify it by saying that they may not have a *sufficiently developed* syntax to articulate their experiences of injustice in a way that positions them as equal interlocutors in public debates about the societal forces that create the conditions in which they exist. I believe that examining the sociological endeavour as requiring a form of commitment that works to foster and deepen the pre-existing ethical relationships between authors, readers, and social problems can work to provide the tools for augmenting the languages that members of society have for understanding, critiquing, and changing the social forces that impact upon their lives. In the same way that Sartre's literature of commitment posited that "the novelist as social leader must constantly seek to *lift* the intellectual level of his readers" (Whiting 1948, 87), I believe that we need to re-engage the sociological endeavour to pay more mind to our ethical obligation to lift the intellectual level of our readers – in essence, to put our analyses in service to the larger society in a pedagogical manner, to fulfill the goal of helping society to "stop being the shitty mess that it is," as Sartre put it (Sartre and Lévy 1996, 1964-65). Failing to do so will harm both sides of this equation; as Jacoby (2000, xxi) puts it, "Ultimately, it is not only the larger public that loses when intellectuals turn inward to fetishize their profundity, but intellectuals themselves. Their work turns arid, their arguments thin, their souls parched. In the life of the mind, as in life itself, vitality requires resisting the lure of the familiar and the safe."

Notes

1 One can see the parallels between this kind of engagement and the antiwar actions during the Gulf War, the bombing of Yugoslavia, and the American "war on terror." See, for example, Ali's (2000), *Masters of the Universe*, Žižek's (1999) *NATO as the Left Hand of God?*, and the comments listed in the American Council of Trustees and Alumni report (2002).

2 This question presumes that the frequent interventions in global politics and even the internal affairs of sovereign nations on the part of the US government are worthy, in a manner parallel to the antiwar movements analyzed by Schalk, of intellectual

engagement. Since 1987, there have been at least nine relatively large-scale American military interventions in the world: the invasion of Panama to capture General Manuel Noriega; the Gulf War to "liberate" Kuwait and the continuing enforcement of the "no-fly zone"; the two humanitarian interventions in Somalia and Haiti; the NATO bombing of the Federal Republic of Yugoslavia (FRY) in response to the FRY's attacks on Kosovo; the continuing "war on drugs" and the Colombia plan involving $1 billion of military aid and personnel; the support of anti-terrorist actions in the Philippines; and the invasions of Afghanistan and Iraq as the opening moves in the American "war on terror." Adding the various problems that continue to plague North American society – economic inequality, racial profiling of African Americans and Arab Americans, the economic policies of international monetary organizations, the fundamentalist orientation of the Bush administration, the withdrawal of civil liberties in the face of the 9/11 attacks, and many others – it would appear that there are many opportunities for intellectual engagement in public affairs.

3 Two examples might suffice to support this contention: the rumoured acceptance by Jean-François Lyotard, famous postmodern theorist, of a chair at Emory University endowed by the Coca-Cola corporation; and the establishment of an endowed chair in English at University of Nebraska by the founder of Cliff Notes, the company best known for providing English students a way of getting out of reading assigned texts.

4 It should be noted, though, that Florida Atlantic University has established a PhD program in comparative studies, which is designed to produce public intellectuals who are "theoretically confident and knowledgeable about the world they hope to understand ... and change" (2002, "PhD in Comparative Studies," http://www.publicintellectuals.fau.edu/). This development could be understood in one of two ways: either an admirable attempt to redress the issue I have raised here, or an effort that is already admired in the professionalization of academic work. See also Tittle (2004).

5 For a Canadian model of public intellectualism, see Helmes-Hayes, this volume.

6 I have dealt elsewhere with the issues of responsibility and ethics in Sartre's work and their sociological import. See Schaffer (2004).

7 Bourdieu served in the French military in Algeria from 1955 to 1957, and then served as an *assistant de philosophie* in the Faculty of Letters of Algiers from 1958 to 1960. During his military work, Bourdieu was able to begin the groundwork for his 1958 *Sociologie de l'Algérie*, work he continued along with Abdelmalek Sayad while at the Faculty of Letters of Algiers. Both of these, Bourdieu argued, represented "un terrain d'étude privilégié" (Bonnewitz 2002, 6; Poupeau and Discepolo 2002, 17).

8 The colonial society is a system that requires knowing the logic and the internal necessity of the fact that it constitutes the context to which all behaviours, and in particular the relations between the two ethnic communities, refer. To the transformations inevitably resulting from contact between two civilizations as profoundly different in the economic domain as in the social domain, colonization knowingly and methodically adds the upheavals to assure the authority of the dominant power and the economic interests of its nationals (my translation).

9 From Algeria at war and changing education in the 1960s, to the exposure of the miseries of the world, those of the neoliberal society, and those of the globalized world of the 1990s (my translation).

10 As Havel (1990, 72) explains, "here [in Czechoslovakia] so many demands are placed on the writer that they become a burden. Traditionally in our circumstances, more is expected of writers than merely writing readable books. The idea that a writer is the conscience of his nation has its own logic and its own tradition here. For years, writers have stood in for politicians: they were renewers of the national community, maintainers of the national language, awakeners of the national conscience, interpreters of the national will. This tradition has continued under totalitarian conditions, where it gains its own special coloring: the written word seems to have acquired a kind of heightened radioactivity – otherwise they wouldn't lock us up for it!"

11 There are, of course, forums in which more publicly oriented intellectual writing appears. *Harper's*, the *New Yorker*, and other like magazines are well known; *Bad Subjects* and *Contexts*, the new magazine published by the American Sociological Association, as well as other publications attempt to address their work to the general reader while maintaining intellectual rigour.

References

Abbott, Andrew. 2007. "For Humanist Sociology." In *Public Sociology: Fifteen Eminent Sociologists Debate Politics and the Profession in the Twenty-First Century*, edited by Dan Clawson, Robert Zussman, Joya Misra, Naomi Gerstel, Randall Stokes, Douglas L. Anderton, and Michael Burawoy, 195-209. Berkeley: University of California Press.

Abend, Gabriel. 2008. "The Meaning of 'Theory.'" *Sociological Theory* 26, 2: 172-99.

Ali, Tariq, ed. 2000. *Masters of the Universe: NATO's Balkan Crusade*. New York: Verso.

American Council of Trustees and Alumni. 2002. *Defending Civilization: How Our Universities Are Failing America and What Can Be Done about It.* Washington, DC: American Council of Trustees and Alumni.

Bernard, Philippe. 2002. "Bourdieu, raisons et passions." *Le Monde*, 26 January.

Bonnewitz, Patrice. 2002. *Pierre Bourdieu: Vie, oeuvres, concepts*. Paris: Éditions Ellipses.

Boschetti, Anna. 1988. *The Intellectual Enterprise: Sartre and Les Temps Modernes.* Translated by Richard C. McCleary. Evanston, IL: Northwestern University Press.

Bourdieu, Pierre. 1958. *Sociologie de l'Algérie*. Paris: Presses Universitaires de France.

–. 1977. *Outline of a Theory of Practice*. Cambridge: Cambridge University Press.

–. 1987. *Distinction: A Social Critique of the Judgment of Taste*. Translated by Richard Nice. Cambridge, MA: Harvard University Press.

–. 1990. "The Intellectual Field: A World Apart." In Pierre Bourdieu, *In Other Words: Essays Toward a Reflexive Sociology*, 140-150. Translated by Matthew Adamson. Palo Alto, CA: Stanford University Press.

–. 1992. "Interest, Habitus, Rationality." In Bourdieu and Wacquant, *An Invitation to Reflexive Sociology*, 115-39.

–. 1996. *Contre-feux: Propos pour servir à la résistance contrel'invasionnéo-libérale.* Paris: Éditions Liber.

–. 1998. "To the Reader." In Bourdieu, *Acts of Resistance: Against the Tyranny of the Market,* v-ix. Translated by Richard Nice. New York: New Press.

–. 1999. *The Weight of the World: Social Suffering in Contemporary Societies.* Stanford: Stanford University Press.

–. 2001. *Contre-feux 2.* Paris: Raisons d'Agir.

–. 2002. "Pessimisme sociologique contre fausse science." *Le Monde,* 24 January.

Bourdieu, Pierre, and Günter Grass. 1999. "La tradition 'd'ouvrir sa gueule.'" *Le Monde,* 2 December.

Bourdieu, Pierre, Jean-Claude Passeron, and Monique St. Martin. 1996. *Academic Discourse: Linguistic Misunderstanding and Professorial Power.* Stanford: Stanford University Press.

Bourdieu, Pierre, and Loïc J. D. Wacquant. 1992. *An Invitation to Reflexive Sociology.* Chicago: University of Chicago Press.

Burawoy, Michael. 2005. "2004 Presidential Address: For Public Sociology." *American Sociological Review* 70, 1: 4-28.

–. 2009a. "Disciplinary Mosaic: The Case of Canadian Sociology." *Canadian Journal of Sociology/Cahiers canadiens de sociologie* 34, 3: 869-86.

–. 2009b. "The Public Sociology Wars." In *Handbook of Public Sociology,* edited by Vincent Jeffries, 449-73. Lanham MD: Rowman and Littlefield.

Charle, Christophe, and Daniel Roche. 2002. "Pierre Bourdieu et l'histoire." *Le Monde,* 26 January.

Dawes, Scott. 2009. "Drifting Apart? The Institutional Dynamics Awaiting Public Sociology in Canada." *Canadian Journal of Sociology* 34, 3: 623-54.

De Tocqueville, Alexis. N.d. *Democracy in America.* Vol. 2, sec. 1. *American Studies at the University of Virginia.* http://xroads.virginia.edu.

Fish, Stanley. 2002. "Postmodern Warfare: The Ignorance of Our Warrior Intellectuals." *Harper's* 305, 1826: 33-40.

Hamsik, Dusan. 1971. *Writers against Rulers.* Translated by D. Orpington. New York: Random House.

Havel, Václav. 1990. *Disturbing the Peace: A Conversation with Karel Hvízdala.* New York: Alfred A. Knopf.

–. 1998. *The Art of the Impossible: Politics as Morality in Practice: Speeches and Writings, 1990-1996.* Translated by Paul Wilson. New York: Fromm International.

Helmes-Hayes, Rick, and Neil McLaughlin. 2009. "Public Sociology in Canada: Debates, Research, and Historical Context." *Canadian Journal of Sociology* 34, 3: 573-600.

Honneth, Axel. 2007. *Disrespect: The Normative Foundations of Critical Theory.* London: Polity Press.

Huntington, Samuel. 1998. *The Clash of Civilizations and the Remaking of the World Order.* New York: Touchstone Books.

Jacoby, Russell. 2000. *The Last Intellectuals: American Culture in the Age of Academe.* New York: Basic Books.

Kriseová, Eda. 1993. *Václav Havel: The Authorized Biography*. Translated by Caleb Crain. New York: St. Martin's Press.

Kusin, Vladimir. 1971. *The Intellectual Origins of the Prague Spring: The Development of Reformist Ideas in Czechoslovakia, 1956-1967*. Cambridge: Cambridge University Press.

–. 1972. *Political Grouping in the Czechoslovak Reform Movement*. New York: Columbia University Press.

Maxa, Josef (Journalist M). 1970. *A Year Is Eight Months*. Garden City, NY: Doubleday and Company.

McLaughlin, Neil, and Kerry Turcotte. 2007. "The Trouble with Burawoy: An Analytic, Synthetic Alternative." *Sociology* 41, 5: 813-28.

Merleau-Ponty, Maurice. 1973. "Sartre and Ultrabolshevism." In *Adventures of the Dialectic*, 95-202. Evanston, IL: Northwestern University Press.

Poupeau, Franck, and Thierry Discepolo, eds. 2002. *Interventions 1961-2001: Science sociale et action politique*. Marseilles: Agone.

Said, Edward. 2002. "Impossible Histories: Why the Many Islams Cannot Be Simplified." *Harper's* 305, 1826: 69-74.

Sartre, Jean-Paul. 1948. *Qu'est-ce que la littérature?* Paris: French and European Publications.

–. 1963. *Being and Nothingness: A Phenomenological Essay on Ontology*. Translated by Hazel Barnes. New York: Washington Square Press. First published 1939.

–. 1985. *Critique of Dialectical Reason*. Vol. 1, *Theory of Practical Ensembles*. London: Verso. First published 1960.

–. 1993a. "Freedom and Responsibility." In *Essays in Existentialism*, edited by Wade Basking, 63-66. New York: Citadel Press.

–. 1993b. "The Humanism of Existentialism." In *Essays in Existentialism*, edited by Wade Basking, 31-62. New York: Citadel Press.

Sartre, Jean-Paul, and Benny Lévy. 1996. *Hope Now: The 1980 Interviews*. Chicago: University of Chicago Press.

Schaffer, Scott. 2002. "Introduction: The Mirror Stage." *Journal of Mundane Behavior* 3, 2, http://mundanebehavior.org/.

–. 2004. *Resisting Ethics*. New York: Palgrave.

–. 2012. "Cosmopolitanising Cosmopolitanism? Cosmopolitan Claims Making, Interculturalism, and the Bouchard-Taylor Report." *Rooted Cosmopolitanism: Canada and the World*, edited by Will Kymlicka and Kathryn Walker, 129-55. Vancouver: UBC Press.

Schalk, David. 1991. *War and the Ivory Tower: Algeria and Vietnam*. New York: Oxford University Press.

Soley, Lawrence C. 1995. *Leasing the Ivory Tower: The Corporate Takeover of Academia*. Boston: South End Press.

Tittle, Charles. 2004. "The Arrogance of Public Sociology." *Social Forces* 82, 4: 1639-43.

Truong, Nicolas, and Nicolas Weill. 2012. "A Decade after His Death, French Sociologist Pierre Bourdieu Stands Tall." *Guardian* (UK), 21 February.

Wacquant, Loïc J.D. 1992a. "Epistemic Reflexivity." In Bourdieu and Wacquant, *An Invitation to Reflexive Sociology*, 36-46.

–. 1992b. "Reason, Ethics, and Politics." In Bourdieu and Wacquant, *An Invitation to Reflexive Sociology*, 47-60.

Whiting, Charles G. 1948. "The Case for 'Engaged' Literature." *Yale French Studies* 1: 84-89.

Wolfe, Tom. 2000. "In the Land of Rococo Marxists: Why Is No One Celebrating the Second American Century?" *Harper's* June 300, 1801: 73-82.

Žižek, Slavoj. 1999. *NATO as the Left Hand of God?* Zagreb: Arkzin.

4

Precarious Publics

Interrogating a Public Sociology for Migrant Workers in Canada

JILL BUCKLASCHUK

As Ariane Hanemaayer and Christopher J. Schneider explain in their introduction to this collection, Michael Burawoy (2005a) encourages sociologists to reflect upon their discipline by considering what it means to be a sociologist and why sociological work is important in his now famous 2004 address to the American Sociological Association (ASA). He calls for sociologists to question the purposes of their work, consider for whom they produce knowledge, and focus on goals for social change. The ASA address and its goal to promote and legitimize public sociology have resulted in widespread debate on public sociology. As this volume evidences, Burawoy has prompted scholars to question the role of morals and values in research and the place of social justice in sociology. His work has encouraged us to ask how we, as sociologists, can be more engaged with "publics."[1]

He presents organic public sociology as an avenue for pursuing a sociology that strives for social change and is driven by goals of social justice. By engaging in dialogue with publics, the public sociologist engages in "a process of mutual education" that will make the invisible visible and the private public (Burawoy 2005a, 8). The organic public sociologist is actively involved with publics in a process of social transformation aimed at "elaborating local imaginations of what could be" (Burawoy 2005b, 430). The underlying assumption of organic public sociology, as presented in the ASA address and Burawoy's subsequent works (e.g., 2006, 2007a, 2007b), is that such work is largely intended to address social inequality and empower the powerless. Therefore, in this form of public sociology, publics are understood as those who occupy social positions of little power and are marginalized from the mainstream. While the intentions of organic public sociology seem to be relatively well developed, how public sociologists go about identifying and engaging such publics remains ambiguous. Furthermore, while Burawoy acknowledges that there are multiple and diverse publics, he has not fully considered that particular publics may trouble his conceptual framework.

I argue that to achieve its goals and develop into a more inclusive framework for conducting sociology, organic public sociology must explore the implications and complexities of engaging marginalized groups as publics. Examining marginalized groups as publics unsettles the notion of "a visible, thick, active" public that is "understood as people who are themselves involved in conversation" (Burawoy 2005a, 7) because marginality contributes to a situation where particular publics are rendered invisible and disconnected from the mainstream and social networks (Basok 2004; Calavita 1998; Liamputtong 2007). Despite potentially benefiting from engagement in organic public sociology, marginalized groups lack the economic and social resources that are needed to be actively involved in dialogue, and they may face constraints in publicly addressing concerns. I explore the situation of temporary migrants in Canada to illustrate the challenges of this marginalization.[2]

Temporary migrants constitute a marginalized group that would positively benefit from engagement in a project of organic public sociology by having their private struggles become public issues (see Mills 1959) so as to address their often poor living and working conditions. Despite the important economic role of temporary migrants in various labour market sectors in Canada, they often experience social exclusion and constitute an invisible group (Basok 2004; Hu 2009). Their residence in Canada is understood as merely temporary, for the short-term purposes of addressing a labour market need. The parameters and regulations of temporary migration programs deny temporary migrants full rights of citizenship and reinforce dependency on employers.[3] The combination of their temporary status, government policy, and associated lack of citizenship rights contributes to their social exclusion, marginalization, and vulnerability.

Engaging in research with marginalized groups such as temporary migrants must be approached cautiously. Despite the potential benefits that groups may receive from such engagement, making invisible groups visible may have consequences. There are "mechanisms of social control" (Basok

2002, xviii) that contribute to the continued marginalization of temporary migrants, which keeps them in precarious circumstances and impacts how they are able to act to change the conditions of their lives in Canada.[4] These "mechanisms of social control" are shaped by government policy and implicitly or explicitly enforced by employers;[5] for example, if deemed necessary, employers can send temporary migrants home or choose not to hire them again after their contracts expire. Temporary migrants do not wish to jeopardize their employment overseas and therefore often remain quiet about poor living and working conditions, which reinforces their invisibility. Studying temporary migrants through the framework of organic public sociology may move towards addressing their marginality and invisibility, but, given the potential adverse effects of publicly addressing these issues, it is premature to assume that such engagement is always desirable.

If public sociology is to be accountable to its publics and focused on questions of "knowledge for whom" and "knowledge for what" (Burawoy 2005a), further clarification regarding how publics are constituted, understood, and engaged is required. When considering organic public sociology, Burawoy (2005a, 2006) seems to assume that publics are obvious, easy to identify, readily available, and willing to be engaged by (or with) public sociologists. However, some publics may in fact be invisible and reluctant or unable to come forth, define themselves, and engage in conversation with sociologists. Engaging in public sociology is inherently complicated by the complex social circumstances and locations that people occupy, which is an issue that has yet to be thoroughly considered. The circumstances that contribute to social marginalization can constrain the goals of Burawoy's organic public sociology, complicate the act of doing public sociology, and even contribute to the continued marginalization of groups. This chapter demonstrates that public sociology cannot be the "angel of history" or the "saviour of humanity" (Burawoy 2005a) if it is not cautious and acutely aware of the complex and even tenuous circumstances in which some publics may exist and the associated dilemmas of doing organic public sociology.

When considering such dilemmas in the context of Burawoy's organic public sociology, two important questions arise: How do sociologists locate and define publics? And what complications arise in working with publics, especially those that are not readily identifiable? These questions revolve around concerns regarding two central yet inadequately problematized aspects of Burawoy's conceptualization of publics: first, that publics are to be or made to be visible and are able to be engaged in conversation; and second, that the public sociologist's "specialized knowledge" (Burawoy 2007b, 127) is best suited to defining publics and assisting in their pursuits of social change.[6] Such elements of Burawoy's public sociology require further interrogation. A purposeful, socially relevant, and value-driven public sociology, which is what Burawoy (2005a) intends with his organic public sociology, must recognize that publics may not always be identifiable, that many publics may face barriers to engaging in dialogue, and that public sociologists alone may be unable to adequately address the needs of particular publics.

Before discussing marginalized groups in more detail, this chapter presents a brief overview of organic public sociology as well as a discussion of Burawoy's conception of publics and how they are to be engaged. I examine the particular circumstances and social position of temporary migrants to problematize the concept of publics and raise dilemmas for engaging in organic public sociology with groups that are unable or unwilling to be involved in discussion. To elaborate the problems of engaging in organic public sociology and the social constitution of publics, I use feminist scholarship to outline a critique of conducting work that is ostensibly empowering and to elucidate the problems inherent in researching groups outside the mainstream. Finally, I work towards developing a public sociology for temporary migrants, which offers insights into how organic public sociology can be more inclusive of the needs of marginalized publics without compromising their well-being or further contributing to their marginalization. An organic public sociology that allows publics to determine how or if they wish to be visible while recognizing the importance of multiple perspectives and knowledge can be an important step towards unveiling social inequality and working towards social justice.

What Is Organic Public Sociology?

Public sociology, as explained by Burawoy (2005a), has emerged from two areas of frustration and concern in the social sciences and sociology in particular. The first concern is associated with intradisciplinary hesitation in relinquishing the pre-eminence of scientific inquiry and the positivist paradigm. The second concern that shapes Burawoy's public sociology is related to socioeconomic factors associated with neoliberal globalization, including rampant individualism, increased marketization and privatization, growing social inequality, and shifts to the political right. Burawoy envisions public sociology as a way to address such areas of concern by bringing sociology into the public realm and making private issues into public concerns, challenging positivism, and legitimizing morally and politically motivated inquiry, which, incidentally, have been the central goals of feminist scholarship for years (Acker 2005; Creese, McLaren and Pulkingham 2009; Risman 2006). After a period that lauded a disciplinary emphasis on the scientific method, Burawoy (2005a, 5) argues that sociology must now focus on "taking knowledge back to those from whom it came, making public issues out of private troubles, and thus regenerating sociology's moral fiber." Public sociology is an effort to bring concern for social change as well as morals and values back into sociological work.

Furthermore, public sociology seeks to engage wider, non-academic publics through the use of accessible writing and interest in current topics of public concern, which will, therefore, make sociological work more relevant to a larger audience. Also, it emphasizes dialogue and collaboration with organizations and other groups and focuses on addressing issues by using local knowledge in conjunction with the professional expertise of sociologists. Public sociologists seek to engage publics ranging from the mass media to university students and social movements to marginalized groups. To differentiate between different goals and engaged publics, Burawoy outlines two forms of public sociology – traditional and organic. A traditional public sociology promotes the public intellectual and engages with mass audiences, which are largely invisible publics (Gans 2002). In contrast, in organic public sociology, the intellectual works closely with what is often a counterpublic that is visible, engaged, well developed, and local (Burawoy 2005a, 7). Burawoy most passionately advocates organic public sociology because it is most grounded in goals of social change and addressing local issues.

If we read Burawoy's work beyond the ASA address (Burawoy 2005b, 2006, 2007a, 2007b), we learn that his public sociology is very much shaped by a normative valence as it intends "to grapple with the destruction of human community" (Burawoy 2006, 2), the negative implications of neoliberal globalization, and the troubling relationship among state, economy, and society. He argues for a public sociology of human rights that guides social action and seeks to mobilize publics. Burawoy's imagining of public sociology is fuelled by fights against social injustice, questions regarding the role of nation-states, and considerations of the impacts of neoliberal globalization as borders become more flexible to the movement of people and capital. Burawoy makes it clear that public sociology's purpose, as he imagines it, is to develop a framework in which subjectivity, local knowledge, and a concern for social and human rights issues can be understood and given legitimate space within sociology. Ultimately, throughout his works on public sociology, Burawoy is encouraging sociologists to ask a reflexive question: "For whom and for what do we pursue sociology?" (Burawoy 2005a, 11). He emphasizes that sociological work can and should strive for the betterment of society. Public sociology is to be accountable to publics, and, therefore, sociological knowledge should be pursued for publics.

What Are *Publics?* How Are They Engaged?

Burawoy (2005a, 7) broadly defines publics as "people who are themselves involved in conversation." He further explains that publics can be sought, are in flux, and can be created and transformed. In fact, he suggests that in addition to contributing to the creation and transformation of publics, "part of our business as sociologists is to define human categories ... and if we do so with their collaboration we create publics" (Burawoy 2005a, 8). So, publics, in the organic public sociology framework, are those groups that are visible; thick; involved in dialogue both amongst themselves and with sociologists; and can be defined, created, and located by sociologists. There can be multiple publics and, in organic public sociology, they usually involve diverse and organized groups such as human rights organizations, neighbourhood associations, or labour movements (Burawoy 2005a, 7-8).

In Burawoy's definition, it is understood that sociologists' knowledge and expertise have an important role to play in mobilizing publics and helping publics identify and hopefully escape the conditions that contribute to inequality and injustice in their lives. Sociologists, according to Burawoy (2007b, 127), "transmit their specialized knowledge ... to these communities, while the latter in turn mobilize what they have absorbed in order to advance their specific interests – to defend rights to respectful employment, education, and a healthy and safe environment." Organic public sociology is closely and actively engaged with publics through dialogue and collaboration in a process that reciprocally shares knowledge with the purposes of recognizing social injustice and determining ways to address it (Burawoy 2005a, 2007b). Further, Burawoy (2007b, 131) suggests that the public sociologist is in a position to offer publics options and "effective ways forward." Because those engaging in organic public sociology may have particular goals of advocacy at the root of their projects, Burawoy implies that their knowledge and ideas are best suited to guide publics; however, he does not consider the implications associated with such knowledge coming from a privileged and more powerful position. In fact, such guidance and engagement may be harmful or inappropriate to the particular publics one is attempting to help.

Marginalized and Vulnerable Groups as Publics

There remains an imprecision in Burawoy's conceptualization of publics. His definition leaves us with an uncertain understanding of exactly what select publics look like and how they are found and engaged by organic public sociologists. We are simultaneously left to believe that publics are readily identifiable by sociological categories, yet they are counter to the mainstream. And if publics require the professional knowledge of sociologists to advance their interests, then it is assumed that such publics are not in privileged or powerful social positions. In seeking clarity regarding who these publics are, Steven Brint (2005, 52) states, "by 'publics' I think Burawoy has in mind mainly community groups that are challenging the power structure in some way." Publics, then, are usually in disadvantaged positions and, as Burawoy (2005a, 2007a) explains, the publics of organic public sociology can be considered "counterpublics," acting to alter the hegemonic structures that contribute to social inequalities.[7] I argue that marginalized groups such as temporary migrants do not constitute publics or counterpublics because they are not visible and are not already involved in dialogue or conversation. Their issues and concerns are not made public, and, therefore, they continue to exist on the margins of society with few avenues to social change.

Marginalization is complex and multidimensional, involving experiences of structural and systemic inequality, injustice, social exclusion, and exploitation (Brown and Strega 2005). Those in marginalized groups experience a "disadvantaged position in the distribution of social, economic, and political resources" (Williams 2000, 16). There is considerable variety within experiences of marginalization, which may occur because of gender, race, class, citizenship status, or other characteristics that categorize people into social groups, and outcomes often include poverty, substandard housing, inadequate access to health services, and limited participation in the labour market (Buchanan, Fisher, and Gable 2009; Liamputtong 2007; Moore and Miller 1999). Existing in marginal social positions limits individuals' and groups' ability to recognize and enjoy a full spectrum of legal, social, and political rights, which also limits their ability to participate fully in society and further contributes to their social exclusion (Basok 2004; Taket et al. 2009). As such, marginalized groups or individuals are limited in their ability to participate, for example, in visible and active organizations, and they face constraints in voicing public concern for their private issues. Because of their social exclusion and separation from the mainstream, marginalized groups are positioned and understood as invisible, hidden, or hard-to-reach populations, which presents challenges to those who wish to involve such groups in advocacy or sociological work (Abrams 2010; Atkinson and Flint 2001; Van Liempt and Bilger 2009).

Vulnerability is often presented as an outcome of marginalization (Derose, Escarce, and Lurie 2007). According to Linda Moore and Margaret Miller (1999, 1034), vulnerable people "lack the ability to make personal life choices, to make personal decisions, to maintain independence, and to self-determine." A lack of social and economic resources, stigma, and discrimination can contribute to vulnerability as it leads to further marginalization and profound social exclusion, and hinders the ability to act to advance one's position (Liamputtong 2007; Moore and Miller 1999; Taket et al. 2009; Van Liempt and Bilger 2009). For immigrant groups, legal status becomes a very important contributor to vulnerability and marginalization because less than full legal status restricts access to public services such as health care and education and limits opportunities in the labour market (Calavita 2005; Derose, Escarce, and Lurie 2007; Goldring, Berinstein, and Bernhard 2009). Temporary migrants are considered both marginalized and vulnerable because they are precariously and temporarily employed and do not have full legal status in Canada or the opportunity to access permanent residence or full citizenship and the rights therein. Because of the policy mechanisms inherent in temporary migration programs, temporary migrants are also unable to act independently to change their circumstances, and their ability to make personal decisions is hindered by the structures of dependence built into such programs (Goldring 2010; Goldring, Berinstein, and Bernhard 2009; Nakache 2010; Sharma 2008; Stasiulis and Bakan 2005; Van Liempt and Bilger 2009). Vulnerability and precariousness become important conditions and dimensions of social exclusion and marginalization when groups do not have full legal status and live with the continual threat of discrimination, punishment, and deportation.

Marginalized and vulnerable groups cannot constitute publics that are visible, thick, active, and already involved in conversation if they do not have social or economic resources and cannot act independently without fears of repercussion. They remain invisible as they lack the requisite resources to identify and work towards addressing the conditions of their marginality. In their daily lives, marginalized and vulnerable groups live with the fear of job loss, discrimination, or further social exclusion, and as such remain quiet about their struggles and are unable to engage in conversation or discussion (Basok 2004; Liamputtong 2007; Taket et al. 2009). How, then, is public sociology practised with publics that cannot readily participate in dialogic processes? What happens when such publics face consequences for engaging in such discussions?

Temporary Migrant Workers

The case of temporary migrants in Canada offers insights into pursuing organic public sociology with a marginalized and vulnerable public.[8] Researchers studying temporary migrants in Canada contribute to knowledge *for* publics with the purpose of bringing to light the exploitation they face, their daily struggles to make a better life, and how they are adversely affected when unaware of their legal rights or when inadequate policy fails to protect their well-being (Basok 2002; Goldring, Berinstein, and Bernhard 2009; Hennebry and Preibisch 2012; Preibisch and Binford 2007; Sharma 2008; Stasiulis and Bakan 2005).[9] The subject area continues to problematize the concept of publics and challenges the notion that all publics are able to be defined and engaged. Temporary migrants are marginalized and vulnerable because of their permanently temporary status in a country that limits access to many social services, denies rights of citizenship, and restricts labour market participation, all of which results in social exclusion. Furthermore, identifying temporary migrants as visible publics has the very real potential of jeopardizing their employment, safety, rights, and family because of their vulnerable and precarious social, economic, and legal status.

With an aging population and purported labour shortages in various sectors, Canada can be expected to continue to rely on immigration to fuel its economy and fill jobs (Green and Green 1999; Reitz 2004). Since the early 2000s, temporary migration programs have become increasingly common as employers seek expedited methods to address labour shortages and the Canadian federal and provincial governments respond to industry demands for cheap, and often foreign, labour. Temporary migration programs have typically been devised to attract highly skilled workers who bring expertise to the labour force and temporarily fill positions that cannot be filled by Canadians. However, Canada is experiencing a recent shift in employment patterns of foreign workers; work permits issued for low-skilled occupations are outpacing those issued to highly skilled workers, particularly in the domestic service, construction, hospitality, and food-processing industries (Fudge and MacPhail 2009; Hennebry 2008; Hennebry and Preibisch 2012).[10]

Temporary migration programs are criticized by academics and political advocates for their unjust foundation of nonpermanency and exclusion from rights of citizenship, and the sanctioned dependency of employees upon employers (Basok 2002; Byl and Foster 2009; Hennebry and Preibisch 2012; Stasiulis and Bakan 2005). Typically, temporary migrants are bound to the employer that issued their work permit, and if conditions become unacceptable, they face extreme difficulty in finding a more suitable arrangement without concerns of being deported (Basok 2004; Goldring, Berinstein, and Bernhard 2009; Hennebry and Preibisch 2012; Nakache 2010; Sharma 2008). Driven by the desire and need for a better life for themselves and their families, temporary migrants' existence in Canada is fraught with social isolation and loneliness because they are often not allowed to bring their families to Canada during their employment and thus lack social networks. Their social marginalization and dependence upon employers make it challenging to openly express displeasure or advocate for rights, which results in susceptibility to unscrupulous recruiters' demands for inordinate fees or exploitative employers who refuse to uphold contracts and provide abhorrent living conditions (Basok 2002).

Engaging temporary migrant groups in sociological work comes with many challenges, and there are significant barriers to groups' participation in collaborative relationships with academics. Temporary migrants do not often function as a cohesive, publicly organized group, which makes them difficult to identify. In fact, Linda Hu (2009, 260) refers to them as "invisible." Gaining access to temporary migrants is particularly challenging because of obstacles presented by and threats imposed by employers who act as gatekeepers and strictly regulate the daily lives of temporary migrants (Hu 2009; Stasiulis and Bakan 2005). It has been documented that some employers of temporary migrants illegally withhold passports, provide substandard housing, compromise workplace health and safety, and deny payment for overtime hours (Basok 1999; Byl and Foster 2009; Stasiulis and Bakan 2005). Temporary migrants are aware that employers have significant power in determining the conditions and length of their stay in a country and as such may refuse to provide specific information that might document abuses or exploitation to their advocates (Basok 2002; Goldring 2010). If public sociologists are to work for and with temporary migrants to address such issues in a public manner, they must be particularly sensitive to such employment circumstances and acknowledge that temporary migrants may be uneasy or unwilling to participate in conversation with sociologists and sociology and to be made "visible" by their contact with sociological activists and their sociological work.

When conducting work with marginalized and vulnerable groups, the benefits versus risks of participation must be carefully weighed and negotiated. University research ethics boards (REBs) remain the formal authority on assessing such aspects of research projects and seek to protect research participants. However, when seeking to protect research participants, REBs do not always have full knowledge of the circumstances in which some groups exist, and the boards' generalized protocols may hinder research with groups they deem particularly vulnerable (Bosworth, Hoyle, and Dempsey 2011). Seeking to bring issues of precarious legal status into public arenas, Judith Bernhard and Julie Young (2009) encountered significant barriers in gaining ethical approval to study migrant families living in Canada. Anticipating potential obstacles related to engaging a group that is fearful of deportation, Bernhard and Young were surprised to discover that the largest barrier to their work was negotiating the REB's procedure. Persistent concerns regarding the protection of this public's identity and the precariousness of its members' legal status as temporary migrants ultimately resulted in a halt to Bernhard and Young's project. The vulnerability of their publics was of great concern to the REB, and the benefits versus risks proved to be too difficult to negotiate and reconcile. Engaging with marginalized or vulnerable groups as publics must include careful consideration of many ethical concerns and, if necessary, a project may need to be abandoned to protect the well-being of participants.[11] Abandoning projects designed to bring public awareness to their circumstances is not an ideal outcome, but in some cases it may be the most appropriate option given the realities of marginalized groups.

The threat and fear of jeopardizing employment in Canada results in a certain acquiescence that makes temporary migrants hesitant to publicly address concerns and seek social justice (Basok 2002, 2004). Given the parameters of their temporary employment and lack of citizenship rights, temporary migrants cannot be expected to become active and engaged publics without intervention, involvement, and assistance from other actors (Orum and Grabczynska 2006). In addition to increased public awareness and careful negotiation of ethical concerns, paths to social change must also include discussions regarding policy.

Sociologists have a role to play in exploring and collecting the experiences of marginalized groups, but they must be able and willing to collaborate with myriad actors, in addition to publics, if they wish to seek social change. In fact, public sociologists alone do not and cannot hold all of the right answers for defining groups and articulating paths to social change. Burawoy's public sociology has been criticized for being arrogant and dismissive of the value of other knowledges (Tittle 2004; Goldberg and van den Berg 2009), therefore privileging the sociologist and assuming that sociologists are in the best position to define and engage publics as they work towards social change. The sociologist defines publics from a position of privilege based on the assumption that he or she is best situated to identify the realities of publics. Burawoy fails to consider the impacts of such "arrogance" (Tittle 2004) and does not question the implications of imposing one's sociological knowledge and definitions upon others. Joan Acker (2005, 330-31) poignantly suggests that sociologists should "be careful about defining the realities of others ... Publics have to emerge in a political process, they are not invented in the minds of sociologists." Rather than being defined by others, marginalized and vulnerable groups must be afforded autonomy and independence, since this is severely lacking in their lives (Liamputtong 2007; Moore and Miller 1999). Organic public sociology may intend to address the inequalities in publics' lives, but by imposing a singular sociological knowledge and defining others' realities it may lead to further inequality or vulnerability.

Empowerment, Public Sociology, and Feminist Scholarship

Scholars suggest that the most effective strategy for addressing social inequality and effecting social change is to empower marginalized groups so they can independently address the injustices in their lives (Kirby, Greaves, and Reid 2006; Ristock and Pennell 1996). In fact, notions of empowerment are woven into the goals of organic public sociology, which is both implicitly and explicitly highlighted in Burawoy's work (2006, 2007b). Adopting empowerment as a goal has implications for how we think about publics, how they are engaged, and the nature of paths to social change. In his post-ASA-address work, Burawoy (2007b, 131) argues that collaborative engagement is empowering to groups under sociological study and that academics can be a source of information that leads to empowerment because "oppressed peoples do not fully comprehend the conditions of their own subjugation." Helping publics realize the nature of the "structures of domination" (Burawoy 2007b, 132) in which they live and providing them with the tools to understand their social position are central goals of a public social science. However, as much feminist scholarship demonstrates (Bosworth, Hoyle, and Dempsey 2011; Gore 1992; Opie 1992; Patai 1991; Rowlands 1995), such claims of empowerment have significant implications for research and cannot be adopted without reflection and careful consideration by those conducting such work.

Feminist scholarship lends many useful insights to this discussion because its foundation is based on bringing issues of marginalized and vulnerable groups into the public while also engaging in epistemological examinations of knowledge creation and the role of researchers in advancing social change (Doucet and Mauthner 2007; Reinharz 1992; Santos 2012). Emerging from social movements, feminism is imbued with morals, ethics, and values and is driven by goals of social change, not unlike organic public sociology (Ramazanoglu and Holland 2002; Risman 2006). Feminist scholars have grappled with the eminence of positivist paradigms, dualisms, social injustice, and hierarchies of power since long before Burawoy's call for a public sociology that seeks to address the same concerns (Acker 2005; Collins 2007; Creese, McLaren, and Pulkingham 2009; Doucet and Mauthner 2007; Reinharz 1992; Risman 2006). Further, feminist scholarship seeks to incorporate ethics and morals into social research, encouraging reflexive considerations of the purpose of our work and whom we create knowledge for, which is reminiscent of Burawoy's questions "knowledge for whom?" and "knowledge for what?" Seeking social change and making private issues into public concerns are not new goals for feminist scholars who have worked for years with marginalized groups, focused on contributing to knowledge for women and with women (Doucet and Mauthner 2007; Smith 1987).

Feminist scholarship has also argued that espousing certain politics and morals focused on social change does not, however, mean that researchers' work is without consequence. The implications of imposing categorizations and solutions upon marginalized groups has inspired many critiques of predominately Western research, bringing to attention the importance of letting groups speak for themselves rather than through the lens of privileged academics (Bosworth, Hoyle, and Dempsey 2011; Oakley 1998; Opie 1992; Patai 1991; Smith 2006). The very nature of working with marginalized and vulnerable groups, as Daphne Patai (1991, 139) explains, is "embedded in a situation of material inequality," and potential for exploitation is "built into almost all research projects with living human beings." There are inherent structural complexities and epistemological dilemmas that exist throughout the process of knowledge creation, and such dilemmas exist regardless of our sociological goals.

So, in addition to considering the mechanisms of social control that can hinder marginalized groups' ability or willingness to act and become visible, it is also important to consider how the process of actually engaging in a research process can be influenced by inequalities between the researcher and publics. There are persistent imbalances and unequal structures in the research process that challenge how we think of our research goals and how we reconcile such goals with the notion that academics are at the top of a knowledge hierarchy. Empowering marginalized groups through a process of collaboration and engagement can assist in developing strategies to address social inequality, but how such empowerment is achieved or carried out remains a significant dilemma for those doing organic public sociology.

In the case of temporary migrants, projects that seek their engagement must be wary of unilaterally defining categories and imposing solutions to social injustice. Providing one of the most thorough accounts of the dilemmas encountered throughout the process of working with temporary migrants, Tanya Basok (1999, 2002) critically explores the social and economic impacts of the seasonal migration of thousands of agricultural workers to a small town in southern Ontario, Canada. What began as an economic-impact assessment evolved into a project that unearthed the poor living and working conditions of Mexican seasonal migrants.

Basok was careful not to define or create publics. She recognized early in her project that questioning temporary migrants about their living and working conditions could jeopardize their employment, so she deliberately avoided inquiry focused on these issues. However, through a process that involved multistaged discussions with migrant workers in both Ontario and Mexico, her publics emerged and identified her as a source of information and assistance as they sought to understand the nature of their marginality. Without actively attempting to place herself in an advocacy position, Basok was acknowledged by temporary migrants as someone who would listen to their troubles and hopefully, in her privileged position, address the conditions of their marginalization. Prior to Basok's conversations with temporary migrants, they remained largely unaware of what few rights they were entitled to in Canada and therefore did not exercise their right to overtime pay, life insurance, or sickness pay, for example. Without knowledge of such entitlements, temporary migrants would continue to work if they were ill or injured, compromising their health and well-being. Not having access to a basic modicum of rights contributes to their precariousness and vulnerability.

Demonstrating the complicated nature of working with publics while attempting to empower temporary migrants, Basok's goals of social justice were not enough to ensure that the temporary migrants with whom she worked were able to actively and publicly address their poor working and living conditions. Furthermore, despite their initial enthusiasm for collaboration and participation in dialogue, Basok's publics eventually pulled away from actively engaging. As she explains,

> Much to my frustration, my attempts to solve the problems of Mexican workers bore no fruit. The first meeting in the church basement was attended by some two hundred workers. But only some fifty of them showed up for the second meeting ... At the first meeting I asked the workers, who could not stop giving me examples of abuses they had suffered, to make a list of farms and indicate whether their *patrones* offered them vacation pay and public holiday pay and whether they used unsafe work practices. Not a single person volunteered to make such a list. (2002, xvii)

As a sociologist and an advocate, Basok felt disappointed, angered, and betrayed by her publics, since she went to considerable lengths trying to help them, only to witness apprehension and reluctance. Her experience, however, demonstrates that even though publics may be marginalized and disempowered, sociologists cannot assume that they are best situated to determine the process by which such publics should address the social injustices in their lives. Furthermore, it cannot be assumed that marginalized publics have the ability or even courage to organize and demand what is socially just, despite what sociologists may consider to be in their best and immediate interest. In the case of temporary migrants whose social position is mired in mechanisms of social control, recognizing what is socially just and challenging employers can lead to deportation and may compromise their opportunity to work in Canada in the future.

A Public Sociology for Temporary Migrants

Is it possible to engage temporary migrants as publics given the problems associated with identifying and engaging such groups? How is it possible to work as advocates for such publics while also being sensitive to the conditions of their marginality and vulnerability? Is it counterproductive to acknowledge marginalized and vulnerable groups as publics if engagement may lead to their further marginalization? Given Burawoy's consideration of "knowledge for whom" and "knowledge for what," such questions are essential in pursuits of work with publics that exist in such complex and precarious economic and social positions. Public sociology, in principle, is ideally situated to guide marginalized groups through a process that will identify and work towards addressing the inequalities that constitute their lives, but how we understand, identify, and engage publics has important implications for how organic public sociology is actually done. In some cases, the vulnerability and social exclusion that permeates the lives of marginalized groups may lead to a shift in project goals or even abandonment of a project that may jeopardize the well-being of publics (Basok 2002; Bernhard and Young 2009). The example of temporary migrants illustrates the complexities of engaging marginalized and vulnerable groups and demonstrates that publics may be difficult to identify, remaining largely invisible because of their conditions of marginalization.

There is no simple or prescribed way to identify and engage invisible publics. Ideally, publics should emerge through a process that is built on respect, trust, and collaboration between publics and the public sociologist, as they did in Basok's study (2002). This process must be appropriate to the needs, desires, and realities of publics rather than actively created or prescribed by sociologists (Acker 2005). Marginalized and vulnerable groups lack autonomy and independence, are largely excluded from decision-making processes, and have few opportunities to be engaged in dialogue and conversation. Allowing publics to define the parameters of their visibility, engagement, and actions towards social change is an important part of a public sociology for marginalized groups, since such self-definition will contribute to empowerment and ideally an escape from vulnerability and social exclusion.

When projects are guided by goals of empowerment, however, the organic public sociologist must be aware of and carefully negotiate the inherent limitations he or she faces in prescribing avenues to social change.[12] As Jo Rowlands (1995, 105) explains, engaging marginalized groups in a process of empowerment "cannot be effective if the methodology is 'top-down' and directive, or encourages dependency. Empowerment is a process that cannot be imposed by outsiders." Marginalized and vulnerable groups lack the economic and social resources to pursue social change on their own. The organic public sociologist can play an important role in exploring and collecting their experiences and bringing public awareness to the inequalities and injustices they face. However, there are limitations to what sociologists can and should do on their own. Sociologists may "'get it wrong' in assuming we know what would be empowering for others ... No matter what our aims or how we go about 'empowering,' our efforts will be partial and inconsistent" (Gore 1992, 63). Our organic public sociology can "get it right" if it is flexible and respectful of the vulnerabilities people face in their daily lives and if it is aware of its limitations in achieving social change. We cannot impose solutions or strategies onto publics. Nor can we make them visible just because we believe they would benefit from such a process. Marginalized and vulnerable groups too often face impositions from others and must be afforded autonomy and independence in defining the contours of their visibility and engagement in conversation.

Empowerment and social change cannot be pursued by marginalized groups and sociologists alone; these things involve collaboration and co-operation amongst the multiple actors that contribute to and address conditions of marginalization and vulnerability, as has been demonstrated in feminist scholarship (Bosworth, Hoyle, and Dempsey 2011; Brady 2004; Creese, McLaren, and Pulkingham 2009; Kirby, Greaves, and Reid, 2006; Risman 2006; Ristock and Pennell 1996). More particularly, a public sociology for temporary migrants must be based upon a thorough awareness of the economic, social, and policy structures in which government programs aimed at the migrants exist. As Basok (2002, xviii) recognizes, there are "'mechanisms of social control' that assure temporary migrants' compliance with poor working and living conditions regardless of the extent of their mistreatment." Such compliance contributes to their invisibility, marginalization, and social exclusion and is tied up in the particular contours of temporary migration programs, which influence how and if publics are able or willing to be engaged in conversation and dialogue. For example, Basok's (2002, 150) "aborted activism" demonstrates that, despite intentions, our sociological work may not have the outcomes we desire or expect and that we must let publics determine the best way to address the inequalities in their lives. In her postscript, Basok explains that the private issues of temporary migrants became public concerns only once a newspaper exposé, combined with a labour walkout, brought the attention of labour unions and social justice organizations to their plight, heightening public awareness and attracting advocates to put pressure on employers and government to change policies and enhance the workers' protection.

A public sociology for temporary migrants cannot ignore the role that multi-actor collaboration and policy and government engagement can have in attempts to achieve social change and alleviate the struggles of marginalized and vulnerable publics. Sociologists cannot work alone, and public sociologists cannot solely assume the role of defining and engaging publics. Combining academic, policy, and advocacy goals is an effective way to make private troubles into public issues by bringing relevant circumstances to the attention of broad audiences through widely disseminated reports, conference presentations, and the mass media.[13] On their own, marginalized and vulnerable groups lack the social and economic resources required for full public engagement and participation, which compromises their ability to influence decision-making processes (see Fraser 1990 and 2007 for a discussion of the characteristics of strong and weak publics). Linking such groups with both policy makers and public sociologists has the potential to address the ramifications of their unequal social positions. Despite what Burawoy may contend, such a process involves more than just public sociologists. As Diane Vaughan (2006, 390) suggests, "the raison d'être of public sociology is not in its successful implementation of specific policy prescriptions, but in its ability to influence policy by the very fact of its becoming public, thereby contributing to public discourse and policy debate." Influencing local processes, empowering publics, and bringing public awareness to social inequalities are positive outcomes and worthwhile pursuits of organic public sociology, if done through a process that respects publics' precarious circumstances and realities.

In conclusion, a public sociology for marginalized and vulnerable groups cannot be restricted to pursuing the means and ends prescribed by sociologists alone (Goldberg and van den Berg 2009). Public sociology is not the only arena in which to pursue social change and societal betterment through academic pursuits. There must be collaborative interdisciplinary and cross-sector efforts to reach the goals of public sociology and achieve any modicum of social change. An organic public sociology for marginalized and vulnerable groups, and public sociology more generally, would greatly benefit from the invaluable insights and guidance provided by a multitude of areas, especially feminist scholarship (Acker 2005; Collins 2007), which would problematize how we think of those we are creating knowledge for. Public sociology has a unique opportunity to develop new ways of understanding social problems, bringing the experiences of marginalized and vulnerable groups to the attention of a broader audience, with the hopes of changing policies and people's lives. Further epistemological reflections are necessary to more fully develop the pursuit of a public sociology that is truly accountable to the sociological constitution of publics.

Notes

1 For a discussion of "engaged intellectuals" in Canada, see Schaffer, this volume.

2 Canada has many types of temporary migration programs that allow employers to access foreign labour, including the Live-In Caregiver Program, Skilled-Worker Programs, visas for international students, the Seasonal Agricultural Worker Program, and the Low-Skill Pilot Project. I focus on temporary migrants arriving through the Live-In Caregiver Program, the Seasonal Agricultural Worker Program, and the Low-Skill Pilot Project because they constitute the largest programs and are most commonly cited in the literature as those groups that suffer poor living and working conditions, work in low-paying occupations, and have low skill and education levels (Basok 2002; Bernhard and Young 2009; Byl and Foster 2009; Goldring 2010; Hennebry 2008; Hennebry and Preibisch 2012; Nakache 2010; Preibisch and Binford 2007; Stasiulis and Bakan 2005).

3 Citizenship status is an important consideration when examining immigration. It represents membership in a nation-state and it contains legal and moral rights as well as active and passive participation. Citizenship, according to Bauböck (1994, 28), "is a set of rights, exercised by the individuals who hold the rights, equal for all citizens, and universally distributed within a political community, as well as a corresponding set of institutions guaranteeing these rights." When discussing rights in this chapter, I will be referring to the rights entitlements included in citizenship, which, in Canada, generally include legal, mobility, equality, and democratic rights. Temporary migrants are not entitled to full rights of citizenship.

4 The term *precarious* is used here following the work of Goldring (2010) and Goldring, Berinstein, and Bernhard (2009) to describe the situation of migrants with statuses that do not include access to citizenship or permanent residence. Precarious status is understood as multidimensional with multiple avenues to such a status; in general, though, it refers to "'less than full' migration status" for documented and undocumented migrants and includes legal or authorized statuses (Goldring 2010). Precariousness is linked to the "presence/absence of rights and entitlements" (Goldring, Berinstein, and Bernhard 2009, 240). Further, precarious status can lead to "precarious well-being and differential inclusion and social exclusion" (Goldring 2010, 53).

5 Temporary migration programs are regulated and managed by the Government of Canada. Each temporary migration program has unique policies that outline the roles and responsibilities of employers. In most programs, employers are required to ensure that there is suitable housing available for workers, that there is an employer-employee contract in place whereby workers receive the prevailing wage, and that workers receive provincial health care when eligible. Government policy outlines workplace safety and employment standards as well (Nakache 2010).

6 For a discussion about the roles and duties of the organic public sociologist, see Mesny, this volume.

7 Such a conceptualization harkens to Nancy Fraser's work on strong publics and weak publics, where she puts forth the notion of "subaltern counterpublics" as subordinate groups that provide an alternative discourse to hegemonic ideas and interpretations (Fraser 1990, 2007).

8 In fact, Burawoy (2006, 11) has written about migrant labour in the United States, demonstrating migrants' vulnerability and marginalized position by stating that migrant workers "own nothing but their labor power."

9 For more on Canadian research into temporary migration, see the spring 2010 issue of *Canadian Issues,* published by the Association for Canadian Studies and available through http://canada.metropolis.net.

10 The Low-Skill Pilot Program, which is more formally known as the Pilot Project for Occupations Requiring Lower Levels of Formal Training (National Occupation Categories C and D), or the NOC C and D program, is designed to bring low-skill foreign labour to those industry sectors that require labourers with at most high school education or two years on-the-job training. The program is not limited by quotas, and, in 2009, nearly 66,000 temporary migrants entered Canada via the Low-Skill Pilot Program, up from 32,000 in the previous year (Government of Canada 2009, 2010).

11 For more on research ethics in public sociology, see Mesny, this volume.

12 It is also important to note that, despite such negotiation and considerations, we can never entirely control how findings are used, interpreted, or disseminated (Channels 1993).

13 For example, a report by the Alberta Federation of Labour (Byl and Foster 2009) provides detailed empirical evidence of the sudden rise in numbers of temporary migrants to the province of Alberta as well as an account of the abuses and exploitative treatment they face. While the report is neither sociological nor academic, it presents invaluable information that further complicates the situation of temporary migrants in Canada. The report illustrates temporary migrants' precarious circumstances vis-à-vis employers and the government and provides an informed and empirically grounded foundation upon which to base advocacy work and struggles for policy change.

References

Abrams, Laura S. 2010. "Sampling 'Hard to Reach' Populations in Qualitative Research." *Qualitative Social Work* 9, 4: 536-50.

Acker, Joan. 2005. "Comments on Burawoy on Public Sociology." *Critical Sociology* 31, 3: 327-31.

Atkinson, Rowland, and John Flint. 2001. "Accessing Hidden and Hard-to-Reach Populations: Snowball Research Strategies. *Social Research Update* 33: 93-108.

Basok, Tanya. 1999. "Free To Be Unfree: Mexican Guest Workers in Canada." *Labour, Capital and Society* 32, 2: 192-222.

–. 2002. *Tortillas and Tomatoes: Transmigrant Mexican Harvesters in Canada.* Montreal: McGill-Queen's University Press.

–. 2004. "Post-national Citizenship, Social Exclusion and Migrants Rights: Mexican Seasonal Workers in Canada." *Citizenship Studies* 8, 1: 47-64.

Bauböck, Rainer. 1994. *Transnational Citizenship: Membership and Rights in International Migration*. Brookfield, VT: Edward Elgar Publishing.

Bernhard, Judith K., and Julie E. Young. 2009. "Gaining Institutional Permission: Researching Precarious Legal Status in Canada." *Journal of Academic Ethics* 7, 3: 175-91.

Bosworth, Mary, Carolyn Hoyle, and Michelle M. Dempsey. 2011. "Researching Trafficked Women: On Institutional Resistance and the Limits of Feminist Reflexivity." *Qualitative Inquiry* 17, 9: 769-79.

Brady, David. 2004. "Why Public Sociology May Fail." *Social Forces* 82, 4: 1629-38.

Brint, Steven. 2005. "Guide for the Perplexed: On Michael Burawoy's 'Public Sociology.'" *American Sociologist* 36, 3: 46-65.

Brown, Leslie. A., and Susan Strega, eds. 2005. *Research as Resistance: Critical, Indigenous and Anti-oppressive Approaches*. Toronto: Canadian Scholars' Press.

Buchanan, David R., Celia B. Fisher, and Lance Gable, eds. 2009. *Research with High-risk Populations: Balancing Science, Ethics, and Law*. 1st ed. Washington, DC: American Psychological Association.

Burawoy, Michael. 2005a. "2004 Presidential Address: For Public Sociology." *American Sociological Review* 70, 1: 4-28.

–. 2005b. "Response: Public Sociology: Populist Fad or Path to Renewal?" *British Journal of Sociology* 56, 3: 417-32.

–. 2006. "A Public Sociology for Human Rights." In *Public Sociologies Reader*, edited by Judith Blau and Keri E. Iyall Smith, 1-18. Toronto: Rowman and Littlefield Publishers.

–. 2007a. "The Field of Sociology: Its Power and Its Promise." In *Public Sociology: Fifteen Eminent Sociologists Debate Politics and the Profession in the Twenty-First Century*, edited by Dan Clawson, Robert Zussman, Joya Misra, Naomi Gerstel, Randall Stokes, Douglas Anderton, and Michael Burawoy, 241-58. Berkeley: University of California Press.

–. 2007b. "Private Troubles and Public Issues." In *Collaborations for Social Justice: Professionals, Publics, and Policy Change*, edited by Andrew L. Barlow, 125-33. Lanham, MD: Rowman and Littlefield.

Byl, Yessy, and Jason Foster. 2009. *Entrenching Exploitation: The Second Report of the Alberta Federation of Labour Temporary Foreign Worker Advocate*. Edmonton: Alberta Federation of Labour.

Calavita, Kitty. 1998. "Immigration, Law, and Marginalization in a Global Economy: Notes from Spain." *Law and Society Review* 32, 3: 529-66.

–. 2005. *Immigrants at the Margins: Law, Race, and Exclusion in Southern Europe*. New York: Cambridge University Press.

Channels, Noreen. 1993. "Anticipating Media Coverage: Methodological Decisions in Criminal Justice Research." In *Researching Sensitive Topics*, edited by Claire M. Renzetti and Raymond M. Lee, 267-80. Newbury Park, CA: Sage.

Collins, Patricia Hill. 2007. "Going Public: Doing the Sociology That Had No Name." In *Public Sociology: Fifteen Eminent Sociologists Debate Politics and the Profession in the Twenty-First Century,* edited by Dan Clawson, Robert Zussman, Joya Misra, Naomi Gerstel, Randall Stokes, Douglas L. Anderton, and Michael Burawoy, 101-13. Berkeley: University of California Press.

Creese, Gillian, Arlene Tigar McLaren, and Jane Pulkingham. 2009. "Rethinking Burawoy: Reflections from Canadian Feminist Sociology." *Canadian Journal of Sociology* 34, 3: 601-22.

Derose, Kathryn P., José J. Escarce, and Nicole Lurie. 2007. "Immigrants and Health Care: Sources of Vulnerability." *Health Affairs* 26, 5: 1258-68.

Doucet, Andrea, and Natasha S. Mauthner. 2007. "Feminist Methodologies and Epistemologies." In *Twenty-First Century Sociology: A Reference Handbook,* edited by Clifton D. Bryant and Dennis L. Peck, 36-42. Thousand Oaks, CA: Sage.

Fraser, Nancy. 1990. "Rethinking the Public Sphere: A Contribution to the Critique of Actually Existing Democracy." *Social Text* 25/26: 56-80.

–. 2007. "Transnationalizing the Public Sphere: On the Legitimacy and Efficacy of Public Opinion in a Post-Westphalian World." *Theory, Culture, and Society* 24, 4: 7-30.

Fudge, Judy, and Fiona MacPhail. 2009. "The Temporary Foreign Worker Program in Canada: Low-Skilled Workers as an Extreme Form of Flexible Labor." *Comparative Labor Law and Policy Journal* 31: 101-39.

Gans, Herbert. 2002. "More of Us Should Become Public Sociologists." *Footnotes* 30, 6: 1-16.

Goldberg, Avi, and Axel van den Berg. 2009. "What Do Public Sociologists Do? A Critique of Burawoy." *Canadian Journal of Sociology* 34, 3: 765-802.

Goldring, Luin. 2010. "Temporary Worker Programs as Precarious Status: Implications for Citizenship, Inclusion and Nation Building in Canada." *Canadian Issues, Temporary Foreign Workers* Spring: 50-54.

Goldring, Luin, Carolina Berinstein, and Judith K. Bernhard. 2009. "Institutionalizing Precarious Migratory Status in Canada." *Citizenship Studies* 13, 3: 239-65.

Gore, Jennifer. 1992. "What We Can Do for You! What Can 'We' Do for 'You'? Struggling over Empowerment in Critical and Feminist Pedagogy." In *Feminisms and Critical Pedagogy,* edited by Carmen Luke and Jennifer Gore, 54-73. New York: Routledge.

Government of Canada. 2009. *Facts and Figures 2008. Immigration Overview: Permanent Residents and Temporary Foreign Workers.* Ottawa: Citizenship and Immigration Canada. http://www.cic.gc.ca/english/pdf/research-stats/facts2008.pdf.

–. 2010. *Temporary Foreign Worker Program: Labour Market Opinion Statistics.* Ottawa: Human Resources and Skills Development Canada. http://www.hrsdc.gc.ca/eng/workplaceskills/foreign_workers/stats/index.shtml.

Green, Alan G., and David Green. 1999. "The Economic Goals of Canada's Immigration Policy: Past and Present." *Canadian Public Policy/Analyse de Politiques* 25, 4: 425-51.

Hennebry, Jenna. 2008. "Bienvenidos a Canadá? Globalization and the Migration Industry Surrounding Temporary Agricultural Migration in Canada." *Canadian Studies in Population* 35, 2: 339-56.

Hennebry, Jenna, and Kerry Preibisch. 2012. A Model for Managed Migration? Re-examining Best Practices in Canada's Seasonal Agricultural Worker Program." *International Migration,* 50: e19-e40.

Hu, Linda. 2009. "Integrating the Four Sociologies: The 'Baigou Project' in China." In *Handbook of Public Sociology,* edited by Vincent Jeffries, 245-62. Lanham, MD: Rowman and Littlefield.

Kirby, Sandra L., Lorraine Greaves, and Colleen Reid. 2006. *Experience Research Social Change: Methods beyond the Mainstream.* Peterborough, ON: Broadview Press.

Liamputtong, Pranee. 2007. *Researching the Vulnerable: A Guide to Sensitive Research Methods.* London: Sage.

Mills, C. Wright. 1959. *The Sociological Imagination.* New York: Oxford University Press.

Moore, Linda W., and Margaret Miller. 1999. Initiating Research with Doubly Vulnerable Populations. *Journal of Advanced Nursing* 30, 5: 1034-40.

Nakache, Delphine. 2010. "Temporary Workers: Permanent Rights?" *Canadian Issues, Temporary Foreign Workers* Spring: 45-49.

Oakley, Ann. 1998. "Gender, Methodology and People's Ways of Knowing: Some Problems with Feminism and the Paradigm Debate in Social Science." *Sociology* 32, 4: 707-32.

Opie, Anne. 1992. "Qualitative Research, Appropriation of the 'Other' and Empowerment." *Feminist Review* 40: 52-69.

Orum, Anthony M., and Arlette Grabczynska. 2006. "Migrants, Rights, and States." In *Public Sociologies Reader,* edited by Judith Blau and Keri E. Iyall Smith, 173-90. Oxford: Rowman and Littlefield.

Patai, Daphne. 1991. "U.S. Academics and Third World Women: Is Ethical Research Possible?" In *Women's Words: The Feminist Practice of Oral History,* edited by Sherna B. Gluck and Daphne Patai, 137-53. New York: Routledge.

Preibisch, Kerry, and Leigh Binford. 2007. "Interrogating Racialized Global Labour Supply: An Exploration of the Racial/National Replacement of Foreign Agricultural Workers in Canada." *Canadian Review of Sociology* 44, 1: 5-36.

Ramazanoglu, Caroline, and Janet Holland. 2002. *Feminist Methodology: Challenges and Choices.* London: Sage.

Reinharz, Shulamit. 1992. *Feminist Methods in Social Research.* New York: Oxford University Press.

Reitz, Jeffrey G. 2004. "Canada: Immigration and Nation-Building in the Transition to a Knowledge Economy." In *Controlling Immigration: A Global Perspective,* edited by Wayne A. Cornelius, Philip L. Martin, and James F. Hollifield, 91-133. 2nd ed. Stanford, CA: Stanford University Press.

Risman, Barbara. 2006. "Feminist Strategies for Public Sociology." In *Public Sociologies Reader,* edited by Judith Blau and Keri E. Iyall Smith, 281-92. Oxford: Rowman and Littlefield.

Ristock, Janet L., and Joan Pennell. 1996. *Community Research as Empowerment: Feminist Links, Postmodern Interruptions.* Don Mills, ON: Oxford University Press.

Rowlands, Jo. 1995. "Empowerment Examined." *Development in Practice* 5, 2: 101-7.
Santos, Ana C. 2012. "Disclosed and Willing: Towards a Queer Public Sociology." *Social Movement Studies* 11, 2: 241-54.
Sharma, Nandita. 2008. "On Being Not Canadian: The Social Organization of 'Migrant Workers' in Canada." *Canadian Review of Sociology* 38, 4: 415-39.
Smith, Dorothy E. 1987. *The Everyday World as Problematic: A Feminist Sociology.* Toronto: University of Toronto Press.
Smith, Linda Tuhiwai. 2006. *Decolonizing Methodologies: Research and Indigenous Peoples.* London/Otago: Zed Books/University of Otago Press.
Stasiulis, Daiva K., and Abigail B. Bakan. 2005. *Negotiating Citizenship: Migrant Women in Canada and the Global System.* Toronto: University of Toronto Press.
Taket, Ann, Beth R. Crisp, Annemarie Nevill, Greer Lamaro, Melissa Graham, and Sarah Barter-Godfrey. 2009. "Introducing Theories of Social Exclusion and Social Connectedness." In *Theorising Social Exclusion,* edited by Ann Taket, Beth R. Crisp, Annemarie Nevill, Greer Lamaro, Melissa Graham, and Sarah Barter-Godfrey, 1-34. London: Routledge.
Tittle, Charles R. 2004. "The Arrogance of Public Sociology." *Social Forces* 82, 4: 1639-43.
Van Liempt, Ilse, and Veronika Bilger, eds. 2009. *The Ethics of Migration Research Methodology: Dealing with Vulnerable Immigrants.* Brighton: Sussex Academic Press.
Vaughan, Diane. 2006. "NASA Revisited: Theory, Analogy, and Public Sociology." *American Journal of Sociology* 112, 2: 353-93.
Williams, Melissa S. 2000. *Voice, Trust, and Memory: Marginalized Groups and the Failings of Liberal Representation.* Princeton, NJ: Princeton University Press.

5

Reflections on the Theory and Practice of Teaching Public Sociology

SUSAN PRENTICE

Michael Burawoy (2005, 5) identified a special role for teaching when he challenged sociologists to "embark on a systematic back-translation, taking knowledge back to those from whom it came, making public issues out of private troubles." "Students," he wrote, are our "first and captive public" (7), and, as a result, "as teachers, we are all potentially public sociologists" (9). Yet surprisingly little has been written about *teaching* public sociology, despite the nominal centrality of teaching to the public sociology enterprise (Hattery and Smith 2006; Hays 2009; Persell 2009).

In 2010, I designed and taught a graduate course called Theory and Practice of Public Sociology.[1] To my knowledge, this was the first graduate or undergraduate Canadian public sociology course, if by *public sociology* we take the name and Burawoy's fourfold typology as determinant. Three months after the course ended, I moved to France for a year. Living in the Hexagon's second-largest city during Sarkozy's pension reforms gave me a new set of insights into North American sociology. My experience in France prompted deeper reflection on public sociology and my teaching.

Drawing on these insights, this chapter lays out a reflexive account of how my graduate course was structured and why it was organized as a space of critical sociological inquiry. As context, I first explore the public sociology teaching and learning field and the conflation of service learning with public sociology. Much of what makes public sociology seem so innovative – and contested – is specific to (North) American social relations, which my year abroad brought home to me quite forcefully. I assess how the political particularities of American sociology undergird many of the general theoretical claims about public sociology and suggest that this parochialism needs problematizing. I further draw on feminist insights to trouble the romanticization of civil society, which is the flip side of the dismissal of the state that characterizes much of the public sociology literature. In the end, I propose that, for theoretical as well as applied reasons, a public sociology classroom is best thought of as a critical space of "traditional" learning and teaching.

What Is a Public Sociology Course?

As I set out to design the course, I sought examples of public sociology syllabi as well as reflections on its teaching. In both searches, I came up largely empty-handed. I started with the Canadian Sociological Association (CSA) and the American Sociological Association (ASA). The CSA, much smaller than the ASA, is not organized by sections, and its website contains no links to curriculum resources such as syllabi. The ASA, by contrast, created a Task Force on Institutionalizing Public Sociologies in 2004: its sole recommendation related to teaching was to "Develop a workshop course, curriculum and/or manual on public sociology for the department" (ASA Task Force 2005). The teaching page of the Task Force website remained "under construction" for a long time, and, as of February 2012, still contained no teaching resources or links. A search of the ASA Teaching Resources and Innovations Library for Sociology (TRAILS), which was established in 2010, for the term *public sociology* generates eighty-nine syllabi, none of which use *public sociology* in their title (accessed 29 July 2011). None of TRAIL's seventeen categories or any of its eighty-one elaborations lists *public sociology.*

Thus, neither the Task Force nor the ASA provides much assistance in mapping out the contours of the teaching of public sociology. *Teaching Sociology,* the primary journal for scholarship on the sociology classroom (Howard 2010), contains very few articles on public sociology and even fewer on teaching public sociology (DeCesare 2009).[2] In the small literature that does exist, the general trend is of nontraditional learning. The most common approaches are combinations of experiential or action learning, service learning, or practicum/field courses. My scan of the scant literature leads me to conclude that where public sociology courses exist, they nearly all ask students to "do" public sociology rather than to study it. This observation is underscored by the new Sage Publications website on public sociology, for those "who are interested in public sociology movement in particular or service learning and civic engagement in general."[3]

In comparison with other disciplines, sociology is at the forefront of service learning (Marullo 1996). Service learning has been defined as educational experiences designed to link community service to the academic curriculum. Such courses may include internships, needs assessments, and participatory action research as well as other academic endeavours. In service learning, students typically participate in an activity designed to respond to community needs and then analyze and reflect on that service in a program of educational development. Like many other forms of experiential learning (Mooney and Edwards 2001), service learning usually places students largely or wholly outside the classroom. Sam Marullo (1996, 2) celebrates service learning as a pedagogy that bridges theory and practice, offering a crucible for learning that enables students to test theories with life experiences and forces upon them an evaluation of their knowledge and understanding grounded in their service experience.

Burawoy (2005, 26) proposes that service learning is the "prototype" of public sociology. Service learning has enthusiastic proponents beyond the former ASA president. Marullo (1996, 3) reports that such courses have "revolutionary potential" because "it is precisely these activities that will reveal the systemic, social nature of inequality, injustice, and oppression. It is also revolutionary to the extent that it creates a partnership for change among community and university actors." Service learning and similar teaching has been described as "transformative" and "cathartic" (Grauerholz and Copenhaver 1994; Myers-Lipton 1996).

There is no question that service learning courses can offer students a rich educational experience, taking learners out of their comfort zone to experience social realities with which they are unfamiliar or which enable them to see familiar settings through new eyes. For all its benefits, however, service learning can also be problematic. Such activities can raise ethical questions, even in their more modest forms; in more intense service learning courses, learning requirements can confront students with physical conditions that demand both courage and physical rigour, and may even be psychologically distressing (Edwards 2010; Grauerholz and Copenhaver 1994; Hattery and Smith 2006; Roberts, Mason, and Marler 1999). Experiential learning is a highly contested terrain, often motivated more by benevolence and philanthropy than organic relationships with mobilized publics.[4] Although I once designed and offered a practicum course (in women's studies), I never considered offering a graduate seminar on this model.

What Did I Teach and How Was It Taught?

I organized the Theory and Practice of Public Sociology as a conventional graduate seminar. The course was anchored by the debates sparked by Burawoy, his allies, and his critics. As the syllabus stated, the course objectives were to examine the theory and practice of public sociology through tackling questions about "the nature and purpose of sociological inquiry, probing the relationship between commitments to social justice and to modes of science, and considering how and why differing schools of sociological theorizing have responded to the call for more public sociology." The course began with epistemological and normative interrogations of a wide literature and then moved to four close readings of public sociology cases: environmental justice and questions of nature, bureaucracy, expert witness practice, and social movements and public policy interventions. The seminar was designed to explore the possibilities, potentials, contradictions, and challenges of public sociology in its many forms.

The one-semester (three credit hours) graduate seminar met once a week for twelve weeks in a three-hour session. It had no assigned book, but instead used twenty-nine articles or chapters, which averaged about forty-four pages of assigned reading per week. To encourage engaged reading and foster discussion, students were required to prepare comments and/or questions about each week's readings. Response papers were to be submitted by 9 a.m. the day before each class to give both me and that week's student seminar facilitator time to reflect on what students had identified as key ideas and issues in the readings. On the first day, I asked students to determine how many response papers should be required for the nine sets of readings; the eventual consensus was that it should be seven. Students earned 30 percent of their grade through response papers.

The seminar began with a full class dedicated to a close reading of Burawoy's 2004 ASA address. The second class then addressed a selection of articles that lay out key landmarks in the debate over public sociology. In the third session, students tackled readings that preceded Burawoy in a study of the historical roots of the public sociology debate (also see Hanemaayer, this volume). Students read Marx and Weber as well as Mills and Becker in order to appreciate that the questions posed anew by Burawoy have long characterized the lively disciplinary conversation about the meaning and practice of sociology.[5] From there, three seminars were devoted to debates for and against public sociology. Just after the halfway point, students presented their research proposals for peer and instructor feedback. Weeks eight through eleven concentrated on practice, as students engaged with readings on nature and the environment, bureaucracy, legal and expert witness, and social movements and public policy. During the seminar on social movements, I assigned one of my own articles, in which I reflect on the contemporary childcare movement and its strategic uses of the "business case" (Prentice 2009). Since I am a participant in, as well as an observer of, childcare advocacy, I wanted to offer up my own practice and assessments for student engagement and critique. On the final day, students presented their research papers.

Beginning with the second class, students led the seminar discussions, and the task of facilitating was formally assigned (students volunteered for their preferred date). Each seminar facilitator was asked to distribute written questions and comments to the class to structure the discussion. The day before each class, I forwarded a copy of student responses to that week's readings to the scheduled facilitator(s). This allowed them time to review responses and anticipate or develop areas for seminar discussion and exploration. Additionally, I asked seminar facilitators first to summarize the key points in the materials, and then pose questions or reflections emerging from the readings. Seminar facilitation comprised 15 percent of the course grade.

Ten MA and PhD students enrolled in the course, eight from Sociology and two from other schools or faculties. The assessment scheme was designed to allow students to demonstrate their grasp of key theoretical debates as well their familiarity with a specific arena of public sociology, as demonstrated through a research paper.

In a handout detailing the research essay process, I explained that students were "free to take any stance in relation to public sociology – from endorsement to rejection or other assessment. What research papers must do, however, is demonstrate an in-depth familiarity with the debates within and over public sociology and an ability to integrate, synthesize, and apply insights from this debate." Eligible topics included, among others: conceptual or theoretical explorations of public sociology; a particular social issue or problem approached or assessed from the perspective of public sociology; a consideration of the discipline and practice of sociological training through the lens of public sociology (drawing on adherents, sympathizers, or critics); and a consideration of how a public sociology approach might shape a research project, to either productive or nonproductive ends. The research essay project had three parts. Students first presented a short proposal of their intended project at the midpoint of the term (5 percent of total grade) and then presented their paper at the last class (10 percent). The essay itself was worth 25 percent of the course total.

Fifteen percent of the course grade came from student participation. The syllabus made an explicit request for "sustained participation throughout the term to demonstrate preparation, careful reading, and active classroom citizenship." It also asked students to provide peer feedback: students exchanged comments on their peers' early essay proposal and then provided written feedback to each other on the final presentation. I distributed a presentation-grading rubric that permitted the evaluation of content as well as "professional skills." On content, students were asked to evaluate theoretical, empirical, and methodological criteria, including integration of course readings. On professional skills, they were to assess coherence, quality/usefulness of the handout, use of time, and delivery and presentation effectiveness. Both the content and professional skills used a scale of one to ten for a total of eleven indicators. In open-ended feedback, students were asked to provide one positive comment and one "area for improvement." For each of the ten students, therefore, there were nine peer evaluations, in addition to my commentary as instructor. I calculated average grades for the peer feedback indicators and assembled the qualitative narrative comments – giving each student the feedback provided by her peers.

Overall, the ten students seemed to appreciate the course and were satisfied with how it was structured, as measured by Standardized Student Evaluation of Educational Quality (SEEQ) scores collected by the department. Students saw the course as having an average (40 percent) to demanding (60 percent) difficulty level. While 50 percent strongly agreed that the assigned readings were valuable, the remaining were neutral or agreed. No negative results were given for grading or assessment measures, which were all neutral to positive. On their participation, students were exceptionally content. On the four SEEQ group interaction measures, 90 percent "strongly agreed" that they were encouraged to participate, invited to share their ideas, encouraged to ask questions, and encouraged to express their own ideas.

Over the term, I organized two activities that complemented the course. First, I arranged a faculty panel titled "Practicing Public Sociology?" and invited students in the seminar to attend. To set up the forum, I circulated a call to departmental colleagues, inviting any proposal that engaged in some way with public sociology, including presentations that disputed the approach (hence the interrogation mark in the panel's title). Three colleagues accepted the offer, notwithstanding the poor timing of organizing a colloquium during the busy beginning of term. Each faculty member engaged with the theory and practice of public sociology in a panel whose audience overflowed the room. For the first time, we digitally video recorded a colloquium presentation for posting to the department's website. In so doing, we created a space on par with what Christopher Schneider calls e-public sociology (this volume), potentially allowing an even wider audience to watch the presentations.[6] The public sociology colloquium conversation, which first existed in real time, now also exists in virtual time, both within and beyond the academy.

The second activity to complement the graduate seminar was a workshop. Over the 2009-10 academic year, I was graduate chair. In that capacity, I organized a series of workshops for graduate students and also sought opportunities for more exchanges between graduate students and faculty. In March 2010, the Sociology Department in collaboration with the Manitoba Research Data Centre (one of the more than two dozen Statistics Canada "data liberation" sites), mounted a two-day research development workshop for graduate students. We brought a facilitator to Winnipeg for an intensive workshop expressly designed for graduate students. At the Research Data Centre (RDC) in Ottawa, Dr. Heather Juby (knowledge transfer [KT] coordinator) was prepared to tailor KT sessions for different audiences. We asked Juby to offer a two-day "Communicating Social Science Research" workshop, open to all graduate students in sociology, economics, psychology, health, or any social science discipline. Fifteen graduate students participated in the free workshop, which was the first time the RDC knowledge transfer coordinator had led a session primarily oriented to qualitative and social science researchers. Participants learned about, and had hands-on practice in, communication of their research. The graduate seminar was scheduled to meet during the event, and so class was cancelled and the course extended by a week so all students could participate.

Thus, inside the classroom during the seminar as well as in the department colloquium and RDC workshop, students were exposed to the theory and practice of public sociology with a strong focus on communication. The course and the cognate learning opportunities structured around it were designed to introduce students to the substantive debates (re)raised by Burawoy, and then to figure out their own stance in relation to public sociology. Students were explicitly told that in their learning activities they were free to adopt their own perspective – from endorsement, through

FIGURE 5.1 This image appeared on a poster advertising the March 2010 Research Development Workshop, "Communicating Social Science," co-organized by the Department of Sociology and the Manitoba RDC.

modification, to rejection of public sociology. I was particularly happy to have found a visual image that captured this nonsectarian approach (see Figure 5.1).

As this detailed description makes clear, I opted to introduce graduate students to public sociology through a *critical* sociology – one that challenged students to ask probing questions about values, methods, epistemologies, and foundational principles of sociology as an intellectual practice. Thus, as I approached the theory and practice of teaching public sociology, the classroom looked remarkably ordinary: not a site of service learning or extramural activism. The graduate seminar was a place of scholarly teaching and learning.

Reflections from France: A Feminist Abroad

Burawoy's gauntlet is particularly challenging to Americans, I would argue, where its ideas are "largely absent from the country's political thinking" (Gans 1989, 1). Like others, I agree that many of Burawoy's recommendations for more public sociology are uncontroversial and already widely practised in Canada, including by many feminist sociologists (Creese, McLaren, and Pulkingham 2009; Goldberg and van den Berg 2009). Canadian sociologists have a long tradition of the kind of engaged work recommended by Burawoy (Helmes-Hayes and McLaughlin 2009).

And yet the "national culture" (Wallerstein 2007) of Burawoy's recommendations only really struck me after I taught the course and began my year-long sabbatical in France. In the first weeks of settling in with my family, we went to a cinema to see the just-released Angelina Jolie film, *Salt.* While standing in line for the *version originale sous-titrée* screening, we began chatting with others in the queue. When, in my halting French, I explained who I was and why I was spending the year in France, one man exclaimed warmly, "Ahhh, I love sociology and how it sees the world. I especially love Pierre Bourdieu. We all do," he finished, grinning broadly. I was *bouche bée* (literally, "open-mouthed"; figuratively, "stunned"). While a sample of one is never representative, I am equally sure that the odds of standing in a Canadian film lineup and discovering someone who had read Bourdieu are virtually nil. The point is that the public profile of sociologists and sociology is nation-specific. Burawoy can deplore the absence of social science public intellectuals in the United States, but the situation is very different in France.

The value of cross-national reflexivity was brought home by other experiences. I was in France during the particularly tumultuous months of September to November 2010, when the country experienced fierce clashes over competing visions of pension "reform." The public face of the debate turned on the question of increasing the minimum age of retirement, and the main objective of Sarkozy's government was to lengthen the contribution period. The labour movement led the campaign against pension reforms, with strong support from civil-society actors.

The key issue for the labour movement and community associations was the pushing back of the retirement age by two years – to sixty-two (for early pensions, up from age sixty) or to sixty-seven for full pension (an increase from age sixty-five). Public reaction was intense: at least fourteen national days of protest between 23 March and 23 November 2010, half of which involved more than two million people (according to syndicalist accounts). Protests produced severe disruptions, from gas shortages to transportation delays – including cancelled trains and truckers' Opération escargot on the autoroutes. Nevertheless, polls reported 71 percent of the population approved the protests, with public opinion solidly against the government (BBC 2010; Irish 2010). Postsecondary as well as high school students came out in large numbers to support the public demonstrations. Protesters directly targeted the state as they sought to prevent the rollback of pension entitlements, which were regularly framed as a social movement victory to be protected.[7]

It is one thing to know about European social movement activity theoretically, and it is quite another to watch the riot lines of police outside one's apartment window. There are, I learned, direct links between the national specificity of sociology as a public practice and the teaching of sociology. Where students see sociologists as socially engaged participants in public and political discourse, they scarcely need to be persuaded of the discipline's relevance. Thus, France is unlike the United States, or even Canada.

As many observers have noted, academics have an active role in political discourse and public life in France (Bowen 2007). Public intellectuals – conservative and progressive – play a significant role in French society (Christofferson 2004; Drake 2005). Alain Touraine (2007) uses his vantage point as an "outsider" to observe that sociology, as a professional field of teaching and research, was particularly important in Europe after the First World War. Touraine (2007, 73) argues that the relative importance of Burawoy's four orientations depends, to a large extent, on the organization of social actors and power structures. Touraine recommends more comparative sociology, including more cross-national and cross-context fieldwork.

Burawoy's (2005, 20) model fails to recognize its Americanism, even as he calls for a "21st century public sociology of global dimensions" and encourages the decentring of America. While acknowledging that the very term "public sociology" is an American invention, Burawoy misrecognizes the scope of the phenomenon. He is clear-eyed enough to identify that American sociologists have a "special responsibility to provincialize our own sociology, to bring it down from the pedestal of universality and recognize its distinctive character and national power" (Burawoy 2005, 22), but he takes his own national context for granted. Social structure shapes the foundations of sociology, and this means our discipline is historically and politically contingent, something that is easily lost in the sweep of claims that presume the specificities of American realities are universal.

A critical awareness of the parochialism of North American sociology – even in its public form – demands some practical responses from teachers (Quah 2005). Aside from the ambitious suggestions of Judith Stacey (2007), I've not yet found any other programs practically aimed at internationalizing learning and teaching public sociology. Like Stacey, I endorse the value of international exchanges and recognize the importance of the language training that is required for effective collaborations. I look back with considerable regret at my own department's decision to drop a second language requirement for doctoral students. In French and other European universities, thanks to mobility policies, the student body is international and cosmopolitan. I spent a year at the École Normale Supérieure in Lyon. As one of the best-known *grandes écoles*, it is unusually elite, but its students were more diverse than those in my Canadian classrooms. As I participated in four *français langue étrangère* classes, the rich communication resources of the students impressed me; for most, French was a third or fourth language. I was struck by the linguistic chauvinism of North Americans and grew embarrassed to have to frequently explain that while, yes, Canada is part of the Francophonie, outside Quebec and regional francophone pockets, a very large majority of Canadians are monolingual English speakers.

As graduate chair, I stress the importance of language training and do my best to make sure students have better access to language course opportunities and international exchanges. This activity blends into the "service" component of faculty activity. For example, almost a dozen Canadian universities have signed *cotutelle* agreements with France to permit doctoral students to undertake coursework concurrently at a Canadian and French university, to complete a dual degree.[8] At my home university, I have participated in meetings with the French scientific and cultural attachés and have urged my university to enter into an agreement so our graduate students can also participate in such exchanges. My work as a teacher will be facilitated if such agreements are in place.

Burawoy's parochialism has further implications for his conception of public sociology, with further consequences for teaching. The fourfold division of sociology makes sense in only some settings, and is far from a transnational reality, an assumption relied upon by Burawoy and many of his adherents. For my purpose, I am most concerned about what this means for his understanding of policy sociology. Burawoy's rejection of the state, and hence of policy sociology that he sees as its servant, makes some sense in the context of a liberal welfare regime. It is, however, surprisingly unhelpful where nation-states act differently and so – as both cause and consequence – publics engage differently with the state. Although many social movement actors see the state as a site of remedy for social problems, Burawoy reproduces the neoliberal conviction that the state is always and only beleaguering, coercive, and despotic.

Burawoy is "thoroughly hostile" to the state (Brady 2004). He demonizes the state largely as a counterpoint to his celebration of civil society. I dispute the dismissal of the state, the archetype and most public of publics. Even as his presidential address lauded the collaboration of sociology, civil society, social movements, and governance in South Africa, Scandinavia, and the former Soviet Union, Burawoy remained convinced that the "best possible terrain for the defense of humanity" (2005, 25) is civil society. In making this claim, he fails to recognize the many social movements that make the state the object of their struggle and the policy sociology that collaborates in these campaigns. It is, at the least, incoherent for Burawoy to dismiss the public movements he sets out to defend, but this is what happens when he valorizes civil society through a rhetorical and conceptual opposition to state-focused activism and thus dismisses sociology that engages critically with public policy.

European social scientists have developed strong relationships with public policy and the many movements that target the state. In "conservative" France, with its wealth of family-friendly policies, policy and public sociology are far more alike than distinct. Ariane Hanemaayer (this volume) argues that it is the distinction between policy and public sociology that allows Burawoy to clearly state the programmatic mandate of public sociology. Even setting aside the metatheoretic commitments entailed by this move, I dispute the separation of policy and public sociology (see also Mesny, this volume).

Reflecting on policy and public sociology as a feminist abroad intensified another of my concerns about the theory and practice of public sociology. Beyond demonizing the state, Burawoy also romanticizes civil society. His two-by-two grid (of audiences and types of knowledge) both draws upon and reinforces the public/private dichotomy so prevalent in male-stream political economy and Western societies. In this, and other aspects, public sociology fails to seriously engage with feminist scholarship.[9] As Myrna Marx Ferree, Shamus Rhaman Khan, and Shauna Morimoto (2007) bluntly signal, a significant gender polarization still characterizes sociology as a discipline. As a result, they point out, it is not surprising that men can still publish work that recapitulates or draws invisibly on earlier feminist work in the field and by doing so convert a "women's" issue into one that is now "general." Thus, for example, decades of feminist research on women's community organizations and activism are now seen as merely precursors to the real (men's) discovery of civil society (Ferree, Rhaman Khan, and Morimoto 2007, 478).

Feminists have critiqued the inattention to feminist sociology in public sociology scholarship, despite their generally welcoming response to the call (Acker 2005; Creese, McLaren, and Pulkingham 2009; Stacey 2007). Patricia Hill Collins (2007, 102-3) captures the sentiment in her wry observation: "I should be happy that the type of sociological practice that has so long preoccupied me is now gaining recognition," she writes: "What has long been 'out' now has a rare invitation to attend the party within American sociology, which has not been particularly inclined to changing its ways" (103). It is likely the Matilda effect. As Ferree and colleagues (Ferree, Rahman Khan, and Morimoto 2007) explain,

> The cascading consequences for women's status that derives from men's failure to acknowledge women's contributions has been dubbed the "Matilda effect" in honor of suffragist author Matilda Joslyn Gage, who both described and endured this denial of credit. The Matilda effect is a counterpoint to the Matthew effect, which was ascribed to Robert Merton but (as he himself later acknowledged) actually was described by Harriet Zuckerman and him together. (454)

It takes a great deal of intellectual graciousness for a community of feminist scholars to celebrate a disciplinary debate about public sociology that largely disregards its extensive contributions. (For a Canadian overview, see Robbins, Eichler, and Descarries 2008.) Many feminist sociologists have been theorizing and practising – and teaching – a form of public sociology for years, yet their contributions are virtually invisible in the debates that assume the enterprise was launched by Michael Burawoy.

As I taught the graduate seminar Theory and Practice of Public Sociology, I partially resisted the male-streaming of public sociology. Yet, retrospectively, I regret that I introduced feminist critics late in the theory section of the course. Sharon Hays (2009), Joan Acker (2005), and Pat O'Connor (2006) appeared on the syllabus only in week seven (with Dorothy Smith as a recommended but not required reading). The second part fared better, with two of the four weeks on the practice of public sociology, including feminist content. The session about expert witness began with Judith Stacey's (2004) remarkable account of testifying for same-sex marriage. It also included readings about the Sears case, which predated Burawoy's 2004 address and introduced arguments long-debated by feminist scholars and activists.[10] The week on public policy and social movements examined childcare advocacy through the lens of gender justice. However, when I teach the course again, I will aim to integrate more feminist content up front, as well as more material from writers in the Global South.

Final Reflections: Ethics and the Teaching of Public Sociology

Public sociology courses, conceived of as experiential or service learning, can be considered to belong to the scholarship of application in the Carnegie Foundation typology (Boyer 1990, 21). In her 2007 Hans O. Mauksch award speech, Bernice Pescolido (2008) also noted the "remarkable consistency" and convergence of Burawoy's model with the typology identified by the foundation's former president. It was Ernest Boyer who famously identified four different professorial foci, which he named the scholarship of discovery, integration, application, and teaching. It is in practising a scholarship of application that the scholar asks, "How can knowledge be responsibly applied to consequential problems? How can it be helpful to individuals as well as institutions?" And further, "Can social problems themselves define an agenda for scholarly investigation?" (Boyer 1990, 21). From a perspective that sees the convergence between Boyer and Burawoy, we should expect to see a very high priority placed on teaching. The reality of an underdeveloped state of scholarship on "the promise and challenge" of public sociology signifies, among other troubles, an unreflexive national perspective and gender-blindness.

I take as axiomatic that sociologists write about what matters to them. As Caroline Persell (2009, 213) notes, taking the scholarship of teaching and learning seriously requires a focus on making teaching public, "so that it can be critiqued, improved and ultimately validated by peer review." It requires activities such as publishing and what she calls "thoughtful" annotated course syllabi to explicate the rationale for organizing and constructing a course in a particular way. Virtually nothing of this kind exists for the teaching of public sociology (distinct from service learning and experiential courses). It is thus hard to seriously claim that teaching public sociology is a disciplinary priority. The paucity of scholarship on teaching/learning sociology must stand as a rebuke to the idea that public sociology has a special relationship to our "first and captive" public.

Despite encouraging service learning as the prototypical form of public sociology teaching, Burawoy is not responsible for the discipline's curricular trajectory. As a teacher of graduate courses, however, I take sociological cautions about how we teach quite seriously. I am fully sympathetic to engaged and activist scholarship. As a researcher who both participates in and writes about social movements, my own career has been inextricably defined by my commitment to engaged application. Many feminists, both inside and outside sociology, share this commitment to a scholarship of relevance. Participatory, action-oriented, and community-based engagements define the academic careers of many colleagues, who agree – in different ways – with the sentiment expressed in Marx's famous observation, "the philosophers have only interpreted the world, in various ways; the point is to change it." Certainly, the careers of colleagues in programs and departments such as women's and gender studies, sexuality studies, Native studies, labour studies, political economy, development studies, dis/ability studies, and other fields with a social justice orientation amply demonstrate the phenomenon.

But commitments on the part of the scholar as researcher must be carefully considered in relation to the scholar as teacher. Max Weber provided a still-apt caution when he warned that demagogues and prophets do not belong in the classroom (Weber 1991). My own theoretical commitments are scarcely Weberian, but I fully agree with him about the obligations of teachers not to indoctrinate students. To be sure, as Weber clarified, in democratic settings of political contest, one ought not to hide one's personal standpoint; "indeed, to come out clearly and take a stand is one's damned duty" (1991, 149). But equally, teachers have ethical obligations, and one of them is not to "imprint" their personal political views because such moves are irresponsible, coercive, and undemocratic in the context of a classroom where a teacher's power cannot effectively be opposed. (Also see van den Berg, this volume.) Like Weber (1991, 147), I believe my task is to teach students to "recognize inconvenient facts ... [and] there are facts that are extremely inconvenient for my own opinion, no less than for others."

I see teaching a graduate course in public sociology as belonging to the scholarship of discovery and integration. If we take the characterization of critical sociology as the practice of examining the foundations – explicit and implicit, normative and descriptive – of our discipline, then as a practising public sociologist, I teach as a critical sociologist. Burawoy clarifies that it is critical sociology that gives us "the two questions that place the four sociologies in relation to each other" (Burawoy 2005, 268). My answer to the question "knowledge for whom?" is clear. We teach for our students, who need to begin with foundational knowledge explored through open debate. From there, as teachers, we respect our students' answers to the question "knowledge for what?" In a public sociology classroom, we do our best sociology when we teach our students to interrogate the foundations of social science inquiry, including those of public sociology itself.

Acknowledgments

I gratefully acknowledge the generous support of the Collegium of Lyon, IEA, housed at the École Normale Supérieure, which supported me during the first drafting of this chapter. The Collegium of Lyon's supportive environment was so exceptional, in fact, that I stayed there over March 2011 instead of attending the exciting UBC workshop on which this anthology is based. I am grateful to editors Ariane Hanemaayer and Christopher Schneider for making space for me despite my absence and for their thoughtful comments on earlier versions of this chapter. I also extend my warmest thanks to Elizabeth Comack, specifically, for talking this chapter through with me, but even more importantly for many years of fine discussions about the complex relationships between teaching, research, and activism.

Notes

1 Despite its name, the course was numbered SOC 7160, my department's generic selected topics "holding" number; thus it remains for another public sociology course to be permanently offered under it own stable course entry. To see the course syllabus, see Appendix 1.

2 A search of *Teaching Sociology* for *public sociology* from 2004 to 2011 generates twenty-two hits, including fifteen articles and seven book reviews (28 July 2011).

3 See the Sage Pine Forge Public Sociology Community site, http://www.sagepub.com/publicsociology/.

4 It is beyond the scope of this chapter to interrogate the relationship of service learning and public sociology. For a blistering critique of service learning as providing "political cover for neoliberal state retrenchment," see Arena (2010, 121).

5 And a good thing too. Few of the graduate students recognized that Burawoy modeled his address on Marx's *Theses on Feuerbach*. Nor did they realize the importance of Number XI, sociologist as partisan.

6 The talks by Christopher Powell ("How Can I Change the World with My Mind: Dilemmas of a Materialist"), Mark Hudson ("Public Sociology and the 'Ruthless Criticism of All That Exists'"), and Lance Roberts ("A Sociologist Confronts the Engineers: How to Renew the Public School Facilities") can be viewed at http://umanitoba.ca/faculties/arts/departments/sociology/links.html.

7 In 1983, Socialist President François Mitterrand reduced the pension age to sixty, down from sixty-five.

8 Details of the *cotutelle* program can be found at http://www.canada.campusfrance.org/.

9 Am I the only person to notice that in Vincent Jeffries's (2009) 473-page *Handbook of Public Sociology*, the words "feminist," "gender," and "women" appear in none of the twenty-five chapter titles, nor in the index? Where the fault belongs is hard to know, but at least one article (Elizabeth Leonard's "From Data to Drama: Returning Research to Convicted Survivors") ought to have been listed under these terms, since the chapter tackles Leonard's career studying women convicted of the deaths of their abusers.

10 The Sears case is considered an important moment in feminist and public history, which raises the important question about public sociology's relationship to inter- and transdisciplinarity – another rich avenue I set aside in this chapter.

References

Acker, Joan. 2005. "Comments on Burawoy on Public Sociology." *Critical Sociology* 31, 3: 327-31.

Arena, John. 2010. "The Contested Terrains of Public Sociology: Theoretical and Practical Lessons from the Movement to Defend Public Housing in Pre- and Post-Katrina New Orleans." *Societies without Borders* 5, 2: 103-24.

ASA Task Force on Institutionalizing Public Sociologies. 2005. Public Sociology and the Roots of American Sociology: Re-establishing Our Connections to the Public – Interim Report and Recommendations. American Sociological Association. http://www.asanet.org/.

BBC. 2010. "Q & A: French Strikes over Pension Reform." *BBC*. 10 November. http://www.bbc.co.uk/.

Bowen, John R. 2007. *Why the French Don't Like Headscarves: Islam, the State and Public Space*. Princeton, NJ: Princeton University Press.

Boyer, Ernest. 1990. *Scholarship Reconsidered: Priorities of the Professoriate*. Stanford, CA: Carnegie Foundation for the Advancement of Teaching.

Brady, David. 2004. "Why Public Sociology May Fail." *Social Forces* 82, 4: 1629-38.

Burawoy, Michael. 2005. "2004 Presidential Address: For Public Sociology." *American Sociological Review* 70, 1: 4-28.

Christofferson, Michael. 2004. *French Intellectuals against the Left: The Anti-totalitarian Movement of the 1970s*. New York and Oxford: Berghahn Books.

Collins, Patricia Hill. 2007. "Going Public: Doing the Sociology That Had No Name." In *Public Sociology: Fifteen Eminent Sociologists Debate Politics and the Profession in the Twenty-First Century*, edited by Dan Clawson, Robert Zussman, Joya Misra, Naomi Gerstel, Randall Stokes, Douglas L. Anderton, and Michael Burawoy, 101-13. Berkeley: University of California Press.

Creese, Gillian, Arlene Tigar McLaren, and Jane Pulkingham. 2009. "Rethinking Burawoy: Reflections from Canadian Feminist Sociology." *Canadian Journal of Sociology* 34, 3: 601-22.

DeCesare, Michael. 2009. "Presenting Sociology's Four 'Faces': Problems and Prospects for the High School Course." In *Handbook of Public Sociology*, edited by Vincent Jeffries, 187-204. Lanham, MD: Rowman and Littlefield.

Drake, David. 2005. *French Intellectuals and Politics from the Dreyfus Affair to the Occupation*. New York: Palgrave MacMillan.

Edwards, Nelta M. 2010. "Using Nail Polish to Teach about Gender and Homophobia." *Teaching Sociology* 38, 4: 362-72.

Ferree, Myrna Marx, Shamus Rhaman Khan, and Shauna Morimoto. 2007. "Assessing the Feminist Revolution: The Presence and Absence of Gender in Theory and Practice." In *Sociology in America: A History,* edited by Craig Calhoun, 438-79. Chicago: University of Chicago Press.

Gans, Herbert. 1989. "1988 Presidential Address: Sociology in America: The Discipline and the Public American Sociological Association." *American Journal of Sociology* 54, 1: 1-16.

Goldberg, Avi, and Axel van den Berg. 2009. "What Do Public Sociologists Do? A Critique of Burawoy." *Canadian Journal of Sociology* 34, 3: 765-802.

Grauerholz, Elizabeth, and Stacey Copenhaver. 1994. "When the Personal Becomes Problematic: The Ethics of Using Experiential Teaching Methods." *Teaching Sociology* 22, 4: 319-27.

Hattery, Angela, and Earl Smith. 2006. "Teaching Public Sociologies." In *Public Sociologies Reader,* edited by Judith Blau and Keri E. Iyall Smith, 265-80. New York: Rowman and Littlefield.

Hays, Sharon. 2009. "Stalled at the Altar? Conflict, Hierarchy, and Compartmentalization in Burawoy's Public Sociology." In *Public Sociology: Fifteen Eminent Sociologists Debate Politics and the Profession in the Twenty-First Century,* edited by Dan Clawson, Robert Zussman, Joya Misra, Naomi Gerstel, Randall Stokes, Douglas L. Anderton, and Michael Burawoy, 79-90. Berkeley: University of California Press.

Helmes-Hayes, Rick, and Neil McLaughlin. 2009. "Public Sociology in Canada: Debates, Research, and Historical Context." *Canadian Journal of Sociology* 34, 3: 573-600.

Howard, Jay R. 2010. "2009 Hans O. Mauksch Address: Where Are We and How Did We Get Here? A Brief Examination of the Past, Present, and Future of the Teaching and Learning Movement in Sociology." *Teaching Sociology* 38, 2: 81-92.

Irish, John. 2010. "Students and Families Join French Pension Protests." *Reuters,* 2 October. http://uk.reuters.com/.

Jeffries, Vincent, ed. 2009. *Handbook of Public Sociology*. Lanham, MD: Rowman and Littlefield.

Marullo, S. 1996. "Sociology's Contribution to the Service Learning Movement." In *Service-Learning and Undergraduate Sociology: Syllabi and Instructional Materials,* edited by Morten Ender, Brenda Marsteller Kowalewski, David A. Cotter, Lee Martin, and JoAnne DeFiore, 1-13. Washington, DC: American Sociological Association.

Mooney, L., and B. Edwards. 2001. "Experiential Learning in Sociology: Service Learning and Other Community-Based Learning Initiatives." *Teaching Sociology* 29, 2: 181-94.

Myers-Lipton, Scott. 1996. "Service-Learning: Theory, Student Development, and Strategy." In *Service-Learning and Undergraduate Sociology: Syllabi and*

Instructional Materials, edited by Morten Ender, Brenda Marsteller Kowalewski, David A. Cotter, Lee Martin, and JoAnne DeFiore, 21-31. Washington, DC: American Sociological Association.

O'Connor, Pat. 2006. "Private Troubles, Public Issues: The Irish Sociological Imagination." *Irish Journal of Sociology* 15, 2: 5-22.

Persell, Caroline Hodges. 2009. "Teaching and Public Sociology." In *Handbook of Public Sociology,* edited by Vincent Jeffries, 205-21. Lanham, MD: Rowman and Littlefield.

Pescolido, Bernice. 2008. "The Converging Landscape of Higher Education: Perspectives, Challenges, and a Call to the Discipline of Sociology." *Teaching Sociology* 36, 2: 95-107.

Prentice, Susan. 2009. "High Stakes: The 'Investable' Child and the Economic Reframing of Childcare." *Signs: Journal of Women in Culture and Society* 34, 3: 687-710.

Quah, Stella R. 2005. "Four Sociologies, Multiple Roles." *British Journal of Sociology* 56, 3: 395-400.

Robbins, Wendy, Margrit Eichler, and Francine Descarries, eds. 2008. *Minds of Our Own: Inventing Feminist Scholarship and Women's Studies in Canada and Quebec, 1966-1976*. Waterloo, ON: Wilfrid Laurier University Press.

Roberts, Robin W. J. Walter Mason, and Penny L. Marler. 1999. "A True Specialist: Teaching Sociology through a Service-Learning Project Involving the Construction of a Pit Latrine." *Teaching Sociology* 27, 4: 407-16.

Stacey, Judith. 2004. "Marital Suitors Court Social Science Spinsters: The Unwittingly Conservative Effects of Public Sociology." *Social Problems* 51, 1: 131-45.

–. 2007. "If I Were the Goddess of Sociological Things." In *Public Sociology: Fifteen Eminent Sociologists Debate Politics and the Profession in the Twenty-First Century,* edited by Dan Clawson, Robert Zussman, Joya Misra, Naomi Gerstel, Randall Stokes, Douglas L. Anderton, and Michael Burawoy, 91-100. Berkeley: University of California Press.

Touraine, Alain. 2007. "Public Sociology and the End of Society." In *Public Sociology: Fifteen Eminent Sociologists Debate Politics and the Profession in the Twenty-First Century,* edited by Dan Clawson, Robert Zussman, Joya Misra, Naomi Gerstel, Randall Stokes, Douglas L. Anderton, and Michael Burawoy, 65-78. Berkeley: University of California Press.

Wallerstein, Immanuel. 2007. "The Culture of Sociology in Disarray: The Impact of 1968 on U.S. Sociologists." In *Sociology in America: A History,* edited by Craig Calhoun, 427-37. Chicago: University of Chicago Press.

Weber, Max. 1991 [1918]. "Science as a Vocation." In *From Max Weber: Essays in Sociology,* edited by H.H. Gerth and C. Wright Mills, 129-58. London: Routledge.

PART 3

BLURRING THE LINE BETWEEN POLICY AND PUBLIC SOCIOLOGY

6

Public Sociology and Research Ethics

ANNE MESNY

The recent debate about public sociology has stimulated a renewed reflection about social scientists' roles and duties and, more specifically, about the opportunity to combine scholarship with public commitment and political advocacy. Public sociology means both that sociological knowledge should reach the general public and that it should serve to improve society and the well-being of its members (Brady 2004, 1630). Both aims imply that sociologists develop close connections with the people who are simultaneously the "subjects" of sociological research and also its targeted "public," in the sense that research is supposed to benefit them and be useful to them. This is especially the case in organic public sociology (Burawoy 2005, 7-8), which refers to various forms of collaborative research between the researchers and particular groups or "counterpublics" in society. The practice of public sociology, especially its organic type, raises a number of complex ethical issues about the relationship between sociologists and their subjects, and between sociological knowledge and its publics.

A logical starting point for exploring these ethical issues is the policy about ethical conduct for research involving humans. As scientists whose subjects are human beings, sociologists share with many other researchers in other fields, including of course biomedical research, the duty to treat these research subjects in an ethical way. In Canada, the Tri-Council Policy Statement (TCPS) establishes the principles and regulations that scientists should follow in their relationship to the people they research. The key concern is the protection of research participants, and the core principles are respect for persons and concern for welfare and justice. Application of these principles aims at maintaining the participants' free and informed consent and ensuring the adequate sharing of the benefits of research.

Scientific research often implies risks for research participants; a balance has to be found between protecting participants and promoting research. Although risks for participants may vary from one scientific field to the other, another important assumption of the TCPS is that it is both possible and desirable to define principles and regulations that can apply to all types of research. In social science, it is acknowledged that the risks are generally less severe than in biomedical research. The risks in social science concern "the invasion of privacy, loss of confidentiality, psychological trauma, indirect physical harm, embarrassment, stigma and group stereotyping" (Oakes 2002, 449). Another important assumption embedded in the TCPS is that the researchers themselves, well-meaning as they are or should be, are not the best persons to correctly assess the risks posed by their own research projects and to find the proper balance between protecting participants and carrying on their research. For that reason, the mandatory review of research projects by REBs (research ethics boards) was introduced in the TCPS1 in 1998. Twelve years later, after a two-year process involving a vast amount of public consultation, a revised and updated version of the policy (TCPS2) was issued and adopted.

A number of scholars, especially among social scientists, have stressed the discrepancy between the ethical issues that are acknowledged and discussed in the TCPS and the ethical issues that they actually encounter. The argument in this chapter, however, differs from the already numerous complaints about the TCPS. Researchers of all types have been complaining about the policy itself, about REBs' roles and practices (Gunsalus et al. 2007), and about the fact that REBs' real concern seems to be to protect universities from being sued rather than to protect research subjects (Bonacich 2007, 88). Social scientists have been especially prompt to argue that this policy has been written for and by biomedical researchers who are trying to protect subjects from the physical risks of surgical and pharmacological experiments (Bosk and De Vries 2004; Connolly and Reid 2007; De Vries, DeBruin, and Goodgame 2004; Oakes 2002) and to stress issues regarding written consent, the lack of social science expertise of REB members, or the lack of fit between the policy and certain social science methods (De Vries, DeBruin, and Goodgame 2004, 353; Owen 2002).

Beyond these legitimate complaints, the aim of this chapter is to expose major points of friction between two fundamentally different ways of conceiving the relationship between researchers and their human subjects. On one side, the policy about ethical research with humans is based on a conception of the research subject as a vulnerable individual who needs to be protected from the risks carried by the research process itself, exemplified by experimentation in clinical biomedical research and standard clinical trial (Bosk and De Vries 2004, 252). Here, research participants refer to the people who are directly involved in the research process as experimental subjects. On the other side, social scientists, and organic public sociologists in particular, deal with not-so-powerless participants who are targeted as representatives or members of organizations, groups, associations, or particular publics. The risks entailed by social research occasionally concerns the research *process* itself but, more often, they rather concern the diffusion of the research *results* and the impacts of these results on direct *and* indirect participants.

Several implications will follow from this systematic comparison between the traditional, mainstream conception of research participants and research ethics as it appears in the TCPS, and the particular ethical conundrums faced by organic public scientists. First, the current policy about research ethics, by being based upon such a narrow conception of research participants, jeopardizes the very possibility for social scientists to address ethical issues in any sound and appropriate way. Second, the idea of public sociology, as it has been defined and discussed in recent years following Michael Burawoy's presidential address in 2004, will also come under scrutiny. The distinctions between public sociology and policy sociology, as well as the locus of critical inquiry, will be reexamined. Finally, the project of public sociology will be examined in light of the current context that urges scholarly research to be more "relevant."

Organic Public Sociology

The notion of public sociology was popularized by Herbert Gans (1989) as a call to improve sociologists' relations with the lay public. With Burawoy (2004, 2005), public sociology has come to encompass many things, from writing in the opinion pages of national newspapers to engagement in political activities and collaborative research with various publics or counterpublics (Clawson et al. 2007; Goldberg and van den Berg 2009; Nichols 2007; Tittle 2004). These various practices all refer to ways sociological knowledge can reach people, and be useful to them, outside professional and academic circles. Public sociology strives to "engage multiple publics in multiple ways" (Burawoy 2005, 4). In times of pressing demands for greater relevance of social science knowledge, the idea of public sociology is also an answer, or a mosaic of answers, as to how sociology can be relevant for today's society, apart from the more traditional type of policy sociology.

Burawoy's (2005) call for public sociology reaffirmed the legitimacy of a type of sociology that, in his view, differs from other types, specifically professional sociology, policy sociology, and critical sociology. Both policy and public sociologies target extra-academic audiences, but they involve two different types of knowledge – instrumental in the case of policy sociology, reflexive in the case of public sociology: "Policy sociology is sociology in the service of a goal defined by a client. [Its] *raison d'être* is to provide solutions to problems that are presented to us, or to legitimate solutions that have already been reached ... Public sociology, by contrast, strikes up a dialogic relation between sociologist and public in which the agenda of each is brought to the table, in which each adjusts to the other" (Burawoy 2005, 9).

Public sociology itself is a mix of different kinds of sociology, which reflect "different types of publics and multiple ways of accessing them" (Burawoy 2005, 7). Traditional public sociology essentially consists of diffusing sociological knowledge through non-academic channels (books, lectures, newspaper commentaries, and so on) in order to reach the general public and spur public debate (Bonacich 2007, 74). There is no direct interaction with the publics being addressed, who are "generally invisible in that they cannot be seen, thin in that they do not constitute a movement or organization, and they are usually mainstream" (Burawoy 2005, 7-8). Organic public sociology, in contrast, implies interaction and dialogue between sociologists and particular publics, through political engagement, problem solving, collaborative research, and so on. Organic public sociologists "work in close connection with a visible, thick, active, local and often counterpublic." Burawoy insists that the recognition of public sociology "must extend to the organic kind, which often remains invisible, private and is often considered to be apart from our professional lives" (8).

Organic public sociology thus involves interaction with various publics during the research process itself. It differs from traditional public sociology, in which knowledge is produced by sociologists (with or without direct fieldwork) and *then* conveyed to and appropriated by the public. Much like the so-called new modes of knowledge production (Nowotny, Scott, and Gibbons 2003), in organic public sociology, dichotomies between knowledge production and knowledge use, and between research subjects and research users, tend to dissolve. Here sociology's publics are particular groups or individuals with whom the researcher interacts sometimes very early in the research process in order to define a research project, negotiate access to the field and to research participants, convince research participants of the research project's significance, discuss research results and implications of results with them, and so forth.

Organic public sociology is a new label to refer to a range of far-from-new types of social research, such as action research, participatory research, participatory action research, cooperative inquiry, or advocacy research. Although significant differences exist between these various types, they share at least two common characteristics: first, they consider research participants as both subjects and co-researchers, which means that the researcher works *with,* rather than *on,* the researched; second, they aim to foster the interests of the people under study (Whyte 1991). Participatory research thus involves two kinds of participation from the researched: "epistemic participation," which refers to "the relation between the knower and the known," and "political participation," which refers to the relation between the subjects of the research and the decisions that affect them (Heron 1996, 20). In all these forms of participatory research, participants commonly belong to minorities and disadvantaged groups, and the researcher assumes that they lack the resources to foster their own interests by themselves (Weber and McCall 1978). In these traditional versions of organic public sociology, the researcher is deemed more powerful than the researched, an assumption that will be questioned in the next section.

Differential Power between the Researcher and the Researched

Research participants are vulnerable people who should be adequately protected from the potential harms of scientific research. This assertion is the undisputed core of research ethics. Regulating scientific research became imperative following the numerous cases of abuse of research participants in medical research but also in social science research (Mertens and Ginsberg 2009). From the medical experiments on prisoners by the Nazis to the Tuskegee syphilis study; from Milgram's experiments to Humphreys's study about "tearoom trade," cases abound about researchers' misconduct with research participants. The opening chapter of the TCPS2 (Canadian Institutes of Health Research et al. 2010, 7) evokes these "unfortunate examples where research participants have been needlessly, and at times profoundly, harmed by research, sometimes even dying as a result." In the

1960s and '70s, "advocacy anthropology" emerged precisely as a response to the criticism that anthropologists had been the passive advocates of the colonial state, and had served indirectly to perpetuate colonial rule. Social scientists are now aware that "the person being studied typically has less power than the researcher and must be accorded the protections that render this inequality morally acceptable" (Sieber 1992, 13).

A large part of social research, however, does not fit the traditional conception of research in which powerless research participants face powerful researchers. This traditional conception may remain true in biomedical research but it should come under severe scrutiny in social science. Two different arguments can be distinguished here. First, generally speaking, participants are more educated and more likely to be organized in various groups and communities that make them less vulnerable to abuse by researchers, and they are more knowledgeable about the logic of scientific research (Mesny 2009). Lay people increasingly resist being subjects of inquiry, especially when they do not see how the inquiry can serve their own purposes (Hymes 1974), and they tend to impose conditions before agreeing to be studied in order to have some control over the research projects in which they participate (Barnes 1979; Bonacich 2007, 86).

Second, a significant number of social scientists do research that involves participants who are powerful members of society. Although sociologists have traditionally been concerned with studying the "underdog" (Barnes 1979, 34; Barrett 1984, 4), that is, underprivileged groups of society, and to speak "on behalf of the poor and dispossessed" (Brint 2007, 237), their research interests are not, and should not be, confined to the study of the powerless. The "interests of the powerful and the weak, the rich and the poor, and the idealized and the stigmatized all should be reflected in our research questions" (Brief and Cortina 2000, 11).

If sociologists want to better understand society, then they have to study all its components and demonstrate, as all researchers should, a "scholarly openness" (Goldberg and van de Berg 2009, 788) for studying "the whole social world" (Brint 2007, 255). There is no logical reason why sociologists, including organic public sociologists, should concentrate only on particular, generally underprivileged, counterpublics, or even only on "civil society" (Brint 2007, 246). Sociological research implies understanding "the multiplicity of experiences and actors operating with civil society" and should thus engage "the full range of actors and political possibilities revolving around the problem under study" (Goldberg and van den Berg 2009, 788).[1]

Studying only the powerless is also problematic from the perspective of a vision of sociology that aims at a "deepening of democracy" (Bonacich 2007, 83). Understanding the roles and functioning of apparently powerful constituents of society is certainly necessary to properly raise and address social issues. For example, Edna Bonacich, who sees herself as an organic public sociologist (2007, 74), recounts how she decided to work with the Writers Guild of America (WGA), a union that represents "privileged, mainly white, Hollywood artists," in contrast to her former projects which involved "low-wage, immigrant workers" (81). Working with the WGA enabled her to raise the issue of the role of the powerful media in society and to denounce the pernicious degree of advertising penetration in TV reality shows.

Pushing the argument farther, other social scientists have called for a switch from the traditional, powerless subjects of research towards the powerful and affluent to make a better use of the inherently subversive nature of social inquiry. These forms of social inquiry raise a number of ethical issues that are seldom exposed in the literature or debate about research ethics, let alone in the TCPS. Stanley Barrett (1984, 4), for example, argues that exposing the inner working of a group or a system amounts to indicating how these people can be controlled. In his view, social research thus implies that the power of the people that are investigated often becomes undermined. Therefore, he chose to study white extremists rather than the victims of racism. Barrett (1984, 7) writes, "In view of the lack of substantial research on victimizers compared to that on the victims, and the possibility that research actually is negative in its consequences, my judgment was that a greater scholarly and social contribution could be made by plugging into the other side, so-to-speak." In a related vein, Bonacich (2007, 87) researches middle-management, whom she sees as "servants of the capitalist class," with a view of herself as "a Robin Hood researcher, stealing information from the privileged to give to the poor." Although she feels that "most of the middle-management people that [she] talk[s] with are decent, sincere, sensitive, well-meaning people," she feels authorized to "betray them" by hiding her true intentions about her research (87).

These cases illustrate conundrums faced by organic sociologists. These conundrums are unlikely to be resolved by the TCPS. More importantly, they also escape the debate about organic public sociology as defined by Burawoy since it is assumed that organic sociologists study powerless individuals and groups. Ethical issues that emerge from researching powerful people have no place in the official politics about research ethics. In Burawoy's perspective, powerful publics refer to policy sociology and *not* to organic sociology. Yet, as exemplified above by Bonacich and Barrett, studying powerful people does not necessarily amount to serving them as "clients." Organic public sociology involves all types of research participants, from the underprivileged and powerless to the wealthy and powerful. If we want to pursue Burawoy's argument about the value of a sociology based on a direct interaction between the researcher and the researched, then we need to enlarge our conception of the politics of fieldwork that underlies this interaction. A conception of fieldwork based on the assumption that research commonly implies vulnerable participants who should be protected from powerful researchers is bound to be at odds with the practice of a significant number of organic social scientists.

As these researchers very well know, social research very often resembles a political minefield between not-so-powerless participants and not-so-powerful researchers (Bryman 1988). Researchers need to negotiate research access to all sorts of organizations (unions, movements, associations, governmental agencies, private or public companies, etc.) and to respondents or informants in a context in which this access has become more and more difficult to obtain. Organizations are often overloaded with requests for research access, and executives have little time and interest for academic research (Buchanan, Boddy, and McCalman 1988, 55). Besides, members of organizations can be very suspicious of social researchers, and they employ all kinds of means to exclude researchers and block access to respondents and data by retaining data as confidential, constraining the time allowed to researchers, regulating the information they provide, and so on (Beynon 1988, 21; Buchanan, Boddy, and McCalman 1988, 55).

The growth of organic public sociology and, more generally, of a sociology grounded in in-depth fieldwork with a diversity of publics, should be based on a renewed conception of the power relationships between the researcher and the researched. I have argued that this conception is much more complex and multifaceted than the biomedical model of powerful researchers studying powerless participants. In the next section, I turn to another aspect of the politics of social research that refers to the increasing number of stakeholders who wish to own and control one or several parts of the research process.

Scholarly Research, Academic Freedom, and Research Integrity

Academic social research is increasingly collaborative in the sense that researchers tend to collaborate with a diversity of stakeholders, such as funders, users, respondents, or governments, at various stages of the research process, including the design of the research project and research question, data collection, data analysis, and the diffusion of results (Goldberg and van den Berg 2009, 770; Holmwood 2007; Mesny and Mailhot 2007). Besides, an increasing part of social research activity is taking place outside academia per se. A large range of organizations, groups, or institutions understand the benefits of systematic investigation for better comprehending the social phenomena that pertain to their actions and interests. They routinely employ the methods used in academic research and sometimes have research teams on their own (Bonacich 2007). They also often ask for the help of academic researchers to carry on these research endeavours. Academic researchers may intervene as academic consultants, counsellors, or subcontractors. Their involvement can range from taking charge of the entire research project to merely provide a symbolic endorsement to a research process that largely escapes their control.

In such a context, it becomes increasingly difficult to clearly distinguish between social research performed by academic researchers in the realm of academic freedom and academic integrity and other research practices that escape the ethos of science, although they might involve academic scientists at various stages of the process. This distinction is especially important if we want to reinforce the legitimacy of public organic sociology. In my view, an important condition for maintaining this legitimacy is for academic researchers to have a say in all the stages of the research projects in which they agree to participate.

A large range of social scientists are very familiar with the risk of becoming "servants of power" (Baritz 1960; Brief 2000; Brief and Cortina 2000), that is, of giving up their academic freedom as well as duty to serve the "public good" by becoming, willingly or unwillingly, the servants of particular interests or particular publics. Public sociology's opponents have accused organic public sociologists of selling – literally or symbolically – their expertise and knowledge to particular interest groups. In their so doing, organic public sociology becomes another form of policy sociology in the sense that it aims at serving particular clients, policy makers, or others. The fact that the clients of organic sociologists are generally less visible than the clients of policy sociologists does not change the fact that the risk of subsuming scholarly research to particular interests exists in both cases. There is no easy way to reduce this risk, and there is no clear-cut definition of scholarly research to settle the matter.[2] However, guidelines are both possible and necessary.

In her extensive research with labour unions, Bonacich (2007, 76) offers a clear account of the way she has managed to set clear lines regarding academic freedom and integrity: "I do not like being told what to do. I value the freedom to study whatever I want to study, and to take an independent stance. So I do not take money from unions, and I am not subject to their determining what I do." She also stresses how her – very organic – sociological practice straddles the line between public and policy sociology: "One can define Policy Sociology more broadly as research that is done for a client (a practice that I generally try to avoid), or as research that is conducted to foster a particular social goal. Using this latter meaning, I think my work can be said to be influenced by this tradition a bit" (93).

Academic freedom, the possibility of critical inquiry, and research integrity all refer in part to the degree of control that the researcher is able to maintain over the research process, whether or not this research is done for a client. In this regard, some forms of collaborative research appear highly problematic. As one stakeholder among others in the research process, academic researchers sometimes have little to say about the definition of the research project itself, the methodology, data collection, or data analysis. Yet academic integrity should involve minimal requirements regarding the researcher's control or implication in the research process. Outside these minimal requirements, the research should not be considered academic research, and we should probably question academic researchers' involvement in these projects.

Although the definition of these minimal requirements is tricky, the task of defining these requirements, especially those that concern data collection, should probably fall within the scope of the TCPS. Academic researchers are now frequently asked to participate in research projects designed by groups or organizations that take charge of data collection and only require the researcher's input for data analysis. Organizations, groups, and institutions run their own empirical investigations about their employees, clients, stakeholders, or markets, and have recourse to academic researchers only after the collection of data is completed. Some of these researchers, however, consider these projects as academic ones, they sometimes get public funds for them, and they get academic publications out of them. Having to explain these projects to their REBs, they would claim that the projects are based on second-hand data originally not intended for academic research and that they had no role or responsibility regarding the reliability and ethics of the collection process.

Conversely, academic researchers are sometimes asked to intervene solely as "methodology experts" for data collection but are not involved in the analysis or in the conclusions. Their role is to ensure that data collection meets the standards of scientific inquiry, but they leave to the client the responsibility of analysis and interpretation. This situation is very different from the one in which data analysis is jointly carried out by the researchers and the research participants, which is a very common situation in collaborative research and action research. Organic public sociology often implies that researchers discuss their results with research participants and the particular publics concerned with the results. They often expect these results to be reinterpreted and diffused in ways that sometimes amount to a clear distortion of what they actually meant. All of this is "part of the game" of doing public sociology. These practices should be clearly distinguished, however, from research projects in which social scientists are simply not involved in the analysis and interpretation of data or act only as external consultants or counsellors. In the absence of a definition of minimal requirements regarding scholars' control of the research process, all these practices – both the legitimate and the dubious – become mixed. There is the risk that organic public social science and other forms of collaborative research, which have normally proven to adhere to high standards of integrity, become depreciated by the scientific community in the absence of guidelines for distinguishing scholarly research from commercial research.

In the context of multiple stakeholders involved in various ways in scholarly research, organic public sociology should be firmly distinguished from other practices in which academic researchers forsake their control of, and responsibility for, large parts of the research process. Minimal requirements for researchers' involvement should probably include data collection and data analysis. Having to negotiate these research phases with other stakeholders is fraught with difficulties and ethical conundrums, but leaving these research phases to other stakeholders simply amounts to a clear breach of scholarly ethics and integrity. The former situation is organic public sociologists' daily lot; the latter should have no place in sociology.

Sociology for Whom? Benefits of Research for Direct Participants

The "sociology for whom" question is a central issue in the debate about public sociology. It is also at the core of the TCPS about research ethics with humans. The TCPS's answer to that question is that "direct participants" should be the first to benefit from scientific research. When research entails risks for participants, researchers must demonstrate how these risks are balanced with potential benefits. Yet "much research offers little or no direct benefit to participants"; rather, "in most research, the primary benefits produced are for society and for the advancement of knowledge" (Canadian Institutes of Health Research et al. 2010, 22). As research with Aboriginal peoples has amply demonstrated, a number of groups and communities have developed mistrust towards research for they feel it has not benefited them (Mabry 2009, 108). Researchers are therefore urged to clearly state the potential benefits of their research and to pay particular attention to short-term benefits for participants in order to give them "something in return for their efforts" (Sieber 1992, 101). From the perspective of research ethics, it is assumed that these short-term benefits are "not only easy to bring about, but are also owed and may facilitate future research access to that population" (97). From this perspective, immediate benefits for participants include "valuable relationships," "knowledge or education," "material resources," "training," and the "opportunity to do good and to receive the esteem of others" (104).

Sociologists involved in action research, collaborative research, emancipatory research, or advocacy research have always been very concerned about impacts of the research process on direct participants. In fact, these impacts are one of the main objectives of these forms of research – along with the production of scholarly knowledge. In contrast with traditional research, the "disturbing" or transformative impact of research on its subjects is considered to be a strength, rather than a flaw, of social research.

Yet benefits for direct participants are not always easy to achieve and, most importantly, they partly escape the researcher's control. In occasional cases, research benefits for direct participants can go as far as improving their health or even saving their lives. For example, Thomas Wright and Vincent Wright report how organizational research about stress at the workplace has sometimes enabled participants to realize their state of stress and to make the decision to quit "before it was too late" (Wright and Wright 2002, 173). Considering the many cases of workplace suicide that are due to high levels of unacknowledged stress, Wright and Wright (2002, 176, 179) have developed what they call a "committed-to-participant research perspective," which consists of "demonstrating compassion and empathy toward research participants" and considering participants' health and betterment as "worthwhile consequences or ends in themselves."

In many cases, however, urging people to participate in social research by promising them direct benefits seems a rather dubious strategy. As

Barrett (1984, 3) puts it, "Perhaps there was a time when we were able to persuade our subjects, and believed ourselves, that our research efforts would be of great practical benefit to them. But most people are too sophisticated to swallow this line now. The residents of ghettos, for example, have become apprehensive about researchers, and often unwilling to accept them into their communities."

A "committed-to-participant research perspective" should be a characteristic of social research in general. This perspective is in line with the current principles of ethical conduct in research as exposed in the CS2TP. However, benefits for direct participants, such as those anticipated by action researchers and other "organic" researchers, depend on two conditions that do not fit easily with current principles of research ethics. First, these benefits are jeopardized if research participants are promised confidentiality and anonymity. As Wright and Wright (2002, 180) rightly note, "the promise of confidentiality makes it impractical, whereas anonymity makes it practically impossible, for the researcher to meaningfully interact with the participants." Without the possibility to connect data (for example, answers to a questionnaire about stress) to the persons who provided them and to interact with these persons with full knowledge of the particular data they provided, the potential benefits that the research could have for these participants are lost. The tendency to rely increasingly on data banks made of anonymous, nonidentifiable information is also in direct opposition with the very principle of research benefits for direct participants.

Second, potential benefits are also potential risks. However thorough and well-informed the ethical review of a research project is, the fact remains that, in social science, the way participants will react to the research process or to research results remains largely unpredictable. To come back to the above example about stress at the workplace, one could imagine that a research participant, instead of feeling empowered by the research results about her own level of stress, becomes seriously disturbed by these results to the point that her health and well-being deteriorate. Close interactions between researchers and participants are thus essential to monitor the various reactions that participants may have during the research process or when faced with the research results. For that reason, online experiments, in which it is impossible for researchers to monitor the participants' reactions to the research process, can be problematic (Wright and Wright 2002, 181). More fundamentally, what should be acknowledged is that there are always risks involved when social scientists make it one of their priorities to really treat research participants as subjects who, by virtue of being reflexive human beings, will necessarily be transformed by their participation in the research process, for good but also, sometimes, for worse.[3]

The unpredictability of research impacts on direct participants cannot be easily reconciled with the current policy regarding research ethics. The TCPS focuses on the necessity to protect research participants from unpleasant consequences resulting from their participation in scholarly research. From this perspective, the ideal situation would be one in which research participants would be untouched and unaltered by the research process. Such a perspective stands in clear opposition with the epistemological foundations of public sociology and all the other approaches in social science that are based on the transformative effect of social science knowledge. The price to pay for protecting research participants from potential harms is to forsake these transformative effects altogether or, rather, to renounce trying to influence them.

The concern for benefits to research participants is also directly connected to the above discussion about the power relationships between the researcher and the researched. Research participants may represent particular interests, and the issue of research serving these particular interests rather than "the public good" is not easily resolved. When they are organized and have the means to speak for themselves, research participants can increasingly impose the kind of direct benefits they expect from the research. For example, researchers studying Native American culture may be expected, as a requirement for continuing research, to testify in support of land claim litigation (Clifford 1986, 9). Such a requirement may be at odds with the objectives of a particular research project; in that case, researchers are simply denied the possibility to conduct their research projects because the projects do not fit the subjects' short-term objectives and interests.

With respect to the "rule" that social research should benefit direct participants, organic public sociologists have to reconcile two phenomena: on one hand, people increasingly resist being "researched," and when they do agree to participate, they expect the research process or results to be of some direct value to them. On the other hand, it is often impossible for researchers to deliver direct, short-term benefits to participants, and when they do, they risk becoming the "servants" of particular interests at the expense of "public interest."

Sociology for Whom? The Impact of Research Results on Lay Publics

The insistence on visible, short-term benefits for research participants tends to undermine the larger view about less visible, long-term benefits of research for society at large or for the general public. Concern with the protection of participants, combined with the current pressure towards greater relevance of scientific research (Goldberg and van den Berg 2009, 770) leads to a narrowed conception of research benefits. The broader view about benefit to society becomes dubious: "When researchers vaguely promise benefit to science and society, they approach being silly. These are the least probable of good outcomes" (Sieber 1992, 97).

As invisible and long-term as it may be, the impact of social science knowledge on society cannot be dismissed so easily (Brady 2004, 1630). This impact has been studied and documented from a number of perspectives, from the diffusion of social science knowledge through mass media, its appropriation by lay people, its enlightened effect on policy makers, or its transformation into common sense and social representations (Berger 1965; Farr 1993; Merton and Wolfe 1995; Mesny 2009; Moscovici 1961; Weiss 1977; Wrong 1990). Just because these indirect effects and uses of research results are difficult to trace does not imply that they do not exist. Effects of social science knowledge are often indirect, subtle, and even unconscious (Brief 2000; Mesny 2009). Lay people do not label some of their knowledge about society sociological knowledge, but part of this knowledge nevertheless comes from sociological research (Gans 1989). Yet attempts to obtain "clear-cut proof of the direct utility of our research, based on the self-reports of likely users, probably are doomed to fail or, at a minimum, to yield to suspect findings" (Brief 2000, 350).

The uncontrollability and untraceability of research impacts (Mesny and Mailhot 2012) raise important ethical issues. Public sociologists who have tried to influence the way their work has been disseminated in the mass media are acutely aware of these ethical issues. Sociological knowledge is never "transferred"; rather, it is "transformed" through its diffusion in the mass media and can end up fuelling the public debate in ways that are in complete opposition with the researchers' purposes and beliefs (Brady 2004; Stacey 2004; Tumin 1970). Researchers share the responsibility of the impact of social science knowledge with many other stakeholders, such as journalists, policy makers, legislators, educators, and so on. By urging researchers to concentrate on short-term, visible, and predictable impacts of their research on clearly identifiable people, the current TCPS on research ethics tends to promote a position that can be seen as morally questionable: researchers should not be concerned with uncontrollable effects of their research on society through the diffusion and dissemination of the research results in non-academic channels. I suspect a number of social scientists would find such a position morally untenable. For public sociologists who are concerned precisely with those effects, this means that ethical guidance fails them exactly where they need it the most.

Summary and Implications

Public sociology is about making sociological research relevant and useful to the public or to various particular publics. Principles of research ethics are about protecting participants from the harms induced by scientific research. At first sight, there is a strong affinity between the two perspectives. I have argued, however, that organic public sociology raises ethical issues that are utterly absent from the TCPS or, more critically, that the conception of social research on which the TCPS is based makes it impossible to shed some light on these issues.

Direct and Indirect Research Participants, Research Sponsors, and Research Users

There is a fundamental inconsistency between the way research participants are conceived in the current policy about research ethics and the way social scientists, and public sociologists especially, relate to their own subjects.

In biomedical research, risks associated with direct participation to the research process are often very acute. In social science, in contrast, these risks are less important compared to another category of collective risks that refer to "the harm a study might cause to others beyond the individual subject himself" (Bower and de Gasparis 1978, 12). These risks spring from the research's results rather than the research's process, and they concern indirect as much as direct participants. The latter are part of a larger public, and it is this entire collective that might be put at risk of suffering some setback as a result of a particular research study. "Research participants," thus, does not refer only to the individuals who actually take part in the research process: it also includes the larger groups, organizations, and publics to which research participants belong. Restricting researchers' ethical duty to the protection of the sole individuals who directly participated in the research (often as respondents) is untenable. Researchers who study organizations must ponder the protection of these organizations along with the protection of the individuals who are the subjects of the research as members of these organizations (Mirvis 1982).

In social science, especially in organic public social science, the category of research subjects becomes blurred with other categories: research beneficiaries, research users, and research sponsors. Sometimes all these categories refer to the same people or public. The people who participate in the research are also those who support it (not necessarily by funding it, but, at least, by enabling the researcher access to the field), those who are supposed to benefit from the results, and those who may actually use the research results. In many other cases, these various categories refer to different groups: researchers may study a particular group, but the people who sponsor the research belong to another public and so do the people who could benefit from the results. It is important, thus, to clarify who the direct participants, the indirect participants, the research sponsors, and the research users are.

Public Sociology versus Policy Sociology

The distinction between public sociology and policy sociology draws upon a clear demarcation between two types of publics: policy makers and, more generally, people in positions of power in society; and silent minorities, social movements, and, more generally, grassroots publics that lack power and a voice in civil society. The former are targeted by policy sociologists while the latter are organic sociologists' primary public. In Burawoy's perspective, policy sociologists produce instrumental knowledge for the benefits of conservative clients while public sociologists produce reflexive and critical knowledge for the benefits of ready-to-be-enlightened, progressive groups.

Burawoy's notion of public sociology has been criticized for its exclusively left-wing conception of organic public sociologists and the "presupposition that only the activism of the groups and communities of the progressive left represents the true democratic and social justice interests and aspirations of disenfranchised citizens everywhere" (Goldberg and van den Berg 2009, 786). The argument made in this chapter expands this line of criticism on several counts. First, organic sociologists study and collaborate with a large variety of publics that extends far beyond "silent minorities." Public sociologists work with all kind of publics, some of them highly organized, some of them rather powerful. Simply stating that the public we should engage with are those "that are challenging the power structure in some way" (Brint 2007, 245) overlooks the fact that what constitutes power or what constitutes a challenge to power is highly controversial, including among sociologists. Second, the public itself says nothing about the type of sociological knowledge – instrumental or reflexive – that will be produced. As organic public sociologists very well know, the risk of "instrumentalization" is as real with some grassroots publics as it is with policy makers and powerful subjects. The distinction between public sociology and policy sociology is certainly not as clear-cut as Burawoy suggests. Any form of organic research runs the risk of being subsumed by a goal defined by participants who take the role of a client (Brint 2007, 241; Tittle 2004, 1643). This is by no means restricted to research explicitly aimed at policy makers or "mainstream" publics. Research participants want to be the primary research users and, to that extent, "want impeccable academic research to prove their point" (Bonacich 2007, 86). Researchers often "find themselves in the position of having to choose between their version of the truth and that which is held by the subjects they study and support" (Goldberg and van den Berg 2009, 791). In that sense, a lot of organic research straddles the line between public sociology and policy sociology and, more precisely, between reflexive and instrumental knowledge, as defined by Burawoy. Close interaction and dialogue between the researcher and "grassroots counterpublics" does not necessarily produce reflexive knowledge. It can very well produce instrumental knowledge at the satisfaction of both sides. In other words, organic public sociology may produce instrumental knowledge. Conversely, policy sociology – working with mainstream groups or organizations that explicitly consider themselves clients – may sometimes produce reflexive knowledge, that is, knowledge that triggers a "dialogue about matters of political and moral concern" (Burawoy 2004, 1607).

Conclusion: Sociology and Relevance

Beyond public sociology, we need to acknowledge the multiple ways and channels whereby sociological knowledge becomes diffused and used outside the academic field. Enriching "public debate about moral and political issues by infusing them with sociological theory and research" (Burawoy 2004, 1603) can be done in many ways outside the practice of public sociology. Conducting research that is immediately relevant for research participants should be seen as *one* type of research among other equally legitimate types of research. In fact, restricting the usefulness of social science knowledge to short-term and observable uses by research participants jeopardizes the very project of social science (see Hanemaayer, this volume). Social science knowledge may well be at first considered useless and sometimes harmful by particular publics, as Bucklaschuk also points out in Chapter 4. It is precisely by paying no heed to this accusation of worthlessness that such knowledge ends up being useful and highly relevant. Arthur Brief (2000, 346) makes the point quite clearly regarding management knowledge by showing how "useful" is mixed up with "controllable": "The desire to conduct managerially useful research disrupts the scientific enterprise.

Those seeking to do managerially useful research are advised to be concerned with independent variables in the control of management; however, doing so could limit theory development by deemphasizing or excluding those variables that management cannot manipulate but that may be potent with explanatory power."

In his famous account of the way social scientists who studied industry in the first half of the twentieth century became "servants of power," Loren Baritz (1960) shows that the research participants (employees) were not the research users (companies' middle- and top-management). Researchers concentrated exclusively on the problems of employees' productivity and loyalty because these problems were deemed "relevant" for the management community and to some extent to society at large. Today, Brief and Cortina (2000) draw the same type of conclusion when they note, for example, that organizational research about downsizing has concentrated on the survivors of layoffs but rarely on the victims themselves. The public good, which we tend to take too much for granted, is not always easy to define. It virtually always takes the form of particular goods. It might be easy to condemn blatant forms of "servant research" when the interests served are clearly those of "the powerful," such as the management community. In many other cases, however, it takes quite a dose of moral clarity and modesty to admit that, as sociologists, we can never be assured that the particular publics to which we want to give a voice do indeed represent the public good. It also takes some form of courage to accept that what sociologists should sometimes produce are "discomfiting truths" (Brint 2007, 240) that few people among the public will find relevant.

Notes

1 In that regard, Burawoy's exclusively left-wing–oriented conception of organic public sociology, according to which only left-wing publics are worthy of research, becomes problematic (Brint 2007; Goldberg and van den Berg 2009; Holmwood 2007; Nielsen 2004).

2 The TCPS is not very helpful in this regard. The TCPS (Canadian Institutes of Health Research et al. 2010, 7) defines research as "an undertaking intended to extend knowledge through a disciplined inquiry of systematic investigation." This definition does not enable us to distinguish between acceptable and dubious forms of systematic investigation. Regarding activities "that have traditionally employed methods and techniques similar to those employed in research," such as "quality assurance and quality improvement studies, or program evaluation activities," the policy states that "they do not constitute research" for the purposes of the TCPS2 and fall outside the scope of REB review, although they may raise ethical issues (19-20).

3 For further discussion of the unanticipated harms of doing organic public sociology, see Bucklaschuk, this volume, and her discussion of temporary migrant workers in Canada.

References

Baritz, Loren. 1960. *The Servants of Power: A History of the Use of Social Science in American Industry*. Middletown, CT: Wesleyan University Press.

Barnes, John A. 1979. *Who Should Know That? Social Science, Privacy and Ethics*. Cambridge: Cambridge University Press.

Barrett, Stanley R. 1984. "Racism, Ethics, and the Subversive Nature of Anthropological Inquiry." *Philosophy of the Social Sciences* 14: 1-25.

Berger, Peter L. 1965. "Towards a Sociological Understanding of Psychoanalysis." *Social Research* 32: 26-41.

Beynon, Huw. 1988. "Regulating Research: Politics and Decision Making in Industrial Organization." In *Doing Research in Organizations,* edited by Alan Bryman, 21-33. New York: Routledge.

Bonacich, Edna. 2007. "Working with the Labor Movement: A Personal Journey in Organic Public Sociology." In *Public Sociology: The Contemporary Debate,* edited by Lawrence T. Nichols, 73-94. New Brunswick, NJ: Transaction Publishers.

Bosk, Charles, and Raymond G. De Vries. 2004. "Bureaucracies of Mass Deception: Institutional Review Boards and the Ethics of Ethnographic Research." *Annals of the American Academy* 595: 249-63.

Bower, Robert T., and Priscilla de Gasparis. 1978. *Ethics in Social Research: Protecting the Interests of Human Subjects*. New York: Praeger.

Brady, David. 2004. "Why Public Sociology May Fail." *Social Forces* 82, 4: 1629-38.

Brief, Arthur P. 2000. "Still Servants of Power." *Journal of Management Inquiry* 9, 4: 342-51.

Brief, Arthur, and José Cortina. 2000. "Research Ethics: A Place to Begin." *Academy of Management: Research Methods Division Newsletter* 15, 1: 1, 4, 11, 12.

Brint, Steven. 2007. "Guide for the Perplexed: On Michael Burawoy's 'Public "Sociology.'" In *Public Sociology: The Contemporary Debate,* edited by Lawrence T. Nichols, 237-62. New Brunswick, NJ: Transaction Publishers.

Bryman, Alan, ed. 1988. *Doing Research in Organizations*. New York: Routledge.

Buchanan, David, David Boddy, and James McCalman. 1988. "Getting In, Getting On, Getting Out and Getting Back." In *Doing Research in Organizations,* edited by Alan Bryman, 43-67. New York: Routledge.

Burawoy, Michael. 2004. "Public Sociologies: Contradictions, Dilemmas, and Possibilities." *Social Forces* 82, 4: 1603-18.

–. 2005. "2004 Presidential Address: For Public Sociology." *American Sociological Review* 70, 1: 4-28.

Canadian Institutes of Health Research, Natural Sciences and Engineering Research Council of Canada, and Social Sciences and Humanities Research Council of Canada. 2010. *Tri-Council Policy Statement: Ethical Conduct for Research Involving Humans* (TCPS2).

Clawson, Dan, Robert Zussman, Joya Misra, Naomi Gerstel, Randall Stokes, and Douglas L. Anderton, eds. 2007. *Public Sociology: Fifteen Eminent Sociologists Debate Politics and the Profession in the Twenty-First Century.* Berkeley: University of California Press.

Clifford, James. 1986. "Introduction: Partial Truths." In *Writing Culture. The Poetics and Politics of Ethnography,* edited by James Clifford and George E. Marcus, 1-26. Berkeley: University of California Press.

Connolly, Kate, and Adela Reid. 2007. "Ethics Review for Qualitative Inquiry: Adopting a Values-Based, Facilitative Approach." *Qualitative Inquiry* 13, 7: 1031-47.

De Vries, Raymond, Debra A. DeBruin, and Andrew Goodgame. 2004. "Ethics Review of Social, Behavioral and Economic Research: Where Should We Go from Here?" *Ethics and Behavior* 14, 4: 351-68.

Farr, Robert M. 1993. "Common Sense, Science and Social Representations." *Public Understanding of Science* 2: 189-204.

Gans, Herbert J. 1989. "1988 Presidential Address: Sociology in America: The Discipline and the Public." *American Sociological Review* 54: 1-16.

–. 2002. "More of Us Should Become Public Sociologists." *Footnotes* July/August, http://www.asanet.org/footnotes/.

Goldberg, Avi, and Axel van den Berg. 2009. "What Do Public Sociologists Do? A Critique of Burawoy." *Canadian Journal of Sociology* 34, 3: 765-802.

Gunsalus, C. Kristina, Edward M. Bruner, Nicholas C. Burbules, Leon Dash, Matthew Finkin, Joseph P. Goldberg, William T. Greenough, Gregory A. Miller, Michael G. Pratt, Masumi Iriye, and Deb Aronson. 2007. "The Illinois White Paper: Improving the System for Protecting Human Subjects: Counteracting IRB 'Mission Creep.'" *Qualitative Inquiry* 13, 5: 617-49.

Heron, John. 1996. *Cooperative Inquiry: Research into the Human Condition.* London: Sage.

Holmwood, John. 2007. "Sociology as Public Discourse and Professional Practice: A Critique of Michael Burawoy." *Sociological Theory* 25: 46-66.

Hymes, Dell. 1974. "The Use of Anthropology: Critical, Political, Personal." In *Reinventing Anthropology,* edited by Dell Hymes, 3-79. New York: Vintage Books.

Mabry, Linda. 2009. "Governmental Regulation in Social Science." In *The Handbook of Social Research Ethics,* edited by Donna M. Mertens and Pauline E. Ginsberg, 107-20. London: Sage.

Mertens, Donna M., and Pauline E. Ginsberg, eds. 2009. *The Handbook of Social Research Ethics.* London: Sage.

Merton, Robert K., and Alan Wolfe. 1995. "The Cultural and Social Incorporation of Sociological Knowledge." *American Sociologist* (Fall): 15-39.

Mesny, Anne. 2009. "What Do 'We' Know That 'They' Don't? Sociologists' versus Non-Sociologists' Knowledge." *Canadian Journal of Sociology* 34, 3: 671-95.

Mesny, Anne, and Chantale Mailhot. 2007. "The Difficult Search for Compromises in a Canadian Industry/University Research Partnership." *Canadian Journal of Sociology* 32: 203-26.

–. 2012. “Control and Traceability of Research Impact on Practice: Reframing the ‘Relevance Gap’ Debate in Management.” *M@n@gement* 15, 2: 180-207.

Mirvis, Philip. 1982. “Know Thyself and What Thou Art Doing: Bringing Values and Sense into Organizational Research.” *American Behavioral Scientist* 26, 2: 177-97.

Moscovici, Serge. 1961. *La psychanalyse: Son image et son public – Étude sur la représentation sociale de la psychanalyse.* Paris: PUF.

Nichols, Lawrence, ed. 2007. *Public Sociology: The Contemporary Debate.* New Brunswick, NJ: Transaction Publishers.

Nielsen, François. 2004. “The Vacant ‘We’: Remarks on Public Sociology.” *Social Forces* 82, 4: 1619-27.

Nowotny, Helga, Peter Scott, and Michael Gibbons. 2003. “‘Mode 2’ Revisited: The New Production of Knowledge.” *Minerva* 41: 179-94.

Oakes, J. Michael. 2002. “Risks and Wrongs in Social Science Research: An Evaluator’s Guide to the IRB.” *Evaluation Review* 26, 5: 443-79.

Owen, Michael. 2002. “Engaging the Humanities? Research Ethics in Canada.” *Journal of Research Administration* 33, 3: 5-12.

Sieber, Joan E. 1992. *Planning Ethically Responsible Research: A Guide for Students and Internal Review Boards.* Newbury Park, CA: Sage.

Stacey, Judith. 2004. “Marital Suitors Court Social Science Spin-sters: The Unwittingly Conservative Effects of Public Sociology.” *Social Problems* 51, 1: 131-45.

Taylor, Charles. 1983. “Political Theory and Practice.” In *Social Theory and Political Practice,* edited by Christopher Lloyd, 61-85. Oxford: Clarendon Press.

Tittle, Charles R. 2004. “The Arrogance of Public Sociology.” *Social Forces* 82, 4: 1639-43.

Tumin, Melvin M. 1970. “Some Social Consequences on Racial Relations.” In *The Impact of Sociology: Readings in the Social Sciences,* edited by Jack D. Douglas, 116-33. New York: Appleton-Century-Crofts.

Weber, George H., and George J. McCall, eds. 1978. *Social Scientists as Advocates: Views from the Applied Disciplines.* London: Sage.

Weiss, Carol H. 1977. *Using Social Research in Public Policy Making.* Lexington, MA: DC Heath.

Whyte, William Foote, ed. 1991. *Participatory Action Research.* London: Sage.

Wright, Thomas A., and Vincent P. Wright. 2002. “Organizational Researcher Values, Ethical Responsibility, and the Committed-to-Participant Research Perspective.” *Journal of Management Inquiry* 11, 2: 173-85.

Wrong, Dennis H. 1990. “The Influence of Sociological Ideas on American Culture.” In *Sociology in America,* edited by Herbert J. Gans, 19-30. London: Sage.

7

Coral W. Topping, Pioneer Canadian Public Sociologist

"A Veteran Warrior for Prison Reform"

RICK HELMES-HAYES

In "For Public Sociology," Michael Burawoy's 2004 now iconic presidential address to the American Sociological Association (Burawoy 2005c), he proposed that sociology cast aside its commitment to value freedom, long regarded as one of the key principles of scientific practice. He made this startling proposal – and has reiterated it in many subsequent essays – because, in his view, sociology had lost its critical edge. As Burawoy saw it, too many sociologists had stopped engaging the truly difficult and pressing social problems of our times in favour of professional scientific "busy work" and puzzle solving aimed at the understanding of manageable but comparatively trivial questions about the workings of the social world. If we wanted to make sociology more relevant, he argued, we needed to return to the historical roots of the discipline. We needed to abandon the regnant disciplinary model of the discipline that venerates "value-free" science because, while valuable in the 1930s, '40s, '50s, and '60s as sociology developed a set of fruitful and reliable theoretical and methodological frameworks and practices, this model had become outmoded and counterproductive. In today's ubiquitously neoliberal political-economic environment, Burawoy argued, and continues to argue, sociology must become a "value science" committed to social democracy and universal human rights so that it can assume a central role in the fight against the spread of what he regards as massively ruinous neoliberal economic and social policies and practices around the world.

Not surprisingly, Burawoy's "accusation" – that much of sociology is irrelevant and/or trivial – and his proposed solution – namely, the abandonment of value freedom and the adoption of social democratic political principles and practices – touched a nerve. Colleagues around the world took up the cudgels for and against his proposal, and since his 2004 address we have witnessed an impassioned, sometimes vitriolic, debate over two fundamental questions: "sociology for whom?" and "sociology for what?"

My purpose in this chapter is not to argue for or against Burawoy's position, though, to be clear, I have expressed my support for it elsewhere (Helmes-Hayes 2009). Rather, my goal is to look back in time – specifically, to the first half of the century in Canadian sociology – and add some support to Burawoy's claim that a different ethos once pervaded the discipline. This was the case not just in the United States, as Burawoy notes, but in Canada as well. Indeed, a conception of sociology that saw it as a value-committed science was once an accepted and useful part of mainstream sociological practice.[1] I illustrate this claim via an examination of the life and work of Coral Wesley Topping (1889-1988), the first and only sociologist at the University of British Columbia between 1929 and 1954. Topping, who did his PhD in the United States (Columbia 1929), is a fascinating and significant figure in the history of Canadian sociology in his own right. He was a steward and builder of the discipline for over thirty years during a period when sociology had only a precarious foothold in the Canadian university system. He is relevant to our discussion of public sociology because of his efforts as a tireless and effective advocate of what was referred to at the time as the "New Penology." The New Penology, which was imported to Canada from Britain and the United States in the 1930s, was a progressive trend in the treatment of criminals and juvenile delinquents. It was based on the then novel notion that during the time prisoners were incarcerated they were to be "rehabilitated" – resocialized and educated rather than just punished – so that, upon release, they would become productive, law-abiding members of society. The New Penology was slow to win a place in Canada's justice and correctional systems, in part as a consequence of resistance afforded by those in positions of authority and influence who clung to the retributive conception of penology, and in part as a result of delays produced by the Depression and the Second World War. Eventually, however, the efforts of Topping and like-minded scholars, activists, and politicians across the country were successful. By the 1960s, the New Penology was institutionalized, profoundly altering the organization and running of the nation's carceral institutions. Indeed, in many respects, the New Penology is the basis of Canada's current correctional system. It is somewhat curious that Topping, one of the chief advocates of the New Penology in Canada, is so little known. His name crops up occasionally in accounts of the history of prison reform in Canada, alongside those other prominent figures, such as J. Dinnage Hobden, Agnes Macphail, Justice J. Archambault, John Kidman, and Ralph B. Gibson,[2] and I have discovered a newspaper account of Topping's role that refers to him as a "veteran warrior for prison reform" (Edmison, 1969-70, 548; see *Vancouver Sun*, January 12, 1970, in UBC Archives, C.W. Topping Fonds, vol. 4, file 15, folder 2), but he is less well known than he should be.

Bearing the foregoing in mind, my purpose in this chapter is twofold. First, I aim to discuss Topping's contributions and "style" as public sociologist in Burawoy's sense of the term. Second, the chapter illustrates the many respects in which Topping's style reflected a culture of scholarly engagement that was popular among British, American, and Canadian intellectuals of the era. From the late 1800s until well into the 1940s, in Canada, indeed, North America and the West more broadly, the university, like the rest of society, struggled to come to terms with a set of contentious, divisive issues raised by the publication of Charles Darwin's *On the Origin of Species* (1988 [1859]). If, for their part, universities generally became more scientific and secular after this momentous event, religion nonetheless remained a powerful source of taken-for-granted knowledge within (and outside) the academy (Allen 1971; Cook 1985; Marshall 1992; McKillop 1994). The sociology of the period reflected these tensions, features, and trends. It first emerged as a highly moralistic, often religion-based enterprise with a practical or applied "social work" orientation but became increasingly secular, professional, and "scientized." Notwithstanding the fact that religious understandings of the world were increasingly supplemented, if not supplanted, by secular ones, values – usually some form of rational humanism – remained central to the discipline. A close look at Topping's career provides a window on these developments.

The chapter is based on information gleaned from five main sources: (1) the C.W. Topping Fonds (CWT Fonds) housed in the UBC Archives, which contain (among other things) many of his unpublished scholarly manuscripts, a good deal of his correspondence, and, most importantly, a three-hundred-page unpublished autobiography titled "Quest" (CWT Fonds, vol. 2, file 9); (2) other archival sources; (3) government documents and reports; (4) Topping's published work; and (5) selected secondary literature.

The balance of the chapter is written in four sections. I begin by providing a biographical sketch of Topping's life, including a brief description of his major publications. I then turn to a selective review of his writings, focusing particularly on those publications that highlight his pioneering contributions as a scholarly and political advocate of the New Penology. These efforts place Topping squarely in the camp of those who would today regard themselves as public sociologists. Of course, the setting in which Topping worked differs radically from the current setting, and these differences should be clarified. Thus, in the penultimate section of the chapter, I describe the scholarly and political influences – science, religious and secular values, developments in sociology, a period-specific conception of the role of the scholar as activist – that contoured and guided his activities as a public sociologist during the second quarter of the twentieth century. I conclude by returning to Burawoy's current concerns, discussing Topping's work as exemplary of an historically specific style of New Liberal intellectual/political practice that accords well with Burawoy's conception of a properly engaged public sociology.

Coral W. Topping: A Brief Biography

Born 30 July 1889 near Ottawa, Ontario, Topping was the youngest son of the Reverend Nassau Bolton Topping (DD), a Methodist clergyman, and his wife, Catherine (née Cooke).[3] He completed secondary school in Perth and took a bachelor of arts degree in Greek and philosophy at Queen's University in part under the influence of Scottish Hegelian John Watson (Topping, n.d., 44-45, 131). After spending some time on the Prairies as a teacher and preacher and following a period of active service in the Canadian Army during the First World War, he became Governor of Kingston Jail (1917-19) (Topping, n.d., 83-91). While serving as governor, he took a bachelor of divinity at Queen's University Theological College (1919). During the next ten years, he studied at McGill University and Wesleyan Theological College in Montreal and Union Theological Seminary and Columbia University in New York, along the way earning master's degrees in theology and sociology (1921) (Topping, n.d., 98, 101-2, 117; Simpson 1988, 846). He remained at Columbia for the PhD, simultaneously studying for a doctorate in theology at Wesleyan Theological College (Topping, n.d., 103, 105-7). He completed the former in 1929 and the latter in 1925. His dissertation, "Canadian Penal Institutions," was a comprehensive study of the programs and living conditions in Canada's federal, provincial, and city prisons (104, 109, 123-27).

From 1923 to 1929 he taught at the College of Puget Sound, in Tacoma, Washington (Topping, n.d., 111), where he constituted a "one-man Department of Sociology" and taught social work (113; see 112-21). In 1929, he got a job at UBC. There he spent the next quarter-century. His was not an easy task, for he had to build sociology in the face of very straitened conditions brought on by the Depression and the Second World War while at the same time not only directing the department's program in social work but also teaching courses in economics, political science, philosophy, and social work (Topping, n.d., 127-31; 1980c, 27; see also CWT to H. Hiller, March 29, 1978, CWT Fonds, vol. 4, file 16, folder 2). As at Puget Sound, at UBC, he remained a one-man "department within a department."[4]

Topping died in Vancouver on 21 February 1988, at ninety-eight years of age (Fonds description, CWT Fonds). His many scholarly, practical, reform-oriented contributions garnered him considerable attention and earned him many accolades during his lifetime. I mentioned his reputation as a prison reform advocate, but he made a mark in social work as well. Though he had no formal training in the profession and referred to the responsibility of running the social work program at UBC as a "millstone" (Topping, n.d., 298, 121), he was identified in local Vancouver newspapers as an "outstanding, pioneer" social worker (*News Herald* [Vancouver], June 14, 1950, CWT Fonds, vol. 4, file 13, folder 2; *Vancouver Sun,* n.d. [ca. 1943], CWT Fonds, vol. 4, file 13, folder 1).[5]

Topping's Curriculum Vitae

Topping's research productivity is perhaps modest by current standards, but impressive under the circumstances: three brief books, four government reports, about a dozen scholarly journal articles and book chapters, and a number of short articles in social work and church journals. As well, he wrote dozens of newspaper columns and editorial pieces and gave scores – indeed, I suspect hundreds – of public talks on social issues and problems (see, e.g., Topping, n.d., 295-96; and CWT Fonds, vol. 4, file 13, folder 2; vol. 4, file 14, folders 1 and 2; vol. 4, file 15, folder 1).

Though he had a deep interest in marriage and the family and published in the area (see Topping 1953), he focused above all on the fields of criminology, juvenile delinquency, and penology. His interest in these fields grew in part from scholarly curiosity but also in part from a genuine concern for the disadvantaged, which is clearly evident in his involvement in the practical, "social betterment" activities of the many church and community organizations. The most important of these organizations was the John

Howard Society of BC (founded by the Rev. J. Dinnage Hobden in 1931), but he was also an active member of the Elizabeth Fry Society, the League of Nations Society of BC, the Vancouver Social Workers Club, and the Student Christian Movement. As well, he served on a number of United Church bodies, including its Institutional Council and Board of Evangelism and Social Service (CWT to R. Cousins, February 16, 1964, CWT Fonds, vol. 4, file 15, folder 1; Topping, n.d., 204), and contributed time and expertise to the BC Committee on Unemployment and Relief and the BC Board of the Social Service Council of Canada (Simpson 1988, 846; Topping, n.d., 114-16, 219, 221-24, 247, 248; CWT to H. Hiller, March 29, 1978, CWT Fonds, vol. 4, file 16, folder 2).

In the field of crime and penology, Topping produced five substantial works: *Canadian Penal Institutions* (1929 [1930 in the United States]); the *Report of the Commission of Inquiry on the Provincial Industrial School for Boys* (Pepler and Topping 1934); the *Report of the Commission on the British Columbia Prison Farm at Oakalla* (1935); the *Report of the Commission Appointed by the Attorney-General to Inquire into the State and Management of the Gaols of British Columbia* (Pepler, Topping, and Stevens 1950); and, *Crime and You* (1960).

Before I discuss these works, I should briefly characterize Topping's conception of his role as a scholar, for I want to comment below on his activities as a public sociologist in the sense that Burawoy uses the term. Most importantly, just like Burawoy, Topping regarded sociology as a properly value-laden yet scientific enterprise. Though an evangelist for "science" and "social engineering," Topping always employed these terms within – indeed, subordinated them to – a broader perspective that combined secular humanism and Christian values. And, though he was professor throughout his career, he did not see the university as an ivory tower. Rather, he operated as a traditional and organic public sociologist from the outset; he regarded social engagement at the local, provincial, and national levels as intrinsic to being a good teacher and scholar. "To be effective," he said, "[a teacher has] to become a scholar ... [H]e must get out where the action [is] taking place, get to the heart of the matter, absorb it and report it in the media of the time and the occasion" (Topping, n.d., 132). In his view, political involvement was a personal commitment that should drive one's scholarly agenda; "I have always, somehow, been mixed up with the problem of the minute" (304); "With me, teaching ... [and] social reform took precedence over basic research" (132). He regarded J.S. Woodsworth as a role model and noted that, like Woodsworth, he "enjoyed being out there in the trenches with the scouts" fighting for social justice (CWT to Rev. L. Wilson, April 12, 1978, CWT Fonds, vol. 4, file 16, folder 2).

Topping's Work in the Fields of Criminology and Penology

Canadian Penal Institutions (1929 [1930 in the United States])

Topping's first substantial publication was *Canadian Penal Institutions,* a scholarly book based closely on his PhD dissertation of the same title (see Topping, n.d., 171). The dissertation was extremely ambitious: it provided a comprehensive description of the philosophy, organization, and functioning of Canada's penal system in the late 1920s.[6] His research focused on prison programs and living conditions, a picture of which he painted using data he gathered via the administration of two one-hundred-item questionnaires, numerous site visits, and many interviews with politicians and prison officials (Topping 1930, ix-xii; Topping, n.d., 125, 301-2). While he was somewhat heartened by his major finding that conditions in Canada's federal penitentiaries had improved greatly since the turn of the century, he discovered that much remained to be done. Provincial and local jails especially had not improved to anywhere near the standard set by the federal penitentiaries (1930, 88-91, 91-92) and little progress had been made federally in the area of parole (1930, 83-88; see also Canada 1938; and Canada, Parole Board of Canada, n.d., 6-7). The solution to these problems, in his view, was the immediate and enthusiastic adoption of the principles and practices of the New Penology.

The New Penology for which Topping advocated was a humanitarian and constructive alternative to the brutal, inhumane, punishment-oriented philosophy and practices that had dominated Canadian carceral institutions since before Confederation. That system had been guided from the outset by the principles of punishment and retribution. Prisoners were intended to have few rights, and prison life was made as onerous as possible: physical labour during the day, solitary confinement during leisure time, perpetual silence, and severe corporal punishment for minor transgressions of innumerable rules (Cellard 2000; Canada, Parole Board of Canada, n.d., 7). By contrast, the New Penology was deeply grounded in two sets of ideas that diverged sharply from the traditional approach. The first was a novel philosophy regarding corrections based on the writing and advocacy work of the eighteenth-century British prison reformer John Howard (1726-90) (see Wilton 1973); the other was a set of "reform liberal" political and philosophical ideas.

As early as the 1770s, Howard had argued that it was necessary to rethink the entire approach to corrections. For him, as well as for later generations of like-minded reformers in Europe, the United States, and Canada, the new watchword – the core notion of the New Penology – had to be rehabilitation. But rehabilitation was possible only if the extant retribution-based philosophy was replaced by a new, humane approach based on "vigilance, gentleness, patience, persuasion, education, example, and religion" – all informed and guided by humanely applied scientific knowledge (*Annual Report of the Superintendent of Penitentiaries 1920*, 10, qtd. in Topping 1930, 28).

The slow rise to hegemony of an interventionist liberal view of the proper nature and role of the state in Canada created a receptive environment for such an approach beginning in the late nineteenth century, but it reached full flower only in the 1960s and '70s (Ferguson 1993; Granatstein 1982; Owram 1986).[7] According to this postclassical version of liberalism – the so-called New Liberalism – issues such as crime, juvenile delinquency, and penal reform were seen to be in need of a comprehensive scientific prevention and treatment strategy devised and administered by a scientifically informed and benevolent managerialist state.

At the time that Topping researched and wrote *Canadian Penal Institutions,* there was no systematic Canadian treatise on the New Penology to which he could refer.[8] Nonetheless, the basic premises of the approach were clear. Prisoners were to be treated humanely while in jail and then assisted after they left custody by a scientifically informed program of aftercare. At the heart of the approach was the principle that the "reformation" of criminals into "law abiding citizens" (Topping 1930, 12) rested on the application of four scientific procedures: observation, classification/segregation, treatment, and aftercare (10-17, 83).[9] A panel of applied scientists would assess each prisoner on entry and then help to develop a program of targeted treatment designed "to turn him from his evil ways and make a positively contributing citizen out of him" (Topping, n.d., 183-84). The elements of the program of treatment included vocational, religious, moral, and citizenship training combined with full-time work throughout the period of incarceration (Topping 1930, 14-15). A further goal, very slow to be realized in Canada, was adequate aftercare in the form of parole (25, 92-93).[10]

Report of the Commission of Inquiry on the Provincial Industrial School for Boys (1934)

Five years after the publication of *Canadian Penal Institutions,* Topping served with Colonel Eric Pepler, deputy-general of British Columbia, on a provincial commission that examined the management of and conditions in the BC Boys' Industrial School (*Report of the Commission of Inquiry on the Provincial Industrial School for Boys,* 1934, CWT Fonds, vol. 4, file 3). The conclusion at which Pepler and Topping arrived, based in part on their observations at the school and in part on an international survey of expert opinion in the field, was unequivocal. The BC facility was "out of step with what was going on in the rest of the world" and, thus, could not "do the job it was set up to do" (Topping, n.d., 147). The school's superintendent was dismissed and the school was set on a new course; its philosophy and operations were reformed in line with the New Penology. As it turned out, Pepler and Topping's recommended reforms proved exceedingly difficult to implement because of space constraints and management problems, and, in the short run, they did not work. To Topping's dismay, the Industrial School for Boys did not become the "outstanding institution" the commissioners had hoped (153).

The Report of the Commission on the British Columbia Prison Farm at Oakalla (1935)

A year later, Topping carried out a similar study, this time on his own, at the provincial prison farm at Oakalla, BC.[11] Again, however, he became frustrated. His report, which came to conclusions similar to those of the report on the BC Industrial School for Boys, had no impact. "Filed away" by the government of the time, Topping (n.d., 171) said, it "did not come up for air" until 1950, a decade and a half later. It must be borne in mind that, in this respect, Topping's report was in good company. In 1935, the same year that he submitted his report on Oakalla, progressive reformers led by Liberal MP Agnes Macphail, founder of the Elizabeth Fry Society, forced the new Liberal government of Mackenzie King to launch a Royal Commission on the state of Canada's penal system. Authored by Justice J. Archambault, the *Royal Commission Report on Penal Reform in Canada* came out in 1938. Among the most consequential documents on Canadian penal reform ever written, it argued in favour of a philosophically progressive set of penological principles based on "strict but humane discipline" and "reformation and rehabilitation of prisoners" (Canada 1938, 355).[12] Indeed, Archambault made scores of recommendations intended to put the specifics of the New Penology into place. However, his report, like the others, had little immediate impact. Just like the Depression had stalled prison reform in the late 1920s and early 1930s, the Second World War all but halted prison reform in the late 1930s and early 1940s.

The Report of the Commission Appointed by the Attorney-General to Inquire into the State and Management of the Gaols of British Columbia (1950)

Years later, Topping helped strike yet another blow in support of the (no longer new) New Penology. In 1950, when British Columbia formed a commission to assess the province's prison system, Topping was one of three commissioners appointed to undertake the study; Pepler and E.G.B. Stevens were the others. Stevens and Topping were directors of the John Howard Society at the time (Wilton 1973, 102). In the aftermath of the BC Commission of Inquiry, the government established the Advisory Committee on Juvenile Delinquency. Topping was appointed a member (Topping, n.d., 189-91). The three began their report by noting that "with the exception of the Borstal-type institution known as 'New Haven,' no major improvement ha[d] taken place" in the BC prison system since 1919, despite "great advances" that had occurred in the United States and other parts of Canada (Pepler, Topping, and Stevens 1950, 5). In the previous decade and a half, they said, the New Penology had emerged as "the central trend" in the philosophy and practice of corrections. They underscored the fact that there was a lot of scholarly literature in support of "constructive treatment" of lawbreakers – youth and adults alike – and that under Ralph B. Gibson, the new Canadian commissioner of penitentiaries, much progress had been made in instituting the "new" philosophy (6-7). Their key recommendation was that the core elements of California's Borstal-type system – the most advanced and progressive one in North America – should be adopted in BC (27-31; see Topping, n.d., 171-84). They were gratified when the provincial government acted on their recommendations and, many years later, Topping was pleased to report that the results, especially for those inmates in the juvenile justice system, were "notable, perhaps even spectacular" (Topping, n.d., 192, see 190-95).

Crime and You (1960)

In 1954, after retiring from UBC, Topping taught for three years at United College in Winnipeg. He wrote a set of articles about crime, punishment, and rehabilitation for the *Winnipeg Tribune* (Topping, n.d., 228; see also CWT Fonds, vol. 4, file 14, folder 2). In 1960, these articles were collected and published as *Crime and You,* a volume aimed at a popular rather than scholarly audience. Even more strongly than *Canadian Penal Institutions, Crime and You* spoke out in favour of a progressive penology. Of much assistance to Topping in his quest at this point was that, following the Second

World War, the American Correctional Association had developed *A Manual of Correctional Standards* (1946 and 1959), a bible of sorts of the new approach (see Topping 1960, 17-18). The manual was continually in a process of revision as scientific research and field experience dictated (Topping 1960, 18), but its core principles were sufficiently similar to those Topping had outlined in 1930 that he simply reiterated them in *Crime and You* (15-18). After reprising the principles of the New Penology, Topping reviewed trends in correctional practices and outcomes in Great Britain, the United States, Sweden, and Canada for the period 1930-60 and concluded that the new approach had spread rapidly and with great success (19-50; see also Topping 1955, 161-64).[13] Surveying the scene in 1960, Topping argued even more confidently than in 1930 that knowledge, scientifically gathered, was the key: "The job of curing crime, like the job of curing cancer, is a scientific procedure in a scientific age" (1960, 60).[14] "Men could be "buil[t] ... from the ground up," he wrote, using "education at its best and religion at its best" (2).

Topping as a Public Sociologist: Combining Science, Progressive Values, and Activism

Topping's research in the areas of criminology and penology was guided and contoured by several intellectual influences: (1) the theory and empirical practices of the social Darwinist Franklin Henry Giddings; (2) a set of progressive economic, political, and social values rooted in a combination of the Protestant Social Gospel and secular reform liberalism (the New Liberalism); and (3) a belief in the potential of science and social engineering to help realize those values.

The Influence of Giddings

The first time Topping came into contact with an explicitly sociological advocate of scientific liberal reformism was at Columbia University when he took a sociology course from Franklin Henry Giddings. Giddings had a profound impact on Topping. So impressed was Topping by Giddings's "masterful" lectures that he became "fascinated by ... his ideas and proceeded to read anything [he] could get [his] hands on that [Giddings] had written" (Topping 1980c, 5; Topping, n.d., 103). Indeed, in "Quest," Topping notes that while he was studying for his PhD, he came to regard Giddings as the man he "admired most in all the world" (1930, 312, 290). For his part, Giddings had been greatly influenced by the evolutionism of the social Darwinist Herbert Spencer (Hofstadter 1955, 157-58). However, unlike many of Spencer's devotees, Giddings came to be a reform liberal who advocated the adoption of a scientific model of sociology (Gillin 1927, 216-17, 223-25) in the belief that it would allow for the development of more rational and efficient work in the area of social service and corrections (Calhoun 2006, 9-10, 28-29). This is exactly the style of scientific/moralistic sociology Topping employed, and these are exactly the issues Topping addressed. But Giddings was not alone in holding these beliefs. They were especially central to the views of those who were advocates of the Protestant Social Gospel.

The Influence of the Social Gospel

Topping was a deeply religious man, a devout Methodist who held a doctoral degree in theology and served for many years as a clergyman. Indeed, in "Quest" he stated forthrightly that Jesus was his "first and greatest love" (n.d., 2). Given Topping's Protestant background and reformist zeal, it is likely that in his pastoral efforts he would have tried to save individual souls – to get sinners to take personal responsibility for their actions, become good Christians, and follow what he referred to as "the Jesus straight and narrow way" (CWT Fonds, vol. 2, file 3; dedication page; see also CWT to Coretta Scott King, Jan. 14, 1971, CWT Fonds, vol. 4, file 15, folder 2).[15] But likewise there can be no doubt that Topping adopted the basic elements of the Social Gospel, which, at the time, constituted the theological backbone of mainstream Protestant theology. According to the Social Gospel, the personal failings of individuals – problems such as alcoholism, prostitution, poverty, and criminality – had societal origins and could be overcome only via societal-level solutions. Thus, social gospellers took an activist political stance. It was neither necessary nor appropriate, they claimed, to wait until the afterlife to experience Heaven. If, as Christians, they took collective social responsibility for social ills and engaged in progressively oriented reform activities designed to create the conditions within which individual persons would be socialized, make good moral choices, and behave in morally sound ways, Heaven could be created here on Earth.

Curiously, Topping neither used the terminology nor cited the literature of the Social Gospel. I say *curiously* because his actions clearly indicate that he was deeply influenced by its theology. I noted above that he served on a number of United Church boards and bodies during a period when the Social Gospel was central to its philosophy (Allen 1971; Marshall 1992; Christie and Gauvreau 1996). As well, he proudly identified himself as one of the Protestant clergymen of his era who were, in his words, overwhelmingly "left of centre" in their social and political beliefs (CWT to Editor,

United Church *Observer*, Sept. 26, 1965, CWT Fonds, vol. 4, file 15, folder 1). Like his Social Gospel colleagues, he believed he had a duty to work towards the establishment of God's Kingdom here on Earth. Even in the 1970s, fifty years after he began teaching sociology at Puget Sound College, he talked about sociology's mission in exactly these terms. "The Kingdom of Heaven on Earth is both feasible and workable," he said, and requires adherence to Jesus's principle of "brotherhood" (1980c, 9). Continuing in the tradition established by his forebears in the Social Gospel movement, and reflecting Giddings's interests and concerns, Topping focused throughout his career on social problems (e.g., delinquency, crime, drugs, alcoholism, unemployment) and remained a steadfast proponent of the possibilities of social betterment via "social engineering," which is the title of Chapter 8 of "Quest." This is where, in the teachings of the Social Gospel, sociology became the church's ally and tool.

To be successful in their reformist mission, social gospellers argued it was necessary to fortify individual and collective moral will with sound scientific research. As Topping put it years later, "Has not the time arrived for basic research to take the place of propaganda ... ? Truth for truth's sake must become more than a slogan ... if we are to bring order out of chaos ... Man was born with stars in his eyes. Perhaps only basic research can keep them there" (1980c, 9-10). If human beings could engage in collective efforts that would put a man on the moon and solve the riddle of atomic power, he said, then surely they could engage in similar collective actions to solve pressing social problems such as crime (1980c, 9-10; see also CWT to Rev. N. Foster, April 5, 1978, CWT Fonds, vol. 4, file 16, folder 2). The most powerful tool they had at their disposal was science.

The Influence of Science

Sociological theory was important to Topping, and he regarded himself as a human ecologist in this regard (Topping, n.d., 114, 116, 132), but he was even more committed to data. "[The sociologist's] first question," he wrote, "must be that of the imported German scientist who was the curse of meetings at Chicago University: 'Vass ist da pruff?'" (Topping, n.d., 132). Topping stressed the same point every year in the first lecture of his Sociology of Canada course:

> We shall not begin with the complicated and controversial question, "How does God reveal himself?" ... Such questions are not for sociologists, fascinating as they are. The sociologist as a sociologist must shut and lock the

> transcendental door. He must, and has, confined his observations and comments to the phenomenal realm, as the great philosopher Emmanual [sic] Kant called it. ("The Sociology of Canada," General Introduction, CWT Fonds, vol. 3, file 3)

Many of his essays and lectures reveal the same orientation. A 1942 essay on the emergence of what he referred to as the "equalitarian family" is a good example. It opens with two pages of data regarding divorce rates before launching into a description of the reasons for the decline of the traditional family and the increase in marital breakdown (Topping 1942b). His 1953 textbook, *The Family and Modern Marriage,* and his book *Canadian Penal Institutions* were likewise based on empirical data, some gathered by Topping himself. His 1948 paper, "Predicting Success or Failure in Marriage," is even more straightforwardly empirical. It is a simple data-reporting exercise with no word of theory or interpretation uttered (Topping 1948). The early 1950s version of Topping's Sociology of Canada course likewise illustrates the point. It begins with two lectures extolling the virtues of a scientific version of sociology, drawing almost exclusively on the work of neopositivist George Lundberg. Each of the subsequent subsections of the course begins with an overview titled "The Contributions of the Scientists," a select bibliography of extant scientific literature on the topic in question. However, even more foundational to Topping's *Weltanschauung* than science was his moralism.

The Influence of Moralism: Christian and Secular

Topping, doctor of sacred theology, was above all a moral man – a Christian and a humanist, driven by what he referred to as his "Puritan conscience."[16] In the opening pages of his autobiography he justifies his life's activities in terms of an effort to be "kind and good" in a world filled with people intent on pursuing their own "self-interest" (n.d., 3). Topping believed that, unfortunately, it was part of human nature for people to be self-interested and, thus, to "exploit" one another. The tendency, he wrote, "comes as naturally as breathing." However, he also believed that such behaviour was sinful and could and should be controlled (CWT to R. Manning, Nov. 15 and Dec. 6, 1978, CWT Fonds, vol. 4, file 16, folder 2). Religion and scientific/rational enlightenment provided potential means for doing so. In fact, for Topping, the degree to which members of society collectively succeeded in controlling self-interestedness and mutual exploitation was a measure of the degree to which they could claim to have created the Good Society. In other words, the successful suppression of exploitation was, in his view, a litmus test, "an objective test for sorting bad from good" (CWT to R. Manning, Nov. 15 and Dec. 6, 1978, CWT Fonds, vol. 4, file 16, folder 2).

The notion that collective salvation could be achieved appeared in Topping's first publication, an essay in the *Wesleyan Mirror*, published 1924. There, in a discussion of the nature and prospects in "civilization," by which he meant a version of the Good Society, he draws on John Dewey to argue that "the most rational society will be that ... which recognizes, faces and most adequately organizes itself to meet the universal problems of mankind" (1980d, 3). Years later, he wrote that the first and most basic decision, the one that would set the stage for the rest of any particular society's collective efforts to create a humane society, was the collective decision to adopt Christianity. "The future of humanity is as simple as that for me ... Either we adopt Christianity or we get blown to Hell" (CWT to H.E. Fosdick [Union Theological Seminary], May 14, 1959, CWT Fonds, vol. 4, file 14, folder 2).

However, while he framed his solution to humanity's ills primarily in religious terms, he remained firm in his conviction that science had to play a complementary role. In fact, flying in the face of the dominant modern conception of the relationship between science and values, he argued that the proper application of the scientific method would allow for the identification of a definitive set of values that would make plain how society should be organized in order to maximize social rationality and justice:

> If a system of Canadian values is to be identified, isolated, described and propagandized, the total Canadian situation must be studied until it is understood ... If the total situation was clearly and fully elucidated for any specific area, then sound judgements concerning that area and a sound philosophy of the matter under consideration ... could be anticipated and predicted. *Sociology,* more than any other academic discipline, since it aims at objective analysis and synthesis of total situations, *can provide a solid groundwork for the creation of a system of values and of rational behaviour in Canada or anywhere else.* ("Sociology 430," Lecture 1: Research and Value, 2, CWT Fonds, vol. 3, file 3, emphasis added)

With respect to this strategy for identifying and acting to solve social problems, he professed the value of a balanced, "practical" outlook that involved a spirit of Christian generosity and compromise (Topping, n.d., 309). As humans, people were prone to sin, bound to make mistakes. The alcoholic, one of his favourite topics, is a good example. Topping himself was an adamant believer in prohibition and could easily have chosen to condemn alcoholics as morally weak and defective. However, rather than preach at those who drank to excess, he became a student of alcoholism and for years spoke in favour of the compassionate and scientific treatment of alcoholics (289-92).

This moral logic and a deep-seated faith in the power of science to promote the social good were basic to Topping's worldview and integral to his efforts in the field of penal reform. But he was not alone in holding such beliefs. In a less specifically religious form, this faith in the power of science wedded to a set of progressive humanistic values rested at the core of much of the social change agenda in Canada (and the West) in the early twentieth century. This where we must consider the nature and impact of the New Liberalism.

Michael Burawoy on Moving Forward While Looking Back: Science, Values, and the Historicization of Professional Sociology

In a 2005 essay, Burawoy argued that American sociology had passed through a number of phases. During the first phase, which covered the last part of the nineteenth century and the first part of the twentieth, social reformism was part and parcel of the essential impetus and *habitus* of the discipline. It was an era of "primitive public sociology," which Burawoy referred to – not disparagingly – as "charity sociology." In this iteration, science and reform were "one," joined together at the heart of the discipline (2005f, 71). During phase two, 1920 to 1960, American sociology professionalized and, with considerable (though not complete) success, "sought to secure its legitimacy as a social science" (68-69). As a part of this process, sociology all but retreated into the academy (saving the development of links to government policy work [69]), and adopted an allegedly "value-free" or "value-neutral" political stance, while simultaneously sundering its relations to the publics and political activities that had constituted its original animus and raison d'être (70). During the 1960s and '70s, it entered a third phase. Critical sociologies, often closely tied to social movements aimed at overcoming racial, ethnic, gender, class, and other forms of inequality and oppression, vigorously challenged the comfortable complacency and parochialism of mainstream professional sociology, eventually forcing it to incorporate critical perspectives and deal seriously with the argument that sociology should give up its pretensions to being/becoming a social science on the model of the natural sciences (70-71; see also Burawoy 2005b).

Since then, however, much of the ground gained in this partial victory has been lost. As Burawoy describes it, during the period since 1980 or so, mainstream professional sociologists *inside* the discipline, those who regarded the "scientizing" of sociology as a legitimate and desirable intellectual goal became increasingly assertive about – and successful at – imposing their views. They lamented the counterproductive "politicization" of the discipline that occurred in the 1960s and '70s (see Turner and Turner 1990; Coleman 1990-91; Horowitz 1993; Cole 2001) and, in recent years, in the context of the global spread of neoliberal economic and political philosophy and practices (which Burawoy refers to as the ascension to power of the "market panacea" [2005f, 71]), they became increasingly concerned about sociology's prospects. Their fears were a consequence not just of their collective desire to adhere to the canons of science but also of their concern over the personal, disciplinary, and institutional consequences of such a move. During a period when universities have been forced to turn increasingly to corporate sponsors and private donors, mainstream scholars stressed the need to "do science" and stay out of "politics." To engage in the latter, they argued, would be a regressive step; it would return the discipline to the period before it became a bona fide professional social science. The result would be disastrous. Sociology would suffer a huge loss in stature, and sources of funding for scientific research would be jeopardized (see Boyns and Fletcher 2005; Brint 2005; re: Canada, see Davies 2009).

Burawoy argues precisely the opposite. In a number of essays written since 2005, he has steadfastly urged the development of a new type of public sociology, a "mature public sociology" built on the existing "secure foundation of theory, methodology and research" developed in large part by professional sociologists during the middle decades of the twentieth century (2005f, 71, 83). This new "mature" public sociology would be animated by and infused with exactly the same concern with values, especially issues of social justice, as the "charity sociology" that originally lay at the heart of sociology, including American sociology, a century ago. To his critics, who would argue that such a strategy would pervert value freedom, one of the first principles of science, he has steadfastly replied that professional sociology is not and never has been apolitical (2005f, 78-79). This is especially the case, he says, at present. In a neoliberal era when the university and the discipline are beset by privatization, corporatization, and marketization, it is necessary to "rethink the foundations of [the] discipline," including value freedom (2005f, 71; see also 2005a, 516). He claims that it is necessary to dismiss the handwringing of those who want to retain an outmoded positivist conception of the discipline and to enter into a new disciplinary era. Indeed, he maintains that such a move is not just appropriate in these changed social and political conditions, but a "necessity" (2005f, 83). In his estimation, this new version of public sociology, one with social democratic principles at its core (2005b, 325; 2005d), could then be used as both "a defence against politicization thrust upon [the university and the discipline] from without" (2005f, 75, 76; see also 2005a, 523; 2008b, 359; 2008b) and as a crucially necessary means of engaging with oppressed publics outside the academy (2005b, 319; 2005f, 77-78). Only by such means, he says, can we help to realize what he refers to as "humanity's interest," that is, a civil society characterized by universal and truly powerful human rights capable of resisting the ravages of the "unregulated markets" and "unilateralist states" that constitute "rapacious" neoliberal capitalism (2005a, 522, 521, 524; 2005b, 319; 2005f, 77-78; 2006, 2).

And it is possible to jettison the problematic aspects of professional, scientific sociology, he argues, without compromising its strengths. For this to happen, though, sociology has to adopt a "postpositivist" model of scientific philosophy and practice, beginning with the realization that the discipline is "implicat[ed] in the world it studies" (Burawoy 2005a, 516). He expands on this argument by claiming that sociology must "provincialize positivism without losing science," one aspect of which is to "provincialize universalism without resorting to particularism" (516-17). Though American professional sociologists proceed on the assumption that the discipline must follow the model of the natural sciences, Burawoy claims that sociology lies at the intersection of the natural sciences and the humanities and, thus, cannot adopt a pure natural science model of theory and practice. One key to his argument here is the notion of provincialization. He argues that advocates of mainstream, professional sociology must come to appreciate that what they see as the only legitimate model for sociology – a natural science model – came to occupy hegemonic status in American sociology in the period 1920-60 only because of historical circumstances peculiar to the United States that no longer exist (2005f, 69, 79). Moreover, they must come to understand that in other parts of the world, particularly but not exclusively the Third World, other conceptions of the discipline that are overtly political and critical, which stress public engagement by sociologists in progressive causes, are appropriately dominant. The dominance of these conceptions is threatened only insofar as those in the First World wrongly and inappropriately try to impose professional sociology as a universal model of disciplinary philosophy and practice. The success of attempts to universalize a positivist model of the discipline were successful in the past, and are successful now, Burawoy (2005a, 516-18) says, not because the model is correct, but because those who prefer it have the financial and intellectual resources to impose it.

In the pages to follow, I conclude my essay by describing Coral Topping's efforts as an engaged public intellectual in terms of Michael Burawoy's analytic framework. Part of this discussion involves thinking about Burawoy's claim that if, one hundred years ago, sociology was less scientifically sophisticated than it now is, it was at least animated by a set of progressive, humanist values hostile to the inequalities inevitably generated by a capitalist economy.

Topping and the New Penology: Through the Lens of Burawoy's Public Sociology

For reformers like Topping, *the New Penology* was a catchphrase for a new conception of the way the community and the state should deal not just with crime but with social problems in general. Crime was simply the problem to which the term referred most directly. As a more general orientation, the New Liberalism that underpinned the New Penology referred to activities undertaken by the Protestant churches, community organizations, and, above all, the state intended to help the "underdog" (CWT to R. Bonner, March 3, 1978, CWT Fonds, vol. 4, file 16; see also Topping, n.d., 93, 203). By the "underdog," Topping and other New Liberals meant not just the juvenile delinquent or criminal, not just the prostitute (Topping, n.d., 110), the drug addict (198) or the drunk (204), but working people in general and, in particular, all those who were in some respect disadvantaged or exploited in modern, urban, industrial society.

The New Liberalism, as it came to be influential in Canada, was developed in England between 1880 and 1930 (see Allett 1981; Clarke 1978; Collini 1979; Freeden 1978). Developed further by John Maynard Keynes, it was intended as an improvement on classical liberalism, retaining the basic moral and political principles of the classic doctrine – equality, freedom, toleration, rights, universality – but reconfiguring the market and the rights of private property to minimize the inequities of wealth and power that appeared to attend the operation of the free market and the laissez-faire state. A more powerful, managerialist state would be put into place, charged with the responsibility of maximizing the collective social good via interventionist policies and practices on a whole range of issues (see Ferguson 1993; Owram 1986; Granatstein 1982).

Topping did not see himself as a protagonist of the welfare state. In fact, the opposite often appears to have been the case (Topping, n.d., 71, 93, 294). Nonetheless, his comments on issues such as unemployment, poverty (294, 320; 1980a, 12-17), the Depression (n.d., 292-93), unemployment insurance (293) and health insurance (295, 320), when considered in light of his career-long support for the Social Gospel, the Cooperative Commonwealth Federation, the New Democratic Party, and, later in life, the Trudeau Liberals, suggest that while he was a believer in self-reliant individualism, he was deeply influenced by progressive New Liberal ideas about interventionist social policies, especially as they concerned the provision of "social insurance" (Topping, n.d., 243; 1980a, 16-17). Like many Canadians who had suffered through the Depression and the Second World War, he believed that government intervention, if not overly intrusive, and if undertaken on the basis of programs and policies developed by scientifically informed experts (researchers, trained civil servants, social workers, professional counsellors, etc.), was a good thing. It could play an important role in identifying, understanding, and preventing or helping to solve societal problems. So, despite the fact that he professed to be an opponent of "Socialism or State Capitalism," and opposed "State Religion, State Education and State Medicine" on the grounds they were too expensive for the taxpayer and had not done enough to help the poor (Topping, n.d., 294), there is clear evidence in his autobiography that he held New Liberal or social democratic views on the nature and role of the state. For example, towards the end of "Quest," he outlines a nine-point plan designed to minimize unemployment and thereby reduce poverty. The means he suggests are exactly the sort of thing an interventionist New Liberal or social democrat would propose: stabilize prices with the help of a Central Bank; provide alternative jobs for the seasonally unemployed; offer retraining programs to workers displaced by technological change; bring in unemployment insurance; and develop government "make work" programs financed by loans that banks are reluctant to provide to individuals and private industry (293).

Topping's professed distrust of state capitalism (and the like) was rooted in part in a deep-seated mistrust of power holders in general. This put him in an awkward position. He was in many respects a traditionalist and supporter of the status quo. Yet, at the same time, he demonstrated clear animosity towards those he referred to as "the Establishment" and had grave doubts about the status quo they strove to preserve. It is not always clear to whom the term "the Establishment" refers in his writings, but it is safe to say that it included all those who were wealthy and powerful, especially those who used their positions of power and privilege to serve their own personal interests rather than the collective good. Rapacious business people in particular drew his scorn. Note the following from a 1961 letter in which he approvingly cites an acerbic quip about thieves penned by the Fabian socialist George Bernard Shaw: "A thief is a man who steals in ways that are not customary. He takes a loaf of bread from a baker's window and, straightaway, we run him into jail. Another steals the bread from the mouths of millions of women and children who do not understand the ways of company promoters and, straightaway, we run him into Parliament" (CWT to R. Bonner, Sept. 24, 1961, CWT Fonds, vol. 4, file 15, folder 1).

Even the organized church was not above criticism. Topping argued that it had often strayed from Jesus's teaching and set a poor example. For example, in the closing pages of his master's thesis, he wrote that "the Church was *not* the organ of the Kingdom of God." Indeed, it had often been "anything but" (Topping, n.d., 101; see also "The Church as the Organ of the Kingdom of God," CWT Fonds, vol. 3, file 4). Similarly, years later, he outlined in an approving tone a critique of the church's stance on marriage written by Judge B.B. Lindsey, one of his intellectual heroes. According to Lindsey, the moral code of the church vis-à-vis marriage was "so rigorous" that even church leaders could not obey it. Worse still, so "uncharitable and hypocritical" had been the attitudes of church people towards taboos related to marriage that the clergy had "lost that magic touch for mending wounded lives and broken homes that once was theirs by right of calling" (Topping 1953, 5).

Despite these criticisms of and misgivings about those in positions of power and privilege, Topping harboured a strong belief that positive social change was possible and that sociology would play a central role in creating it. The clearest and most extended expression of his views on the matter can be found in his 1936 article, "Sociological Research and Political Leadership," in which he argues that businessmen were interested not in the social good but in what was good for business (1936, 544). Thus, he said, they would not act in the collective interest. That task, said Topping, was reserved for "statesmen," who, in his mind, were charged with the responsibility of creating "genuine democracy" and "social justice." In trying to reach these goals, Topping argued, statesmen could and should turn to social scientists for help (544). Why? Because social scientists could see social issues and problems in terms of "fundamentals" and assess them with the "poise" and judgment provided by a sense of historical perspective that politicians typically lacked. Moreover, unlike elected officials, social scientists would not be seduced by the temptation to deal only with the "crisis" of the moment (546-47). In fact, Topping put forth some very specific proposals regarding how the statesman/social scientist relationship should be structured. Social scientists, he claimed, could and would develop a long-term research agenda under the direction of a "coordinating research bureau" that would allow them to come to grips with the "great and fundamental problems" of the time (544-45). Moreover, over time, they would be able to develop a program to train an elite of social science engineers who would work in politics and government: "A School of Applied Social Science would graduate social engineers, with, in time, as detailed specialized training as is now found in a School of Applied Science" (546; see also 1937 and CWT to H.E. Allen, May 6, 1980, CWT Fonds, vol. 4, file 16).

For over three decades, Topping worked as a "lone wolf," establishing and stewarding the sociology program at UBC while doing research on fundamental social issues and problems, criminology and penology above all. His approach, a heady but practical mixture of secular humanism and religious faith combined with a belief in the transformative power of science harnessed to the interventionist state, reflected many of the progressive views of his time. A devoutly religious man who held progressive moral and social views that he thought represented "the Jesus straight and narrow way," he was a firm believer in science and a practitioner of what Burawoy would call professional and policy sociology, in particular as they related to questions concerning Canada's penal system. Especially happy when in the limelight, he assumed the role of the social activist and public intellectual, spreading the gospel of the New Liberalism and the New Penology in any way he could. In this respect, he played dual roles as a public intellectual. Most frequently, he acted in the role of the traditional public intellectual, writing books and journal articles both popular and scholarly, penning newspaper columns, and giving public lectures to any group that would listen. At the same time, though less frequently, he served as a member of many church and community groups, donning the mantle of the organic public intellectual.

I noted above that one particularly important aspect of Burawoy's conception of a new vision of sociology, one committed to resisting the spread of neoliberalism and the market mantra, is a willingness to reject value neutrality. Topping's approach is consistent with Burawoy's approach on this score as well. As much as he was an advocate of science and social engineering, and as much as he professed an allegiance to the doctrine of value neutrality, in practice Topping eschewed it. It is no stretch to say that he regarded sociology as what Burawoy has referred to as a "value science." Topping held firmly to the conviction that he had a moral obligation as a Christian and liberal humanist to use sociology as a tool to pursue the interests of the underdog, and, throughout his career, he pressed government figures and other power holders to act in an informed, rational, humane way to better the living conditions of the underprivileged, especially those who were confined in the nation's carceral institutions. And when power holders balked, he used means both public and private (speeches, newspaper articles, membership in advocacy groups, personal letters to influential public figures) to hold their collective feet to the fire.[17] He complemented this scholarly and public advocacy work with practical, applied policy work, especially around his pet project – spreading the doctrine of the New Penology. Finally, while in many respects a traditionalist and believer in the status quo (he was no radical in the sense a Marxist would have been), he espoused what were for the time quite progressive and critical moral views on many social and political issues. Without ever uttering the phrase, he was a New Liberal, concerned to frame a new, more collectivistic and humane relationship between the individual and the state at a time when such ideas were less mainstream than they now are. He does not fit neatly into any of Burawoy's categories, then, but combines them all. It would be hard to find a better period example of Burawoy's public sociologist.

Notes

1 For brief overviews of the historical development of various forms of politically engaged sociology in French and English Canada, see Warren (2009) and Helmes-Hayes and McLaughlin (2009), respectively. The most prominent English-language Canadian sociologist to espouse a view similar to Burawoy's is John Porter, author of *The Vertical Mosaic* (1965). Porter came under the influence of the New Liberalism, a value-laden form of sociology/political economy, at the London School of Economics, where he studied with Morris Ginsberg – a follower of the influential New Liberal L.T. Hobhouse – immediately following the Second World War (Helmes-Hayes 1990, 2009, 2010).

2 For further information about these prominent figures of Canadian prison reform, see the Parole Board of Canada's "History of Parole in Canada," http://www.pbc-clcc.gc.ca/.

3 Regarding Topping's father, see "Rev. Nassau Bolton Topping, 1849-1939" and "Two Generations Back," CWT Fonds, vol. 2, file 10; and "Brief Vita: The Rev. Nassau Bolton Topping," CWT Fonds, vol. 4, file 16, folder 1.

4 Not until 1950, when the university hired Stuart Jamieson (MA, McGill; PhD, California) as a labour economist, was there another person with a sociology background (CWT to H. Hiller, March 29, 1978, CWT Fonds, vol. 4, file 16, folder 2). On the history of sociology at UBC, see Whittaker and Ames (2006) and Department of

Sociology, UBC, 2013, "A Departmental History of Sociology at UBC," available upon request from the department, www.soci.ubc.ca. After retiring from UBC in 1954, Topping signed a three-year contract to teach sociology at United College in Winnipeg (later the University of Winnipeg). There, for a third time, he became "a one-man department of sociology" (Topping, n.d., 225-30).

5 Topping's work as a member of the Vancouver Branch of the Canadian Association of Social Workers helped "form the grassroots of what was later to become the School of Social Work at the University of British Columbia" (Wilton 1973, 79-80). Regarding the founding of the UBC School of Social Work, see Bliss (n.d.), Parkinson (2008), and Topping (1980b).

6 *Canadian Penal Institutions* is only 120 pages long. Topping's PhD thesis research was much more extensive than what is reported in the published volume. Topping claims in the Foreword that the book deals with only 10 percent of his research findings (1930, ix).

7 On the development of the New Liberalism in English Canadian sociology, see Helmes-Hayes (2009 and 2010) and Helmes-Hayes and McLaughlin (2009). Very similar policies and practices were espoused at the same time by other progressive Canadian political and intellectual groups, such as the Fabians (Horn 1980).

8 The principles of the New Penology, probably most clearly realized in the Borstal system established in England in 1902 (Rose 1961, 67), had been around since the 1800s, and had been outlined in books and research reports written in Great Britain, the United States, and continental Europe, often under the influence of the International Prison Congress (Topping, 1930, 9). In Canada, the prime mover of the New Penology was the Rev. J. Dinnage Hobden, who was the founder of the Canadian John Howard Society and an influential member of the Canadian Penal Association (established 1936). Hobden was deeply involved in the establishment of the first Borstal-style institution in Canada, which was in New Haven, BC, in 1938 (Reekie 1958, 32-33). He was also instrumental in bringing the modern system of parole to Canada in 1959.

9 In 1956, Topping listed treatment measures: psychiatric assessment, the separation of young offenders from seasoned criminals, adequate treatment facilities, and opportunities for work and education ("Topping Hails Two Reports: New Penology at Its Best," *Winnipeg Free Press,* March 15, 1956, CWT Fonds, vol. 4, file 14, folder 1).

10 The question of aftercare was an especially important part of the new philosophy but one that was slow to be institutionalized in Canada. Not until 1959 was it established on a national basis. Other aspects of the aftercare program included services such as legal aid, forensic clinics, halfway houses, and so on (Topping, n.d., 203).

11 Despite the efforts of four librarians – at Waterloo, UBC, the Vancouver Public Library, and the Province of British Columbia – I could not unearth a copy of this report. The remarks in this section are thus based solely on Topping's discussion in "Quest."

12 As a part of their background research for the report, Archambault and his fellow commissioners visited several European countries, in particular England, where they consulted extensively with Alexander Paterson, who they regarded as "one of the world's foremost penologists and the outstanding authority on the 'Borstal system'" (Canada 1938, 5).

13 In 1959, following recommendations made in the Fauteux Report of 1956, the government established the Canadian National Parole Board (Canada, "History of Parole in Canada," 14-15).

14 In a comprehensive essay, "Crime," published in 1942 (the most detailed review of the literature Topping wrote), he stressed the importance of the increasingly scientific basis of the understanding and treatment of delinquency and crime, giving a prominent place in his account to Cesare Lombroso. In Topping's view, Lombroso richly deserved the title the "founder of scientific criminology" (1942a, 544). In this essay and other works, Topping claimed that it was possible to fix or cure criminality because it was learned, socially induced behaviour (581-83). That said, he sometimes suggested that criminality was rooted in biology: "Crime [has] a biological basis that the culturalists and ecologists cannot sponge out" (n.d., 306). It was not clear whether he regarded it as determined by heredity or as a possible consequence of various biological causes (body chemistry, illness, low intelligence, etc.).

15 Topping used this phrase in dedicating *Jewish Flower Child* (1970) to Henry David Thoreau, Mohandas Gandhi, and Martin Luther King, men he believed were "true followers of the Jesus straight and narrow way."

16 On the cover of the copy of "Quest" in the UBC Archives, there is a brief annotation in Topping's handwriting that reads, "damned Puritan."

17 Topping was not shy about offering unsolicited advice (and copies of his work) to prominent Canadian and American politicians and public figures. Among many others, the list includes Prime Ministers William Lyon Mackenzie King (King to CWT, March 21, 1944, CWT Fonds, vol. 4, file 13, folder 2) and Pierre Trudeau (CWT to Trudeau, March 21, 1968, CWT Fonds, vol. 4, file 15, folder 2; and CWT to Trudeau, 23 March 1977, CWT Fonds, vol. 4, file 16, folder 1), as well as Rene Levesque (CWT to Levesque, n.d. [October 1971], CWT Fonds, vol. 4, file 15, folder 2; CWT to Levesque, Nov. 21, 1976, June 27, 1977, and Sept. 14, 1977, CWT Fonds, vol. 4, file 16, folder 1), and Coretta [Scott] King (CWT to C.S. King, January 5 and 14, 1971, CWT Fonds, vol. 4, file 15, folder 2).

References

Allen, Richard. 1971. *The Social Passion*. Toronto: University of Toronto Press.

Allett, John. 1981. *New Liberalism*. Toronto: University of Toronto Press.

American Correctional Association. 1946. *Manual of Suggested Standards for a State Correctional System*. New York: American Correctional Association.

–. 1959. *Manual of Correctional Standards*. New York: American Correctional Association.

Bliss, J. N.d. "A History of the School of Social Work at the University of British Columbia, 1929-54." UBC Archives, Social Work Fonds, Box 1, General History Series 1, file 1.

Boyns, David, and Jesse Fletcher. 2005. "Reflections on Public Sociology: Public Relations, Disciplinary Identity, and the Strong Program in Professional Sociology." *American Sociologist* 36, 3: 5-26.

Brint, Steven. 2005. "Guide for the Perplexed: On Michael Burawoy's Public Sociology." *American Sociologist* 36, 3: 46-65.

Burawoy, Michael. 2004. "Public Sociologies: Contradictions, Dilemmas, and Possibilities." *Social Forces* 82, 4: 1603-18.

–. 2005a. "Conclusion: Provincializing the Social Sciences." In *The Politics of Method in the Human Sciences,* edited by George Steinmetz, 508-25. Durham, NC: Duke University Press.

–. 2005b. "The Critical Turn to Public Sociology." *Critical Sociology* 31, 3: 313-26.

–. 2005c. "2004 Presidential Address: For Public Sociology." *American Sociological Review* 70, 1: 4-28.

–. 2005d. "Rejoinder: Toward a Critical Public Sociology." *Critical Sociology* 31, 3: 379-90.

–. 2005e. "Response: Public Sociology: Populist Fad or Path to Renewal?" *British Journal of Sociology* 56, 3: 417-32.

–. 2005f. "The Return of the Repressed: Recovering the Public Face of American Sociology, One Hundred Years On." *Annals AAPSS* 600, July: 68-85.

–. 2006. "Introduction: A Public Sociology for Human Rights." In *Public Sociologies Reader,* edited by Judith Blau and Keri Iyall-Smith, 1-18. Lanham, MD: Rowman and Littlefield.

–. 2008a. "Rejoinder: For a Subaltern Global Sociology." *Current Sociology* 56, 3: 435-44.

–. 2008b. "What Is to Be Done: Theses on the Degradation of Social Existence in a Globalizing World." *Current Sociology* 56, 3: 351-59.

–. 2009. "Disciplinary Mosaic: The Case of Canadian Sociology." *Canadian Journal of Sociology* 34, 3: 869-86.

Calhoun, Craig. 2006. "Sociology in America: An Introduction." In *Sociology in America,* edited by Craig Calhoun, 1-38. Chicago: University of Chicago Press.

Canada. Parole Board of Canada. N.d. "History of Parole in Canada." http://www.pbc.clcc.gc.ca.

–. Royal Commission to Investigate the Penal System of Canada. 1938. *Royal Commission Report on the Penal System of Canada.* Ottawa: Queen's Printer.

Cellard, Andre. 2000. *Punishment, Imprisonment and Reform in Canada, from New France to the Present.* Booklet no. 60. Ottawa: Canadian Historical Association.

Christie, Nancy, and Michael Gauvreau. 1996. *A Full-Orbed Christianity.* Montreal: McGill-Queen's University Press.

Clarke, Peter. 1978. *Liberals and Social Democrats.* Cambridge: Cambridge University Press.

Cole, Stephen. 2001. *What's Wrong with Sociology?* New Brunswick, NJ: Transaction Publishers.

Coleman, James. 1990-91. "On the Self-Suppression of Academic Freedom." *Academic Questions* 4, 1: 17-22.

Collini, Stefan. 1979. *Liberalism and Sociology.* Cambridge: Cambridge University Press.

Cook, Ramsay. 1985. *The Regenerators.* Toronto: University of Toronto Press.

Darwin, Charles. 1988 [1859]. *On the Origin of Species.* London: Pickering and Chatto.

Davies, Scott. 2009. "Drifting Apart? The Institutional Dynamics Awaiting Public Sociology in Canada." *Canadian Journal of Sociology* 34, 3: 623-54.

Department of Sociology, UBC. 2013. "A Departmental History of Sociology at UBC." Available upon request from the department, www.soci.ubc.ca.

Edmison, J. Alex. 1969-70. "Perspective in Corrections." *Canadian Journal of Corrections* 12: 534-48.

Ferguson, Barry. 1993. *Remaking Liberalism*. Toronto: University of Toronto Press.

Freeden, Michael. 1978. *The New Liberalism*. Oxford: Clarendon.

Gillin, John. 1927. "Franklin Henry Giddings." In *American Masters of Social Science*, edited by Howard Odum, 189-228. New York: Henry Holt.

Granatstein, J.L. 1982. *The Ottawa Men*. Toronto: Oxford.

Helmes-Hayes, Rick. 1990. "'Hobhouse Twice Removed': John Porter and the LSE Years." *Canadian Review of Sociology and Anthropology* 27, 3: 357-89.

–. 2009. "Engaged Practical Intellectualism: John Porter and 'New Liberal' Public Sociology." *Canadian Journal of Sociology* 34, 3: 831-68.

–. 2010. *Measuring the Mosaic*. Toronto: University of Toronto Press.

Helmes-Hayes, Rick, and Neil McLaughlin. 2009. "Public Sociology in Canada: Debates, Research and Historical Context." *Canadian Journal of Sociology* 34, 3: 573-600.

Hofstadter, Richard. 1955. *Social Darwinism in American Thought*. Boston: Beacon.

Horn, Michiel. 1980. *The League for Social Reconstruction*. Toronto: University of Toronto Press.

Horowitz, Irving L. 1993. *The Decomposition of Sociology*. New York: Oxford University Press.

Marshall, Donald. 1992. *Secularizing the Faith*. Toronto: University of Toronto Press.

McKillop, A. Brian. 1994. *Matters of Mind*. Toronto: University of Toronto Press.

Owram, Doug. 1986. *Government Generation*. Toronto: University of Toronto Press.

Parkinson, G. 2008. "Recovering the Early History of Canadian Criminology: Criminology at the University of British Columbia, 1951-1959." *Canadian Journal of Criminology and Criminal Justice* 50, 5: 589-620.

Pepler, Eric, and Coral W. Topping. 1934. *Report of the Commission of Inquiry on the Provincial Industrial School for Boys: For the Honourable the Provincial Secretary of British Columbia*. N.p.

Pepler, Eric, Coral W. Topping, and E.G.B. Stevens. 1950. *Report of the Commission Appointed by the Attorney-General to Inquire into the State and Management of the Gaols of British Columbia*. Victoria: Don McDiarmid, Printer to the King's Most Excellent Majesty.

Porter, John. 1965. *The Vertical Mosaic*. Toronto: University of Toronto Press.

Reekie, I.M. 1958. "J.D." *The Rotarian* 52, 6: 32-33.

Rose, Gordon. 1961. *The Struggle for Penal Reform*. Chicago: Carswell.

Simpson, Kieran, ed. 1988. *Canadian Who's Who*. "Topping, Coral Wesley," 846. Toronto: University of Toronto Press.

Topping, Coral W. N.d. "Quest: An Autobiography." CWT Fonds, vol. 2, file 9, UBC Archives.

–. 1930. *Canadian Penal Institutions*. Chicago: University of Chicago Press.

–. 1936. "Sociological Research and Political Leadership." *Sociology and Sociological Research* 20, 6: 543-47.

–. 1937. "The Engineering Approach to the Delinquent and the Criminal." *Sociology and Social Research* 21, 4: 346-50.
–. 1942a. "Crime: Enemies in Our Midst." In *Society under Analysis,* edited by E. Pendell, 540-87. Lancaster, PA: Jacques Cattell Press.
–. 1942b. "The Equalitarian Family as a Fundamental Invention." *Canadian Journal of Economics and Political Science* 8, 4: 595-605.
–. 1948. "Predicting Success or Failure in Marriage." *Research Studies of the State College of Washington* 16, 1: 11-16.
–. 1953. *The Family and Modern Marriage.* Toronto: Ryerson.
–. 1955. "The Rise of the New Penology in British Columbia." *British Journal of Delinquency* 5, 3: 180-90.
–. 1960. *Crime and You.* Toronto: Ryerson.
–. 1970. *Jewish Flower Child.* Toronto: McClelland and Stewart.
–. 1980a. "The Conquest of Poverty." In *Blood on the Snow,* edited by Coral W. Topping, 12-17. Vancouver: College Publishers and Printers.
–. 1980b. "From Social Service to Social Work at the University of British Columbia." In *Blood on the Snow,* edited by Coral W. Topping, 26-27. Vancouver: College Publishers and Printers.
–. 1980c [1974]. "Sociology among the Social Sciences." In *Blood on the Snow,* edited by Coral W. Topping, 4-10. Vancouver: College Publishers and Printers.
–. 1980d [1924]. "Youth and Civilization." In *Blood on the Snow,* edited by Coral W. Topping, 1-3. Vancouver: College Publishers and Printers.
Turner, Stephen, and Jonathan H. Turner. 1990. *The Impossible Science: An Institutional Analysis of American Sociology.* Newbury Park, CA: Sage.
Warren, Jean-Philippe. 2009. "The Three Axes of Sociological Praxis: The Case of French Quebec." *Canadian Journal of Sociology* 34, 3: 803-29.
Whittaker, Elvi, and Michael Ames. 2006. "Anthropology and Sociology at the University of British Columbia from 1947 to the 1980s." In *Historicizing Canadian Anthropology,* edited by Julia Harrison and Regna Darnell, 157-72. Toronto: University of Toronto Press.
Wilton, Jean. 1973. *May I Talk to John Howard?* Montreal: Leclerc Institution.

PART 4

INNOVATIVE ENGAGEMENTS IN PUBLIC SCHOLARSHIP

8

Social Media and e-Public Sociology

CHRISTOPHER J. SCHNEIDER

Facebook, the world's most popular social networking website, was launched in 2004, the same year that Michael Burawoy gave his now (in)famous American Sociological Association (ASA) presidential address, "For Public Sociology." A lot has changed since. Facebook has gained hundreds of millions of users since its launch. There are now over two hundred million Twitter followers that send one billion tweets per week. It is no understatement that we are in the midst of a profound seismic shift in social reality, the collective move into cyberspace, with social media serving as the principal catalyst.

For Burawoy (2008, 354) the increased necessity for sociology is clear "in the face of third-wave marketization," the social conditions of which encourage the "privatization of everything" (Burawoy 2005a, 7) through "market tyranny and state despotism," which leads to the erosion of civil society (24). This collective process promotes, indeed encourages, according to Burawoy, the facilitation of widespread social inequalities. To counterbalance all of this, Burawoy (2008, 354) argues that an "intervention" is necessary in order for sociologists to defend "their interest in society as the interest of all." His position implies that sociologists should embrace and promote a form of value-laden sociology, a public sociology (Burawoy 2005a).

For Burawoy, public sociology is one of four ways that sociologists are able to fend for the interests of all (2004, 2005a, 2008). The other three include *policy, professional,* and *critical* sociology. One finds, however, that these four positions are not the same in terms of moral and ethical commitments, that is, those commitments that are in defence of the "interests of humanity" (Burawoy 2005a, 24). To act as a policy sociologist, for instance, "increasingly means serving the market" (Burawoy 2008, 354). Professional sociologists, on the other hand, embrace a positivistic neutral stance, a position that avoids directly confronting state-sanctioned market tyranny, for fear of upsetting the balance, in lieu of advancing one's career, all while the interests of humanity continue to erode (Burawoy 2005a, 2008). Critical sociologists both abhor and criticize these positions; however, they do so from within the confines of the ivory tower. Lastly, public sociologists serve as "interlocutors with diverse publics" (Burawoy 2008, 355), a position that embraces value commitments that are believed to represent "the interests of humanity – interest in keeping at bay both state despotism and market tyranny" (Burawoy 2005a, 24).

According to Burawoy, there are just two types of public sociology: *traditional* and *organic,* each a vehicle for generating dialogue with publics. Traditional public sociology addresses broad publics and facilitates "interest" (Burawoy 2004, 1607), through oligopolistic mass media (e.g., television, newspapers, books), media that are largely directed by market forces. Organic public sociology, on the other hand, is an unmediated interactional process where sociologists work directly with diverse publics (Burawoy 2005a). I consider herein a third type, what I call *e-public sociology,* a form of public sociology that through the use of social media merges traditional and organic forms of public sociology, allowing sociologists to become simultaneously both a generator and interlocutor of dialogue with publics. To elucidate this form, I situate my discussion of e-public sociology in terms of "our first and captive public" – students (Burawoy 2005a, 7). Hierarchical relations between students and professors complicate the practice of a public sociology in university and college classroom spaces. For instance, while the classroom might consist of a "process of mutual education" (Burawoy 2005a, 8), it always remains the professor that determines a grade; ergo, hierarchy and power relations remain omnipresent in these spaces (which is not addressed in the public sociology debate). For this reason, I frame my discussion of the possibility of an e-public sociology around the question of professionalism – namely, student-teacher relations.

Current research on social media tells us very little about the use that higher education faculty (i.e., those that teach at universities/colleges) make of these media, including in their interactions with students. Nor are there many data regarding the teaching benefits – if any – that might accrue to the use of social media. I explore below what some social science faculty members say about their use of these media in their interactions with students, consider what this might tell us about the practice of teaching, and then explore how this might relate to the development of public sociology.

Social media are a hybrid of social interaction and media. Interactions in this realm rely on user-generated content, a process that can occur in real time. Types of social media can include websites that host user-generated content, such as text, audio, or video and, of course, social networking. Social networking sites like Facebook and Twitter, at the time of this writing, remain the most commonly understood and popular forms of social media. While there is much confusion about how to understand social media, they remain widely used and discussed. Debates about the use of these media by teachers, and how their use might affect face-to-face relationships with students, remain unresolved.

In April 2011, the Ontario College of Teachers, the regulatory body for teaching in Ontario (Canada's most populous province), issued an advisory to its 230,000 members about social media. Among the recommendations, the guide suggested that teachers *not* interact with students through social media (e.g., not accept "friend requests" from students), never communicate with students from a personal email account, never text-message students, and communicate electronically with students only during normal business hours.

The following month, the Ontario College of Teachers issued a follow-up advisory suggesting that teachers immediately terminate any existing "friendships" with students on social networking websites like Facebook (Bielski 2011). Interactions between teachers and students through social media have been discouraged by other regulatory bodies in Canada, including the British Columbia Vancouver Board of Education (Bielski 2011). Many universities, including the University of British Columbia, are increasingly adopting social media guidelines for students, staff, and faculty. (At UBC, I served as part of this process myself.) Many of these guidelines, while they might not necessarily discourage use, do remind employee users (including faculty) to maintain distinct lines between personal and professional use of social media.

Colorado State University, for example, suggests that faculty members "not tag users [on Facebook] or send email invitations to non-users [on Facebook] without their consent" (Colorado State University 2012). Other universities have issued less stern suggestions. Concordia's Office of the Provost, for instance, issued an advisory in 2011 to faculty members to ensure that they "are aware of the implications involving the use of social media such as Facebook in classroom projects and pedagogy" (Concordia University 2011). While teachers are increasingly cautioned to be mindful of their use of social media involving students, and are sometimes discouraged from interacting with students in these spaces, many of these students (and other publics, including faculty) are increasing their interactions in social media spaces.

Sociologists are at a crossroads. The emergence and proliferation of social media in the past few years prompt us to reexamine our roles and commitments as sociologists and teachers. Are we obligated simply to study the impact of these media upon society, or might we also consider utilizing these media to disseminate knowledge and interact with various publics, including our students? What function do these media now play in our role as professional sociologists? Critical sociologists? Policy sociologists? Public sociologists?

In his ASA presidential address, Burawoy (2005a) outlined four types of overlapping sociologies, briefly noted above: professional, critical, policy, and public. To reiterate, professional sociology defines the discipline, from which emerged sociological concepts, theories, and methodologies. This type of sociology is rooted in value-free instrumentality anchored in positivistic science; it is sociology that seeks to discover the universal laws of the social structure. Critical sociology provides alternative frameworks to our understandings about the social world that are developed from professional sociology. Critical sociologists "target their firearms at the very possibility of scientific neutrality" (Burawoy 2008, 354) – a position that in some ways is antithetical to professional sociology. However, this form can also be instrumental (like professional sociology) as critical sociologists "wail within the walls of the academy, incomprehensible to those beyond" (355). Policy sociology provides instrumental knowledge to audiences outside of the academy, often knowledge aimed at fixing social problems. This knowledge serves market forces (Burawoy 2008). Lastly, public sociology promotes the dissemination of knowledge among multiple publics to facilitate discussion and debate among and between publics (Burawoy 2005a). Public sociologists can serve as mediated (traditional) and unmediated (organic) interlocutors among publics about matters of public importance.

Social media allow for the possibility of an omnipresent "dialogic relation between sociologist and public in which the agenda of each is brought to the table, in which each adjusts to the other" (Burawoy 2005a, 9). Sociologists might consider ways to "exploit" these media for the purposes of public sociology (Burawoy 2006, 16). Research indicates that users of social media have not engaged in "prolonged exchanges" (Thelwall and Wilkinson 2010, 393). Moreover, no research has yet explored whether sociologists use social media to bring "sociology into a conversation with publics ... who are themselves involved in conversation" – including students (Burawoy 2005a, 7).

Burawoy (2005a, 4) does not clarify what he means by "engage multiple publics in multiple ways" or specify the means by which sociologists might address publics. What Burawoy (2004, 1608) does make clear, however, is that students are "our first public," and, "[a]s teachers, we are all *potentially* public sociologists" (Burawoy 2005a, 9, emphasis added). Surprisingly, almost no research examines public sociology and teaching (DeCesare 2009), and no research has yet examined how social media connect with teaching practices and public sociology. In fact, with few exceptions, very little has been said about public sociology *and* teaching (Brady 2004; Pfohl 2004; Vaughan 2004; Bonacich 2005; DeCesare 2009; Persell 2009).

Teaching is a core component of our obligations as professional sociologists, an endeavour that for some of us constitutes the majority of our university-related commitments. Teaching is also the area in which professional sociologists receive the least formal training. Caroline Hodges Persell (2009) and others (e.g., Burawoy 2005a; DeCesare 2009) argue that teaching is in fact a form of public sociology because the practice of teaching brings sociology into conversation with "new publics" and "professional audiences" (Persell 2009, 207).[1] An element of teaching is to bring sociological expertise into conversation with various student publics, including high school students (DeCesare 2009; Persell 2009).

Social media provide sociologists with the opportunity to better facilitate, promote, and develop teaching-related commitments, including bringing sociology into conversation with various student publics within and beyond the walls of the academy. Understandably, how (or if) this could be accomplished remains an open question if sociologists are unable (or unwilling) to agree on the parameters of teaching the four forms of sociological practice (Persell 2009), including public sociology. Nevertheless, if at a minimum we accept students as "our first public," as Burawoy (2004) suggests that we should, sociologists should also then reflect upon the presence and growing importance of social media in connection with our overlapping roles as teachers *and* sociologists – and the potential for public sociology to develop in these spaces.

This chapter considers what some social science higher education faculty members say about their use of social media in their interactions with students. I explore what this might tell us more generally about the practice of teaching sociology, in particular, ways that public sociology might be developed in social media spaces, what I refer to as e-public sociology. I outline this process below. I then conclude with a short discussion on social media and the future of public sociology.

Conceptual Issues

While the terms *social networking* and *social media* are most often used interchangeably, the latter term encompasses a broader range of technologies and activities, one of which is the use of social networking sites.[2] Furthermore, survey data indicate that "virtually all higher education teaching faculty are aware of the major social media sites" (Moran, Seaman, and Tinti-Kane 2011, 3).

Research has explored the development of these technologies in education, including course design (Mason and Rennie 2008), their role in "power/knowledge relations" between students and faculty (Al-Harthi and Ginsburg 2003), and vis-à-vis faculty/student perceptions of social networking sites (Roblyer et al. 2010). Other research has considered the use of social networks for teaching students about professionalism (Cain, Scott, and Akers 2009; Ferdig et al. 2008). Yet while these studies indicate an awareness, and somewhat limited application (employment) of social media (and social networking) by faculty members, this research tells us little about how faculty members *actually* use social media in higher education.

There is very little research on faculty use of social media in higher education (see Moran, Seaman, and Tinti-Kane 2011; Roblyer et al. 2010; Tinti-Kane, Seaman, and Levy 2010). In "Social Media in Higher Education," Hester Tinti-Kane, Jeff Seaman, and Justin Levy (2010) found that nearly 100 percent (of 939 respondents) had "heard of" social networking and that 80 percent of higher education faculty had a social networking account (the authors use the term *social networking* rather than *social media*). The survey also revealed that approximately one-third reported that they used social networking to communicate with students or educators. The most reported use of social networks, both personal and teaching, consisted of watching online videos and listening to podcasts. Social network use was highest among the humanities and social sciences faculty members (Tinti-Kane, Seaman, and Levy 2010).

While research suggests that social media platforms are "reshaping publics" (boyd 2009) and "educational curricula" (McNely et al. 2010), this literature does not explain how faculty members actually use social media for these purposes. In perhaps the most detailed survey assessment to date, "Teaching, Learning and Sharing: How Today's Higher Education Faculty Use Social Media," the authors note that "faculty are big users of and believers in social media" (Moran, Seaman, and Tinti-Kane 2011, 3). However, the authors neither define social media nor specify what is meant by use of these media. While the survey does attempt to better understand personal, professional, and classroom uses of these media, it does not indicate, for instance, how or if faculty members interact with students using these media or identify ways that social media might be used to enhance pedagogy.

To reiterate, a basic shortcoming of the existent literature is that it usually says very little about how social media are understood or defined by those that use these media. Part of the problem with defining social media is that they are continually evolving. While many university policies now exist to govern faculty use of social media, few policy statements actually define these media. There are, of course, exceptions. Ball State University (2009), for instance, defines social media as "media designed to be disseminated through social interaction, created using highly accessible and scalable publishing techniques." Scalability refers to the ability to provide data to meet growing online demand. Social networking sites (e.g., LinkedIn, Twitter, Facebook, YouTube, and MySpace) are then listed as examples of social media.

In a survey of over six hundred respondents, Lon Safko and David Brake (2009) found that, when asked to define social media, 66.4 percent were unable to do so, and that the other third "lied" (Safko 2010, 4). While there appear to be problems with the data (e.g., they do not indicate how the term *social media* was defined), and with the subsequent interpretation of the data (e.g., was this survey scientific? What exactly do the authors mean by "lied"?), the data do, at the very least, provide some empirical evidence to support the claim that people are generally confused about the meaning of the term *social media.*

In *The Social Media Bible,* Safko and Brake (2009, 6) define social media as "activities, practices, and behaviors among communities of people who gather online to share information, knowledge, and opinions using conversational media." The authors continue, noting that "conversational media" includes "Web-based applications that make it possible to create and easily transmit content in the form of words, pictures, videos, and audios" (6). Conceptual issues notwithstanding, the existent research on social media tells us very little about why exactly faculty use social media, the nature of student–faculty relationships that develop through social media, and whether or not social media and social networking sites are beneficial for teaching sociology.

Data

The data to which I refer in the balance of this chapter come from a research questionnaire consisting of one descriptive question and four short response questions designed to elicit information regarding the uses that higher education faculty make of social media in their interactions with students and what this could tell us about the practice of teaching. These data also permit us to consider the development of public sociology and the idea of students as our first public in social media spaces.

After I received university research ethics board (REB) approval for the study, I posted a short questionnaire and accompanying consent form (as Microsoft Word documents) to listservs (not named herein to further ensure confidentiality) located through the American Sociological Association (ASA) webpage. A listserv is a subscription-based email list that contains the names of similar or like-minded people (e.g., sociologists), who subscribe to receive information about a topic or subject matter (e.g., race, class, gender, Marxism, etc.). With over fourteen thousand members, the ASA is by far the largest professional sociological association in North America.

In an email to those subscribed to each listserv (separate emails were sent to each listserv), I invited all social science faculty members on each selected listserv to complete the posted questionnaire and accompanying consent form. Upon completion, I requested that each respondent email these documents directly to me (i.e., not post them to the listserv for others to see) at their earliest convenience. As well, I asked them to forward my questionnaire and consent forms to other potentially interested sociology faculty members who were not subscribed to the listserv.

Seventy-five faculty members from eleven countries (Brazil, Canada, Denmark, England, Germany, Israel, Netherlands, Norway, Singapore, Switzerland, and the United States) completed and returned the questionnaire. The majority of responses came from the United States (from twenty-eight states and Washington, DC) and Canada (from four provinces). Those who submitted responses ranged from non-tenured part-time faculty members to tenured full professors; years of teaching experience ranged from one to thirty-seven. Respondents included those employed at small (9,999 and fewer students), mid-sized (10,000-19,999 students), and large (more than 20,000 students) postsecondary educational institutions.

There are a few important limitations worth noting about this sampling procedure, most importantly that the sample is not representative. However, these data are valuable, for the point of the study is to better understand what faculty use of social media can tell us about the practice of teaching, not to extrapolate from these data to make predictions about the entire sociology faculty population. Moreover, it is important to consider that those who responded may have had more experience using online technologies than, say, other less Internet-savvy faculty members (i.e., who might be less likely to have volunteered for this study).

No identifying information (e.g., faculty name or university/college name) was requested in the questionnaire. Identifying information (e.g., name) was, however, requested in the accompanying consent form. To safeguard respondent confidentiality, forms were downloaded and placed into two separate file folders. The responses from the questionnaires were sorted by question into a single document, which made it impossible to connect the responses with any individual respondent. These data were then examined for key phrases, terms, and themes consistent with use of social media to interact with students, and coded accordingly. The concept of e-public sociology emerged from my analysis of these data. Emergence, as a process, "refers to the gradual shaping of meaning through understanding and interpretation" (Altheide and Schneider 2013, 16).

Faculty Use of Social Media

The emergence, development, and expansion of social media allow for the greater possibility of bringing sociology into conversation with publics. Since there is no agreed-upon definition of *social media,* it was important *not* to define the term in the questionnaire. This would allow respondents to indicate what they understood by *social media* and to indicate the ways in which they incorporated social media into their teaching practices, that is, brought sociology to "our first public." This also provides some insight into conceptual understandings of social media.

While not directly asked to define *social media,* respondents by and large identified publicly accessible social networking sites as *social media.* Understandings about these media were typically consistent with extra-academic socializing. Nearly all the respondents reported that they did not use these media to interact with students in their courses. A full professor at a large university in Ohio reported, "I see the attraction [of social media]. I have taught online courses and do use discussion boards in my current courses, but I have not set up a social network." If a social network is understood as a set of mediated relationships, then one could readily assume a classroom discussion board to be a social network, a feature of social media. The notable distinction here concerns the use of a restricted, private (i.e., university students only) social network.

More than one-third of respondents noted a specific, publicly accessible social networking site by name (e.g., Facebook or Twitter). Others referred to private, university-endorsed educational social networks (e.g., Blackboard and WebCT); consensus as to whether these constituted social media or social networks was less clear. An assistant professor from a large university in Missouri reported, "I do not use Facebook or Myspace in my courses. I use Blackboard regularly, but I know that is not exactly social media." Similarly, an assistant professor from a large university in Illinois stated, "No, have not seen a need for it. I do use Blackboard which I don't believe would be considered social media."

Most faculty members reported that they chose not to interact directly with students in publicly accessible social media spaces; however, there were circumstances in which respondents elected to use examples drawn from social media as teaching aids, a finding consistent with survey data (Tinti-Kane, Seaman, and Levy 2010). For example, many respondents reported using YouTube, a popular video-sharing website, to illustrate course content, often from the perspective of "critical" sociology. The role of critical sociology is to establish a counterapproach to challenge dominant, professional sociological narratives, as discussed by Prentice in Chapter 5 of this volume. Selected video clips taken from social media sites enable teachers to facilitate the discussion of normative understandings about social phenomena. These exercises serve to "examine foundations – both explicit and implicit, both normative and descriptive" (Burawoy 2005a, 10). A full professor from a large university in Indiana reported, "Students appreciate videos. I ask students about the song "Born in the USA," for their thoughts on it. Then I show some video of crowds chanting the chorus, and then show Springsteen singing it. Then, we go over the lyrics, which show the song is not about how proud Springsteen is of the USA. This is part of an exercise in critical thinking." Others reported that they had students reflect in class on their use of social media and how their individual experiences with these media connected with learned sociological concepts. These "teaching moments" likely help students ponder and question normative assumptions associated with social media as social phenomena; however, whether these instances connect student publics beyond private physical and virtual classroom spaces remains uncertain.

Perhaps not surprisingly, faculty responses indicate confusion about social media around questions of interaction with students; these data reveal that faculty members prefer the use of university (private) online media when interacting with student publics. Respondents considered these media efficient enough for teaching and pedagogical purposes. Interacting with students using these media might then aid with the promotion of professional sociology, that is, what is taught in the classroom, including the incorporation of theory and methods into coursework. This form of interaction with students could also aid with the promotion of critical sociology, that is, provide a means for questioning and challenging the status quo. The development of policy sociology in this space remains limited, as does public sociology, for the simple reason that this space remains restricted to a select public; in other words, other publics are incapable of participating.

Social Media and Faculty Relations with Student Publics

If one element of teaching is bringing sociology into conversation with student publics, and private university social media accomplish this task, to what degree might faculty interact with different student publics in publicly social media spaces? Little is known about this process. Most respondents felt very uncomfortable at the thought of interacting with students in publicly accessible media spaces. One of the most commonly cited reasons was the perceived erosion of the student-teacher relationship, particularly use of the word "friend" to describe this relationship.

Friendship can constitute a great many things depending on social circumstances, but at a minimum represents a personal relation with another. Faculty members always viewed their relationships in the physical and virtual worlds with students in strictly academic (i.e., professional) terms, especially those relations with currently enrolled undergraduate students. Student-faculty relationships outside of an academic context were thought to undermine professionalism. A full professor at a large university in Nevada reported, "I avoid all 'friending' of students through Facebook as part of my general approach to keeping my student relationships professional and so outside any personal activities, including social networking." Some faculty noted very strict personal policies of not accepting "friendship" invitations from current and sometimes former students. Soliciting a "friendship" with current students was unequivocally and universally viewed as inappropriate. While less common, some faculty reported accepting "friend" requests from former undergraduate students, including those currently enrolled at their university. A lecturer at a mid-sized university in Kentucky explained, "As far as 'friending' students: I would never initiate a Facebook friendship with a student, current or past. Only if a student is NOT currently in my class I will accept a friend request from them (former students only)." More often, faculty reported establishing these connections with students once they had graduated. An instructor with twenty-two years of teaching experience from a small liberal arts university in Illinois wrote, "Initially, I responded to some student 'friend' requests on Facebook and LinkedIn, but have now stopped adding students as friends/links until they are alumni." Accepting these requests was usually limited to former students previously known to faculty, usually "favourite students" or, at a minimum, those with whom the faculty member had formed a relationship in a face-to-face context.

A clear delineation existed between undergraduate and graduate students. The decision for several faculty members to interact with undergraduate students in social media spaces often related directly to whether the faculty member had an existent professional (i.e., academic) relationship with the student. Several faculty members reported using publicly accessible mediated spaces to interact with graduate students. Many welcomed this interaction as they agreed it would be necessary in the overall interest of graduate student development. An associate professor at a mid-sized university in Washington, DC, reported, "Faculty ought to be careful of sending the wrong impression by 'friending' undergraduate students. I generally wait until such students graduate and then let them initiate. Grad students are a different beast, since they're junior colleagues; friending them is like friending any other member of the faculty." An associate professor from a large university in Georgia noted, "I do not think it is a good idea for faculty to mix personal life with student teaching life unless it is a mentoring situation with a TA/RA graduate student or research assistant." Similarly, an assistant professor from a small university in British Columbia reported,

> My personal guide for student-faculty relationships on Facebook is to not "friend" undergraduate students who are currently taking my classes. If they have graduated and they asked me to be their friend and I feel like I know them fairly well (i.e., they have taken many of my courses, they worked for me as a R.A., etc.) I would add them. If I had only had them in

> one class, I probably wouldn't. I do however add graduate students as friends. I feel that graduate students are junior colleagues and enjoy networking with them in this way. They can see what types of things I am doing (conferences, marking, paper revising, etc.) via my status updates to some extent, and perhaps have a better understanding of how things proceed in academia. I can also see if they are commenting on their own work or challenges or successes in academia and provide comments or suggestions etc.

e-Public Sociology

Burawoy (2005a, 8) notes that we are "still at a primitive stage of our project" – that is, the development of public sociology – and it seems certain that social media will feature prominently in the development of "our project." The use of social media connects the traditional and organic forms of public sociology where "the sociologist is vehicle for generating dialogue within and among publics as well as public sociology in which the sociologist is the interlocutor" (Burawoy 2006, 16). I refer to this form as e-public sociology.

In making his case for public sociology, Burawoy (2004, 2005a, 2005b) contends that sociologists should engage in more "communicative action" (Habermas 1984), a process of questioning social values through open public discussions. As teachers, are we all really "potentially public sociologists" as Burawoy (2004, 2005a) and others (e.g., DeCesare 2009) suggest? What might faculty use of social media tell us about this relation in terms of "communicative action" with students (our first public)?

While "difficult to achieve in practice" (Burawoy 2004, 1606), the type of "communicative action" depends on "the nature of the public and mode of communication" (Burawoy 2005b, 511). Burawoy (2004, 1607) suggests that "public sociology comes in many different forms" and that "we can distinguish different forms of dialogue (mediated or unmediated, unilateral, bilateral, or multilateral) and different types of publics (national and local, thin or thick, hegemonic or counter-hegemonic, active or passive)." A form of public sociology includes teaching students (Burawoy 2004, 2005a), and some of these students can become "participants in public debates they carry beyond the classroom" (Burawoy 2006, 15). Forms of dialogue can include (but are certainly not limited to) unmediated (e.g., classroom) and mediated (e.g., digital interaction). Burawoy (2005b, 2006), nevertheless, limits his various discussions of use of media for public sociology to oligopolistic (i.e., mainstream) mass media, even noting that a "most obvious" obstacle to public sociology concerns the "commodification of communication, especially the media, not just in terms of who runs them but also in terms of their mode and structure of transmission" (Burawoy 2008, 359).

The potential of social media (which is freely available to many students and faculty) to bring sociology from the private sphere out into the open is unsurpassed by that of any other medium. However, rather than presume, as Burawoy (2005a, 8) does, that at the best of times "traditional public sociology frames organic public sociology," we should instead begin to consider the ways that social media might connect and direct these two public sociologies into a singular space where the academic and extra-academic collide, a place that presents new possibilities for public sociology. Social media bridge the two genres of public sociology, advancing a new component, one that consists simultaneously of both organic and traditional elements of public sociology, or e-public sociology.

Let us briefly reconsider the two components of public sociology, traditional and organic (Burawoy 2005a). Traditional public sociology can consist of books, newspaper articles, and other publicly accessible statements designed to "set a new agenda for the discussion of public issues" and written for "a wide lay audience" (Burawoy 2005c, 71). These statements are most often made via one-way directed forms of media where public interaction tends to be very limited. Using social media – for example, publishing an online blog – these statements can be immediately made available to publics worldwide. Organic public sociology, on the other hand, relies almost exclusively on direct interaction with publics (Burawoy 2005a, 7-8). This type of public sociology facilitates an open dialogue with publics. Using social media, publics can respond (i.e., post comments) to faculty statements (i.e., blogs), and faculty can then respond to these comments, a process that enables faculty to facilitate, engage, and *interact* in (online) dialogues open to publics around the world, whenever and wherever, often in real time. Social media consist of a hybrid of traditional and organic forms of public sociology, a form of social media interaction among publics that can be either public or private.

Social media provide opportunities for sociologists to be public sociologists, bringing sociology into conversation with student and other publics beyond the walls of the academy. Few faculty members, according to the data herein, seem eager to utilize these media for such purposes, especially with student publics. While understandings of and about social media varied among faculty respondents, faculty shared a common view that it was important to maintain a clear separation between private and public social media spaces. Private relations with groups of undergraduate student publics, for instance, were widely considered acceptable and conducive to learning, whereas private relations with these same students in public social media spaces were not acceptable.

Faculty use of social media reveals a merging of professional and critical sociologies. On the one hand, social media are used as an extension of classroom interaction to teach theory and methods, the two cornerstones of professional sociology. On the other hand, while theory and methods are equally important components of critical sociology, examples taken from social media sites are used more often to teach elements consistent with critical sociology (rather than to interact). Using publicly accessible media to engage students in public spaces among respondents was reserved strictly for graduate student development, a public that serves to maintain the professional sociology labour force.

Despite its potential, the use of social media to connect with student publics further confines sociology within university spaces (physical and digital) where norms of professional sociology are upheld. Interacting with student publics in public media spaces has the potential to bring professional sociologists into contact with a vast array of publics that are not directly involved in academia without necessarily compromising the integrity of scholarly materials. In addition to bringing concepts, ideas, and sociological knowledge to others, publics could, among other things, develop an informed understanding about the kinds of academic and political pursuits that interest professional sociologists.

While student publics are among a diverse range of publics, they are arguably our most important public for the simple reason that they create the conditions necessary for our existence as professional sociologists. Do the foreseeable risks of interacting with student publics in public media spaces outweigh the benefits of not doing so? Concerns associated with a perceived loss of professionalism, which might compromise faculty authority over students do little to promote sociology among publics. While faculty engage with students in social mediated spaces, they do so almost exclusively in private, confined spaces, such as the classroom and private social media extensions of the classroom. What should it mean, then, that students are "our first public" if sociologists also tend to engage this public in private spaces beyond the academy? Faculty use of social media indicates that we should reconsider the circumstances in which teaching might (or might not) serve as a form of public sociology.

Concluding Thoughts and the Future of Public Sociology

Faculty members use social media to connect with student publics on a restricted basis. Interactions with undergraduate students using these media are usually reserved for private (restricted from the public) university web boards. In some ways, the use of these media is beneficial for teaching and mentoring purposes, especially graduate student mentorship, but remains somewhat limited for practices consistent with public sociology.

While social media evolve and new social networks emerge as old ones become less relevant, it is probably safe to assume that social media are not going away. The opportunity for sociologists to engage in open and accessible dialogues with students is greatly enhanced by various social media platforms, notably those that allow and encourage interaction – that is, social media that consist of both organic and traditional components of public sociology, or what I call e-public sociology.

Interacting with students in publicly mediated spaces beyond private university spaces propels sociological dialogue into the public realm. While we cannot be empirically certain at this point, we can speculate that these interactions may also encourage nonstudent publics to contribute to the dialogue, thereby further validating the legitimization of sociology in public spaces. Future research might explore this matter. The unwillingness to engage with undergraduate student publics in these mediated spaces is not necessarily conducive to bringing sociological knowledge to wider extra-academic audiences. This is not to suggest that all hope is lost for the future of e-public sociology.

For instance, using publicly accessible social media spaces might serve as good places to host a sociology club or promote other similar campus-related events and activities. This would allow student publics to congregate in designated social media spaces reserved for conversation more in line with academic dialogue. Making such spaces accessible to other non-student publics might serve as a way to remedy some of the shortcomings (i.e., loss of privacy, professionalism, etc.) associated with extra-academic interaction with student publics in public social media spaces.

While the response was less common, some faculty did report that they had considered setting up such spaces for current students. An assistant professor at a large university in Missouri reported, "I suppose I would not be against setting up a Facebook page specifically for a class, student organization, or project." Additional and unnecessary time constraints were a consistent theme associated with such responses. The concern is that using social media to interact with student publics would be more time-consuming in lieu of other more important university-related commitments, such as research, teaching, and service.

As universities continue to increase their presence on social media sites, the incentives for individual faculty members to do so remains unclear. Faculty use of social media to interact with students and other publics does not factor very much (if at all) into consideration for tenure and promotion. This lack of recognition makes it especially unlikely that pre-tenured faculty will "indulge the commitment to public sociology from the beginning and that way ignite the torch of professional sociology" (Burawoy 2005a, 15). It also remains to be seen if an increased faculty presence on social media sites might then "emerge as a new form of tracking [surveillance, particularly for promotion and tenure consideration] within the discipline" (Collins 2007, 103).

Interacting in publicly accessible social media spaces with students and other publics that consist of both organic and traditional components of public sociology was not reported as a common practice. Use of publicly mediated spaces was more in line with traditional forms of public sociology. Audio and video recording of classroom lectures, for instance, posted online (e.g., iTunes U or YouTube) for publics puts sociological knowledge "out there" for public consumption. While public users might offer comment via online postings in these spaces, this does not constitute a truly "dialogic relation between sociologist and public" (Burawoy 2005a, 9). Few reported using popular social media site Twitter as a one-directional publication platform for this purpose – that is, to avoid dialogic relations. This form of (traditional) mediated public sociology allows faculty members to maintain a professional distance from publics, a position arguably antithetical to the public sociology mandate.

The use made of social media by some faculty members to connect with student publics, even if limited, nevertheless suggests that faculty members are not completely opposed to the idea of student-faculty interaction in these spaces, especially for general teaching purposes and mentoring graduate students. In this regard, a full professor at a large university in Nevada noted, "I think we're in a position of figuring out the answer to this question." Developing new ways to utilize public spaces provided by social media to interact with multiple publics, students among them, remains a part of the continuing debate in the public sociology research literature.

Hierarchical relations between faculty and students complicate the practice of e-public sociology with "our first publics." This chapter contributes to better understanding this process. While these relations may be beneficial for some teaching purposes, such interactions with students in extra-academic settings appear to threaten professionalism associated with value neutrality (i.e., students are not our "friends"). Therefore, as teachers, the "potential" (Burawoy 2005a, 9) for public sociology in classroom spaces remains limited. The hierarchical relations between faculty and students are preserved and maintained through the very practice of professionalism, and extra-academic interactions undermine professional sociology. The practice of e-public sociology in the professional setting, then, is not entirely conducive to Burawoy's (2005a, 16) version of public sociology, one that "understands politics as democratic dialogue." The extent to which our students remain "our" publics in extra-academic spaces is debatable. Future work should explore this relation. Future research might also further explore the use of e-public sociology through the other three forms of sociological practice: critical, policy, and public. Other research might address the relation of e-public sociology to strong publics that might include what Marc Prensky (2001) calls "digital natives," a reference to students that are "native speakers" of a digital language, and weak publics such as those "digital immigrants" that include others "not born into the digital world." The "challenge" of public sociology as Burawoy (2005a, 4) tells us "is to engage multiple publics in multiple ways," and additional work is necessarily to understand (and answer) this challenge by further exploring developments in public sociology in relation to multiple online publics. Considering the prominence of social media, the future of "our project" may very well depend on it.

Acknowledgments

I gratefully acknowledge Rick Helmes-Hayes, Ariane Hanemaayer, and Jessica Stites Mor for their very helpful suggestions on earlier versions of this chapter.

Notes

1 For a discussion of ways to engage with new publics and new audiences in multimodal ways, see Vannini and Milne, this volume.

2 For a contextual and historical overview of social networking, see boyd and Ellison (2007).

References

Al-Harthi, Hamood, and Mark B. Ginsburg. 2003. "Student-Faculty Power/Knowledge Relations: The Implications of the Internet in the College of Education, Sultan Qaboos University." *Current Issues in Comparative Education* 6, 1: 5-16.

Altheide, David L., and Christopher J. Schneider. 2013. *Qualitative Media Analysis.* 2nd ed. Thousand Oaks, CA: Sage.

Ball State University. 2009. "Social Media Policy." 17 November. http://cms.bsu.edu/-/media/WWW/DepartmentalContent/UMC/pdfs/BallState_SocialMediaPolicy.pdf.

Bielski, Zosia. 2011. "Sorry, Kids: I Can't Be Your Friend; Teachers Must Be Extra-cautious Online. Friending Students on Facebook Is a No-no. So Is Venting about Them in a Blog or Answering Their E-mails from Home." *Globe and Mail,* 29 April, L1.

Bonacich, Edna. 2005. "Working with the Labor Movement: A Personal Journey in Organic Public Sociology." *American Sociologist* 36: 105-20.

boyd, danah m. 2009. "Social Media Is Here to Stay. Now What?" *Microsoft Research Tech Fest,* 26 February. Redmond, WA. http://www.danah.org/.

boyd, danah m., and Nicole B. Ellison. 2007. "Social Network Sites: Definition, History, and Scholarship." *Journal of Computer-Mediated Communication* 13, 1: 210-30.

Burawoy, Michael. 2004. "Public Sociologies: Contradictions, Dilemmas, and Possibilities." *Social Forces* 82: 1603-18.

–. 2005a. "2004 Presidential Address: For Public Sociology." *American Sociological Review* 70, 1: 4-28.

–. 2005b. "Conclusion: Provincializing the Social Sciences." In *The Politics of Method in the Human Sciences,* edited by George Steinmetz, 508-25. Durham, NC: Duke University Press.

–. 2005c. "The Return of the Repressed: Recovering the Public Face of American Sociology, One Hundred Years On," *Annals AAPSS* 600 July: 68-85.

–. 2006. "A Public Sociology for Human Rights." In *Public Sociologies Reader,* edited by Judith Blau and Keri E. Iyall Smith, 1-18. Lanham, MD: Rowman and Littlefield.

–. 2008. "What Is to Be Done: Theses on the Degradation of Social Existence in a Globalizing World." *Current Sociology* 56, 3: 351-59.

Brady, David. 2004. "Why Public Sociology May Fail." *Social Forces* 82: 1629-38.

Cain, Jeff, Doneka R. Scott, and Paige Akers. 2009. "Pharmacy Students' Facebook Activity and Opinions Regarding Accountability and E-Professionalism." *American Journal of Pharmaceutical Education* 73, 6: article 104. http://www.ncbi.nlm.nih.gov/.

Collins, Patricia Hill. 2007. "Going Public: Doing the Sociology That Had No Name." In *Public Sociology: Fifteen Eminent Sociologists Debate Politics and the Profession in the Twenty-First Century,* edited by Dan Clawson, Robert Zussman, Joya Misra, Naomi Gerstel, Randall Stokes, Douglas L. Anderton, and Michael Burawoy, 101-13. Berkeley: University of California Press.

Colorado State University. 2012. "Social Media, Best Practices." 3 March. http://www.socialmedia.colostate.edu/page/Facebook-best-practices.aspx.

Concordia University. 2011. "Classroom Social Media Policy Developed." 11 January. http://www.concordia.ca/now/university-affairs/governance/20110117/classroom-social-mediapolicy-developed.php.

DeCesare, Michael. 2007. "Presenting Sociology's Four 'Faces': Problems and Prospects for the High School Course." In *Handbook of Public Sociology,* edited by Vincent Jeffries, 187-204. Lanham, MD: Rowman and Littlefield.

Ferdig, Richard E., Kara Dawson, Erik W. Black, Nicole M. Paradise Black, and Lindsay A. Thomson. 2008. "Medal Students' and Residents' Use of Online Social Networking Tools: Implications for Teaching Professionalism in Medical Education." *First Monday* 13, 9, http://firstmonday.org/article/view/2161/2026.

Habermas, Jurgen. 1984. *The Theory of Communicative Action.* 2 vols. Boston: Beacon.

Mason, Robin, and Frank Rennie. 2008. *E-Learning and Social Networking Handbook: Resources for Higher Education.* New York: Routledge.

McNely, Brian J., Christa B. Teston, Garret Cox, Bolutife Olorunda, and Noah Dunker. 2010. "Digital Publics and Participatory Education." *Digital Culture and Education* 2, 2: 144-64.

Moran, Mike, Jeff Seaman, and Hester Tinti-Kane. 2011. "Teaching, Learning and Sharing: How Today's Higher Education Faculty Use Social Media." *Pearson Learning Solutions and Babson Survey Research Group.* Boston, MA: Pearson Learning Solutions. http://www.pearsonlearningsolutions.com/educators/pearson-social-media-survey-2011-bw.pdf.

Persell, Caroline Hodges. 2009. "Teaching and Public Sociology." In *Handbook of Public Sociology,* edited by Vincent Jeffries, 205-24. Lanham, MD: Rowman and Littlefield.

Pfohl, Stephen. 2004. "Blessings and Curses in the Sociology Classroom." *Social Problems* 51: 113-15.

Prensky, Mark. 2001. *Digital Natives, Digital Immigrants.* http://www.marcprensky.com/writing/.

Roblyer, M.D., Michelle McDaniel, Marsena Webb, and James Herman. 2010. "Findings on Facebook in Higher Education: A Comparison of College Faculty and Student Uses and Perceptions of Social Networking Sites." *The Internet and Higher Education* 13, 3: 134-40.

Safko, Lon. 2010. *The Social Media Bible: Tactics, Tools, and Strategies for Business Success.* 2nd ed. Hoboken, NJ: Wiley and Sons.

Safko, Lon, and David K. Brake. 2009. *The Social Media Bible: Tactics, Tools, and Strategies for Business Success.* Hoboken, NJ: Wiley and Sons.

Thelwall, Mike, and David Wilkinson. 2010. "Public Dialogs in Social Network Sites: What Is Their Purpose?" *Journal of the American Society for Information Science and Technology* 61, 2: 392-404.

Tinti-Kane, Hester, Jeff Seaman, and Justin Levy. 2010. Social Media in Higher Education: The Survey. *Pearson Learning Solutions and Babson Survey Research Group.* Boston, MA: Pearson. http://www.babson.edu/Academics/Documents/babson-survey-research-group/social-media-in-higher-education.pdf.

Vaughan, Diane. 2004. "Public Sociologists by Accident." *Social Problems* 51: 115-18.

Public Ethnography as Public Engagement

Multimodal Pedagogies for Innovative Learning

PHILLIP VANNINI and LAURA MILNE

As part of a global popular advertising campaign plastered in more of the world's airports than we have been able to count, financial giant HSBC tells us that our planet is full of untapped resources and investment possibilities. In one particular ad, we are told that there are more people learning English in China today than there are native English speakers in the whole United Kingdom. We see potential of a related kind: there are arguably more students learning the language of the social sciences today than there are journalists, documentarians, think-thank researchers, and policy pundits combined. That is not all. There are probably more professional researchers writing scholarly monographs and articles on social issues than there are authors penning trade books and paperbacks on the same subjects. Yet neither social science students nor professional social scientists are particularly apt at speaking the language of the many publics they study and at speaking louder and more clearly than their better known, pop counterparts. We view this as a missed opportunity for the social sciences. Without wanting to sound too "entrepreneurial," we indeed view this as a great "investment opportunity" for the new public scholarship of the future.

Public audiences have a great deal to gain from the critical messages contained in social scientific research, as eminent public sociologists such as Michael Burawoy (2005) have articulated. Indeed, a more public scholarship is the key to a more advanced democratic society (while others disagree, see van den Berg, this volume). So, how can social scientists – learners and scholars alike – make their voices heard? How can students and academics work together to popularize their work? What opportunities for the public to learn from social scientific research are made possible by different ways of communicating knowledge? We argue that one of the ways in which social scientific research can play a greater role in public discourse and in shaping the popular imagination is by taking inspiration from some of the qualities of an important social scientific tradition: ethnography. Ethnography, we believe, is potentially endowed with rhetorical and substantive characteristics that are of great appeal to the general public. When carried out with the information and entertainment needs and wants of the public in mind, ethnographic research can reach beyond the confines of academic discourse and can position social scientific knowledge at the nexus of public debate, current affairs, and popular culture. Through a fully public ethnography, social scientific research can better engage multiple stakeholders and play a key role in the critical pedagogy of the general public. But, for that to happen, social scientists must first learn to understand the grammar of twenty-first-century public ethnography. They must recognize the importance of student involvement and collaboration and the pedagogical affordances of multimodal communication languages and technologies.

We believe that multimodality is not an option for ethnography but a necessity. To be sure, writing is an effective mode for communicating with specialists. Writing and its typical academic media – for example, the journal article and the book – allow for technical information to be conveyed in great depth and terminological sophistication. But writing journal articles and books alone is not an effective strategy for reaching a wider audience. Traditional mass media, such as magazines, radio, newspapers, and television, as well as new media, such as the Internet and mobile communication devices, provide the general public with information that is more aesthetically captivating, less time-consuming, cheaper, more accessible, and more user-friendly than typical academic media. The result is that it is much more convenient for Joe Citizen to watch a documentary on Netflix, Vimeo, or cable TV than it is to spend an hour poring over an article downloaded from JSTOR (provided he, somehow, had access to JSTOR or a similar database). If academics want their research to be relevant and to have an impact on society and culture, then they need to learn to compete with other sources of information and employ more effective communication strategies. Thus, they need to learn to offer more than simply unimodal products such as writings. Because of its deep immersion in lifeworlds, ethnography is particularly well positioned to communicate multimodally and it behooves us do so (see Pink 2009).

By *ethnography* we mean the in-depth study of people's ways of life, of cultures. There are many different kinds of ethnography, but in its most basic terms ethnography is research focused on describing and understanding social life from the perspective of the people who take part in it. All ethnographic research is potentially public in nature, but this potential is rarely exploited. As we explain later, this potential arises from the ways of knowing typical of ethnography, its tropes, and its typical contents. This potential is seldom exploited in full, however, for a variety of reasons. Public ethnography is ethnographic research that fully exploits this potential. We begin our chapter by introducing the field of public ethnography. We situate public ethnography in a broader paradigmatic shift in ethnography towards reflexive, sensuous, interpretive, narrative, arts-informed, and more-than-representational qualitative research (Vannini, n.d.). Subsequently, we anchor our view of public ethnography in the technological currency of the times. That is, rather than in an exclusively print-based world, we believe that public ethnography can thrive in a public domain inspired and informed by diverse popular media, genres, and communication modes. We then shift our attention to pedagogy by outlining possibilities for collaboration between professional scholars and students. The students' role in scholarly research is often limited to dirty work. But in a rapidly evolving technological context in which students' communication skills are often superior to – or at the very least different from – those of scholars, academic learning and research can offer new opportunities for collaboration. We conclude with a brief reflection on institutional support and by referencing resources for the interested reader. We argue that universities can facilitate the growth of public scholarship by promoting transdisciplinary collaboration, applied research, innovative pedagogies, and community-based criteria of scholarship relevance. As a co-authoring team composed of an academic and a student with professional expertise in the field of knowledge mobilization and community-based research, we hope that our diverse experiences, visions, and reflections presented in this chapter will hold value for university faculty, administrators, and learners, as well as the multiple audiences outside of academia that stand to gain from an innovative approach to research production, distribution, and consumption.

Public Ethnography

Throughout the first decade of the twenty-first century, several social sciences, including sociology, have experienced various pulls and pushes for more publicly engaged forms of scholarship. Sociologists have debated at great lengths the merits and perils of a different social function for their discipline and found numerous reasons to disagree with each other.[1] Ultimately, we find that most of these differing viewpoints can be traced back to the competing differing epistemologies – such as positivist, humanistic, and critical – that, for so long, have fragmented the discipline. Other social scientific fields and disciplines have responded to calls for public scholarship in different ways. Human geography, for example, has been much less divided over its public role. As several commentators have noted, geographers have much to gain and very little to lose by playing a greater role in public discourse (Castree et al. 2008; Davis and Dwyer 2008; Fuller 2008; Fuller and Askins 2010; Murphy et al. 2008; Ward 2006, 2007, 2008). Dissent from this view, indeed, has been minimal. To be sure, the discipline of human geography is in a unique position due to the enormous influence of the "cultural turn" amongst its practitioners.[2] Amongst other dynamics, the cultural turn has influenced the subject matter of human geography's research agendas, research methodologies, and dissemination strategies – freeing human geography of many of the anxieties caused by traditional value-free research (for an example and broader formulation of these ideas, see Dear et al. 2011). Also thanks in large part to the diffusion of more-than-representational theoretical ideas, human geographers are now at the forefront of methodological experimentation, collaboration with the arts and humanities, and theoretical innovation.

Cultural anthropology enjoys a similar state of affairs. Due in large part to the historical acceptance and traditional relevance of general audiences-friendly approaches such as visual ethnography – with a foot firmly planted in the academic realm and a foot planted in the documentary film tradition, or the type of photographic documentary coverage made popular by wide distribution magazines such as *National Geographic* – cultural anthropologists are potentially well equipped to play a visible public role (Borofsky 2000; Lamphere 2004; McClancy and McDonaugh 1996; Purcell 2000; Scheper-Hughes 2009). Indeed, pronouncements on the importance of a public anthropology have been met with little or no resistance, and wherever resistance has been manifested, it has centred more on the identity of public anthropology than around its inherent value.[3] So, in short, the degree of acrimonious debate over the worth of public scholarship that has taken place within sociology seems to be less of a norm and more of an exception to the generally positive recognition of the value of a public scholarship. Sociology's internecine struggles between quantitative and qualitative research are unknown in anthropology and a thing of the past in human geography. To appreciate the potential of public social scientific research, therefore, one has to learn from pandisciplinary trends and circumstances. This is why, unlike many other contributors to this volume, we do not even pose ourselves the normative question of whether we should do it. In fact, we are already doing it (see Vannini 2011, 2012). And it is from this practical – not normative – and postdisciplinary point of view that we begin with our treatment of public ethnography.

Ethnographers work differently from most other researchers by virtue of key qualities of their research, such as its ability to portray people, places, and times in vividly descriptive detail, and its emphasis on the researcher's immediate and direct involvement with, participation in, and experience of the lifeworld object of study. These qualities are typical of all ethnographic research, but recent trends in ethnographic forms of representation have further honed these qualities, emphasizing the narrative, sensuous, embodied, participatory, confessional, impressionistic, and interpretive value of some of the more arts-inspired ethnographic genres (see Knowles and Cole 2008). By *public ethnography,* therefore, we mean here a type of ethnographic research that – not unlike conceptual art – imaginatively enlivens and animates lifeworlds, evoking cultural dynamics that creatively render the strange familiar, and the familiar strange, for the purpose of better capturing the attention of wider audiences.

Ethnography is a simple and intuitive way of knowing. Many in the general public recognize it as an established way of doing empirical social scientific work. Joe and Jane Average may not be able to define ethnography, and may even never have heard the word before, but the idea of a researcher becoming immersed in a community to learn the ways of life of its members is a powerfully captivating and broadly understood idea. As Herbert Gans (2010) has outlined, all of ethnographic research is potentially in a unique position to command the attention of the general public. Ethnographic description and tropes resemble those of the novel. Ethnographic portraits of cultures, people, times, and places speak to the general public's predilection for intimate, personable, context-bound, curiosity-evoking renditions of life. Ethnography's anchoring in everyday life dialogues and interactions is also liable to make sense to a public that may otherwise be baffled by the abstruse conventions of laboratory experiments or the jargon of discourse analysis. And ethnography's tackling of contemporary topics speaks well to public needs for in-depth coverage of current affairs as they affect them and their local communities. In short, ethnography's treatment of culture and places would seem to resonate well, at least potentially, with audiences broader than academic ones.

Ethnography has enjoyed good recognition in sociology, anthropology, and geography – there should be no mistake about it. But in sociology – more than in anthropology and human geography – ethnography has suffered from a somewhat contested status. Sociology's dominant nomothetic and realist epistemologies have often translated in the underprivileging of the ethnographic tradition, which has more or less therefore remained castigated in a minority position. From such a position, sociological ethnographers have had to fight hard to defend their legitimacy. These struggles have yielded various kinds of ethnographic techniques, procedures, and stratagems that have often lent sociological ethnography a certain aura of "scientificness." Triangulation, various kinds of checks, grounded theorizations, anonymous and formal representations, and the like have often made ethnographic research more similar, rhetorically, to the hypothesis-testing flavour of its positivist and postpositivist counterpart than to more captivating travelogues and novels (see Adler and Adler 2008). As a result, despite its potential to attract the attention of the reading public, sociological ethnography has not fully realized its promise and has had only mixed success at the bookstore (as any cursory look at the shelves of popular bookstores, or bestseller lists, will attest, ethnographies are not very likely to be "hot" items). Because of the broad relevance of sociology as a discipline to the rest of the social sciences, sociological tendencies in ethnographic methodology have become relatively widespread. So, because of the science wars happening in sociology, ethnography as a whole has often felt uncomfortable in its own skin and has often missed opportunities to play a greater public role.

Today, more and more advocates of a fully – that is, more self-secure – public ethnography, however, are stepping forward (see Tedlock 2005 and the examples cited therein). For example, within sociology, Gans (2010, 98) has argued that public ethnography appeals to the public "more effectively than other ways of doing sociology at least when it reports on topics and sites of general interest." Not only does ethnography make for a better read than most research, according to Gans (99), but it also brings out some of the best virtues of social scientific research, as it is "about the lives and problems of ordinary people, and because it obtains much of its data directly from such people." For Gans, ethnography *has to* be relevant and accepted by the general public. Carefully chosen topics, timely coverage, accessible writing (which often translates into research that is less theory-driven), and the ability to speak to issues that the public deeply cares about can make public ethnography more relevant and attention-demanding than what can be found in the news. Indeed, what he calls public ethnography can offer more depth than news and documentary journalism. Its in-depth treatment of issues can aid in explanation and understanding, which journalism often has neither the means nor the interest to provide. Similarly, Vaughan (2005) and Becker and colleagues (2004) have argued that public ethnography can capture the attention not only of the reading public but also of policy makers.[4]

The communication strategies of public ethnography have similarly been the subject of reflection within public anthropology. For example, in a recent collection by Waterston and Vesperi (2009), several ethnographers reflect on the tactics they needed to make their writing more engaging and broaden their audiences. For Scheper-Hughes (2009), making ethnographic work more accessible and accountable requires pleasant writing as well as collaboration with journalists and the popular media. Thus, whereas for Gans journalists and authors of trade books represent a form of competition to both learn and take distance from, for Scheper-Hughes (2009, 1) the news world is potentially an ally characterized by "thoughtfulness, thoroughness, dedication to accuracy, and ... ethical and political sensibilities." While she recognizes some of the dangers at stake in playing a public role, rather than "contaminating" oneself by meddling with journalists and the masses, a public ethnographer has much to gain from making one's research public.

In sum, ethnography writ large has traditionally been – at least potentially – in a unique position to command the audience of the general public. Because of insecurities fuelled by academic diatribes, however, not many ethnographers have taken advantage of the potential of their work to enter public discourse. But as calls for public scholarship and public ethnography continue to mount, and as trends especially within cultural anthropology and human geography continue to pull ethnographic research farther away from some of its positivist tendencies, more ethnographers find themselves better actualizing the potential of their work by writing in more appealing styles and by engaging in public discourse together with journalists and popular media. The next step for the growth of this public ethnography as a form of public scholarship, we argue, is to take advantage of the continuing changes in the acceptance of multimodality, as well as the expanding possibilities for producing and distributing appealing and wide-reaching multimodal research.

Multimodal Ethnography

Traditional ethnographies are unimodal. That is, they are communication products that make use of only one mode of communication: writing. In simple words, modes are the ways in which people, objects, or animals communicate. Speech is a mode of communication, for example. Gesturing and singing are other modes. Modes are not synonymous with media. Media are the channels that carry our communication modes. For instance, a book, which is a particular medium, can carry writing, but so can other media, such as a newspaper, a website, a peer-reviewed journal, and so on. There is nothing wrong with unimodal communication; indeed, it has served rather well the intent of communicating complex and abstract ideas clearly. Unimodality, however, is only one option for communicating. There are other valuable options, such as bimodality and trimodality. There are, in other words, possibilities to combine ethnographic writing with other modes (Dicks, Soyinka, and Coffey 2006). As more communication technologies become cheaper and user-friendly, these options demand we take them into serious consideration. We are not suggesting that ethnographers abandon writing or that they take on other modes of communication simply because they are available. But we believe that multimodal communication can serve the aims of public ethnography effectively. Thus, whenever it makes sense for it to be so, we argue that public ethnography ought to be multimodal.

Multimodal ethnography can be many things. Visual ethnography, for example, can be a combination of writing and photography (see Pink 2009). Such has been the most typical multimodal research expression in the social sciences. But other multimodal possibilities exist. Writing, for instance, can be combined with video. In this case, an ethnographer can write a paper and produce a film that can be distributed through a website. By doing so a researcher can easily satisfy both career imperatives (which often demand that research be written and published in a peer-reviewed printed journal) and calls for public engagement (for example, by uploading one's video on a popular website like YouTube or Vimeo). Indeed, even a photography-based ethnography can be shared in similar ways: with a paper ending up in a journal and photography being distributed through a website like Flickr, or better yet, a personal photoblog. Since print journals often severely restrict the number of publishable photos, and since they can only reproduce them in black and white, publishing them independently on a website makes sense. Of course, the need to publish photos or a video separately from a written article ceases to exist when a journal is published on the web. In those cases, whether a journal is published in HTML or in a PDF version, photos and video can be embedded directly into one's writing.

While photography needs writing to convey a more thorough message, video is immediately multimodal when it conveys multiple forms of communication such as speech, gesture, movement, other sounds, and so on. Since ethnography is intended to convey sensations of a lifeworld, video can do so quite efficiently, as Sarah Pink (2009) outlines in her methodological reflections on the possibilities and techniques of sensory ethnography. Think about how many words it can take to describe an object, or a person's facial expression, or a place, and compare that with the number of seconds it can take video to convey the same thing. But video's role in ethnographic research is not just to allow ethnographers to accommodate for larger quantities of their thick descriptions to be shared, or to render through writing sensations, practices, and experiences otherwise difficult or impossible to capture. Video can also be used as a secondary multimodal technology to reproduce and report on other multimodal research productions.

Some public ethnographers lately have made effective use of theatrical performances to share their research (for a review of these projects, see Tedlock 2005).[5] The work of D. Soyini Madison (2005), for example, has shed light on diverse issues such as the struggle for clean and accessible water, the struggle between traditional religion and modernity in Ghana, and the oral histories of University of Carolina labourers and service workers. These performances can benefit from a secondary, wider audience if cameras are employed to record theatrical shows. Video can also be used to report – in journalistic style – on other kinds of multimodal productions. For instance, some researchers organize exhibits, gatherings, festivals, and other events that are essentially bound by space and time – that is, by the necessity of being there in person. Video can be used to record these events and share them widely, via the web or television. As local TV stations continue to struggle with budget cuts and find themselves limiting the original content they can produce, it becomes easier for research teams to have their productions (which represent "free content" for TV stations) featured on television channels, either as a short story as part of a newscast or as a full-length special feature (perhaps for a community or public access channel).

In these cases, the video does not need to capture every single message that the research intends to convey. Rather, a short video can simply be used to "advertise" the complete project (e.g., a book, article, etc.) accessible elsewhere.

Whether it is a still photography-based essay, a documentary video, an event or performance, or a short video reporting on such event or performance, we believe that multimodal products resonate well with public audiences for at least four reasons. First, multimodal communication products such as video and photographic essays can be easier to find than most traditional academic products. Journals, except for the few that are open access, demand expensive individual or institutional subscriptions. Single-article downloads can be pricey, too. Books, which can be equally expensive, are also rather hard to find for most people, as they are neither marketed widely nor sold at large commercial bookstores. On the other hand, accessing websites is inexpensive. By placing a multimodal ethnographic research study on a high-traffic website, or at least by carefully selecting strategic keywords and republishing non-final versions of peer-reviewed work on a personal or university site, or a widely used one like academia.edu, an ethnographer can reach out to more people.

Second, multimodal communication products borrow from genres that are familiar to the public. Consider how widely read current affairs magazines are in comparison to peer-reviewed journals. Despite the fact that many magazines welcome submissions from freelance writers (such as academics and students), they are hardly ever the target of academics' submissions. A photo essay about one's research study, properly "translated" for the magazine format, would undoubtedly be more appreciated by general audiences – indeed, better understood – than a long and complex peer-reviewed journal article. Of course, such a magazine piece would not need to replace a journal article; it could simply be produced in addition to the former as a way of publicizing findings more widely. The same could be said about producing a video. Documentaries are widely consumed these days on the Internet, Netflix, satellite and cable TV, and DVD. Multiple publics *enjoy* watching a documentary video, much more than they might enjoy reading a journal article on the same topic. The fame of documentarians like Michael Moore – judged in comparison to social scientists who write on the same topics – is quite revealing of this phenomenon.

Third, multimodal communication products can make our research more visible and more accountable to our very own informants. Much too often people donate ethnographers their time, stories, and experiences without receiving anything in return. We have all heard informants complain that nothing came out of their research participation, even when a peer-reviewed journal article or two were published on the subject. On the other hand, the ability to share one's research with informants – and through them, their personal networks – by the means of an accessible multimodal product can somewhat repay our debt to them. The first author of this essay, for example, has shared research with his informants by publishing their photographs on his book's accompanying website and distributing research outcomes through a digital audio documentary that was aired on two widely listened regional radio stations (Vannini 2011).[6] This has made the research more accountable (a politically important outcome since the research was taxpayer-funded), and it has even generated more informants because listeners and viewers contacted the researcher to volunteer to be interviewed after hearing about the research.

Fourth, multimodal communication products can allow our research to enter the hypermedia realm – a realm that enjoys great popularity as more and more individuals spend greater amounts of time online, either on their desktops and laptops or mobile devices. Hypermedia research consists of scholarly work that makes use of Internet-based hyperlinks (Dicks et al. 2005). Therefore, an ethnographic study can feature files and external websites and various applications embedded within the text, which the user can access by following links. This kind of hypermedia product is likely to become increasingly popular as more and more users of academic research become accustomed to consuming research through electronic files only, without accessing print. Thus, an e-book, for example, can allow a reader to play sound files, view photos and videos, correspond with a book author via a book-related blog, and utilize other links. As more ethnographers learn to "compose" (not just "write") for e-book readers, and as more book publishers look to e-book publishing to reach wider audiences, the possibilities to make ethnography more publicly accessible by virtue of its richer multimodal offering will continue to expand. All of this, of course, opens the issue of collaboration. It can be technically difficult, at times, and certainly time-consuming to do this kind of public outreach. But newer opportunities open up if we tap into the resource of a large army of students who are often both eager to help and skilled enough to do it.

Students and Public Ethnography

Conducting and disseminating public ethnography necessitates an open door between our academic institutions and the public. It is not enough to simply push research products – innovative and creative as they may be – out to the general public in the hope that they may catch someone's attention. Rather, the door must swing in both directions. We argue that the logical gatekeepers at this door – the actors who can move most gracefully between the university and the public – are students. Today's students are a relatively untapped resource available to universities keen to engage in public scholarship. Indeed, they are not only academics' first public, as Burawoy (2005) puts it, but our first allies and collaborators. Working outside of the deeply worn treads of the tenure track, graduate (and to a lesser degree undergraduate) students blur the boundaries between the university and the public. With one foot in academia and one foot in "mainstream society," students can act as the structural support for the "bridge" that many universities have been attempting to build through various civic engagements, knowledge exchange, and knowledge mobilization initiatives. This has particular implications for public ethnography, whereby various forms of student expertise can be put to use in the creation of innovative and collaborative research products. With an increase in blended, applied, part-time, and distance-learning graduate programs at universities, an influx of diverse, talented, and creative early- and mid-career professionals are bringing to these programs an array of skills and experiences. The opportunity to further one's education without having to stop working, relocate, or generally put life on hold is appealing, and universities are catering to this demographic of potential students by offering less traditional graduate programs that do not focus on producing career academics. Artists, musicians, photographers, broadcasters, journalists, consultants, designers, entrepreneurs, filmmakers, bloggers, activists, and others are seeking graduate degrees, and many are hoping to leverage their talents by blending their educational and professional experiences. The outcome of this can be innovative, stylish, and relevant public ethnographies that have appeal both inside the academy and with the public.

As discussed earlier, ethnographic research has in recent years moved away from the traditional practice of passive, participant observation, and now emphasizes involvement, interconnectedness, and open dialogue (Tedlock 2005). This new celebration of transparency has encouraged contemporary ethnographers to embrace subjectivity and engagement – a trend that lends itself to the production of public ethnography, as well as creating an opportunity for our academic institutions to respond to topics that are relevant to mainstream society and local communities. But the question of how to determine what is relevant to the public must first be asked. Although interviews or consultation through various media can give indications as to what the public deems important, students, who are embedded within public cultures already, can offer insights into popular issues and help determine what various publics may or may not respond to. Students have unique perspectives that are useful in the design and dissemination of public ethnography, as they can judge the relevance of the subject matter from both an academic and a nonacademic standpoint. The varied agendas of faculty researchers – funding, publication, tenure, promotion, and so on – can cloud their judgment and alter what they view as relevant research material. Students, on the other hand, can judge a topic's relevance differently because of their relatively different position in society. Also, while within the academic community, students can debunk inaccurate myths about popular issues and challenge what is accepted as conventional academic wisdom. In sum, students can represent a new breed of academics and positively alter the way that most people view the ivory tower.

New discourses on public engagement, knowledge mobilization, and community-based programming are exercising pressure on universities to be more transparent and accessible. Granting agencies, postsecondary education administrators, policy makers, and the public are all demanding clear returns on investment; they are asking what exactly is being done with both research dollars and in-kind contributions. Universities are, after all, public institutions. Hence, the challenge today is for the academy to prove its relevance to the public, and to reassure society that they are listening. So, to begin with, universities would do well to consult, involve, empower, and make use of their students. Students, unlike most tenured faculty, can skip back and forth from academic discourse to popular discourse. They can push and pull knowledge from both sectors and pool wisdom in the creation of collaborative, relevant, multimodal public ethnography. Graduate students enter programs equipped with a range of experiences, talent, ideas, insights, connections, and, perhaps most importantly, wide-eyed enthusiasm. They do not doubt the relevance of their ideas because, more often than not, they evolve out of participation in mainstream society, pop culture, and the public sector. In short, students are already a part of the culture to which public ethnographers aim to appeal. Because of this, their perspective should be recognized as extremely valuable.

Popularizing ethnographic research requires capturing and holding the public interest. Media outlets, as well as the lay public, will decide which public ethnographies are recommended, liked, shared, blogged about, tweeted about, and so on. Students are a part of this powerful public sphere, and as such they are a lifeline between the universities that they attend and the public that they represent and comprise. This is not to say that faculty members are disconnected from public culture. Indeed, the walls that have been built up around and between institutions, disciplines, departments, and methodologies are arguably becoming somewhat permeable, with interdisciplinary and intersectoral research partnerships becoming more common. However, the differences between academic culture and public culture remain vast. A common complaint about academic research is that it is often written in an esoteric language that is only decipherable by other academics. And what good is cultural and social research that cannot be understood by the diverse publics that it aims to appeal to? More so than career academics, students can easily translate research findings into a language – or a multimodal format – that appeals to audiences outside the walls of our institutions.

Public scholarship and civic engagement are terms that are now regularly used within universities, funding agencies, and research councils. Academic institutions have set up knowledge transfer, knowledge mobilization, and knowledge exchange initiatives in an attempt to demonstrate the relevance of academic research to the public, policy makers, and practitioners. The translation and dissemination of academic research to the public has become an activity that university administrators and researchers can spend countless hours on. Whereas universities once coached students to write in a specific, regulated, rigidly structured academic style, now the struggle is in back-translating research for lay audiences – a process often referred to as knowledge translation. As discussed in the previous section, multimodality in public ethnography offers one type of translation necessary to communicate with diverse audiences, as it challenges the privilege of the written word by offering alternative modes of presentation. But another simple and obvious way to produce public ethnography is to leverage the diverse talents of students through collaboration and consultation. Often, the talents of students result in multimodal research products that do not even need to be "translated" at all to be useful.

For example, the student co-author of this essay coordinated a grant-funded knowledge mobilization initiative at a university for several years. As a part of this initiative, a community-based research internship program that financially supported graduate students to work in partnership with a public organization of their choice was developed. Students who participated in the internship program were encouraged to shape the focus of their internship in collaboration with both their academic supervisor and the public organization they were partnering with. Some of the partnering public organizations included various advocacy groups, a magazine, a youth organization, a food cooperative, an adult education institution, and a First Nations community. The products of these internships were varied and multimodal, ranging from high-quality documentaries to theatrical productions, from public events to marketing plans, blogs, and website design. These types of products were useful, interesting, and relevant to the public, as well as complementary to graduate students' academic pursuits. By making the results of their research internships publicly available and by presenting them in more popular formats (blogs, videos, etc.), these students were producing public ethnographies. The benefits of this program were multifaceted: the students got experience working outside the classroom, the organization got a capable and enthusiastic intern free of charge, and the university increased its visibility and engagement with the public. Rather than getting paid to write academic literature reviews or grade undergraduate papers, these graduate students were able to put their expertise to work in creative, inclusive, and inspiring ways.

The economic realities of our time mean that most graduate students have to work either full- or part-time while in school. However, teaching and research assistantships are no longer the only posts held by graduate students. While such on-campus jobs generally offer students a decent wage, they often demand a large volume of sometimes unacknowledged labour, and they tend to focus on skills that are useful only within the confines of academia. Many graduate students are now early- or mid-career professionals and choose to maintain nonacademic jobs while in school. Students who work in the public sector, for example, have access to a community of stakeholders who stand to benefit from academic research and are also a receptive audience for public ethnography. Additionally, this public audience can communicate its perspectives and needs to universities through working students, influencing research agendas, creating synergies for exchange and collaboration, and weighing in on what is and is not relevant. Students who work in creative fields can not only apply their artistic talents to the production of multimodal ethnography in their educational endeavours but can also facilitate the dissemination of public ethnography outside the academy through their professional networks in the creative industry. A graduate student who keeps a photoblog, for example, will have a very different readership from that of an academic researcher who chooses to publish in a traditional journal. If such a student blends her graduate research with her photography and posts it on her blog, her readers will become new viewers of public ethnography. Students with experience in music production, graphic design, filmmaking, or creative writing can contribute to academic research by diversifying the media we choose to communicate through, and by adding multimodal elements to projects, which faculty members may not have the expertise to do. Professors in the social sciences would be smart to recognize the value that graduate students can add to the design and dissemination of public ethnography, and should empower and consult with students, engaging them in their funded research as collaborators and communicators.

New audiences for public ethnography can be reached through students who actively participate – either through their nonacademic jobs or through their diverse interests – in community events, art shows, festivals, workshops, creative seminars, rallies, volunteer events, theatre, and so on. The diverse relationships, social circles, and connections that students maintain in their personal and professional lives offer tremendous opportunities for public ethnography. Students are a type of knowledge broker, acting on behalf of the academic institutions that they study at as well as on behalf of the public they are a part of. Of course, this is not to say that social science professors are unable or unwilling to engage the public in their projects. Indeed, many faculty members do, and even more are looking for ways to do so. However, students are able to operate outside of the institutional bureaucracy and academic red tape that constrains many grant-funded and tenure-track professors. Moreover, they are able to bring valuable skills and resources (such as time) to the service of public ethnography. This suggests the need for some fundamental changes in the way that academic institutions view both the role of students and the value of multimodal forms of public scholarship.

The Road Ahead for Public Ethnography

Throughout this chapter we have examined ways in which multimodality, innovative public ethnography, and the engagement of students can bolster public scholarship. Conference delegates, academic associations, and funding agencies have traditionally been the privileged audience for social science research products – products that have come overwhelmingly in the form of academic books, empirical journal articles, technical reports, and conference presentations. Diverse audiences for public ethnography want to see research wrapped in new packaging and in forms that make sense to them. One of our key arguments has been that universities would do well to engage students as collaborators for this project. Institutional support for this shift requires that teachers and administrators view courses – especially graduate courses – as collaborative projects with well-defined outreach aims. That is, instead of asking students to recite and reproduce academic knowledge for the sake of their teachers' assessment, coursework could focus on mobilizing research outside of the classroom whenever appropriate.

Indeed, we suggest that the role of students in public scholarship should extend beyond co-op programs and classes that offer experiential learning. Although these types of programs should of course continue and be expanded upon, they often get collapsed into broad institutional civic engagement mandates rather than existing as opportunities for students to demonstrate their unique abilities. The vast and eclectic forms of student expertise need to be recognized, valued, and utilized by universities. Creative, applied, postdisciplinary, public assignments, projects, and theses should be encouraged by professors so they can be relevant to students' lives and the greater public, and should leverage their various skills and talents. Diverse topics and approaches that relate to students' professional and personal activities should become central to the work produced in the classroom (e.g., see student epilogue, this volume), and opportunities for students to contribute to faculty research in multimodal capacities should be supported. Research dissemination should not be the final activity undertaken at the end of a project. From the very start, social science research should be designed, conducted, and articulated in clear language and with strategic communication plans that both hold the public interest and are easily understood. The public audience can no longer be an afterthought. As our institutions face the challenge of public accountability and remaining relevant to mainstream society, we need to think about how this public outreach can be more easily accomplished in the future with the resources that we already have. Many graduate students are in fact future faculty members, and this new demographic of young scholars will be better positioned to engage in public scholarship if rewarded and encouraged to do so early in their academic careers. Our departments, institutions, and funders need to actively support – financially as well as politically – student and faculty involvement in public ethnography and multimodal research. Faculty projects as well as student theses that engage creative research methodologies, collaborative public partnerships, and multimodal dissemination need to be encouraged and rewarded. Debates about expanding criteria for tenure and promotion need to continue, and the peer review process needs to be restructured to include experts from outside academia.

And finally, academics keen on connecting with the public need to approach the research communication process in creative and innovative ways (e.g., e-public sociology, see Schneider, this volume). This means going beyond the status quo, where the written word reigns supreme. While writing should continue to be a priority, composing multimodally opens numerous opportunities for public research and public ethnography in particular. As book and journal publishers gradually shift away from the monopoly of traditional, written-word, printed products, academics can look towards students as knowledgeable teachers. Students can teach career academics, journal editors, and university administrators why and how communicating differently can make a difference. Students are already within the "industry" – their energies simply need to be rechannelled. Their new roles and responsibilities might even attract new students, increasing enrolment and pleasing university executives. It is a very simple and potentially very rewarding investment opportunity – even business un-savvy and unfriendly social scientists can recognize that.

In conclusion, we wish to leave the interested reader with a useful set of resources he/she can apply in doing public ethnography. There is no space here to do a literature review of relevant projects, and we are afraid that even if such space were available our list would grow rapidly outdated. Therefore we want to invite the reader to consult the resources available at the Public Ethnography website (www.publicethnography.net). On that website – made possible thanks to the Canada Research Chair in Innovative Learning and Public Ethnography – we host a set of useful materials, including how-to resources and examples of students' own public ethnographic research, as well as a series of websites that showcase the empirical public ethnographic work carried out for the Routledge Innovative Ethnographies series and for a methodological text-cum-website project titled "Popularizing Research." Links to other public ethnographic projects and how-to books and articles, events, and interesting news items are also available and constantly updated. Readers are invited not only to consult this material but also to network together with us and produce and share with us material of their own.

Notes

1 The interested reader is invited to consult the myriad debates on this issue, conveniently inventoried on Michael Burawoy's webpage: http://burawoy.berkeley.edu/PS.htm.

2 Within the context of the social sciences, the *cultural turn* refers to a paradigmatic shift away from viewing culture as a bounded domain of society (tantamount to the arts- and humanities-centred heritage of a group) and towards viewing it as an all-encompassing "way of life."

3 Alma Gottlieb (1997), for instance, argues that public anthropology is valuable, but it is not significantly different from the well-established tradition of applied anthropology, and therefore the new *public anthropology* moniker risks glossing over that tradition.

4 Vaughan's ethnographic research on the NASA Space Shuttle program, for example, has been tremendously influential in the reshaping of NASA organizational structures and procedures (see Vaughan 2005).

5 Despite their promise, however, the "live" nature of performance ethnography means that it has a rather limited audience. This audience is limited even more by the fact that most performance ethnographies are nowadays nothing but scripts published in academic journals or enacted for scholarly audiences only.

6 The research project investigated the roles played by ferry boats in the lives of coastal British Columbia's ferry-dependent communities. As the research unfolded over the years, it became more and more clear that, besides interpretation and conceptualization, the topic demanded committed public documentation of the social problems caused by escalating ferry fares. As the issue is of great regional relevance, it turned out to be rather easy for the author to influence public debate and policy making through regular media appearances. In addition, even in its less political and controversial aspects, the research subject is of such obvious mundane relevance to islanders' and coasters' lives that it easily demands local publics' curiosity and attention. See ferrytales.innovativeethnographies.net.

References

Adler, Patricia, and Peter Adler. 2008. "Of Rhetoric and Representation: The Four Faces of Ethnography." *Sociological Quarterly* 49: 1-30.

Becker, Howard, Herbert J. Gans, Katherine Newman, and Diane Vaughan. 2004. "On the Value of Ethnography: Sociology and Public Policy – A Dialogue." *Annals of the American Academy of Political and Social Science* 595: 264-76.

Borofsky, Robert. 2000. "Public Anthropology: Where To, What Next?" *Anthropology News* 45: 9-10.

–. 2012. "Public Anthropology: A Personal Perspective." *Public Anthropology.* http://www.publicanthropology.org/.

Burawoy, Michael. 2005. "2004 Presidential Address: For Public Sociology." *American Sociological Review* 70, 1: 4-28.

Castree, Noel, Duncan Fuller, Andrew Kent, Audrey Kobayashi, Christopher Merrett, Laura Pulido, and Laura Barraclough. 2008. "Geography, Pedagogy, and Politics." *Progress in Human Geography* 32: 680-718.

Davis, Gail, and Claire Dwyer. 2008. "Qualitative Methods II: Minding the Gap." *Progress in Human Geography* 32: 399-406.

Dear, Michael, Jim Ketchum, Sarah Luria, and Doug Richardson, eds. 2011. *GeoHumanities: Art, History, Text, at the Edge of Place.* New York: Routledge.

Dicks, Bella, Bruce Mason, Amanda Coffey, and Paul Atkinson. 2005. *Qualitative Research and Hypermedia: Ethnography for the Digital Age.* London: Sage.

Dicks, Bella, Bambo Soyinka, and Amanda Coffey. 2006. "Multimodal Ethnography." *Qualitative Research* 6: 77-96.

Fuller, Duncan. 2008. "Public Geographies: Taking Stock." *Progress in Human Geography* 32: 834-44.

Fuller, Duncan, and Kye Askins. 2010. "Public Geographies II: Being Organic." *Progress in Human Geography* 34: 654-67.

Gans, Herbert J. 2010. "Public Ethnography; Ethnography as Public Sociology." *Qualitative Sociology* 33: 97-104.

Gottlieb, Alma. 1997. "The Perils of Popularizing Anthropology." *Anthropology Today* 13: 1-2.

Knowles, Gary, and Andra Cole, eds. 2008. *Handbook of the Arts in Qualitative Research.* Thousand Oaks, CA: Sage.

Lamphere, Louise. 2004. "The Convergence of Applied, Practicing, and Public Anthropology in the 21st Century." *Human Organization* 63: 431-43.

Madison, D. Soyini. 2005. "Critical Ethnography as Street Performance: Reflections of Home, Race, Murder and Justice in Ghana, West Africa." In *Handbook of Qualitative Research,* edited by Norman K. Denzin and Yvonna S. Lincoln, 537-46. Thousand Oaks, CA: Sage.

McClancy, Jeremy, and Christian McDonaugh. 1996. *Popularizing Anthropology.* New York: Routledge.

Murphy, Alexander, H.J. deBlij, B.L. Turner II, Ruth Wilson Gilmore, and Derek Gregory. 2008. "The Role of Geography in Public Debate." *Progress in Human Geography* 29: 165-93.

Pink, Sarah. 2009. *Sensory Ethnography.* London: Sage.

Purcell, Trevor. 2000. "Public Anthropology: An Idea Searching for a Reality." *Transforming Anthropology* 9: 30-33.

Scheper-Hughes, Nancy. 2009. "Making Anthropology Public." *Anthropology Today* 25: 1-4.

Tedlock, Barbara. 2005. "The Observation and Participation of and the Emergence of Public Ethnography." In *The Sage Handbook of Qualitative Research,* edited by Norman Denzin and Yvonna Lincoln, 151-71. Thousand Oaks, CA: Sage.

Vannini, Phillip. n.d. "Non-Representational Theory and Ethnographic Research." Online presentation. http://ferrytales.innovativeethnographies.net.

–. 2011. *Ferry Tales: Mobility, Place, and Time on Canada's West Coast.* New York: Routledge.

Vannini, Phillip, ed. 2012. *Popularizing Research: Engaging New Media, New Genres, New Audiences.* New York: Peter Lang.

Vaughan, Diane. 2005. "On the Relevance of Ethnography for the Production of Public Sociology and Policy." *British Journal of Sociology* 56: 411-16.

Ward, Kevin. 2006. "Geography and Public Policy: Towards Public Geographies." *Progress in Human Geography* 30: 495-503.

–. 2007. "Geography and Public Policy: A Recent History of 'Policy Relevance.'" *Progress in Human Geography* 29: 310-19.

–. 2008. "Geography and Public Policy: Activist, Participatory, and Policy Geographies." *Progress in Human Geography* 31: 695-705.

Waterston, Alisse, and Maria Vesperi, eds. 2009. *Anthropology off the Shelf: Anthropologists on Writing*. New York: Wiley-Blackwell.

Conclusion

ARIANE HANEMAAYER AND CHRISTOPHER J. SCHNEIDER

At the outset of this book, we inquired about the normative commitments of the discipline of sociology and how these commitments inform or influence conceptions of the relationship between sociological research and recommendations for social transformation in the public sociology debates. Responses to these issues are not clearly divided, as evidenced in the ensuing public sociology debate, and as outlined in preceding chapters of this volume. A basic theme of these debates concerns the practice of sociology and its obligation (if any) to publics and, more generally, civil society. As raised (both explicitly and implicitly) in many of the chapters here, questions concerning the moral worth of sociology and its foundational and organizing principles guide ethical judgments both in the discipline and beyond. For instance, our pedagogical commitments and practices can and do stretch beyond professional settings.

Pedagogy and Its Principles

Prentice, Schaffer, Schneider, and Vannini and Milne each reiterate and collectively renew interest in "students [as] our first public," building upon Burawoy's (2004, 1608) earlier proclamation, to the enterprise of sociology. Overall, these chapters illustrate how our pedagogical commitments and choices matter for the way that sociological research is translated to those that are in contact with the university (and beyond). Others, like Hanemaayer, contend that the contours of one's public sociology are always constituted by the metatheoretical commitments that ground one's sociological judgments. Translating (i.e., teaching) sociological research into possibilities for desirable social change and action within the broader social sphere requires, she argues, ethical judgments that are consistent with one's sociological practice and principles. Her chapter illustrates that classical thinkers Weber and Durkheim both anticipated the normative dimensions of the public sociology debates. Both Weber and Durkheim conceived of the discipline as the demonstration of thinking sociologically and doing sociology (respectively), whether in the classroom or dealing with the pressing issues of their time.

Similarly, in reflections and discussions about her teaching as an example of the kind of critical sociology she values and practices, Prentice highlights that her decision to conduct a new graduate seminar at the University of Manitoba as an inquiry into public sociology and its debates (rather than community service learning) serves as an example of this kind of sociologically (and metatheoretically) principled pedagogy. Prentice notes that more resources are necessary for thinking about teaching public sociology in a way that maintains its relationship to the critical tradition, echoing Burawoy's (2005) position that critical sociology is the backbone of public sociology and its program. The relationship between teaching (demonstration) and the kind of oeuvre (sociology) one practices, as well as how this relates to questions surrounding the potential that sociological research may (or may not) have for inciting and inspiring social change, remains open for further examination.

Schaffer points to three examples of how "public" theoretical work can be principled by one's disciplinary and metatheoretical commitments. By discussing the philosophical activism of Sartre, the sociological "combat" exemplified by Bourdieu, and the artistic works of Havel, Schaffer provides sociologists and social theorists with paths to consider when moving their work beyond the ivory tower and the institutional conditions that may otherwise impede their abilities to do so. Further contributions to this thread of pedagogy principled to its theoretical and disciplinary commitments may consider other innovations to bridge research, theory, and teaching to sociology students and beyond.

In line with the desire to disseminate and translate sociological research and the sociological imagination to students and the public beyond the university, its jargon, and insular, private nature, both Schneider and Vannini and Milne offer ways to engage in public scholarship within and beyond university class settings. Schneider notes how the emerging prominence of social media and online interaction have created the conditions for a new medium for student-teacher interaction to occur. Bridging the traditional and organic divide of the Burawoyan public sociology category, Schneider suggests that not enough (public) sociologists are online, and, like Schaffer, discusses the conditions that may hinder sociologists and teachers to make the move beyond "private" online university spheres. The potential exists in social media to move the sociological imagination online, Schneider contends, in a way to engage with and teach publics through e-public sociology.

Similarly, Vannini and Milne discuss the potentials of multimodal research for both instructing students and giving them the skills to think about their research and its relevance to the public, and moving it beyond the classroom through various media. Noting that other disciplines have already considered the possibilities that multimodal research brings to public scholarship, Vannini and Milne argue that sociology is behind the times when it comes to translating and disseminating its research beyond the written medium. By giving students and publics the opportunity to see, hear, and/or participate in sociological research, this process opens up not only discussions about the happenings of the social world, but also new forms for interacting with various parties in those discussions. Further engagements with teaching and engaging publics beyond the classroom through multimodal and online approaches might consider how these acts are extensions of our pedagogical commitments.

Just as multimodal research and e-public sociology may offer publics more opportunities to participate in the democratic practice of research, our pedagogy and its principles must remain under critical reflection to retain the foundational commitments to the democratic exchange of ideas in sociology and the social sciences. Van den Berg argues that any form of (public) sociology that jettisons these principles risks reproducing the kind of fascist authority that markets or other structural conditions cause when they eliminate the potential for everyone to question the assumptions or inclusivity in any scientific endeavour or undertaking. Normative instruction by public sociologists, be it online, through activism, or in the classroom, may infringe on the ability for the voices of the public to be heard, which, van den Berg asserts, is the nature of democratic (social) science. Therefore, any discussion of teaching and public sociology that takes as its objective the democratic exchange of ideas would need to consider these potential implications and consequences.

Policy and Public Sociology: Activism and the Discipline

Another theme emerging from this volume concerns the relationship between policy and activism. A few dynamics exist in this relationship between doing sociological research and making recommendations for desirable change – dynamics that can be developed in further discussions. Bucklaschuk notes how the conditions that shape government policies may not only make it difficult to identify publics but also create resistance in the groups themselves to any change, for they may set forth undesirable consequences. Temporary migrant workers in Canada are one example that illustrates the tenuous relationship between activism and public sociology and policy change. Labour actions incited and supported by sociological engagement may actually cause these labourers to lose their jobs and render them unable to support their families or reproduce their own social being. By noting how other researchers have encountered issues when attempting to advocate on the behalf of these groups, Bucklaschuk shows how the field of public sociology has yet to consider the potentially negative effects that public sociology may cause as sociologists "get their hands dirty," to borrow from Schaffer (see Chapter 3).

In his intellectual biography of Coral W. Topping, Helmes-Hayes shows how Topping's sociological activism, in particular the manner in which Topping influenced the penal reform of his day, anticipated Burawoy's public sociology. By doing sociological work, Topping was able to advocate for more humane treatment of prisoners in Canada, which led to changes in policy and legislation. Further research might consider how public sociology may lead to policy change, which demonstrates that the line between public and policy sociology in Burawoy's categories may be more blurred than this typology suggests.

Mesny observes another example of the relationship between public and policy sociology in her discussion of the Tri-Council Policy Statement, which regulates what constitutes ethical research with human subjects, to suggest that institutional conditions may deter sociologists from actually doing public sociology. Mesny's chapter aligns with Bucklaschuk's research, which illustrates how national policies and legislation hinder public sociology. Mesny also shows how public and policy sociology may be more interconnected than initially suggested by Burawoy, both in how activism may contribute to actual policy creation and in how institutionalized policies may infringe on our ability to advocate or participate in policy creation.

Future research that builds upon this book might continue to consider, as a basic characteristic of the public sociology debate, how and why we do sociology. It might also inquire into the relationship between sociological research and ethical judgments at the theoretical level – the normative commitments of the discipline – and at the institutional and individual levels of its practice. Additional avenues might include directing these questions towards various offshoots of public sociology, such as "service sociology" that aims to improve society through the resolution of critical social problems (Treviño 2012), a service that includes public teaching (Schneider, Hanemaayer, and Nolan 2014). Other offshoots include criminology and related developments such as e-public criminology (Schneider, forthcoming), as approaches that debate the role of its criminological practitioners in the realm of politics and public policy (Loader and Sparks 2010).

In Burawoy's foreword to this volume, he notes that the public sociology debate will not stop. We agree. It is our hope that this volume will forward the debate in new directions that will encourage others to inquire about the normative commitments of the discipline of sociology and what is at stake for how sociology is practised. On the one hand, the range of responses provided in this collection speak, not surprisingly, to the predictable normative commitments that underlie the public sociology debate, while, on the other hand, the responses provide an unexpected array of approaches towards developing our understandings of the normative practice of sociological inquiry. We leave the reader here to ponder the questions this volume contributes to the public sociology debate: What kind of sociology are you committed to? And how does this commitment inform ethical judgment in your own sociological practice?

References

Burawoy, Michael. 2004. "Public Sociologies: Contradictions, Dilemmas, and Possibilities." *Social Forces* 82, 4: 1603-18.

–. 2005. "2004 Presidential Address: For Public Sociology." *American Sociological Review* 70, 1: 4-28.

Loader, Ian, and Richard Sparks. 2010. *Public Criminology? Key Ideas in Public Criminology*. London: Routledge.

Schneider, Christopher J. Forthcoming. "Public Criminology and the 2011 Vancouver Riot: Public Perceptions of Crime and Justice in the 21st Century." In *Crime, Deviance and the City: Public Criminologies,* edited by Carrie Sanders and Lauren Eisler. Toronto: Pearson.

Schneider, Christopher J., Ariane Hanemaayer, and Kyle Nolan. 2014. "Public Teaching as Service Sociology." In *Service Sociology and Academic Engagement in Social Problems,* edited by A. Javier Treviño and Karen McCormack. Farnham, UK: Ashgate.

Treviño, A. Javier. 2012. "The Challenge of Service Sociology." *Social Problems* 59, 1: 2-20.

Epilogue

Student Reflections on a Public Sociology Course at UBC, Okanagan Campus

KYLE NOLAN

This epilogue builds upon the concluding chapter of this volume and connects with a basic theme of this book – namely, the ways that we think about and practice (by way of obligation to publics) public sociology. Michael Burawoy (2005, 7) insists that students like me are the first "public" for academic and sociological work, and the emphasis that the field of public sociology puts on the relationship between professor and pupil deserves further consideration. As class sizes across the country continue to increase, the potential for research to translate into real-world recommendations is threatened. The role of the professor becomes less about fostering critical thinking skills in his or her students and more about publishing, teaching awards, and tenure promotions.

As Burawoy contends, the dialogue between professor and student is essential for the conceptualization of public sociology. This dialogue, however, differs from the typical lecture-recite-regurgitate pattern that has become the dominant classroom and examination structure within many university courses. Instead, Burawoy (2005, 9) suggests that there must exist "a dialogue between [professors] and students, between students and their own experiences, among students themselves, and finally a dialogue of students with publics beyond the university" for the discipline to flourish. This multilevel conversation allows for private troubles to emerge as public issues (see Mills 1959). Through the identification and explanation of the happenings in the social world, students may begin to think about translating sociological research into recommendations for social action. These ideas informed the development and implementation of a course that both encouraged and created a space for students and non-enrolled members of the public to gather and discuss a plethora of social issues, problems, and phenomena.

In the winter term of 2011, a special topics class (Sociology 295) called Public Sociology was created and initiated by Dr. Christopher Schneider at the University of British Columbia, Okanagan Campus. The course was premised on bringing together individuals from the Okanagan Valley, located in beautiful British Columbia, Canada, and approximately forty enrolled students in an effort to foster a space for the nonhierarchical exchange of ideas among students, academics, and members of the public.[1] The course was free for any outside students and faculty, as well as any members of the public. The inclusion of "multiple publics" was developed as a means of bridging the gap between the university and public spheres, encouraging conversations between professors, students, teaching assistants, and public participants. The course objectives built upon Burawoy's (2005, 7) notion of "organic public sociology," cultivating conversation between the public sociologist and members of the public, based on the principles of mutual education. Here, "the project of such public sociologists is to make visible the invisible, to make the private public, to validate these organic connections as part of our sociological life" (Burawoy 2005, 8). As the teaching assistant of the course, I offer my brief reflections below.

Each week, during a three-hour period, a different invited sociologist presented a lecture to the class. The course lectures and topics were publicized in advance through local public-access television (Shaw TV), print (*Kelowna Capital News,* and Castanet Media), and radio (CBC 88.9FM, AM1150, and 103.9FM The Juice) as well as online through Twitter and WordPress. Typically, each talk would occupy the first portion of the class (around seventy-five minutes), with the other half of class time devoted to small-group discussions. The aim was to deliver an informative and publicly accessible presentation (this also helped set the topic or theme of the ensuing discussion), while allowing the public, enrolled students, and professors, class time to engage in small-group conversation. Topics covered during the semester included music cultures, emergency services and interoperability, surveillance, terrorism and popular culture, police representation in mass media, subcultural identity formation, sexuality and youth culture, and conspicuous consumption, to name a few. Each presentation was then followed by small-group discussions that were generally guided by four or five prepared questions developed by the presenter (and Dr. Schneider) in an effort to stimulate conversation about the presentation among members of the public, students, and the presenter. One of my roles as the teaching assistant was to move from group to group, both listening in on the conversations and contributing to the discussion. The significance of this course especially revealed itself to me during these small-group conversations as the blending of ideas from students and non-enrolled members of the public allowed for conversations that entertained an extremely diverse range of life experiences and ways of knowing the world. Let us consider Dr. Aaron Doyle's presentation.

Dr. Doyle's presentation regarding news and entertainment images of crime, policing, and criminal justice focused on the relationship between mass media and the criminal justice system. Specifically, Dr. Doyle's research employed the television show *Cops* as an empirical example to examine this relationship. In addition to his lecture involving the theoretical relationships among mass media, audience understanding, and social interaction, the class was shown two clips of *Cops* as a means of setting up the subsequent discussion questions. Following the presentation, the class broke into various groups. One of these groups included a retired member of the Royal Canadian Mounted Police (RCMP), along with five students who ranged in age from eighteen to twenty. The conversations that took place in this group were quite different from those in the other groups that day, in part because of the lived experience of the retired RCMP officer. The students were able to offer a sociological perspective to the retired officer, presenting a conceptual twist to his individual experience as an officer and his personal relationship to the institution of policing. For example, the students pointed out that the officers had engaged an individual prior to reading their Miranda rights (which were applicable to the show because of its location in the United States). To this, the retired RCMP officer pointed out that the Miranda rights are not applicable in Canada, and that perhaps the officers had read the rights off camera. The media, he explained, can provide interesting perspectives on police work. This conversation was more than a simple summary of Dr. Doyle's arguments and interpretations. The group questioned the way(s) individuals perceive police work, as insiders and outsiders, and the role of media in the process. Without the inclusion of students, professors, and members of the public, this conversation between professor, student, and citizen would not likely have taken place in this way.

This example, in conjunction with various other experiences as a teaching assistant during the semester, gave me insight into the objectives of this kind of public sociology. In the course syllabus for students (see Appendix 2), Dr. Schneider lists the following as the intended themes and principles associated with the public sociology course: (1) To explore the relationship between sociology and political projects; (2) To consider the sociologist's ethical obligations to acting based on sociological knowledge; (3) To understand how personal troubles are related to broader public issues; and (4) To engage with members of the public and invite their voices to inform and incite political and sociological discussion. Taking these four objectives into consideration, the platform of the course was built on tracking down sociological experts whose various fields would be relevant to a diverse population of students, faculty, and members of the public. Let us consider one more brief example to demonstrate these course objectives.

Dr. Jeff Ferrell's presentation on "dumpster diving" – a sociological subculture where individuals live on materials and food they find in dumpsters – was grounded in his discussion of conspicuous consumption and the global economy of waste. Group discussions were often based on personal experience, such as the need to replace "old" items and technology with new ones, despite the "old" items' retained utility. The age gaps apparent in each discussion group challenged members of the public and students to see how their personal beliefs and lived experiences differ based on different generational and cultural norms. In one group, a student noted how she purchased a new cell phone from "necessity," even though her old cell phone continued to work (i.e., function properly). This personal trouble – as an identified concern of the student (i.e., the student's need to have new technology) – connected to some of the broader public issues that Dr. Ferrell highlighted, such as social status, conspicuous consumption, and the political economy of waste, and led to an engaging discussion between the various group members and participants.

Perhaps the most inspiring aspect of this course was its ability to connect sociological research with such a diverse set of publics. Each presentation was structured in such a way that made the communication of theory, method, and practice understandable and relatable, regardless of the previous exposure to or training in sociology. This was crucial to the overall success of this course; the use of academic jargon might have dissuaded both students and non-enrolled members of the public from thoroughly engaging with the course content.[2] Instead, the atmosphere invited personal experience and knowledge as a fruitful means of mutual education through conversation. This dialogue, as Burawoy (2005) suggests, is crucial to the goals of public sociology, and the development and implementation of this course demonstrates the potential successes of such dialogue.

Notes

1 To browse the syllabus, please see Appendix 2.

2 The popularity of the course can be measured, in part, by the fact that each week between forty and seventy members of the public attended the lecture, and some members of the public attended every single class. Design effectiveness is evidenced in the course Teaching Evaluation Questionnaires, administered at the end of the semester to enrolled students. The mean (across nineteen questions) was 4.73 (with 5.00 being the highest score). Additionally, fifty-eight letters attesting to the success of the course design were collected by Dr. Schneider from course participants and community members on a voluntary basis.

References

Burawoy, Michael. 2005. "2004 Presidential Address: For Public Sociology." *American Sociological Review* 70, 1: 4-28.

Mills, C. Wright. 1959. *The Sociological Imagination*. New York: Oxford University Press.

Appendix 1

Theory and Practice of Public Sociology Syllabus, University of Manitoba

The University of Manitoba
Department of Sociology
Winter Term (January-April) 2010 (3 credit hours)

SOC 7160: Theory and Practice of Public Sociology

Instructor	Dr. Susan Prentice
Office	329 Isbister Building
Telephone	474-6726 (voicemail)
Office Hours	Posted to office door, and by special appointment
Class	Tuesday, 1:00-4:00
	Room 335 Isbister Building
Email	Susan_Prentice@umanitoba.ca

Course Objectives

This course will examine the theory and practice of "public sociology." In particular, we will be tackling questions about the nature and purpose of sociological inquiry, probing the relationship between commitments to social justice and to modes of science, and considering how and why differing schools of sociological theorizing have responded to the call for more public sociology.

As a course examining the "theory and practice" of public sociology, we will begin with epistemological and normative debates, and then move to a small number of selected case studies: environmental justice and questions of nature, social movements, expert witness practice, and public policy interventions. Students will be expected to demonstrate their grasp of key theoretical debates as well as their familiarity with a specific arena of public sociology, as demonstrated through their research paper.

Like all seminars, this course will rely on the active participation of all seminar members to be successful.

Readings

There are no required textbooks – students will need to independently seek out each week's readings. Some readings may be photocopied and placed on reserve in the department. Students should bring a print copy of all readings for each week's seminar to class with them.

Grading Scheme

Seven response papers ***30 percent***

To encourage engaged reading and to foster lively, productive discussions, students must prepare comments and/or questions on (at least) seven sessions' readings. Each commentary must be 1.5-2 pages (not a précis), and should touch on each reading, although it may go into more depth on some. Papers should be typed, double-spaced, include the student's name and date, and be submitted to the instructor by email as an attachment, by 9:00 am the day before each class. Response papers submitted less than 28 hours prior to class commencement but prior to the start of class will be considered late, and assessed at 50% of the maximum grade. If papers are submitted after class begins, they will be assessed as zero. Even if late, a student must submit a minimum of seven papers or forfeit double the value of each missed paper. Missed response papers cannot be for sequential weeks – for example, if a student opts not to write up the readings of week 10, he/she must have written up week 9 and must submit on week 11.

Seminar facilitation ***15 percent***

Each student must facilitate one seminar discussion. You should distribute written questions and comments to the class to structure the discussion. Facilitators should summarize the key points in the materials, and then concentrate on exploring issues, themes, questions, contradictions or reflections on the readings. Excellent facilitation will also integrate previous readings and discussions for context. A student who misses their scheduled facilitation without advance notice and permission will forfeit the grade.

Participation ***15 percent***
Sustained participation throughout the term to demonstrate preparation, careful reading, and active classroom citizenship. Students are expected to attend all classes.

Research Paper ***40 percent***
Students will prepare a paper of about 20 pages outlining a public sociology type of approach to an empirical/social topic of interest to them. The research paper allows students to make a more in-depth investigation of a particular problem, topic, or case, and may work for other courses and/or with their thesis. Topics will need to be reviewed with the instructor.

Students will make a short presentation on their proposed research paper in class for review and discussion (5 percent), will prepare a final paper due the last day of class (25 percent), and will make a short in-class summary of their argument and findings (10 percent). Papers will be assessed on a range of factors, including integration of course materials, new research, expository strength, and correct citation. Please follow the most recent APA style guide for citations and bibliography.

All students must submit a paper for grading on April 6th. If this is not the final paper, students must have earlier provided a reasonable rationale for why they need a time extension, and must have received advance permission from the instructor for their request for extra time.

Voluntary Withdrawal
March 19 is the last day for voluntary withdrawal from this course. Students will have evaluative feedback by this date.

Academic Integrity
Students should acquaint themselves with University policies on academic integrity.

See Sections 7.1 and 7.2 in the *Graduate Calendar*.

Schedule (subject to change with advance notice)

Week 1 Burawoy's Challenge – Jan 12

Burawoy, M. (2005). 2004 American Sociological Association Presidential Address: For Public Sociology. *British Journal of Sociology, 56*(2), 259-294.

Week 2 Burawoy's Challenge – Jan 19

Best, J. (2003). Killing the Messenger: The Social Problem of Sociology. *Social Problems, 50*(1), 1-13.

Gans, H. (2002). More of Us Should Become Public Sociologists. *Footnotes, 30*(6).

Brint, S. (2005). Guide for the Perplexed: On Michael Burawoy's "Public Sociology." *American Sociologist, 36*(3-4), 46-65.

Reminder: Department of Sociology research forum on public sociology – January 22nd, 1:00-2:50, Room 335 Isbister.

Week 3 Historical Roots and Classic Debates – Jan 26

Marx, K. (1845 [1969]). Theses on Feuerbach. *Marx/Engels Selected Works: Volume 1* (pp. 13-15). Moscow: Progress Publishers.

Weber, M. (1948). Politics as a Vocation. In H. H. Gerth & C. W. Mills (Eds.), *From Max Weber: Essays in Sociology.* London: Routledge.

Weber, Max. (1949). Excerpts from "'Objectivity" in Social Science and Social Policy" Pp. 50-63 in *The Methodology of the Social Sciences.* New York: The Free Press.

Mills, C. W. (1959). *The Sociological Imagination.* New York: Oxford University Press. Chapters 1 and 3.

Becker, H. S. (1967). Whose Side Are We On? *Social Problems, 67*(3), 239-247.

Recommended: Reisman, D., Glazer, N., & Denney, R. (1950). *The Lonely Crowd: A Study of the Changing American Character.* New Haven: Yale University Press.

Week 4 Debating Public Sociology – Feb 2

Turner, J. (2005). Is Public Sociology Such a Good Idea? *American Sociologist, 36*(3-4), 27-45.

McLaughlin, N., Kowalchuk, L., & Turcotte, K. (2009). Why Sociology Does Not Need to Be Saved: Analytic Reflections on Public Sociologies. *The American Sociologist, 36*(3-4), 133-151.

Tittle, C. (2004). The Arrogance of Public Sociology. *Social Forces, 82*(4), 1639-1643.

Holmwood, J. (2007). Sociology as Public Discourse and Professional Practice: A Critique of Michael Burawoy. *Sociological Theory, 25*(1), 46-66.

Recommended: Goldberg, A., & van den Berg, A. (2009). What Do Public Sociologists Do? A Critique of Burawoy. *Canadian Journal of Sociology, 34*(3), 765-802.

Week 5 Debating Public Sociology – Feb 9

Gans, H. (1989). Sociology in America: The Discipline and the Public – American Sociological Association 1988 Presidential Address. *American Sociological Review, 89*(1), 1-16.

Morrow, R. (2009). Rethinking Burawoy's Public Sociology: A Post-Empiricist Reconstruction. In V. Jeffries (Ed.), *Handbook of Public Sociology* (pp. 47-70). New York: Rowman and Littlefield.

Wallerstein, I. (2007). The Sociologist and the Public Sphere. In C. Dan, R. Zussman, J. Misra, N. Gerstel, R. Stokes, D. Anderton & M. Burawoy (Eds.), *Public Sociology: Fifteen Eminent Sociologists Debate Politics and the Profession in the Twenty-First Century* (pp. 169-175). Berkeley: University of California Press.

Week 6 Reading Week/No Classes – Feb 16

Week 7 Debating Public Sociology – Feb 23

O'Connor, P. (2006). Private Troubles, Public Issues: The Irish Sociological Imagination. *Irish Journal of Sociology, 15*(2), 5-22.

Acker, J. (2005). Comments on Burawoy on Public Sociology. *Critical Sociology, 31*(3), 327-331.

Hays, S. (2009). Stalled at the Altar? Conflict, Hierarchy and Compartmentalization in Burawoy's Public Sociology. In C. Dan, R. Zussman, J. Misra, N. Gerstel, R. Stokes, D. Anderton & M. Burawoy (Eds.), *Public Sociology: Fifteen Eminent Sociologists Debate Politics and the Profession in the 21st Century* (pp. 79-90). Berkeley: University of California Press.

Recommended: Smith, Dorothy (1987). *The Everyday World as Problematic.* Boston, MA: Northeastern University Press.

Week 8 Research Proposals – March 2

Student presentations of research proposals

Week 9 Public Sociology: Nature & the Environment – March 9

Jackson, S., & Rees, A. (2007). The Appalling Appeal of Nature: The Popular Influence of Evolutionary Psychology as a Problem for Sociology. *Sociology, 41*(5), 917-930.

Laska, S., & Morrow, B. (2006). Social Vulnerabilities and Hurricane Katrina: An Unnatural Disaster in New Orleans. *Marine Technology Society Journal, 40*(4), 16-26.

Week 10 Public Sociology: Bureaucracy – March 16

Aronowitz, S. (2005). Comments on Michael Burawoy's "The Critical Turn to Public Sociology." *Critical Sociology, 31*(3), 333-338.

Vaughan, D. (2006). NASA Revisited: Theory, Analogy and Public Sociology. *American Journal of Sociology, 112*(2), 353-393.

Week 11 Public Sociology: Expert Witness – March 23

Stacey, J. (2004). Marital Suitors Court Social Science Spinsters: The Unwittingly Conservative Effects of Public Sociology. *Social Problems, 51*(1), 131-145.

Jellison, K. (1987). History in the Courtroom: The Sears Case in Perspective. *The Public Historian, 9*(4), 9-19.

Milkman, R. (1986). Women's History and the Sears Case. *Feminist Studies, 12*(1), 375-400.

Week 12 Social Movements & the Public Sociologist – March 30

L. Briggs (2008). Activisms and Epistemologies: Problems for Transnationalisms. *Social Text, 26*(4), 79-95.

Prentice, S. (2009). High Stakes: The "Investable" Child and the Economic Reframing of Childcare. *Signs: Journal of Women in Culture and Society. 34*(3), 687-710.

Week 13 Research Presentations – April 6

Student research paper presentations

Appendix 2

Public Sociology Syllabus, UBC, Okanagan Campus

Public Sociology
SOCI 295 Current Topics in Sociology
ASC 130
Tuesday 4:00-7:00PM

Professor:	Dr. Christopher J. Schneider
Office:	A157
Office Hours:	Tuesdays, Thursdays: 11:00-12:15 or by appointment
Office Phone:	250-807-8094
Email:	christopher.schneider@ubc.ca (best way to contact me)
	www.chrisschneider.org

Teaching Assistant:	Mr. Kyle Nolan
Office:	A157
Office Hours:	Wednesdays 12:00-2:00PM
Email:	kyleatnolan@gmail.com

Required Texts
There will be required readings. Information on how to acquire these readings will be provided in class or online on WebCT.

Course Description

According to sociology Professor Michael Burawoy, a basic aim of public sociology is to reach beyond the university in an effort to bring sociology into conversation with multiple publics. To accomplish this task, this course will bring together both university students and non-enrolled members of the public weekly in an attempt to connect theory with practice by bridging the gap between the university and public sphere. *Each student is strongly encouraged to bring a member of the public, e.g., mother, father, sibling, or friend, each week to class.*

Our weekly meetings will consist of an ongoing dialogue between a series of invited sociologists, university students, and members of the public in order to develop a deeper individual understanding of the social and historical contexts that make society possible. This course will develop and advance both the theory and practice of public sociology. We will consider the development of public sociology in the research literature and the practice of public sociology in our direct engagement with sociology scholars in the field.

Central to the public sociology field is a commitment to a political project guided by the sociological knowledge of the conditions and relations of and within the social world. This course invites a number of speakers in the discipline of sociology to speak about their work, its contours, and its relationship to broader society. We will consider and discuss the political implications of the present sociological project each week, focusing on the relationships between the academy and the public, and knowledge and political action.

Learning Objectives

> *The aim of the college, for the individual student, is to eliminate the need in his* [or her] *life for the college; the task is to help* [her or] *him to become a self-educating* [person].
>
> – C. WRIGHT MILLS

One of the primary objectives of attaining a liberal arts education is the cultivation of analytical thinking skills. My goal as an educator is to facilitate the development of critical thinking skills, i.e., the ability to judge the validity of statements that are presented for consideration. Effective teaching, in my opinion, is not where an "expert" tells the "student" how to think. My concern is not what you think but rather *that* you think. Through the assigned readings, lectures, class discussions, and a final essay, it is expected that students will develop the practical skills necessary to demonstrate proficient knowledge of the subject matter. Students then should be able to critically relate the core concepts learned throughout the course not only to themselves, but also to their everyday experiences and political orientations in the immediate and broader social world.

This course is guided by the following themes and principles:

1. To explore the relationship between sociology and political projects
2. To consider the sociologist's ethical obligations to act based on sociological knowledge
3. To understand how personal troubles are related to broader public issues
4. To engage with members of the public and invite their voices to inform and incite political and sociological discussion

Evaluation

Response Essays (3 × 15%)	45%
Web Discussion	15%
Group Discussion/Attendance	15%
Final Essay Assignment	25%

Response Essays

You will submit a total of three response essays. **Response essays are *due the week after* your assigned speaker.**

These essays must be 750 words in length and will be worth a total 45% of your final mark (3 × 15%). We will negotiate your assigned response essays during Week 2. Essays will be graded on the basis of how well you engage with the speaker's materials (readings *and* presentation) in response to the following questions: 1) *Identify the "personal problem"* 2) *Identify the "public issue"* 3) *Develop the relationship between the two.*

Consideration will also be given to organization and grammar. Essays will be due in electronic and hard-copy formats one week after the assigned speaker date, prior to the beginning of the next class. No WebCT web board discussion is due the week of your assigned response essay. Further instruction on reflection essay criteria will be announced shortly.

In order to facilitate a course that truly engages sociology *for the public,* we will be maintaining an online weblog. The online aspect of this course is crucial to our working through the materials of the course and reflecting together on the weekly speakers in a public way. You may be asked for permission to post all or part of your response essay to the public weblog. You reserve the right to decline. The public will have access to this weblog, where they will also be able to post their reflections. Further details of this weblog will be announced shortly and made available on WebCT under "course content."

Course Participation

Your participation is a vital and necessary component of this course. While not mandatory, each student is *strongly encouraged* to bring a member of the public to each course. The web board discussion posts ***and*** group discussions *together are worth up to 30% of your final grade.*

Web Discussion

In addition to our public weblog, our class will have a private web board discussion regarding the course materials on WebCT. **Students must submit one post per week** to the class discussion board **and respond to at least one post per week**. These posts should engage the materials of the course (i.e., course readings, speaker presentations, and discussion in class). Posts are due every Sunday by 2300h. Students are invited to post more than once per week. The reading load of this class is purposefully minimal in order to allow you to have more time to fully engage your classmates on the discussion board, where it is expected that you will critically reflect upon course materials. No credit will be given for posts that do not appear by the deadline. You must also check the web board to verify that your message was successfully received.

Your first post to the web board should introduce yourself to the class. You are invited to comment on your personal interests. For example, what brought you to this class? What attracted you to sociology? What political concerns or social justice issues are you passionate about?

Group Discussion

> *There should be much small group discussion, and at least some of the skills of the group therapist ought to be part of the equipment of the teacher.*
>
> – C. WRIGHT MILLS

We will have a series of *in class* small group discussions throughout the course. These group discussions will draw explicitly from our course materials. Please note that you must be present in class to receive credit for group discussions. *No exceptions*. More details will be provided shortly.

Final Essay Assignment

The final essay will integrate course concepts, theories, and ideas. A handout specifying the requirements will be passed out in the following weeks. The paper is worth 25% of your final course mark.

Instructor and Student Responsibilities

The instructor can be expected to provide accessible information and a safe learning environment where students are encouraged to express their informed views pertaining to particular subject matter. Some ideas discussed throughout the course may be controversial and may differ from your own beliefs. Be prepared to think about and question your own beliefs and assumptions about your political, moral, and ethical obligations in your immediate and broader social world. In this regard, the instructor will show respect, and this respect is expected in return.

Unauthorized use of communication and information devices (i.e., cell phones) in class will result in a marked absence. It is also expected that mutual respect will be displayed within and throughout the course and the classroom; any action(s) that violates the rights (per University of British Columbia policy) of other students will not be tolerated.

Academic Integrity

A more detailed description of academic integrity, including the policies and procedures, may be found at http://web.ubc.ca/okanagan/faculties/resources/academicintegrity.html.

Disability

For more information about disability resources or about academic accommodations, please visit the web site at http://okanagan.students.ubc.ca/current/disres.cfm.

Schedule of Readings and Course Programme

Note: The assigned readings are to be read ***before*** our meeting time.

* Internet links will be provided to these readings and/or they will be distributed in class or placed on reading reserve at the UBC Okanagan library.

Week 1 (January 4)
Course Introduction: The Challenge and Promise of Public Sociology, *with Dr. Christopher Schneider*

Michael Burawoy, "2004 American Sociological Association Presidential Address: For Public Sociology."
C. Wright Mills. 1959. "The Promise" from *The Sociological Imagination.*

This lecture will outline the structure of the course. In 2004, Michael Burawoy, then president of the American Sociological Association, gave an address that generated significant sociological debate. We will explore what is at stake in public sociology, specifically by addressing the relations between sociology and its publics, theory, and its practice. We will begin to develop our sociological imaginations as we consider how personal troubles are related to the societal structure and institutional relations in the social world. We then draw upon Burawoy's 11 *Theses for Public Sociology* to spotlight the current appeal and necessity of public sociology in our contemporary world.

Week 2 (January 11)
On Politics and the Profession, *with Ariane Hanemaayer*

C. Wright Mills. 1959. "On Politics" from *The Sociological Imagination.*
Emile Durkheim. 1973. "The Intellectual Elite and Democracy" from *Emile Durkheim on Morality and Society.*
Antonio Gramsci. 1957. "The Formation of Intellectuals" from *The Modern Prince and Other Writings.*

Burawoy draws on the work of C. Wright Mills to reiterate his call "for" the public sociology agenda. This week we look at the work of C. Wright Mills and his definitive statement on sociology, politics, and the profession. We will consider how the sociological commitments of Mills, Durkheim, and Gramsci differ from those of Burawoy. What is the democratic society? We will also consider the notion of democracy and the political implications of Mills' position in contrast to those of Durkheim and Gramsci. What is the intellectual/sociologist's relation to mass society?

Week 3 (January 18)
Thirty Years of Okanagan Students' Sexual Behaviour: Subcultures and Safety over an Entire Generation, *with Dr. Nancy Netting*

Netting, Nancy S. 1992. Sexuality within Youth Culture: Identity and Change. *Adolescence* 27: 961-976.

Netting, Nancy S., and Burnett, Matthew L. 2004. Twenty Years of Student Sexual Behaviour: Subcultural Adaptations to a Changing Health Environment. *Adolescence* 39: 19-38.

Every ten years, from 1980 to 2010, Dr. Nancy Netting surveyed university students in the Okanagan about their sexual histories and safer-sex practices. Throughout this period, men had more sexual partners, required less of a relationship before having sex, and engaged in riskier practices. By 2010, women were as likely as men to be sexually active, and had more partners than did women previously. In every decade, there have been three distinct sexual cultures: abstinence, monogamy, and experimentation (practising casual sex, or "hooking up"), previously in a ratio of 30-60-10. Now abstainers have decreased to 25% while experimenters have increased to 15%: a change, but not one which challenges the still-dominant pattern of monogamy. Safety measures, such as using condoms, asking potential partners about their past, and requesting them to be tested for STIs (sexually transmitted infections), increased steadily until 2000, then decreased in 2010. Although this likely reflects a fall in new infections and more effective anti-viral drugs, it still leaves students, especially experimenters, open to STIs. Additional education and discussion about health and safety are recommended.

Week 4 (January 25)
Unwed Mothers in 20th-Century Toronto, *with Dr. Paty Tomic*

Murray, Karen B. 2004. Governing "Unwed Mothers" in Toronto at the Turn of the Twentieth Century. *Canadian Historical Review* 85: 253-276.

This lecture focuses on unwed mothers and illegitimate children in Toronto at the turn of the 20th century. The transformation of the city from a small town into a large industrial conglomerate led to the breakdown of existing forms of social cohesion controlling and protecting women from facing the challenges of unwed motherhood alone. In this lecture we study the process of formation of the public system of social welfare for unwed mothers and their children over this period of rapid industrialization. At the beginning, when illegitimate births were considered an individual problem, women were confronted with almost no social resources, which forced them to fend very much on their own, under deplorable conditions. Slowly a system developed, first, through the intervention of charitable organizations in the hands of middle and upper classes, and then, under the control of the state. Although by the early 1920s a system of government intervention was in place, offering legislation and policy for the protection of both mother and child, the effort to "reclaim" the unwed mother and her "bastard" child was still very much in place.

Week 5 (February 1)
Rap Music and the Censorship Frame, *with Dr. Christopher J. Schneider*

Schneider, Christopher J. 2011. "Popular Culture, Rap Music, 'Bitch' and the Development of the Censorship Frame." *American Behavioral Scientist* 55: 36-56.

This research talk suggests that negative public perceptions associated with rap music are in large part informed through both formal and informal censorship agendas and campaigns, what the speaker terms the *censorship frame.* The censorship frame consists of mass media reports that proclaim the cultural association between music and collectively shared and culturally agreed-upon perceptions of deviance. The focus of this presentation concerns rap music and the term *bitch,* a relatively recent common feature of everyday language use. This talk (a) investigates the increased use and acceptance of "bitch" in popular culture; (b) examines this process in relation to the demonization of rap music; and (c) demonstrates the role of both mass media and claims-makers in shaping public opinion of rap music as deviant, even while other similar messages continue to remain virtually unchallenged throughout the popular cultural milieu.

Week 6 (February 8)
Empire of Scrounge, *with Dr. Jeff Ferrell*

Ferrell, Jeff. 2005. "Scrounging Zen" from *Empire of Scrounge.*

In this talk Jeff Ferrell recounts his long-term participation and research in the illicit worlds of urban "dumpster diving," street scrounging, and second-hand living. In telling this story, Ferrell travels from the back alleys of a single city to the global economy of waste. Along the way he explores the late-modern culture of conspicuous consumption and disposability; the legal and political constraints under which urban scroungers operate; and the practices of creative reinvention by which scroungers and recyclers produce art, knowledge, community, and ongoing sustainability.

Week 7 (February 15)
READING WEEK, NO CLASS

Week 8 (February 22)
Understanding Popular Music through the Concept of the Scene, *with Dr. Joe Kotarba*

Kotarba, Joseph, Jennifer L. Fackler, and Kathryn M. Notwotny. 2010. "An Ethnography of Emerging Latino Music Scenes" in *Studies in Symbolic Interaction,* Vol. 35, C.J. Schneider, B. Merrill, and R. Gardner (eds).

This presentation focuses on the ethnographic study of music scenes. The concept of *social scene* is a useful strategy for exploring the various ways people gather publicly to share meanings for the solutions to everyday life issues and problems. The music scenes I will discuss include Latino popular music (e.g., salsa, rock en Espanole, dance, and religious music); teen-age pop music in post-communist Poland (e.g., heavy metal and pop); and Americana music. Two other symbolic interactionist concepts inform these studies. The concept of *idioculture* directs our attention to the ways audience members experience music within small groups in everyday life. The concept of *place* directs our attention to ways music serves to create new social locations for people (e.g., the ways Latino music helps create symbolic places to anchor the self in reference to country of origin, present music communities, or possible symbolic locations such as America or La Raza). We will apply these ideas to an analysis of popular music scenes in Canada.

Week 9 (March 1)
The Design, Use, and Socio-Political Implications of Police and Emergency Response Information Technologies, *with Dr. Carrie Sanders*

Sanders, Carrie. 2006. Have You Been Identified? *Information, Communication & Society* 9: 714-736.

In the wake of such horrific events as school shootings, terrorist attacks and natural disasters, there have been growing concerns over the state and working infrastructure of emergency and protective services. Private high-tech companies around the world are taking this opportunity to design "new" and "improved" technology that makes emergency information readily available to all emergency workers. Significant investments among governments, cities and municipalities have led to the implementation of such technology throughout Canada and the USA. The present talk explores the means by which emergency response technologies are employed *in situ* by Canadian emergency management services (police, fire and Emergency Medical Services (EMS)). I argue that emergency technologies are subject to *individual actions* and *organizational contexts* that can create impediments to emergency interoperability. I contend that the social world practices of police, fire and EMS have led to an *ideological disconnect* between the design and everyday application of these technologies – leading emergency technologies to be used as tools of legitimacy and power over information-sharing devices. I conclude by raising questions about the social and political implications of emergency information technologies – specifically policing technologies.

Week 10 (March 8)
Sociology in Medias Res: On the Question of Public Video Recording,
with Dr. Tara Milbrandt

Milbrandt, Tara. 2010. "On Appearing in Public in the 21st Century City: Ephemerality Surveillance, and the Specter of the Visual Record" in *Cultural Production in Virtual and Imagined Worlds,* T. Bowman and M.L. Nemanic (eds).

This talk will be an invitation to critically and creatively reflect upon a remarkable new dimension of our contemporary world: ubiquitous cameras and unprecedented image mobility. How are we thinking about what it means to share space and time when what takes place is more likely than ever in the history of humankind to be "captured" on camera? How are we thinking about what we are doing when we look at still and moving images of public scenes and (sometimes) disturbing incidents that have been "caught" on camera? Taking these questions as a point of entry, my talk will begin to wade through our contradictory, murky, and contested practices of, and relations to, public visual recording and publicly "captured" visual records. To ground these questions and focus the discussion, particular consideration will be given to the prolific public responses to the incendiary "by-stander video" involving a tragic confrontation between authorities and an unarmed man at the Vancouver International Airport in 2007. This talk will advance an approach to "doing sociology" that treats embeddedness within a complex, contradictory and multi-layered social world as a necessary and desirable starting point for sociological inquiry. It will also explore how *thinking sociologically* can shed particular light onto compelling collective concerns.

Week 11 (March 15)
Cosmopolitanism and Canadian Society: A Neo-Classical Approach to Public Sociology, *with Dr. Paul Datta*

Burawoy, Michael. 2010. "Meeting the Challenges of Global Sociology." *International Sociological Association* September Newsletter.

Beck, Ulrich. 2010. "Kiss the Frog: The Cosmopolitan Turn in Sociology." *International Sociological Association* December Newsletter.

The basic argument of my lecture is that public sociology, if it is to succeed in its aims, would do well to return to the kind of theoretically rich and politically realist approach exemplified in Emile Durkheim's sociology. Recent discussions of the need for both a global and public sociology, and contemporary journalistic debates about immigration, multiculturalism and elitist cosmopolitanism in Canada, serve as a starting point for my lecture. I will stress the importance of continuously engaging in rigorous theoretical work at all levels of abstraction, including empirical research. Attention will be paid to Durkheim's conception of the conditions of emergence and the effects of organic solidarity and why he argues it is necessary to create new political institutions ("corporations"), appropriate to organic societies. This then serves as the basis for examining Paul Hirst's reformulation of Durkheim's ideas as "associative democracy." I will then outline how cosmopolitan social life is arguably generating a new form of solidarity in global cities like Vancouver, Toronto and Montreal. I show why considering the creation of a viable "New-Comers Corporation," able to address significant challenges facing newcomers to Canada, might be desirable. In doing so, I hope to show why the kind of neo-classical sociological approach on which I draw can be a major resource for meeting the difficult challenges of creating both a global and public sociology.

Week 12 (March 22)
Fear, Terrorism, and Popular Culture, *with Dr. David Altheide*

Altheide, David L. 2010. "Fear, Terrorism and Popular Culture." Pp. 11-22 in *Reframing 9/11: Film, Popular Culture and the "War on Terror,"* Birkenstein, J. and Froula, A. and Randell, K. (eds).

Popular culture plays to fear as entertainment. Whether crime, disasters, or wars, popular culture formats promote evocative feelings over reflective analysis. Aiming to please the audiences and key political leaders, news media, and especially major TV networks (with some exceptions) embraced the emotional sweep of 9/11 attacks and blessed the vengeful priests and politico-warriors, who would make war to protect US citizens while building an empire. Notwithstanding the long relationship in the United States between fear and crime, the role of the mass media in promoting fear has become more pronounced since the United States "discovered" international terrorism on September 11, 2001. Qualitative media analysis shows that political decision-makers quickly adjusted propaganda passages, prepared as part of the Project for the New American Century (PNAC), to emphasize domestic support for the new US role in leading the world. These messages were folded into the previous crime-related discourse of fear, which may be defined as the pervasive communication, symbolic awareness, and expectation that danger and risk are a central feature of everyday life. Politicians marshaled critical symbols and icons joining terrorism with Iraq, the Muslim faith, and a vast number of non-Western nations to strategically promote fear and use of audience beliefs and assumptions about danger, risk and fear in order to achieve certain goals, including expanding domestic social control.

Week 13 (March 29)
Dealing with It: Deviant Identities and Everyday Life,
with Dr. Patrick Williams

Hochestetler, Andy, Heith Copes and J. Patrick Williams. 2010. "That's Not Who I Am": How Offenders Commit Violent Acts and Reject Authentically Violent Selves. *Justice Quarterly* 27(4): 492-416.

Public sociologists have three kinds of obligations: to provide intellectual insight into the empirical world; to recognize and clarify the moral implications of our research; and to support the idea of moral goodness when it comes to the politics of everyday life. But what happens when the sociologists' sense of what is right differs from "standard practice"? I argue that what happens is, ironically, the sociologist gets categorized in much the same way as the marginal social groups he or she studies. In this talk I reflect on ten years of research on subcultures and how I have tried to illuminate and validate the perspectives of marginalized individuals and groups. Beginning with my work on the straightedge youth subculture, I consider colleagues' reactions to my conceptualization of subcultural authenticity. I then discuss co-authored research that represents an extension from deviance to delinquency studies and how I had to deal with conflicting senses of "moral goodness" in my writing. Finally, I comment on my academic experiences in Singapore and how my interest in social psychology and youth subcultures has drawn me into public policy discourses about youth gangs and violence which I find problematic. For me, like the participants in my research projects, "dealing with it" has become a basic fact of life.

Week 14 (April 5)
The Media and the Many Realities of Criminal Justice,
with Dr. Aaron Doyle

Doyle, Aaron. 2010. "Cops" and Reality TV. This is a revised and abridged version of an earlier piece. "Cops: Television Policing as Policing Reality," which appeared in the book M. Fishman and G. Cavender (eds.) 1998 *Entertaining Crime: Television Reality Programs.*

Doyle, Aaron. 2010. "Crime, Policing, and the Media" (prepared for this lecture).

In the first half of the talk I discuss patterns and problems that social science research reveals about news and entertainment media images of crime and criminal justice. I discuss some reasons behind these patterns and some of the consequences that result, both in terms of possible influences on audiences as well as the ways in which the media actually sometimes influence the criminal justice system itself. In the second half of the talk, I move on to discussing the example of the very popular and long-running reality TV show "Cops." "Cops" producers claim the show is "unfiltered reality," but is it? What social impacts might a program like "Cops" have?

Contributors

Jill Bucklaschuk is a doctoral candidate at the University of Manitoba in the Department of Sociology. Her research interests are broadly focused on immigration, temporary migration, citizenship rights, and social inequality. Her dissertation research, supported by a Joseph-Armand Bombardier Canada Graduate Scholarship from the Social Sciences and Humanities Research Council of Canada, explores the increasing opportunities for temporary migrants to become permanent residents. Drawing on years of community-based research experience in Manitoba, her research sheds light on the experiences of lower-skilled temporary migrants as they settle and negotiate their temporary status in Canada.

Michael Burawoy teaches sociology at the University of California, Berkeley. His most recent book, co-authored with Karl Von Holdt, is *Conversations with Bourdieu.*

Ariane Hanemaayer is a doctoral candidate in the Department of Sociology at the University of Alberta, Canada. She is a Social Sciences and Humanities Research Council of Canada Joseph Armand Bombardier Canada Graduate Scholar. Her research and publications have focused on the sociology of games, public sociology, and the sociology of medicine and the body. Her dissertation research analyzes how medical judgments are discursively and socially constituted in the face of uncertainty.

Rick Helmes-Hayes is a professor in the Department of Sociology and Legal Studies at the University of Waterloo. He did his undergraduate degrees and MA at Queen's University and his PhD at the University of Toronto. He teaches a course, unique in Canada, on the history of English-language Canadian sociology. His area of scholarly research is the history of sociology, especially Canadian sociology, and he has published articles on key figures in the discipline, such as S.D. Clark, Leonard Marsh, Carl Dawson, and Everett Hughes. In 2009, with Neil McLaughlin of McMaster University, he co-edited a special issue of the *Canadian Journal of Sociology* on public sociology, which included a response by Michael Burawoy. His book *Measuring the Mosaic: An Intellectual Biography of John Porter* (University of Toronto Press, 2010) won the 2011 Canadian Sociology Association John Porter Tradition of Excellence Award for the best book in Canadian sociology published in 2010.

Anne Mesny is a professor at HEC Montreal. She researches and publishes in sociology and management studies. She is mainly interested in the relationships between social scientists and lay people, and between scholars and practitioners. This overarching interest has led to projects and publications about the uses of social science knowledge, the ethics of social research, university-industry partnerships, research collaborations between management theorists and practitioners, and epistemological issues in social science and management science.

Laura Milne holds a bachelor's degree in anthropology and sociology from the University of Victoria and is a graduate of the Royal Roads University Masters in Intercultural and International Communication program. She spent several years coordinating a federally funded knowledge mobilization program that focused on community-university partnerships and has also worked internationally as an educator in China. During her graduate studies, she worked closely with the Canada Research Chair in Innovative Learning and Public Ethnography and contributed to the development of the Ethnography Media Arts Culture network. She is currently working in a development capacity for an environmental nonprofit organization.

Kyle Nolan is an interdisciplinary graduate studies MA student at the University of British Columbia, Okanagan Campus. His current research interests focus on social media, policing, crime, and deviance. His thesis research examines the discourse produced in mass media news documents and how it contributes to the social construction of police violence.

Susan Prentice is a professor of sociology at the University of Manitoba. A feminist sociologist, she specializes in historical and contemporary childcare politics, focusing on the state, public policy, and social movement advocacy. She works closely with community groups on action research projects. Her interests have recently turned to questions about childcare in Europe, particularly France, where she spent 2010-11 as a senior fellow at the Collegium de Lyon, one of the Instituts d'études avancées. In 2011-12, she taught a second public sociology course on graduate socialization titled "Public Sociology and Communication: The Thesis and Beyond."

Scott Schaffer is an associate professor of sociology at the University of Western Ontario, where he specializes in contemporary and global social thought, social ethics, and cosmopolitan social thought. He is the author of *Resisting Ethics* (Palgrave, 2004), and his current research is on the modes of operation of cosmopolitanism and multiculturalism and their roots in imperial and colonial social policy.

Christopher J. Schneider is an assistant professor of sociology at the University of British Columbia, Okanagan Campus. He has co-authored/co-edited three books. His research and publications investigate mass media messages about crime, deviance, and information technologies in daily life. He received the 2013 Distinguished Academics Early in Career Award from the Confederation of University Faculty Associations of British Columbia (CUFA BC). CUFA BC represents 4,600 university professors and other academic staff at the province's five doctoral universities. He was the recipient of the UBC, Okanagan Campus 2010-11 Award for Teaching Excellence and Innovation (Junior Faculty) and the 2009-10 Provost's Public Education through Media Award. He has given hundreds of interviews with news media across North America, including the *New York Times.*

Axel van den Berg is a professor of sociology at McGill University. His research interests include labour markets and labour market policy, sociological theory, and the relationship between economics and sociology. His publications include *The Immanent Utopia: From Marxism on the State to the State of Marxism* (Princeton University Press, 1988; Transaction

Publishers, 2003) and *The Social Sciences and Rationality: Promise, Limits and Problems* (with Hudson Meadwell, Transaction, 2004).

Phillip Vannini is a professor in the School of Communication and Culture at Royal Roads University. His vision of public scholarship engages new and traditional media as a way of communicating social scientific knowledge to popular audiences. He is author or editor of eight books, including *Popularizing Research: Engaging New Media, New Genres, and New Audiences,* an edited collection that explores new technological and methodological possibilities for public scholarship. He is also editor of the Routledge series Innovative Ethnographies, which combines paper-based writing with web-based multimedia representation in order to reach wider publics. His research on the role played by ferry transportation in everyday life in coastal and interior British Columbia (forthcoming as a book with Routledge) has received very extensive national coverage by numerous radio, television, and print outlets, and two of his documentaries on this topic have played on CBC Radio 1.

Index

activism, 4-5, 13-14, 41-48, 124, 247
  political engagement and, xiv-xvi, 21, 35-36
  professional sociology and, 13-14
  Weberian theory and, 41-44
  See also public engagement
advocacy. *See* activism
advocacy anthropology, 158
Algeria, 89, 90, 91
Althusser, Louis, 32, 48n4, 49n6, 49n8
American Sociological Association (ASA), 31, 49n10, 210
  teaching resources, 133
  views of M. Buroway on, 56-57, 64
anthropology, 243n3
Archambault, Justice J., 183
ASA. *See* American Sociological Association (ASA)
audiences of sociology, 100, 101
  See also publics

Basok, Tanya, 121-22, 124
Bello, Walden, xv
bias. *See* value-laden social science; value-neutral social science
Bonacich, Edna, 159
Bouchard, Gérard, 97
Bourdieu, Pierre, 85, 88-92, 98-99, 103n7, 140, 245
Boyer, Ernest, 145
Brint, Steven, 35
British Columbia
  Boys' Industrial School, 182-83
  Commission to Inquire into the State and Management of the Gaols, 184
  Oakalla prison farm, 183
  role of ferries, 243n6
  Vancouver Board of Education, 207
  See also Topping, Coral Wesley; universities, University of British Columbia
Buroway, Michael
  address to the American Sociological Association, 5-6, 7, 108, 175, 208
  context for espousing of public sociology, 7, 111-12, 190-92
  focus on North American context, 140, 141-43

impact of his theories, 77, 108
views on: civil society, 36, 54, 56, 143, 192, 265; commodification of universities, x-xi, xii, xvii; division of sociological labour, 5-7, 78, 100-1, 142-43, 205-6; left-wing activism, 169, 171n1; phases of American sociology, 190-91; the public sociology debate, 69n3, 190-92; the state, 142-43; students as publics, xii, xv, 132, 209
See also public sociology

Canada
Concordia University (Quebec), 207-8
cotutelle agreements, 142, 148n8
Harper administration, 70n18
Ontario College of Teachers, 205
roles of intellectuals, 77-78, 92, 97
sociological engagement, 140
temporary migrant programs, 116-17, 126n2, 126n5, 127n10
University of Manitoba, 132, 135-40, 144-45, 247, 257-62
See also British Columbia
capitalism. *See* commodification; neoliberalism
Civic Forum (Czechoslovakia), 93
Collins, Patricia, 35
colonialism, 90, 103n8
Colorado State University, 207
commodification, xii-xv, 217-18
of universities, x-xi, xii, xvii, 82, 84-85, 103n3, 191
communication strategies
language of scholarship, 81, 85, 98-99, 112, 225-26, 231
multimodality, 226-27, 233-35, 240, 242, 248
See also public ethnography; social media
Communist Party (Czechoslovakia), 93-97
Comte, Auguste, 38-39, 54, 66
Concordia University (Quebec), 207-8
conscience
as culturally defined, 92-93, 94-95, 96, 104n10
corporate ethos, x-xi
cotutelle agreements, 142, 148n8
counterlegal engagement, 81-82, 92-97
counterpublics, 20, 112, 114, 127n7, 156, 158
critical sociology, xvi, 7, 15-18, 21, 99-101, 190-91, 206, 208
as teaching strategy, 139, 146-47, 214, 215, 219, 247
critical theory, 70n17, 78-79, 99-100
cultural anthropology, 228-29
cultural turn, 228, 243n2
Czechoslovakia, 92-97, 104n10

democratic ethos, x-xi, 14-15, 54-70, 248
democratic public sphere, 22, 56-57, 59, 169, 248
Doyle, Aaron, 254
Dreyfus Affair, 80
Durkheim, Emile, 66
ideological method, 36-37
views on: morality, 44-47, 48n3; socialism, 45; sociology, 31, 39-40, 44-47

e-public sociology, 22-23, 206-22
economics
commodification, xii-xv, 215-16; of universities, x-xi, xii, xvii, 82, 84-85, 103n3, 191
neoliberalism, 111-12, 175, 191, 196
See also marginalized groups
Emory University, 103n3
empowerment, 165, 235, 238
marginalized groups and, 108-9, 111, 119-22, 123-25
engaged intellectuals, 48n5, 80, 91, 92-93, 245
Bourdieu, Pierre, 85, 88-92, 98-99, 103n7, 140, 247

Havel, Václav, 85, 92-97, 247
Sartre, Jean-Paul, 85-88, 98-99, 247
See also intellectual engagement; public engagement; Topping, Coral Wesley
epistemology, 48n2
ethical judgment, 4, 6, 10
Durkheimian morality, 44-47
related to action, 7-9, 43-44
related to sociological research, 11, 16-17
See also research ethics
ethnography, 227, 229-30
See also public ethnography
existential philosophy, 86-87
See also Sartre, Jean-Paul
experiential learning, 133-34, 238-39

falsifiability, 60
feminist scholarship, xii, 63, 140, 143-45, 146, 148n9
researching marginalized groups and, 111, 120-21, 124, 125, 126
Ferrell, Jeff, 255
ferries, 243n6
Flecha, Ramon, xvi
Florida Atlantic University, 103n4
France, 132, 140-41
cotutelle agreements, 142, 148n8
engaged intellectuals, 80, 81, 86-92, 140-42, 143

Gans, Herbert, 155, 228-29
Giddings, Franklin Henry, 185-86
Glenn, Norval D., 34-35

Habermas, Jürgen, 70n19
habitus, 89-91
Hanafi, Sari, xv
Havel, Václav, 85, 92-97, 245
Hobden, J. Dinnage, 196n8
Honneth, Axel, 48n5, 102
human geography, 228

ideological science, 36-37, 49n8
illegal engagement, 81-82
immigrant groups, 115
See also marginalized groups; temporary migrant workers
instrumental knowledge, 34, 56, 156, 169-70, 208
intellectuals, 92-93
accessibility/communication style, 83-84, 98-100, 102, 104n11
See also engaged intellectuals; public engagement
intellectuels engagés. *See* engaged intellectuals; public engagement
interest groups, 161-63, 166, 170-71
invisible publics. *See* marginalized groups

Jacoby, Russell, 83-84

Keynes, John Maynard, 193
knowledge
instrumental knowledge, 34, 56, 156, 169-70, 208
"knowledge for what?", ix, 6-7, 120, 123, 147
"knowledge for whom?", ix, 6-7, 120, 123, 147
reflexive knowledge, 7, 34, 49n9, 65, 120, 156, 169-70
theory development and, 170-71

labour commodification, xv
land struggles, xiv-xv

marginalized groups, xiv-xvi, 101, 102, 127n7
counterpublics, 20, 112, 114, 127n7, 156, 158
implications for engaging as publics, xi-xii, 17, 109-11, 113-14, 115-16, 118-26, 247
issues of empowerment and, 108-9, 111, 119-22, 123-25
See also temporary migrant workers
Marx, Karl, 66

Merton, Robert, x
metatheory, 48n2
methodology, 68-69, 69n2
  See also feminist scholarship; knowledge; sociology; research ethics; value-laden social science; value-neutral social science
migrant workers. *See* temporary migrant workers

NASA Space Shuttle program, 243n4
neoliberalism
  public sociology and, 111-12, 175, 191, 196
New Liberalism, 193-95
New Penology, 176-77, 181-85, 193, 196-97, 198n8, 198n9, 198n10

Ontario College of Teachers, 207
ontology, 48n2
organic public sociology, 101, 108, 153-57, 159, 169-70
  collaboration with multiple actors/knowledges, 118-19, 124-25, 153, 168, 204
  engagement of publics, 20-21, 64-65, 108-9, 112, 113-14
  independence of researchers, 160-63, 166
  reflexive knowledge and, 34, 37, 49n9, 65, 169-70
  views of M. Buroway on, 20-21, 31, 56-57, 64-65, 108-9, 111-13, 169-70, 253
  See also public sociology
overdetermination, 49n6
oversight, 48n4

participatory research. *See* organic public sociology
Pepler, Eric, 182-83, 184
performance ethnography, 232-34, 243n5
photographic communication, 232-35
Piven, Frances Fox, xvi
policy sociology, 4, 6-7, 18-19, 206, 208
  compared to public sociology, 19, 101, 142-43, 155, 169-70, 249
political action. *See* activism
political engagement, 77-78, 91-97
Porter, John, 197n1
positivism, 67, 111
  knowledge claims and, 58-59, 64, 66, 67
  See also Comte, Auguste; Durkheim, Emile
post-positivism, 57-58, 67, 70n17, 192
postivism
  related to public sociology, 38
power
  power differentials: research ethics and, 113-14, 118-22, 157-60, 166
  powerful publics, 158, 159-60, 166, 169, 171
  See also empowerment
Prague Spring (1968), 93-96
professional sociology, 12-14, 34, 101
  Buroway definition, 6-7, 69n4, 206, 208
  public sociology and, 14-15, 21, 32-35, 54-68, 101, 248
  value-neutral social science and, 14-15, 59-64, 65, 67
  views of M. Buroway on, 13, 21, 54-55, 57-58, 67, 69n4
public engagement, 78-81, 245
  critical theory and, 78
  cultural conscience and, 81-82, 92-97
  effects of university administration on, xii, 82-85
  experiential engagement, 81, 88-92
  impediments to, 82-85, 92, 97-100, 249 (*See also* marginalized groups)
  models of, 79, 80-82, 85, 86-99
  philosophical/pedagogical engagement, 81, 86-88
  political engagement, xiv-xvi, 92-97
  See also engaged intellectuals; organic public sociology

public ethnography, xi, 23, 227-32
  communication strategies, 23, 229-32, 240, 242
  student expertise and, 236-42
  web resources, 242
public scholarship, 225-27
public sociology, 7, 20-21, 33-34, 47, 101, 153, 156, 208
  activism role, 4-5, 35-36, 41-48
  advocacy by M. Buroway, 5-7, 31-32, 53-57, 111-12, 156, 205-6, 217-18
  compared to policy sociology, 101, 125, 142-43, 155, 156, 169-70, 249
  compared to professional sociology, 14-15, 21, 32-35, 54-68, 101, 248
  critiques of, 14, 21-22, 35-41, 47-48; democratic ethos and, 53-70; Durkheimian theory and, 44-48; guilty reading of, 32-33; Weberian theory and, 41-44, 48, 50n11, 70n12
  disciplinary debate concerning, ix, 9-12, 53-70, 191-92
  e-public sociology, 22-23, 206-22
  inattention to feminist scholarship, 143-44, 148n9
  interest groups and, 161-63, 166, 170-71
  as moral philosophy, 14, 32-33, 34, 41, 47
  role of expertise in, 66-67
  specificity to North America, 132-33, 140, 141-43
  traditional public sociology, 20, 23, 54, 81, 100, 112, 156, 206, 218
  See also organic public sociology; public engagement; public ethnography; publics; research ethics; teaching public sociology
publics, 21, 101, 110-11, 113, 142-43, 157-58
  counterpublics, 20, 112, 114, 127n7, 156, 158
  interest groups and, 161-63, 166, 170-71
  "knowledge for whom?", ix, 6-7, 120, 123, 147
  power differentials, 157, 158, 166, 169-70
  powerful publics, 158, 159-60, 166, 169, 171
  risks and benefits of research, 154, 163-66, 167-69, 170-71
  students as, xii, xv, 23, 132, 209, 215-22
  See also audiences; marginalized groups; public engagement; research ethics
Pun Ngai, xv

reflexive knowledge, 7, 34, 49n9, 65, 120, 156, 169-70
Regnerus, Mark, 4
related to policy sociology
  public sociology, 125, 142-43, 155, 156, 169-70, 249
research activities, 171n2
  impacts on participants, 21-22, 164-66, 168
  stakeholder relationships, 160-69
  See also methodology; public engagement; research ethics
research ethics
  biomedical vs. social science models, 19, 154-55, 158, 160, 168-69
  power differentials and, 113-14, 118-22, 157-60, 166
  risks and benefits for participants, 154, 163-66, 167-69, 170-71
  risks and benefits for public good, 166-68, 170-71
  role of academics in research process, 160-63
  Tri-Council Policy Statement (TCPS), 153-55, 157, 162, 163-64, 166, 167, 168, 171n2
  university ethics boards (REBs), 118, 154, 162
research participants. *See* publics; research ethics

Rodríguez Garavito, César, xv
Royal Commission on the Reform of the Canadian Penal System, 183

Saint-Simon, Henri, comte de, 38
Sartre, Jean-Paul, 85-88, 98-99, 245
Schalk, David, 80-82
service learning. *See* experiential learning
social change. *See* activism
Social Gospel, 186-87
social justice. *See* public engagement; publics
social media, 22-23, 205, 207
  definitions, 210, 211-12, 213
  use by sociologists, 208-9
  use in higher education, 23, 206-8, 210-17, 248; as public sociology, 209-10, 217-22
social networking, 210
  See also social media
social theorists
  scholarly motivation, 99-100
  schools of thought, 99-100
sociology, 3-4, 78, 101, 133
  audiences of, 100, 101 (*See also* publics)
  historical development, 19-20, 38-39, 49n10, 176, 177, 190-91
  natural science model of, 192-93
  See also critical sociology; policy sociology; professional sociology; public sociology
Soler, Marta, xvi
Soley, Lawrence, 84
Stacey, Judith, 142
Stevens, E.G.B., 184
students, 239
  leveraging student expertise, 236-42, 247-48
  as publics, xii, xv, 23, 132, 209, 215-22
  See also teaching public sociology; universities
subaltern groups. *See* marginalized groups
subalternized groups, 102
Sundar, Nandani, xiv-xv
Sztompka, Piotr, 67, 69n1, 69n6

Task Force on Institutionalizing Public Sociologies, 133
Taylor, Charles, 97
TCPS. *See* Tri-Council Policy Statement (TCPS)
teaching public sociology, xii, 10-11, 145-47, 146-47, 207, 246-47
  colloquia, 137-38
  communication skills, 138-39; multi-modality, 226-27, 232-35, 240, 242, 248
  critical sociology and, 139, 146-47, 214, 215, 219, 247
  as e-public sociology, 206-22
  experiential learning, 133-34, 238-39
  internationalization of learning, xiv-xvi, 141-42
  leveraging student expertise, 236-42, 247-48
  neglect of, 133, 145-46
  syllabi, 133, 257-76
  University of British Columbia, 252-56, 263-76
  University of California at Berkeley, xiii-xvi
  University of Manitoba, 132, 135-40, 144-45, 247, 257-62
  See also universities
temporary migrant workers
  Canadian government programs, 116-17, 126n2, 126n5, 127n10
  precarious status, 109-10, 116, 126n3, 126n4, 127n8, 127n13
  research concerning, 109-10, 116-19, 121-22, 124-25
theatrical communication, 232-34, 243n5
Topping, Coral Wesley, 19-20, 176-79, 194-97, 249
  major influences on, 181-82, 185-90, 193-94

penal reform and, 176-77, 180-85, 193, 196-97, 199n14
as a public sociologist, 193-97
research and publications, 179-85, 198n6, 199n14
Touraine, Alain, 37
traditional public sociology, 20, 23, 54, 81, 100, 112, 156, 206, 218
Tri-Council Policy Statement (TCPS), 153-55, 157, 162, 163-64, 166, 167, 168, 171n2

United States
migrant workers, 127n8
military interventions, 103n2
social conditions, 103n2
sociological engagement, 140, 141-42
universities, xiii-xvi, 103n3, 103n4, 205
universities
Colorado State University, 207
commodification/funding and, x-xi, xii, xvii, 82, 84-85, 103n3, 191
Concordia University (Quebec), 207-8
cotutelle agreements, 142, 148n8
engaged intellectuals and, 103n4
Florida Atlantic University, 103n4
guidelines for the use of social media, 207-8, 220, 221
relevancy: role of students in, 236-42, 247-48
research ethics boards (REBs), 118, 154, 162
support of public scholarship, 227
systems of hiring and promotion, xii, 82-85
University of British Columbia, 205; School of Social Work, 198n5; sociology program, 179, 196, 197n4, 252-56, 263-76
University of California at Berkeley, xiii-xvi
University of Manitoba, 132, 135-40, 144-45, 245, 257-62
University of Nebraska, 103n3
See also research ethics; students; teaching public sociology; University of British Columbia

value-free social science. *See* value-neutral social science
value-laden social science
in early sociological ethos, 19-20, 177, 180, 190, 196-97
New Liberalism and, 193-95
scholarly endeavour and, 78, 101-2
See also public sociology
value-neutral social science, x-xi, 60, 61-64
views of M. Buroway on, 57-58, 175, 190-91
Vancouver Board of Education (British Columbia), 207
Vaughan, Diana, 243n4
Velvet Revolution (1989), 93, 94, 96
video communication, 232-35
vulnerable groups, 115
See also marginalized groups

web-based media, 235
See also social media
Weber, Max, x, 50n11
views on sociology, 31, 41-44, 70n12
WGA. *See* Writers Guild of America
Wieviorka, Michel, xvi
Writers Guild of America (WGA), 159
writing. *See* communication strategies

Printed and bound in Canada by Friesens

Set in Segoe, Univers, and Warnock by Artegraphica Design Co. Ltd.

Copy editor: Joanne Muzak

Proofreader: Jillian Shoichet

Indexer: Christine Jacobs